The American Utopian Adventure

HISTORY OF THE HOPEDALE COMMUNITY

Engraved by H.W. Smith

Adin Ballou

HISTORY

OF

THE HOPEDALE COMMUNITY,

FROM ITS INCEPTION TO ITS VIRTUAL SUB-
MERGENCE IN THE HOPEDALE PARISH.

BY ADIN BALLOU.

WILLIAM S. HEYWOOD, Editor.

"It seemed good to me, having had perfect understanding of all things from the very first, to write."— *Luke 1: 3.*

PORCUPINE PRESS, INC.
Philadelphia 1972

Library of Congress Cataloging in Publication Data

Ballou, Adin, 1803-1890.
   History of the Hopedale Community.

   (The American utopian adventure)
   Reprint of the 1897 ed.
   "Constitution by-laws, rules, and regulations of
the Hopedale community": p. [368]-396
   1. Hopedale Community. I. Heywood, William
Sweetzer, 1824-1905, ed.
HX656.H7B2   1972   335'.9'7443   76-187467
ISBN 0-87991-007-0

First edition 1897 (Lowell, Mass.: Thompson & Hill- The Vox Populi Press,
1897)

Reprinted 1972 by PORCUPINE PRESS, INC., 1317 Filbert St., Philadelphia,
Pa. 19107

Manufactured in the United States of America

INTRODUCTION.

THIS volume is the second in the list of those prepared by the author and left in manuscript at the time of his decease, with definite instructions in regard to their publication. It contains the story of an undertaking with which his name was more closely identified than that of any other person, to which he devoted the best years of his life, and for which, out of a disinterested desire to promote the well-being and happiness of his fellow-men, he was willing to "both labor and suffer reproach." Its acknowledged Founder and the Framer of its Constitutional polity, acquainted with all its members and familiar with its methods of operation throughout its entire career, he, above all others, was qualified to be its historiographer and its ambassador to coming generations. Let his record and testimony concerning it be read, appreciated, and honored accordingly.

That undertaking can be fully understood and its significance justly estimated only by considering the circumstances under which it was projected and the relation it sustained to certain great currents of thought and conduct prevailing in the general community at the time when it first claimed the attention of philanthropists and the public at large. Such consideration will give it the proper perspective and assign it to its rightful place in the order of human events and in the work of benefiting and blessing mankind.

The decade of United States history beginning with the year 1840 was characterized, as intimated on a succeeding page, by an unprecedented manifestation among the people at large of that "enthusiasm for humanity" out of which great moral reforms chiefly spring and all endeavors for the amelioration of the condition of the suffering masses of men, and for the betterment of the world. It was during the early por-

tion of that period that the so-called Washingtonian movement
went sweeping through the country, redeeming multitudes
from the thraldom of the inebriating cup and giving fresh
impulse to the cause of Temperance, of which it was a most
effective and inspiring phase. The Anti-Slavery conflict, in
its moral aspect, was at the same time rising into commanding
importance, enlisting the friends of freedom throughout the
North in uncompromising resistance to the aggressions of the
slave-power, and so preparing the way for and making possible
that memorable edict of twenty years later which proclaimed
"liberty throughout all the land to all the inhabitants thereof."
Under new and enthusiastic leadership the barbarism of the
gigantic war system was exposed, and the claims of the cause
of Peace were urged, with a persistency and to an extent
unknown before. Moreover, it was during that period that the
question of the higher education, the larger opportunity, and
the more complete enfranchisement of woman, not only began
to be discussed but assumed organic form, thereby inaugurat-
ing a work of justice and beneficence the already achieved
results of which constitute one of the marvels of this marvel-
producing nineteenth century. Other reforms, providing for
the abolition of capital punishment, the improvement of
prisons and prison discipline, the prevention of crime and
poverty, etc., were also agitated with unparalleled energy and
zeal, and received a wide and hospitable hearing.

It was early in the same decade and under the same philanthropic impulse that numerous evils pertaining to the
existing order of society arrested widespread attention, suggesting to generous and noble minds the inquiry whether
something might not be done to remedy them — to eliminate
them from the realm of human life and put them forever
away. It was seen and felt upon careful observation and
study that many of these evils were not merely incidental to
the established social system — not simply defects or excres-
cences that would be overcome or outgrown with the lapse
of time and by the ordinary processes of human development,
but that they were *organic*, wrought into and forming an
inherent part of the social structure itself, and therefore to
be exterminated only by reorganizing that structure — by
devising and putting in operation an essentially new order of
society based upon and governed by higher and more equita-

ble principles than the old, and relieved of those features and peculiarities which rendered the old system detrimental to the well-being of vast numbers of people and hence worthy of condemnation. Then came, as a logical and practical result of this view of the matter, the work of so-called *Social Reform;* experiments in the reconstruction of the social order, efforts to solve the problem of human society in the light of reason and religion, and according to the dictates of a broad and generous humanity. As Emerson in hyberbolic rhetoric wrote to Carlysle in the autumn of 1840, "We are all a little wild here with numberless projects of social reform. Not a reading man but has a draft of a new community in his waistcoat pocket."

Within a very few years not less than sixty of these efforts or experiments, under the general name of Communities, were entered upon, and systematically operated in different parts of the country. Most of them were projected and carried forward on essentially economical grounds; being designed chiefly to insure relief from the rivalries and competitions of industrial and commercial life by which multitudes of human beings are brought to penury and wretchedness, to establish more just and harmonious relations between the employer and the employed, and to unite in the bonds of mutual co-operation and helpfulness all classes and conditions of people. Others were more largely of an educational character and made the matter of intellectual training and superior culture a prominent if not the crowning feature of their polity. While a few were distinctively religious in their inception, form of organization, and methods of administration. All professed a steadfast devotion to high ethical principles, and sought to maintain a lofty standard of personal character and social righteousness, and all claimed to be inspired by a desire and purpose to benefit mankind in some definite, practical, effective way.

The Hopedale Community was distinctively and emphatically a religious movement. In all essential respects it was the outcome or product of the religion of the New Testament. The first idea of it was generated by a reverent and painstaking study of the teachings of Jesus, and by a conscientious purpose to make such teachings the ruling forces of thought and conduct in all the manifold concerns of life. It was founded in a spirit of loyalty to Christianity, and that spirit characterized the administration of its affairs from the beginning to the end of its history. As stated in the opening sentence of the body of this work, " The Hopedale Community was a systematic attempt to establish an order of Human Society based upon the sublime ideas of the Fatherhood of God and the brotherhood of man as taught and illustrated in the Gospel of Jesus Christ"; an attempt to actualize in this present world under the limitations of time and sense the Scripture idea of a kingdom of God on earth.

Though organized in accordance with the provisions of a carefully prepared Constitution and governed in its various activities by formally adopted Rules and Regulations, it was in no proper sense a scheme for uplifting and saving men by external restrictions and expedients, or a device for bringing in the millenneum by a skilfully contrived set of machinery. The problem it endeavored to solve was not whether men could be made personally what they ought to be and be brought into fraternal relations with each other by a just and happy environment, or whether society could be regenerated by an ingeniously formulated plan, outward conformity to which would serve humanity's need. Not at all. But whether men believing in Christianity, avowing faith in the principles and precepts of the New Testament, and professing to be actuated by the spirit of the Prince of Peace, could and should make those principles and precepts and that spirit dominant in all social and civil relations and concerns as well as in all individual acts and responsibilities. It rested and urged its claims on the assumption that the legitimate outcome and fruitage of Christianity is a regenerated state of society as well as a regenerated personal character, and that its true disciples ought to unite their energies and resources in establishing a form of social life which should illustrate the great idea of human brotherhood, rather than in upholding and supporting one under which that idea is systematically ignored or thrust aside as a rhetorical generality or iridescent dream, pleasant to rhapsodize about but utterly impracticable in this mundane world. In this assumption may be found the reason for its existence and the ground on which it made its appeal for respectable consideration to all philanthropic and noble men and women, whether living in its own day or in subsequent periods of human history.

It may be questioned, perhaps, whether this endeavor to reconstruct the complicated fabric of human society and initiate the transcendant work of social regeneration will ever be repeated, especially in the exact form in which it appeared at Hopedale, or in the form outlined in the elaborate "Constitution of the Practical Christian Republic" with which this volume closes; whether the divine kingdom will come by the particular processes and methods described in the following pages. But that the existing system of society is not to last forever is in the writer's mind beyond all question or peradventure; a system characterized by incessant rivalries and conflicting interests, by artificial class distinctions and fierce antagonisms, by glaring extremes of wealth and poverty, of ease and slavish toil, of luxury and want, of happiness and misery, by manifold nurseries of iniquity, degradation, and shame, by gigantic military establishments, and vast enginery for slaughtering men and multiplying the sorrows of the world. That such a system, in so many ways hostile to the essential spirit and principles of the Christian Religion, and to the unquestionable primal purpose of a wise and good God, has no guaranty for the future, is no finality, but must some day be superseded by one wherein equity, fraternity, co-operation, harmony shall be in the ascendant, is assured by the highest conclusions of reason, the best aspirations of the human heart, the inherent possibilities of the nature of man, the prophetic intimations of the seers of all ages, and the cheering promises of the Gospel of Christ. And when this sublime consummation is reached it will only be a realization of the comprehensive idea that took form and found expression in The Hopedale Community; the fulfillment of the distinguishing purpose that animated the breasts and prompted the labors of the men and women who composed its membership and gave it a name worthy of preservation and of transmission to coming generations.

Of the more than sixty Communities referred to on a former page, not one, so for as is known, now remains. Hopedale was one of the first to be organized and started on its experimental way, and one of the last to be finally abandoned. The incipient steps leading to its formation were taken with no knowledge, on the part of those concerned, of the fact that similar projects were contemplated even not far away by other laborers in the same field of practical reform· It preserved from first to last a comparatively independent and isolated position, doing its own recognized work in its own way. Soon after organizing, however, it was brought into an acquaintance with several of its contemporaries. The relations between them and itself were of a most friendly and harmonious character, though it differed from them in what were regarded as important details, either of organic form or methods of operation. But this was no obstacle to sympathetic interest, mutual respect, and kindly feeling on either hand.

The entire membership of the Community was composed of about two hundred persons. Of these only some twenty are known to be living, six or eight of them remaining on what was formerly the domain of the Association, the others being more or less widely separated therefrom. Of the thirty-two men and women who put their names to the original Constitution on the 27th of January, 1841, only two, it is believed, are still in the flesh; William W. Cook, now of New York city, and Rev. William H. Fish, who has recently removed from the vicinity of Boston to Colorado Springs in the state of Colorado. After leaving Hopedale he spent a few years in Central New York as general missionary, then returned to South Scituate (Norwell), Mass., where he was more than twenty years the active and highly esteemed Pastor of the First Parish, in the fellowship of the Unitarian branch of the Christian Church. Since leaving there he has resided with his son, Rev. Wm. H. Fish, Jr., at Dedham, Mass. He is now in the 86th year of his age, vigorous and interested still in all good causes, widely known and as widely beloved.

The Founder of the Community and author of this work, Adin Ballou, continued to reside at Hopedale unto the end of his mortal pilgrimage. He served the Community as its leading minister while it retained organic existence, and when it was submerged in *The Hopedale Parish* he was elected Pastor of that body, a position which he occupied until he completed the 77th year of his age, April 23, 1880, having been active in his chosen profession nearly sixty years. Subsequently to this date he was accustomed to answer occasional calls to preach in the vicinity, but more frequent ones to officiate on funeral occasions and at the marriage altar. During the later years of his life he was much engaged in literary work of a varied character. A voluminous "History of the Town of Milford" was prepared by him, and published in 1884; also an elaborate "History of the Ballous in America" some four years later. In addition to these, he wrote an Autobiography which appeared in print a year ago; also the present volume, and others in manuscript awaiting publication. A considerable collection of miscellaneous writings in exposition of his views upon religious, moral, and philanthropic subjects, the product of his pen since the dissolution of the Community, testifies to his tireless industry and to the intensity of his devotion to those aims and pursuits which were dear to his heart, and which engaged his thoughts and energies through a long and active life. He died on the 5th of August, 1890, aged 87 years, 3 months, and 13 days. He was a man of commanding bodily presence, of superior intellectual ability, of generous and genial social qualities, and of a character above reproach and without guile. An agreeable companion, an earnest philanthropist and uncompromising reformer, an able and impressive public speaker, a devoted disciple of Jesus Christ, he lived to make the world better, and died steadfast in the faith that ultimately a divine order of society would be established among men according to his long-cherished ideal, and that so the divine kingdom would at length come and the will of God be done on earth as it is in heaven.

It may be stated that the steel engraving of the author fronting the title page was copied from a photograph taken about the year 1854, and represents him as he was in the ripeness of middle life, when the Community was passing through its most prosperous days, and when he was most diligently employed in prosecuting his labors as an apostle of Practical Christian Socialism.

As this book is sent out into the world it is commended to the candid and thoughtful consideration of the ever-increasing number of those who are interested in the well-being of their fellow-men, and in all efforts to improve their condition and enable them to get the best and the most possible out of the life that has been given them. Also of all students of social problems, who, seeing the manifold evils that pertain to the existing order of society, are seeking conscientiously and earnestly for some means and methods whereby that order may be transformed into or superseded by a reign of righteousness, justice, equity, brotherly-kindness, charity. By imparting some light, encouragement, inspiration to such, and to all workers for human good and happiness who may read the narrative it contains, it is hoped that it will contribute somewhat to the solution of the great question of Social Reform and to the furtherance of the praiseworthy objects for the promotion of which The Hopedale Community was devised and established.

WILLIAM S. HEYWOOD.

Boston, Oct. 26, 1897.

NOTE. — For the benefit of those readers of this volume who may desire to know something of what transpired at Hopedale subsequently to the date when the narrative herein contained closes, and of the present status of the place, a brief statement relating thereto seems desirable and is therefore appended.

The material prosperity referred to in the closing chapters has continued, with but slight modifications, to this day. The brothers, Ebenezer D. and George Draper, to whom the bulk of the Community property was transferred, were men of unusual enterprise, business ability, and perseverence in executing their plans. Moreover, they had the control of a fortunate line of manufacture, and knew how to manage it to the best advantage. Upon that they concentrated all their energies and resources. The less productive branches of industry received from the Community, they cut off and set up new ones tributary to their special work. They called into their partnership, or made their coadjutors, persons from elsewhere of inventive genius and capital. They multiplied their facilities for production, brought out and purchased valuable patents, and rose rapidly to eminence in their particular calling. Their associates and successors, men of like capability and spirit, prosecuted to more signal issues the combined activities so auspiciously begun, and so admirably fitted for their appropriate service.

Corresponding results appeared outside. The population increased, new dwellings sprung up, the village grew in size and attractiveness. Public improvements were introduced; water, gas, macadamized streets, and a host of minor necessaries, comforts, and luxuries. At length the idea of an incorporated township took possession of the leading minds, assuming definite form in the spring of 1885 and reaching its culmination a year afterward, April 7, 1886. So that Hopedale now, composed of the original Community Domain and much contiguous territory, with the inhabitants thereon, numbering 1000 persons more or less, constitutes one of the most active, prosperous, beautiful municipalities in the Commonwealth of Massachusetts.

PREFACE.

I HAVE assumed the labor and responsibility of writing this History of The Hopedale Community for the following reasons: 1. Because the fundamental principles and objects represented in the undertaking bearing that name were in themselves pre-eminently good, conducive to the welfare of mankind, and worthy of lasting commemoration. 2. Because I confidently believe that the said Community in its essential features will have a resurrection at no distant day and be honored as the progenitor of numerous kindred institutions — less imperfect, better conditioned, and far more successful. 3. Because the story of its merits, defects, and varied experiences will enlighten a multitude of ingenuous, beneficently-animated minds, stimulate similar enterprises, and afford valuable instruction for the guidance of those engaged in them. 4. Because I was its chief projector, its first President and leading representative throughout its entire career, and am now the principal mourner over the irretrievable disaster that terminated its existence; as I am also custodian of its records and of all the data pertaining to it. 5. Because I have been prompted and encouraged to the performance of the task by sympathizing and trustworthy friends.

The great masses of people are not yet sufficiently indoctrinated and established in pure Christian ethics — not yet raised to a sufficiently elevated moral and spiritual plane of thought and conduct to care much about the rise or fall of such Communities as the one whose annals the present volume enshrines aspired to be, and can scarcely conceive the possibility of any higher order of human society than that illustrated in the existing civilization of the general community to which they belong. Even the more advanced classes in church and state, seeking the progress, the harmony, and happiness of mankind, propose little if anything more than the *gradual*

improvement of society on the old basis of egoism, caste distinctions, competitive rivalry, shrewd and cunning practices,
jealousy and hatred of race and nation, and dernier resorts to
violence and deadly force. Such must be expected to ignore,
underestimate, contemn, or, at best, pity all such attempts to
benefit and bless the world as that embodied in the Hopedale
Community. If they notice their appearance at all it is only
to decry the folly of them and predict their failure, and when
failure comes they complacently and rejoicingly exclaim: "We
told you so."

There is, however, in the world at large a small but, I have
reason to feel, a continually increasing number of morally
illumined and noble minds who see farther into the nature of
things and into the causes of misrule and misery, who aspire
after a radically more fraternal form of social life and understand in some good degree what is needed to insure it, and
who are groping after some practical and efficient method or
system of operations by which it may be actualized. From
these there is much to hope. Sooner or later they will find
what they seek, and their most ardent longings —the travail
of their souls will be satisfied; but their search will no doubt
be long and their gratification be deferred to a somewhat
remote future. It is my wish in this narrative and other
similar writings to contribute what I can to the accomplishment of the greatly-to-be-desired result. If God has entrusted
me with any distinctive mission on earth, it is to aid in showing my fellowmen the way into that Christ-like order of social
life which shall illustrate in marked degree the great ideas of
the Fatherhood of God and the brotherhood of man. I would,
at least, be among the harbingers and heralds of communal
harmony and blessedness, even though I should seem only to
re-echo "The voice of one crying in the wilderness, 'Prepare
ye the way of the Lord!'"

I fondly and confidently trust that my testimonies in this
volume and elsewhere will, under the sheltering care and
kindly providence of my heavenly Father, be as "good seed,
falling," in some cases at least, "upon good ground," and
bringing forth fruit accordingly. But I am now too far
advanced in life, being more than seventy-three years of age, to
behold any harvest therefrom in the flesh. Nevertheless, it will
come in its season, not by any sudden and startling transfor-

mation, not by the literal and visible letting down of a new Jerusalem out of heaven, but according to the laws of progressive development and growth in the divine kingdom, "first the blade, then the ear, then the full corn in the ear." And as I am divinely assured of a spiritual and immortal life in unseen realms of being, I expect to rejoice with the reapers when "the good time coming" shall appear, however distant that blissful consummation may be. Then the truth of the poet's couplet will be realized in my own experience:

> " The blest to-day is as completely so
> As who began a thousand years ago."

The reader will find in the consecutive chapters of this work a truthful and sufficiently minute account of The Hopedale Community and its manifold affairs from the very beginning through all its intervening stages to its final submergence in the organization denominated and known to this day as *The Hopedale Parish.* "Whoso readeth, let him understand," and be profited thereby.

ADIN BALLOU.

Hopedale, Mass., August 5, 1876.

TABLE OF CONTENTS.

CHAPTER VII.

CHAPTER VIII.

CHAPTER IX.

CHAPTER X.

HISTORY.

CHAPTER I.

1839 – 1840.

THE COMMUNITY IDEA — ITS ORIGIN AND GROWTH —
ORGANIC FORM ASSUMED.

THE Hopedale Community was a systematic attempt to
establish an order of Human Society based upon the
sublime ideas of the Fatherhood of God and the Brotherhood of Man, as taught and illustrated in the Gospel of
Jesus Christ. The primordial germ, of which it was the
natural outgrowth and consummation, first manifested itself
in my own mind about the time of the opening of the
year 1839. That germ, in its crude form, was commu-
nicated to a few personal friends, interested, as I was, in
promoting alike the interests of truth and the enduring
welfare and happiness of mankind, who gladly welcomed
it, and united cordially with me in developing it, in giving
it definite form, and in carrying it out to legitimate,
practical results in actual life. The evolutionary process
by which all this was accomplished, this, the opening
chapter of the present volume, is designed to delineate.
Succeeding chapters will recapitulate and put on record, in
their proper order and relativity, the different characteristics and phases of what subsequently transpired.

At the date mentioned I was Pastor of the First Church
and Parish of the town of Mendon, Mass., a position I

1

had occupied during the eight previous years. I had long
before outgrown my early belief that the religion of the
New Testament was chiefly concerned with the condition
of mankind in a future state of being, and that it was
the essential office and mission of Jesus Christ, in the
plan and providence of the Infinite Father, to save men
from damnation and misery awaiting the finally impenitent
after death. I had come to see that the teachings of the
Master were essential to human well-being in this world
as well as in the world to come; that it was one of the
declared objects of Christ's labors to inaugurate the kingdom of heaven *on the earth;* and that it was the imperative duty of his disciples to pray and to work earnestly
for that sublime end, as one of the best preliminaries
to immortal blessedness. The supreme, universal, un-
changeable Fatherhood of God and the universal Brotherhood of Man had become settled articles of my faith, and
whatever contradicted either of them, in theory or practice, I was certain must be false and wrong. Consequently
the seemingly mighty and almost sole concern of the
nominal Christian Church to save souls from the tortures
of never-ending fire and secure heaven for them beyond
the grave, appeared to me a distortion of the Gospel
requirement — a delusion of superstition.

On the other hand, among dissenters from the dogmas
of prevailing theological systems, the then dominant Uni-
versalism, which magnified the doctrine of the salvation
of all men at death and knew of no condition beyond the
grave but that of angelic beatitude, had become to me
a scarcely less irrational and offensive extreme of so-called
liberalism. I belonged to a small Association of Restorationists who had seceded from the Universalist denomination,
and were in a state of controversial protest against both
extremes. About half of this Association felt strongly
that their Restorationism meant radical reform in respect
to personal and social abuses and evils, and had zealously

espoused the Temperance, Anti-Slavery, and Peace movements, as attested by a series of outspoken, uncompromising resolutions passed not long before in public convocation
and published to the world. The rest were more prudent
and conservative, and sincerely thought their brethren rash
and presumptious in their utterances and action—running
ahead too fast in that particular direction.

I was of the progressive wing and longed most ardently
to see New Testament Christianity actualized—made
practically the controlling agency in all the relations and
concerns of life. My sympathizing associates were like-
minded; enthusiastic in pressing forward to a wider and
more authoritative application of Christian principles to
human conduct in all its phases and manifestations, and
our private meditations and mutual conferences soon
brought us out generations in advance of our former
position respecting the absolute requirements of the law
of Christian righteousness. The growth of our ideas and
convictions in regard to pure Christianity and the obligations it imposes upon its confessors was rapid and
intense, perhaps I should say *precocious*, in view of
subsequent disclosures. This will appear from the following remarkable *Confession* or *Declaration of Sentiments*
drafted by me and sent forth as a comprehensive statement of the views which we had come to entertain
touching the truths and duties included and enjoined by
our holy religion, as we understood and believed it.

"Standard of Practical Christianity.

"At a conference of Christian Ministers called Restorationists holden by special agreement at Mendon, Mass., Feb. 19th,
20th, and 21st, and, by adjournment, Apr. 24th and 25th, 1839,
there was a free and solemn discussion of the prevailing
views, feelings, and conduct of professing Christians in comparison with the precepts and example of Jesus Christ and his
apostles; which discussion resulted in the adoption of the
appended testimonial, to wit:

" Humbly desirous of promoting Christian piety and morality in their primitive purity, the undersigned do solemnly acknowledge and embrace the principles, sentiments, and duties declared in the following

STANDARD.

" We are Christians. Our creed is the New Testament. Our religion is love. Our only law is the will of God. Our grand object is the restoration of man, especially the most fallen and friendless. Our immediate concern is the promotion of useful knowledge, moral improvement, and Christian perfection. We recognize no spiritual father but God; no master but Christ. We belong to that kingdom of 'righteousness, peace, and joy,' which is 'not of this world,' whose throne is holiness, whose sceptre is truth, whose greatness is humility, whose pre-eminence is service, whose patriotism is love of enemies, whose heroism is forbearance, whose glory is self-sacrifice, whose wealth is charity, whose triumphs are salvation. Therefore

" We can make no earthly object our chief good; nor be governed by any motive but the love of right; nor compromise duty with worldly convenience; nor seek the preservation of our property, our reputation, our personal liberty, or our life by sacrificing conscience. We cannot live merely to eat, drink, sleep, display ourselves, acquire property, and be accounted great in this world, but to do good. All that we are and have, with all that God shall ever bestow on us, we unreservedly dedicate to the cause of universal righteousness; expecting for ourselves, in the order of divine providence, only a comfortable subsistence until death, and, in the world to come, eternal life.

" Placing unlimited confidence in our heavenly Father, we distrust all other guidance and protection. We cannot be governed by the will of man, however solemnly and formally declared, nor put our trust in an arm of flesh. Hence we voluntarily withdraw from all interference with the governments of this world. We can take no part in the politics, the administration, or the defence of those governments; either by voting at their polls, holding their offices, aiding in the execution of their legal vengeance, fighting under their banners, claiming their protection against violence, seeking redress in their courts, petitioning their legislatures to enact penal laws, or obeying their unjust requirements. Neither can we participate in any rebellion, insurrection, sedition, riot, conspiracy, or plot against any of those governments; nor resist any of their ordinances by physical force; nor do anything unbecoming a peaceable submisssion to the existing powers;—but will quietly pay the taxes levied upon us, conform to all innocent laws and usages, enjoy all righteous privileges, abstain from all civil commotions, freely express our opinion of governmental acts, and patiently endure whatever penalties we may for conscience' sake incur. We cannot employ carnal weapons nor any physical violence whatsoever to compel moral agents to do right or to prevent their doing wrong — not even for the preservation of our own lives. We cannot render evil for evil, railing for railing, or wrath for wrath, nor revenge insults and injuries, nor lay up grudges, nor be overcome by evil, nor do otherwise than 'love our enemies, bless them that curse us, do good to them that hate us, and pray for them that despitefully use us and persecute us.'

"We cannot indulge the lust of dominion, nor exercise arbitrary authority, nor cherish bigotry, nor be egotistical, nor receive honorary titles, nor accept flattery, nor seek human applause, nor assume the place of dignity. We cannot be pharisaical, self-righteous, or dogmatical. We cannot do evil that good may come. We cannot resent reproof, nor justify our faults, nor persist in a known wrong.

"We cannot excommunicate, anathematize, or execrate any apostate or reprobate person otherwise than by withdrawing our fellowship, refusing our countenance, and declining familiar intercourse.

"We cannot be cruel, even to the beasts of the earth. We cannot be inhuman, unmerciful, unjust, unkind, abusive, or injurious toward any being of our race. We cannot be indifferent to the sufferings of distressed humanity, nor treat the unfortunate with contempt. But we hold ourselves bound to do good as we have opportunity unto all mankind, to feed the hungry, clothe the naked, minister to the sick, visit the imprisoned, entertain the stranger, protect the helpless, comfort the afflicted, plead for the oppressed, seek the lost, lift up the fallen, rescue the ensnared, reclaim the wandering, reform the vicious, enlighten the benighted, instruct the young, admonish the wayward, rebuke the scornful, encourage the penitent, confirm the upright, and diffuse a universal charity.

"We cannot go with a multitude to do evil, nor take part with the mighty against the feeble, nor excite enmity between the rich and the poor, nor stand aloof from the friendless, nor court the great, nor despise the small, not be afraid of the terrible, nor take advantage of the timid, nor show respect of persons, nor side with a friend in what is wrong, nor oppose an enemy in what is right, nor forbid others to do good because they follow not with us, nor set up names and forms above personal holiness, nor refuse to co-operate with any man, class, or association of men on our own principles in favor of righteousness, nor contemn any new light, improvement, or excellence which may be commended to our attention from any quarter whatsoever.

"We cannot make a trade or emolument of preaching the Gospel, nor be supported therein by unwilling contributions, nor keep back any truth thereof that ought to be declared, nor consent to preach more or less than God directs us, nor encourage religious devotion in mere worldly show, nor pursue any course of conduct whereby the money, the smiles, or the frowns of corrupt men may overrule the divine testimony. We cannot surrender the right of serving God according to the dictates of our own consciences, nor interfere with others in their exercise of the same liberty.

"We hold it impossible to cherish a holy love for mankind without abhoring sin. Therefore we can give no countenance, express or implied, to any iniquity, vice, wrong, or evil, on the ground that the same is established by law or is a source of pecuniary profit to any class of men, or is fashionable in high life, or is popular with the multitude; but we hold ourselves so much the more bound to testify, plainly, faithfully, and fearlessly, against such sins. Hence we declare our utter abhorrence of war, slavery, intemperance, licentiousness, covetousness, and worldly ambition, in all their forms. We cannot partake in these sins, nor apologize for them, nor remain neutral concerning them, nor refrain from rebuking their various manifestations; but must ever abstain from and oppose them.

"We cannot promote our own advantage at the expense of others, by deceiving, defrauding, corrupting, degrading, overbearing, or impoverishing them. We cannot take away their good name by defamation, nor by retailing the scandal of their enemies, nor by spreading abroad evil reports on mere hearsay authority, nor by wantonly publishing their failings. We cannot be busy-bodies in other people's affairs, nor tale-bearers of domestic privacy, nor proclaimers of matters unsuitable for the public ear. We cannot rashly judge men's motives, nor raise evil suspicions against them, nor join in condemning the accused without a hearing, nor delay reparation to the injured, nor make any one's necessity our advantage, nor willingly render ourselves burdensome to others, nor cause any one unnecessary trouble for our mere gratification; but we will always deem it 'more blessed to give than to receive,' to serve than to be served; sacrificing nothing of holy principle, though, if need be, everything of personal convenience.

"We cannot live in idleness or be carelessly extravagant; nor, on the other hand, be avaricious, parsimonious, or niggardly. We cannot indulge in any feverish anxiety concerning our temporal affairs, nor fret ourselves under disappointment, nor repine at anything which marks our lot. We cannot be austere, morose, or rude; nor capricious, ungrateful, or treacherous. We cannot practice dissimulation, nor offer fulsome compliments, nor use a flattering courtesy. We cannot follow pernicious fashions, nor encourage [immoral] theatrical exhibitions, nor join in frivolous amusements, nor countenance games of chance, nor array ourselves in costly apparel, nor wear useless ornaments, nor put on badges of mourning, nor distinguish ourselves by any peculiar formalities of raiment or language.

"We cannot indulge to excess in eating, drinking, sleeping, recreation, labor, study, joy, or sorrow; nor permit our passions to tyrannize over our reasons. We cannot harbor pride, envy, anger, malice, wrath, ill-will, sullenness, or peevishness; nor cherish any unholy lusts, imaginations, or tempers.

"We cannot swear by any manner of oath, nor make any rash vow, nor offer any extraordinary protestations of our innocence, sincerity or veracity, nor utter any blasphemy, imprecation, falsehood, obscene expression, foolish jest, or profane exclamation.

"We cannot enter into the state of matrimony without grave deliberation and an assurance of divine approval. We cannot neglect or abuse our families, nor evince any want of natural affection towards our bosom companion, our aged parents, or helpless offspring. We cannot imbrute our children by disregarding their education, nor by setting them an evil example, nor by over-fondness, nor by harshness and severity, nor by corporal punishments, nor by petulence and scolding.

" We cannot desert our brethren in their adversity, nor call anything our own when their necessities demand relief, nor be silent when they are unjustly accused or reproached. We cannot speak of their faults in their absence without first having conferred with and admonished them; nor then, if they have promised amendment.

" We cannot over-urge any person to unite with us, nor resort to undignified artifices of proselytism, nor seek debate with unreasonable men, nor protract a controversy for the sake of the last word, nor introduce sacred subjects for discussion in a company of scorners. Yet we will hold ourselves always ready to give an answer to every one that asketh of us a reason for our faith, opinion, or conduct, with meekness, frankness, and patience.

" Finally, as disciples of Jesus Christ, before whose judgment seat all must appear, we acknowledge ourselves bound by the most sublime, solemn, and indispensable obligations, to 'be perfect as our Father in heaven is perfect' in all possible respects; and whereinsoever we come short thereof, to take shame to ourselves, seek divine pardon, repair to the utmost our delinquencies and bring forth fruits meet for repentance. And for all this, 'our sufficiency is of God,' to whom be glory, world without end. Amen.

" ADIN BALLOU, DAVID R. LAMSON, GEO. W. STACY, DANIEL S. WHITNEY, WILLIAM H. FISH, *Ministers:* CHARLES GLADDING, WILLIAM W. COOK, *Laymen concurring.*"

This document was intended to cover the whole ground of personal and social righteousness on the high plane of Practical Christianity. It was accompanied with references to the principal passages of Scripture understood to teach its distinctive principles, sentiments, and duties, and with brief explanatory notes upon the more important and radical points. Thus verified and fortified, it was submitted to the consideration and judgment of those who might deem it worthy of deliberate attention. It was received with widely-varying emotion, and provoked much comment — friends, foes, and neutrals expressing in more or less emphatic terms their opinion concerning it. Some condemned it outright as extravagant, unsound, absurd, impracticable, though few of these attempted to show that it was in any wise hostile to, or inconsistent with, the teaching and example of Christ. Others, more appreciative and hospitable, regarded it with favor; a small number with moral admiration and delight. But the great mass of those claiming to be followers of Christ and believers in his religion gave it little or no heed. As for myself, I accepted it at the time and endorsed it with all my mind and heart and soul, and have remained a firm and unwavering adherent of it, with a few slight and unessential modifications, until this hour. However faulty I may have been concerning it in practice, it has always expressed substantially my profound and settled convictions of pure Christian righteousness; such as the truly regenerate church of Christ will some day believe in, teach, and exemplify.

Having devised and formulated the foregoing *Standard*, the germination and growth of the Community idea in my own mind were as natural and inevitable as are the flowering and fruitage of any productive plant of garden or field when the seed from which it springs is cast into congenial soil. Equally so were its acceptance, development, and ultimate practical realization, in the minds of those who, with me, had in good faith put their names to that manifesto, and of all in cordial sympathy with us. We were "a peculiar people" in the professing Christian world. We had taken a stand unlike that of any of our contemporaries in either church or state — in any existing form of social life. We occupied a new and anomolous situation. We had gathered a fresh and hitherto unknown species of grape from the primitive Christian vintage, and had extracted therefrom a sample

of the "new wine" of the Kingdom of God. But where
were the bottles to hold and preserve it? They were not
to be found. Where was the church, the congregation, the
social organism, prepared to accept, sustain, and illustrate
such principles, virtues, obligations — such high and noble
ideals of duty to God and man as we had avowed and proclaimed far and wide as a new revelation from the infinite
source of all goodness and truth? Nowhere upon the face
of the earth was there one of these — one among all the
sects of Christendom — one among all the schools of
philosophy, or orders of philanthropy, or movements of
reform, prepared to embrace, maintain, defend, *live* by
them in their entirety — in all the length and breadth,
height and depth of their far-reaching meaning and obli-
gatoriness. As popular Christianity *was*, in church and
state and general society, there was for such ideas, convictions, principles as ours, no place of shelter, nurture, and
practical actualization — no congenial and permanent home.
They were too radical, too unconformable to the established
institutions, customs, practices, and fashions of this world
— the world of so-called Christian civilization — to find
anywhere an open hearty welcome and a ready-made
habitation to dwell in and to go forth from as a power
of godliness and redemption to mankind.

In several fundamental particulars were we openly and
uncompromisingly arrayed against the prevailing theory
and practice of the world at large about us.

(1) The great overshadowing *War System*, everywhere
deemed essential to the maintenance of public order and
the security of the common welfare, with its multiplex
enginery of destruction, its appalling record of devasta-
tion, bloodshed, and death; its awful burden of degradation, poverty, and wretchedness, crushing the life out of
vast multitudes of people; its manifold barbarities and
cruelties, subversive of the essential principles and vital

spirit of the Gospel of Christ, we unqualifiedly condemned and repudiated.

(2) The vast complex mechanism of *Politico-civil Government* in its existing form and mode of administration, based upon injurious and death-dealing force as a final resort, and claiming the unquestioning allegiance and support of its subjects, with its ubiquitous agencies, offices, emoluments, excitements, honors, and rewards, its subtle methods of control and usurpations of authority, its disregard of the requirements of the moral law and of the rights of the weak and defenceless, the chicanery and corruption that often enter into its management, shaping its policy and dictating its legislation — all this was transcended and set aside by us in our declared loyalty to that kingdom which is "not of this world," "whose officers are peace and its exactors righteousness," and wherein those that are chief and would be accounted greatest are servants of all.

(3) The abounding *spirit of competition, rivalry, self-aggrandizement, and open antagonism* which dominates industry and trade, whereby mammon worship is perpetually encouraged and mutual helpfulness ignored; whereby the strong make victims of the weak, the cunning and unscrupulous outwit and overreach the honest, simple-minded, and self-respecting, the arrogant and heartless take advantage of the necessities of the poor and unfortunate, resulting in class distinctions, in gross inequalities of condition, in revolting extremes of wealth and poverty, of prodigal luxury and famishing want, of gorgeous display and loathesome destitution, engendering discontent, ill-will, resentment, animosity, hatred, and sometimes the spirit of revenge and open violence; — all this, and especially the state of things producing it, we condemned and repudiated as utterly opposed to our doctrine of human brotherhood, which requires that kindly interest, mutual assistance, and friendly co-operation, according to the

maxim "each for all and all for each," should be the supreme rule of action in all departments and activities of industrial and commercial life.

Minor points of difference between us and those of our contemporaries who were generally satisfied with the world as it was, or at least with the social system under which they were living, of which there were many of more or less significance, it is not needful here to enumerate. Enough have been mentioned to indicate the unique, the peculiar, the virtually isolated situation in which we found ourselves by reason of the new interpretations and applications of Christian truth which we had adopted and testified to in our "Standard." Realizing our condition, it was a serious question with us what we were going to do about it. We could not renounce our faith, abandon our avowed principles as false, visionary, chimerical, impracticable, and go back to the position — to the ecclesiastical, political, social status and fellowship whence we came. That would be to shut out the light that had dawned upon us from heaven and to deny the Lord to whom we owed allegiance. We could not unite with any existing body of people, religious, reformatory, philanthropic, or otherwise, with any assurance that we should find sympathy. co-operation, desirable assistance in maintaining our views of truth and duty or in proclaiming them and making them efficacious in enlightening, uplifting, and redeeming mankind. Nor could we stand in our separate and unrelated individuality — apart from the world and all existing associations, institutions, organizations, and apart from each other. Not at all. We must ourselves, few in numbers as we were, strike hands together, be united in spirit and in action, co-operate, associate our interests, combine our forces, institute a church, a system of society, that should truly represent our convictions; build a new civilization radically higher than the old, which should be in deed and in truth the realization of

a divine order of human life founded on the great ideas
of the fatherhood of God and brotherhood of man. This
would be to put the new wine of our Practical Christianity
into the new bottles of an embryonic kingdom of heaven
on the earth. In this way was conceived and quickened
in us the germinal principle that in a few months was to
become incarnated in *Fraternal Community No. 1*, afterwards known as *The Hopedale Community*.

Another consideration of no trifling importance came in
as a factor of the problem whose solution was commanding our attention, and no doubt had considerable influence
in determining our future course. Our acknowledged
"Standard" comtemplated and required on our part, not
only a devotion to whatever might conduce in a general
way and by the more quiet methods of moral enlightenment and spiritual regeneration and growth to the progress and redemption of mankind, but also a deep and
active interest in those specific reforms which were then
agitating the public mind and pressing their claims home
upon the hearts and consciences of all those who loved
God and their fellowmen. Recognizing and accepting the
obligations imposed upon us in that respect, we had
heartily espoused the Anti-Slavery, Temperance, and Peace
movements, and had borne faithful witness in the pulpit
and elsewhere against the great evils they were designed
to overcome and banish from the world. Our course had
aroused more or less opposition on the part of certain of
our parishioners, some of whom threatened to withdraw
their support from us and secure our discharge from our
post of ministerial duty, as had been done under similar
circumstances elsewhere. This was exceedingly embarrassing and unpleasant for us and led us to see how unfortunate was the position of a minister who was impelled by
his conscience to proclaim unpopular truths and to arraign
and denounce prevailing errors and abuses while dependent
for the means of subsistence for himself and family, in

part at least, upon those who were brought under rebuke
and condemnation by his testimonies. It also suggested
the inquiry whether some way could not be devised or
plan adopted whereby we, as occupants of such a position, could not maintain ourselves outside of our profession, — by week-day agricultural or mechanical labors, or
otherwise — and go out into the community at large on
Sundays or week-day evenings, as opportunity should offer,
and deliver our message upon questions affecting the
interests of humanity, freely and independently, in fidelity
to our highest convictions, whether men would hear or forbear. The proposition to establish a Community seemed
to be in line with that inquiry and to furnish a satisfactory
answer to it. Under such a system as that to which our
declaration of faith was impelling us, all our material
wants would be adequately provided for and we could
proclaim our Gospel of Reform as the Lord's freemen,
uninfluenced by any financial or other worldly considerations, and make war against reigning abominations, fashionable iniquities, and spiritual wickedness in high places,
regardless of the favor or hostility, the smiles or the
frowns of men. So were we confirmed and strengthened in
our purpose to move forward in the way already indicated
— a way which appeared to our thought and faith providentially opened to us.

While in the midst of the inquiries and deliberations
set forth in the foregoing pages, seeking after and waiting for any new light that might be thrown upon our
uncertain path, we commenced the publication of a small
semi-monthly sheet, entitled, *The Practical Christian*, its
first number being dated, "Mendon, Mass., April 1,
1840." It had for a standing motto, "Devoted to Truth
and Righteousness." As stated in the *prospectus*, its
leading design, in general terms, was to be an organ for
"a faithful exposition, defence, and promulgation of

Primitive Christianity, in all the prominent characteristics, aspects, and bearings of its theology, piety, and
morality," and "to bear aloft and magnify the standard of
religious truth and duty for which Jesus of Nazareth died
on the cross." Though naming the town of Mendon as its
place of publication, it was not at first printed there, but
at such localities as were most convenient. Its *Editor in
Chief* and *Publishing Agent* was ADIN BALLOU; with
DAVID R. LAMSON, GEORGE W. STACY, DANIEL S. WHIT-
NEY, and WILLIAM H. FISH, *Contributors.* These assistants
for several years furnished a goodly proportion of the
matter that appeared in its columns. On the last page
of No. 1, was presented in full our "Standard of Practical Christianity" adopted a year before, with all its
Scripture verifications and explanatory notes. In the
same issue I began a series of articles entitled *Exposition
of Faith*, in which I endeavored "to furnish inquiring
minds with a well digested, systematic, and comprehensive
view of Christian theology, as understood by me and
generally by those sympathizing with me in matters of
religious faith and practice." It ran through the entire
volume and near to the middle of the succeeding one.
Concurrently therewith, both my brethren and myself, with
now and then an outside correspondent, were unfolding,
illustrating, and applying the general moral and spiritual
ideas and sentiments that had been imparted to us, in
such a manner as seemed calculated to instruct our readers in the things of the Divine Kingdom, to show them
their duty to both God and man, to arouse in their
breasts a sense of personal responsibility, and so build
them up in the faith and life of Christ. A rational, a
practical, a spiritual interpretation and application of the
Gospel in its relation to the individual and social needs
of our fellowmen constituted the principal theme of our
discussions, the burden of our testimonies. All the virtues
that dignify and adorn human character, all the graces

that enter into the Christian life, all helpful ministries of good, all disinterested philanthropies, all salutary reforms, received encouragement at our hands and the commendation which we felt to be their due.

Meanwhile the Community idea in our minds was struggling to make itself felt, and to gain a commanding place in our thoughts and deliberations. It entered more and more into our social intercourse as we met from time to time, and grew in importance as we dwelt upon it and suggested practical measures to one another in friendly conversation. But it did not seem advisable in its yet immature, undigested state, to make it the subject of deliberative discourse in any of our public convocations, nor even to mention it in our paper, and for quite a while it was scarcely heard of outside our own little circle. At length, having as I thought sufficiently pondered it in my own private meditations and talked about it with my brethren, I was moved to make known our views and feelings upon it, more in the spirit of suggestion and inquiry than of positive conviction, through the columns of *The Practical Christian*, in its issue of Sept. 15, 1840: Vol. I, No. 10. The article will show the still rudimental phase of the matter involved at that date, but as it was the first proclamation of what was fomenting in our own breasts and seeking an outward expression, ere long to be actualized in an organic form and stand forth before angels and men as a noteworthy achievement among the humanitary movements of the middle of the 19th century, it is given here complete.

"COMMUNITIES.

"A good deal has been said among our brethren in their social interviews at various times about the establishment of *Practical Christian Communities*. We have been frequently requested of late to lay the subject before the readers of this paper with a view to a free discussion of the general proposition and its details. We have at length concluded to comply with this repeated request, but in doing so would respectfully premise that the whole matter is in a mere embryonic state as yet, and that little more can be done at present than to suggest, discuss, and consider. Whether in the end any enterprise of the kind will be deemed desirable, or, if desirable, practicable, remains to be seen. We shall submit a rough sketch of a general plan for a Community, and leave it to the criticism and amendment of the brethren at large. The Shakers and the Moravians have established and maintained Communities after their peculiar fashion, neither of which we should at present wholly approve as models, though much might be selected from both worthy of adoption. With us. at present, perfect individuality is a fundamental idea of the true man. We believe that by setting the individual right with his Creator, we shall set social relationships right. We therefore go for unabridged independence of mind, conscience, duty, and responsibility; for direct divine government over the human soul; and, of course, for as little *human* government as possible. We wish to know whether there is any such thing as man's being and doing right from the law of God written on his heart, without the aid of external bonds and restraints. We believe this is possible, and that it is every man's privilege, by the grace of God, to attain to such a state. And more than this, we believe that men in the flesh will yet by thousands actually arrive at that blissful state. Hence, our notions of a Practical Christian Community preclude very much of the governmental machinery employed in both the Shaker and Moravian establishments.

"We are not prepared to embrace the doctrine of the Shakers respecting marriage, nor their plan of entire common property. The Moravians, it is true, retain marriage, preserve family integrity, and secure the individual rights of property, etc. But there is too much detail and complexity in their government. Both of these classes of Christians have taken a noble stand in favor of many points of Practical Christianity, as have also the Friends, Mennonites, and others. They are lights of Christian excellence to which we should do well to give heed: not implicitly as unto perfection itself, but judiciously, as unto lamps lighted at the great sun, Jesus Christ, which yet may be excelled in some respects by still brighter luminaries. Especially would we recommend, should our

brethren ever attempt to found a Community, that some suitable persons be sent to the Shaker and Moravian settlements, for the purpose of investigating the practical working
of their respective systems, in order that whatever is good in
them might not be overlooked or rejected. We say this the
more earnestly because we have made the foregoing remarks
respecting their Communities wholly from book knowledge
and not from actual observation, which last might perhaps
render it necessary to modify our judgment in some respects.
With these preliminary observations, we proceed to the business in hand.

"(1) What is the great leading idea of the proposed Community? Ans.—A compact neighborhood or village of practical
Christians, dwelling together by families in love and peace,
insuring to themselves the comforts of life by agricultural and
mechanical industry, and devoting the entire residue of their
intellectual, moral, and physical resources to the Christianiza-
tion and general welfare of the human race.

"(2) What is the basis on which members are to be admitted
into this Community? Ans.—Assent to the document known
among our friends by the title, *Standard of Practical Christianity.* Those who profess the principles and acknowledge the
duties declared in that Standard (together with their families
and dependents) are to be the inhabitants of the Community,
village, or neighborhood.

"(3) How is a tract of land, or proper quantity of real
estate, to be obtained for such an establishment? Ans.— By
means of a joint stock fund raised by subscription in definite
shares and judiciously expended in the purchase of the
requisite real estate; which estate, having been secured, should
be afterwards partly or wholly divided among the joint proprietors according to the value of their several subscriptions
— unless all were agreed to hold it in common.

"(4) Where shall the Community be located? Ans.— In the
East or West, according to circumstances. It should be on
land capable of the highest degree of improvement at the
least expense, in a healthful location, a little retired from the
bustle of the world, with a good mill privilege, and within
reach of a ready market for vegetable productions.

"(5) What should be the maximum size of the Community?
Ans.— We think it should not comprise more than one hun-

dred families, and perhaps not so many. More good might probably be done by planting new colonies when those wishing to unite in such an enterprise should exceed fifty families, especially if it were to be undertaken in a part of the country where land is not easily obtained. Unforseen circumstances, however, would more definitely settle the question of size. It might vary in different localities. No precise limits can now be prescribed.

"(6) What sort of a Constitution or Compact would be proper for such a Community?   Ans.— Something like the following, viz.:

" We, the undersigned, professing the principles and acknowledging the duties declared in the document entitled *Standard of Practical Christianity*, do covenant with each other and agree as follows:

"That by divine permission and favor we will unite in the formation and establishment of a Community to be called THE FRATERNAL COMMUNION.

" That we will purchase a suitable tract of land, lay out the site of a village, and, as soon as may be, settle thereon by families in a compact neighborhood.

" That to this end we will create by subscription a joint stock fund in shares of fifty dollars each.

" That said shares shall be transferable by the holders at their pleasure, provided only that no share shall be sold out of the Communion until the purchase thereof shall have been refused by all within its membership.

" That when the joint stock fund shall have been invested in real estate, any stockholder shall be entitled, upon demand, to have his or her just portion of the joint property, or any specified part thereof, set off to his or her exclusive possession.   And that it shall forever be at the option of the stockholders, as individuals, to continue in joint partnership with each other, wholly or in part, or to dissolve the same by an equitable division.

" That this Communion shall from time to time elect such official servants as may be deemed necessary, all of whom shall be directly accountable to their constituents, and subject to their instructions and removals at their pleasure.

"That any person professing the principles and acknowledging the duties set forth in the forenamed *Standard*, may become a member by subscribing this Compact.

"That any member of this Communion may be dismissed, or withdraw from the same, at any time, by expressing a desire or purpose to do so in writing.

"That nothing herein contained shall be so construed as to countenance the slightest interference with the conscience, rights, duties, or responsibilities of any individual member.

"That this Communion may at their pleasure amend this Compact, or adopt any rules or regulations for the transaction of business under the same not repugnant to its general object and spirit.

"(7) Finally, What important advantages may be expected from the establishment of the proposed Community? Ans.— Such a Community would furnish a happy home to many pure-hearted Christians now scattered abroad, insulated from each other, enthralled by a corrupt church, and oppressed by the world. It would enable them to secure, with less severe toil and more certainty, a comfortable subsistence for themselves and their family dependents. It would render it much easier for them to reform pernicious habits of living and promote the true physical health of themselves and their children. It would remove them from the dominion of many corrupt and demoralizing influences to which they are now exposed. It would enable them to set up and maintain a purer religious worship, a holier ministry, a more salutory moral discipline, and a better spiritual culture. It would enable them to send forth devoted religious, moral, and philanthropic missionaries into the world for its conversion — men and women who could not be bribed nor frightened into subserviency to popular iniquities, and who, when weary, might return like Noah's dove to the shelter of a peaceful ark and find repose. It would enable them more effectually to prosecute every work of moral reform and improvement, by means of the press, of well-ordered schools, and of trained teachers going out to inculcate their holy principles wherever the people might welcome them. It would enable them to 'bring up their children in the nurture and admonition of the Lord,' away from those loose and degrading influences so prevalent in existing society. It would enable them to build asylums for the orphan, the widow, and the outcast, wherein they might be led into the paths of life.

"In fine, it would be a powerful concentration of moral light and heat which would make Practical Christianity known and felt by all beholders. It would be in the moral and religious world what the sun glass and steam engine are in the physical. If one such Community could be established, the number might be indefinitely multiplied till at length the kingdoms of this world should be absorbed in the glorious kingdom of our Lord Jesus Christ. Thus the reign of ignorance, selfishness, pride, and violence would be terminated among men, and the whole great brotherhood of our race would dwell together in unspeakable peace under the government of Him to whom belongeth the kingdom, power, and glory, forever.

"Shall the experiment be made? Who has faith in such small things? Let the believers speak."

The above article, though the product of my pen, was in its general character a consensus of the sentiments and aspirations of all those whose names had been appended to the Standard. It is worth while to call attention to a few of its distinguishing features. It exhibits a strong determination to maintain unabridged individuality of personal rights and responsibilities, the integrity of the marriage and family relationship, and the great safeguards against communal tyranny and absorption; yet at the same time it holds up the grand desideratum of fraternal unity and co-operation. It contemplates no unnatural, exclusive, monastic retreat from society at large, but only such a concentration of the benign social forces represented by us as should enable us most effectually to reach out a religious and philanthropic hand to all mankind. It proposes a definite moral and religious test of membership, but not a theological, dogmatic, sectarian one. It supposes those entering the association suggested to be Christlike enough to stand upon his super-worldly plane, sufficiently above the common level of existing civilization not to be involved in its semi-barbarism; thus to uplift it instead of being debased by it, as has so long been the case with the nominal Christian Church. The weakest point of the proposition, perhaps, was its over-sanguine assumption that such persons could be found, with the attainments, resources, and noble devotion requisite to the realization of the end in view, — the formation of practical Christian Communities in those times or at some time not far away. The credulity on which such assumption was based may be regarded as a weakness, but can be no crime, and is morally far preferable to that pseudo-Christian skepticism which is forever postponing the advent of a truly Christian dispensation under the plea that in our day it is utterly impracticable. Whatever may be said of the article, it shows very plainly the drift of myself and brethren towards Community life.

But as we advanced in that direction and began to confer together in regard to a plan of organization, almost insuperable obstacles hindered our progress. In the first place we were hardly more than novitiate confessors of our exalted *Standard*. And yet our understandings, convictions, and consciences were far in advance of our circumstances, our habitual spiritual states of mind, and aptitudes for the exemplification of our sublime ideal. Hence we were very liable to trip and stumble in the presence of temptation. Moreover, our knowledge, skill, and experience as social architects was sadly inadequate to the designing and construction of the needed edifice. And then we could command but a fraction of the requisite pecuniary means. Furthermore, we could muster only a handful of coadjutors, and most of these were untrained and undisciplined, and of doubtful capability for the work we were about to undertake. And finally, it was by no means certain that any of our families were disposed to enter heartily with us upon the untried and hazardous experiment. Under these circumstances what was to be done? Our ardent aspirations, our zeal and enthusiasm could not be repressed. Something we must do, if it were only to grope and flounder toward our well-determined object. We could meditate, we could plan, we could agitate the subject if we could do nothing more, and so prepare the way for systematic action when the proper time should seem to have come.

After the publication of the article quoted, which brought the whole matter before our friends scattered abroad and the general public, it came under frequent and earnest consideration at our conferences and social meetings, as well as in our private interviews. Letters of inquiry from interested persons near and far away began to reach us, to one of which I responded in *The Practical Christian* of December 1, 1840, thus:

"I wish the good and the true would give it (the Community question) their most serious and deliberate consideration. I look forward with high expectations of good to mankind through this instrumentality. The matter is maturing and will in due time ripen into cheering results. Encouraging letters have been received from our friends at a distance in relation to the general proposition. I wish to hear from more of those who, I am sure, would be glad to take part in such an enterprise. It has been deemed inexpedient to enlarge much on the topic in our paper, but all persons interested may rest assured that the discussion is going on, and that the project will not be abandoned without some attempt to carry it into execution. I would invite those of our brethren and sisters in various places who think favorably of it to communicate with me on the subject, and especially to signify what amount of means they are prepared to invest in the undertaking, if they can see a rational prospect of success."

In other ways than by correspondence were things moving on towards the practical realization of our fondly cherished hopes. Meetings were held in different localities for the special purpose of bringing together persons known to be favorable to our particular movement, or to the general cause of Social reform, for mutual consultation and suggestion; many individuals, devoted to works of philanthropy and human improvement in a large and unsectarian way, were interviewed and consulted for the purpose of securing their encouragement and moral support, even when they were not prepared to co-operate personally with us or aid us with pecuniary assistance; and certain localities were visited and examined somewhat in order to ascertain their fitness as a site for a Community. Moreover, I had spent much time, thought, and energy upon drafting the form of a Constitution to be submitted to the brethren and sisters when the time for a permanent organization should come. An event of great significance to me personally had also occurred,— the acceptance of the Community idea by my wife. She had demurred for some time, but at length, after a long conversation with me upon the subject, confessed herself satisfied and ready to second my efforts in carrying my plans into execution. This gratified me exceedingly and gave me fresh courage and zeal in pressing forward toward what had become the goal of my most cherished ambition and desire.

It should be remembered by the reader of these pages that the year of which I am now writing, 1840, opened a decade of American history pre-eminently distinguished for the general humanitarian spirit which seemed to pervade it, as manifested in numerous and widely extended efforts to put away existing evils and better the condition of the masses of mankind; and especially for the wave of communal thought which swept over the country, awakening a very profound interest in different directions in the question of the re-organization of society; — an interest which assumed various forms as it contemplated or projected practical results. There were a considerable number of what were known as Transcendentalists in and about Boston, who, under the leadership of Rev. George Ripley, a Unitarian clergyman of eminence, planned and put in operation the Roxbury Community, generally known as the "Brook Farm" Association. A company of radical reformers who had come out from the church on account of its alleged complicity with Slavery and other abominations, and hence called Come-outers, instituted a sort of family Community near Providence, R. I. Other progressives, with George W. Benson at their head, founded the Northampton Community at the present village of Florence, a suburb of that city. During the same period Mr. Albert Brisbane of Philadelphia, an enthusiastic disciple of Charles Fourier, a celebrated French philosopher and inventor of a new system of society, published a work entitled "*Social Destiny of Man,*" etc., which, seconded by the writings and lectures of such men as Horace Greeley, Parke Goodwin, and Rev. Wm. Henry Channing, stimulated the rise of several Phalansterian Associations, as they were termed, in the middle and western states, chiefest of which was "The North American Phalanx" in Monmouth Co., N. J. These and other similar movements of varying type and character, generated by the spirit that was abroad, made the land, especially the Northern portion of it for some years, one vast theater of social theorizing and experimentation.

The undertaking of which I am writing was among the earliest of these referred to, and its origin was wholly independent of them all. It was strictly of Practical Christian genesis, and for some time we who were interested in it scarcely knew of contemporaneous projects of a like nature. We very soon, however, became informed of the ideas and prospective designs of Mr. Ripley and his associates, and entered into correspondence with them, for the free interchange of views and feelings upon the subject of absorbing interest to both parties. It was found that we stood in most friendly relations towards each other, and that in many things we occupied common ground, with common objects to be attained. To such an extent was this the case, with such a mutual attraction between us, that at one time, before we or they were fairly organized for future operations, a proposition for a formal coalition and union of resources and forces was seriously considered. Upon conferring together, however, and going into details, this was decided to be impracticable and undesirable. They would have nothing to do with our Practical Christian Standard, upon which our proposed action was based, and we were unwilling to relinquish its tests and obligations. So we parted, amicably but uncompromisingly. They abounded in educational resources, in literary accomplishments, and æsthetic tastes : and also had in cheering prospect a gratifying amount of capital. In these respects we were poor. But we had a resolute spirit and a determined will. Moreover, we knew what it was to work hard, to live on small means, and to deny ourselves for conscience' and righteousness' sake. But as we could not agree heartily upon what we each deemed vital to our movement, we went respectively our own ways, faithful to our convictions of truth and duty and wishing each other well in the premises. They were nearly a year ahead of us in securing a location and commencing Community life, and about ten years our predecessors in terminating their experiment.

As for ourselves, we made advances towards the organization of our forces and a settlement upon our communal estate as rapidly as circumstances would permit, and more rapidly, perhaps, than wisdom and prudence dictated. Before the meeting of our Quarterly Conference in January, 1841, we held several preliminary gatherings of from ten to thirty persons, discussed means and methods of operation, considered and amended a Constitution which I had drafted, and had given it our approval. So that when that body convened on the 27th of the month, everything was ready for provisional action. Immediately following the customary religious exercises of the occasion came the deliberate and careful consideration of the proposed plan of organization. It was examined, article by article, section by section, discussed in all its details, and, after successive adjournments, unanimously adopted by those prepared to unite together in an attempt to actualize the object it contemplated and carry its several provisions into effect. Its reproduction here will close the first chapter of this History.

"CONSTITUTION

OF THE

FRATERNAL COMMUNION.

"Know all men:

"That in order more effectually to illustrate the virtues and promote the ends of pure religion, morality, and philanthropy; to withstand the vices and reform the disorders of the present social state; to secure to our posterity the blessings of a more salutary, physical, intellectual, and moral education; to establish a more attractive, economical, and productive system of industry; and to facilitate the honest acquisition of individual property for laudable purposes; — We whose names are hereunto annexed do unite in a voluntary Association to be called

THE FRATERNAL COMMUNION;

And we do adopt and ordain for our Association the following

CONSTITUTION.

ARTICLE I.

"SECTION 1. This Association shall be organized in distinct, independent Communities, unitedly maintaining a general fellowship, but exercising within themselves respectively all the social powers, rights, and immunities of Christian commonwealths.

"SEC. 2. The members of this Communion shall meet in Quarterly and General Conferences, for religious improvement and fraternal counsel, at such times and places as may in the progress of events be found expedient.

"SEC. 3. The general meetings shall be regulated and conducted according to such rules of order as two-thirds of the members in attendance for may the time being agree to adopt.

Article II.

" Sec. 1.   Membership in this Association shall be acquired only by admission into some one of its Communities.

" Sec. 2.   No person shall be a member of any Community who does not deliberately and cordially assent to the annexed

DECLARATION.

" I believe in the religion of Jesus Christ, as he taught and exemplified it according to the Scriptures of the New Testament.   I acknowledge myself a bounden subject of all its moral obligations.   *Especially* do I hold myself bound by its holy requirements, never, under any pretext whatsoever, to kill, assault, beat, torture, enslave, rob, oppress, persecute, defraud, corrupt, slander, revile, injure, envy, or hate any human being, even my worst enemy; never in any manner to violate the dictates of pure chastity; never to take or administer an oath; never to manufacture, buy, sell, deal out, or use any intoxicating liquor *as a beverage;* never to serve in the army, navy, or militia of any nation, state, or chieftain; never to bring an action at law, hold office, vote, join a legal posse, petition a legislature, or ask governmental interposition, *in any case involving a final authorized resort to physical violence;* never to indulge self-will, bigotry, love of pre-eminence, covetousness, deceit, profanity, idleness, or an unruly tongue; never to participate in lotteries, games of chance, betting, or pernicious amusements; never to resent reproof nor justify myself in a known wrong; never to aid, abet, or approve others in anything sinful; — but through divine assistance, always to recommend and promote, with my entire influence, the holiness and happiness of all mankind.

" Sec. 3.   Any person eighteen years of age, thus assenting to the foregoing Declaration, may be proposed for membership at any regular meeting of a Community, and admitted by vote.

" Sec. 4.   Any person may cease to be a member by communicating to the Secretary of his or her Community a written notice to that effect.

" Sec. 5.   Any unworthy member, having proved incorrigible, may be disowned by vote.

" Sec. 6.   Every Community shall be distinguished by number, according to the date of its formation, and shall be uniformly entitled, in all written instruments, records, and addresses, *Fraternal Community No.* 1, 2, 3, etc., as the case may be. And every such Community shall keep a book containing this Constitution, with a general Register of all its members annexed; which Register shall exhibit in distinct columns the following particulars, viz.: — their names at full length, place of nativity, time of birth, date of admission, and general calling, together with blank space sufficient to minute their death or disconnection however effected. A book shall also be kept by every Community in which all births, marriages, and deaths shall be carefully recorded.

"Sec. 7. All members of every Community shall stand on a footing of personal equality, irrespective of sex, color, occupation, wealth, rank, or any other natural or adventitious peculiarity.

Article III.

"Sec. 1. The members of each Community in this Association shall own and manage such and so much real and movable estate in Joint-Stock proprietorship as they may from time to time deem best.

"Sec. 2. This Joint-Stock property shall be created by subscription, in negotiable shares of fifty dollars each, and may be increased by new subscriptions indefinitely at the discretion of the Community.

"Sec. 3. All Joint-Stock property thus created shall be considered as existing in the two following named distinct funds, viz.: —the *consolidated fund* and the *floating fund*. The consolidated fund shall cover all investments in real estate of every description whatsoever. The floating fund shall cover all unexpended cash, moneys due the Community, and movable property in possession of every description. And all accounts shall be kept with strict reference to these two funds.

"Sec. 4. No Community shall invest more than five-sixths of its Joint-Stock property in real estate, except for temporary safe keeping under peculiar circumstances. At least one-sixth shall ordinarily remain in the floating fund; and sufficient cash be retained on hand to meet all probable necessities.

"Sec. 5. A regular subscription book shall be opened and kept in every Community, which shall exhibit the terms of subscription, the names of all subscribers, the amount subscribed, the number of shares taken, the time when, a record of all certificates of stock at full length, and a minute of all transfers of shares.

"Sec. 6. Every person, on payment of his or her subscription to the Joint-Stock property of any Community, shall receive a certificate of title to the number of shares taken, signed by the presiding executive officer thereof, and countersigned by the Secretary; which certificate shall be in the form following, to wit : —

" 'For value received, A, B, or order, is hereby entitled to —— shares in the Joint-Stock property of Fraternal Community No. —, valued at —— dollars, etc., together with such dividends as may from time to time be declared thereon.

" 'Given under our hands at —— this day of ——A. D., ——.

C. D., Pres't.
E. F., Sec'y. '

"Sec. 7. Whenever any stockholder shall be desirous of converting his or her stock, or any part thereof, into cash, and no purchaser readily appears to take the same, the Community shall, if possible, purchase it at the par value thereof, and pay the amount out of the money on hand in the floating fund.

"Sec. 8. No member shall ever sell any share of the Joint Stock except to fellow members, without first offering it to the Community.

ARTICLE IV.

"Sec. 1. The members of every Community in this Association shall, *if practicable*, dwell together, on their own soil, in a compact neighborhood.

"Sec. 2. They shall erect in each Community, at their earliest convenience, one or more spacious, well-constructed mansion-houses, with such appurtenant barns, granaries, workshops, mills, manufactories, and other buildings, as they may be able, and deem necessary. These mansion-houses, with their appendages, shall be called *Habitations*, and shall be capable of affording comfortable accommodations to one hundred persons, *at least*, and as many more as may be found expedient.

"Sec. 3. All Habitations, with their surrounding lands and buildings, shall be owned and controlled solely by the Community within whose limits they are comprised.

Article V.

"Sec. 1. It shall be considered the duty and the privilege of all members of this Association in every Community, and of their family dependents, unless absolutely incapacitated, to perform a reasonable amount of productive labor, either manual, mental, or mixed, in some department of useful industry.

"Sec. 2. To this end each Community shall endeavor to provide suitable employment for every individual connected with it; which various employment shall be adapted, as nearly as the case will admit, to the genius and taste of the several operatives.

"Sec. 3. All operatives of every description, whether employed at home or abroad, in manual labor, or as business agents, teachers, or missionaries, eighteen years of age and upwards, shall be allowed one uniform rate of wages, not exceeding fifty cents for every eight hours of actual service. All persons sent out on business agencies shall be furnished with the means of defraying their extra expenses. All literary, philanthropic, moral, and religious teachers, going out into the surrounding world with the approbation and under the direction of the Community, shall be considered as serving forty-eight hours per week, and be credited accordingly. And for all moneys, or other goods, received from the people among whom they may exercise their gifts, they shall account to the Community — retaining to themselves a sufficient amount to cover their reasonable extra expenses.

"Sec. 4. All children and youth under eighteen years of age connected with any Community, shall be allowed wages for all labors performed not exceeding the following rates, viz.: From five to seven years of age, half a cent an hour; from seven to nine, one cent an hour; from nine to eleven, two cents an hour; from eleven to fourteen, three cents an hour; from fourteen to sixteen, four cents an hour; and from sixteen to eighteen, five cents per hour.

"Sec. 5. Time shall always be reckoned only for actual employment, excluding the necessary intermissions of rest and refreshment, and shall be accounted for on settlement by the year, or the quarter, or the next longest term practicable. Where wages are agreed on by the year, quarter, month, or week, the average of eight hours to the day, or forty-eight

per week, shall be the common measure. All lost time worthy of notice shall be deducted, and all extra time added, each at the allowed rate.

" Sec. 6. All work executed by the members of every Community shall be wrought in a thorough, faithful, and neatly finished style, according to its kind; so that it may reflect honor on the Association and command the confidence of the public.

Article VI.

" Sec. 1. All the children and youth connected with any Community in this Association shall be educated in the most approved manner. Their physical education shall commence in a common nursery, furnished and attended in the most appropriate and judicious way; into which they may be received, with the consent of their parents, at the earliest age. From the nursery, at the age of two or three years, they shall be introduced into well-ordered infant school classes, and thenceforth advanced from stage to stage of physical, intellectual, and moral improvement till maturity.

" Sec. 2. All education in this Communion shall be conducted on the manual labor principle, and with a view to qualify every youth for the actual business of life, each according to natural genius, taste, and passion.

" Sec. 3. No charge shall be made by any Community, (except for books and stationery,) on account of education, literary advantages, or religious instruction. These, and all privileges naturally connected with them, shall be free to the individual members with their respective family dependents, and shall be supported by each Community at large, out of its floating fund or ordinary resources.

Article VII.

" Sec. 1. All persons connected with any Community in this Association, except as designated in the 5th section of this article, shall be considered regular boarders and charged a certain price per week for their accommodations.

" Sec. 2. Board shall include suitable house-room, food, lodging, bathing, light, heat, washing and ironing, medicine, medical attendance, (unless called from abroad,) and proper nursing when necessary; and shall be afforded at prices not exceeding the following-named per week, viz.: From birth until seven years of age, fifty cents; from seven years till twelve, seventy-five cents; from twelve years and upwards, one dollar.

"Sec. 3. An ample fare shall be agreed on, provided, and served, by each Community to all its boarders, either in commons, in select messes, or private families, as may have been stipulated.

"Sec. 4. Families served with their food in private apartments or separate tenements, shall furnish their rooms with bedding, chairs, tables, crockery, and every other necessary article of household convenience, at their own expense. In all other respects they shall fare and be treated like those who take their meals in the public eating rooms.

"Sec. 5. Whenever any family belonging to a Community shall anxiously desire to keep house, cook, and board themselves in a separate tenement, they shall be furnished with house-rent, fuel, bread-stuffs, and all the staple necessaries and comforts of subsistence at a fair price.

"Sec. 6. Each Community shall endeavor to grow, manufacture, or purchase at wholesale, all articles of necessary consumption; so as to keep in store an adequate supply for the wants of all its members and dependents. And every item sold out of the Community stores, or furnished at a price, to any member of this Communion, or to any family dependent of such member, shall be afforded at cost, as nearly as the same can be ascertained.

"Sec. 7. All labor performed for any Community shall be credited; board and all other articles furnished shall be charged; and a complete settlement shall be made with every individual, at least once a year.

Article VIII.

"Sec. 1. All losses of real estate from any cause whatsoever, exceeding the sum of three hundred dollars in any one year, shall be borne by the stockholders of a Community, and repaired by an equitable assessment on their shares. All other losses, whether of real or movable estate belonging to the Community, shall be borne by such Community out of its floating fund. The public taxes, ordinary repairs of buildings, and all other incidental current expenses of every description, shall be paid out of the floating fund.

3

" Sec. 2. The clear profits of every Community shall be divided among the members thereof, and members only, according to capital invested and labor performed. The shares of Joint-Stock shall receive five-twelfths of such profits, and labor seven-twelfths. Every member owning shares shall receive a dividend of the profits accruing to capital, according to the number of such shares; and every member shall receive a dividend of the profits accruing to labor, according to the time credited to him or her on the books of the Community.

" Sec. 3. Provided, nevertheless, that capital shall never receive profits exceeding an amount equal to six per cent. per annum, simple interest, for the whole time of its investment in the funds of the Community. Nor shall labor beyond the average of forty-eight hours per week, nor that of minors under eighteen years of age, nor the services of any other person, ever entitle any member to profits.

Article IX.

" Every Community in this Association shall stand forever pledged to the relief and comfortable maintenance of all its members who may become destitute of pecuniary resources; and also of their widows and orphans, so long as they shall conform to wholesome rules and regulations.

Article X.

" Sec. 1. Each Community in this Association shall hold an annual meeting for the choice of official servants, the hearing of reports, and the transaction of other necessary business.

" Sec. 2. All official servants shall continue to discharge the proper duties of their offices till others are chosen and prepared to serve in their stead.

" Sec. 3. Special meetings may be called and holden on seven days notice. And such meetings shall be called and holden whenever seven members may request the same in writing.

" Sec. 4. The manner of calling, notifying, and conducting meetings shall be prescribed by vote of the Community.

" Sec. 5. Every member shall have one and but one vote on all questions; and the concurrence of two thirds of all the members present and acting shall always be necessary to a decision.

"Sec. 6. Nine members shall be requisite to constitute a quorum for the transaction of business, but a less number may adjourn.

Article XI.

"Sec. 1. The official servants annually chosen by every Community in this Association, shall be a President, Secretary, Auditor, and six Intendants, viz.: an Intendant of Finance and Exchange, an Intendant of Agriculture and Animals, an Intendant of Manufactures and Mechanical Industry, an Intendant of Health and Domestic Economy, an Intendant of Education, Arts, and Sciences, and an Intendant of Religion, Morals, and Missions.

"Sec. 2. The President and these six Intendants shall constitute, *ex officio*, a Board of Trustees, in whose name the whole property of their Community shall be holden and managed for the common benefit.

"Sec. 3. These official servants shall also constitute, *ex officio*, the Executive Council of their Community, with plenary authority to select and appoint all managers, foremen, overseers, directors, and agents, necessary to its complete industrial organization. Also to approve and recommend all teachers, lecturers, ministers of the Gospel, and missionaries, going out from the Community under its direction or in its general service.

"Sec. 4. It shall be the duty of the Executive Council to arrange all the business interests and affairs of their Community into six general departments, each having its appropriate branches, in such a manner that every person, thing, and particular matter of concern, may be under the oversight of the Intendant to whom the same most naturally belongs. And the several Intendants shall be considered responsible for the orderly management and good condition of their respective departments.

"Sec. 5. The Executive Council, through the President, shall make a clear detailed report of the standing of their Community in all its departments, at least once a year, and as much oftener as the members may by vote demand.

"Sec. 6. It shall be the duty of the Secretary to act as Clerk of the Community, the Board of Trustees, and the Executive Council, and to keep full, fair, well-ordered records of their proceedings, and of all other matters properly coming within his province.

"SEC. 7. It shall be the duty of the Auditor to examine and attest all pecuniary accounts kept by the Community, and to guard its financial statistics, if possible, from error.

"SEC. 8. The proper duties of the Treasurer, as well as of general Purveyor and Accountant of the Community, shall be performed by the Intendant of Finance and Exchange. He shall receive, safely keep, and justly account for all moneys accruing to the Community, and pay them out, under such regulations as may from time to time be ordained. He shall keep all his accounts by the most approved method, and in such a form and state that his books may at all times exhibit the true financial standing of the Community in its several funds and interests.

"SEC. 9. No official servant, manager, foreman, overseer, director, or agent of a Community, shall ever receive any salary, or other compensation whatsoever, exceeding the established rate of wages allowed to the members at large.

ARTICLE XII.

"SEC. 1. It shall be the settled policy and a fundamental principle with every Community in this Association, never to contract any debt or obligation of suretyship out of the pale of its own membership, nor within that pale beyond temporary occasional necessity in the management of its internal affairs. Nor shall the goods or productions of any Community ever be sold on credit to the surrounding world.

"SEC. 2. All moneys to be expended for land, stock, goods, or any other object, by the Trustees, Executive Council, or Intendants of any Community, shall first be appropriated by vote thereof at some regular meeting.

ARTICLE XIII.

"All matters of serious controversy arising in any Community of this Association, shall be tried and determined in the first instance by a mutual council, and upon failure thereof, finally, by a jury of twelve impartial members.

ARTICLE XIV.

"Every Community in this Association may enact and establish such By-Laws, Rules and Regulations, not inconsistent with the general spirit and object of this Constitution, as may be found necessary to its good order and general welfare.

ARTICLE XV.

" The Constitution of this Communion may be altered or amended by a vote of three-fourths of all its members specially convened for that purpose, either in their respective Communities or in general Conference: provided, always, that every such alteration or amendment shall be proposed in writing, and publicly announced to the members at least thirty days preceeding the time of its regular consideration.

" Now, therefore, in solemn ratification of this Constitution in all its Articles and Sections, and for the formation of Fraternal Community, No. 1, we have severally caused our names to be hereunto annexed.

" Adin Ballou, Lucy Hunt Ballou, David Rich Lamson, Mary Lamson, George Whittemore Stacy, Daniel Sanderson Whitney, William Henry Fish, Ann Eliza Fish, Levi Tower, Henry Lillie, Caroline Hayden Lillie, Samuel Silsbee Brown, Mary Louisa Brown, Amos Wood Pitts, Mary Ann Pitts, Perry Thayer, Charlotte Taft Thayer, Nathan Harris, Martha Harris, William Walker Cook, Abigail Draper Cook, Charles Gladding, Ruth Shove Gladding, Jemima Sherman, Ebenezer Daggett Draper, Anna Thwing Draper, John Wheeler, Miriam P. Wheeler, Lemuel Munyan, Emily Gay, Samuel Colburn, Barbara Barker Colburn."

CHAPTER II.

1841.

IT will have been observed by the careful reader, that, according to the terms of the final clause of the Constitution presented on the last few pages, the act of ratifying that instrument, accompanied by the formal signing of the same, was also the act of forming a working body under its general provisions to be called Fraternal Community No. 1, of which the persons whose names are appended to it, thirty-two in number, were the original members. This being accomplished, those composing the new organization resolved themselves at once into a special deliberative assembly, for the purpose of transacting such other items of business as at the time seemed calculated to promote still further the great objects they had in view. A record of the proceedings of that first meeting of the Community after it was regularly instituted was made and preserved, and is herein presented in full:

"At a regular meeting of the members of Fraternal Community, No. 1, holden in Mendon, Mass., Jan. 28, 1841, David R. Lamson acting as President, and Adin Ballou as Secretary, the following votes were passed unanimously:

"*Voted*, That the choice of our regular official servants be deferred for the present, and that a Provisional Committee of seven members be chosen, with the following special instructions and powers, viz.:

"(1) To procure suitable Record and Account Books, or so many as may for the present be found necessary, and cause the Constitution to be properly inscribed.

"(2) To receive subscriptions to the Constitution and to the Joint-Stock.

"(3) To receive and account for any moneys that may be paid into the treasury.

"(4) To prepare a suitable Exposition of the Constitution.

"(5) To cause 500 copies of the Constitution and Exposition to be printed in *The Practical Christian*, and an equal number in the form of a tract or pamphlet.

"(6) To collect such information as they may be able respecting a location for this Community; respecting the form and construction of buildings; respecting the internal economy of social communities, hospitals, and large boarding establishments; respecting agriculture, manufactures, and education; and respecting any other matters likely to promote the prosperity of our enterprise.

"(7) To purchase such books and treatises, not exceeding the cost of ten dollars, on agriculture, manufactures, education, and other subjects, as they deem particularly necessary.

"(8) To call a meeting of the Community and report their doings as soon as circumstances will in their opinion warrant.

"*Voted*, That the following named members do constitute said Committee, viz.: Adin Ballou, Nathan Harris, Wm. H. Fish, Henry Lillie, David R. Lamson, Daniel S. Whitney, and Geo. W. Stacy.

"*Voted*, That the sum of one hundred dollars be appropriated to the use of the Provisional Committee for the purposes of their appointment.

Voted, That the Joint-Stock subscription terms of this Community be in the form following, to wit:

"SUBSCRIPTION TO THE JOINT-STOCK PROPRIETORSHIP
OF
FRATERNAL COMMUNITY, NO. 1.

"In conformity to the Constitution adopted, ordained, and ratified by the members of Fraternal Community, No. 1, we, the undersigned, do severally subscribe to the Joint-Stock property of said Community and promise to pay into the treasury thereof in current money or some acceptable equivalent at our earliest convenience after demand, the sums designated and covering the shares noted opposite our respective names; the said Joint-Stock property and every share thereof to be forever holden, controlled, regulated, subjected, privileged, and entitled, in all respects, strictly according to the provisions and specifications of said Constitution.

"Names ———. Sums ———. No. Shares ———. Place and Date ———.

"*Voted*, That this meeting be now dissolved."

At a meeting of the Provisional Committee subsequently holden, Adin Ballou was chosen a sub-committee to draft, prepare for the press, and publish an Exposition of the Constitution. I at once addressed myself to the task thus assigned me by my associates, producing a document of great length, explaining and illustrating in detail every article, section, and phrase almost of the instrument, in order that it might be intelligible to the average mind of those likely to be interested in it and in the cause it was designed to advance. Though serving well in its time the purpose for which it was designed, it does not seem needful to reproduce it in the present volume. It was printed as a supplement to the Constitution in *The Practical Christian* of February 15, 1841, and both were reprinted in pamphlet form directly afterward, and scattered far and wide among the friends of reform and in the general community. In this way was our movement, now fairly inaugurated, advertised extensively throughout large sections of the country, intensifying the enthusiasm of those who sympathized with us, exciting the curiosity of strangers, and calling out in various ways the adverse criticism and sometimes scorn of unbelievers and opposers. Besides the publicity which we ourselves gave it, the knowledge of it was considerably extended by the early appearance of our Constitution in the columns of *The Liberator*, through the unsolicited favor of our friend, the editor, William Lloyd Garrison.

It may be questioned whether it was wise to make our humble experiment so generally known at the outset, inasmuch as it naturally raised expectations in many quarters that could not possibly be realized, and multiplied applications for membership with us to an extent beyond our ability to accept them and of a character sometimes calculated to hinder rather than help in our contemplated work. But our hope and zeal overmastered our prudence, and we pressed forward more rapidly, perhaps, than a more cautious sagacity would warrant. And yet had we not done so, our undertaking would very likely have been deferred to an indefinite future, or, more probably, abandoned altogether. This, in my judgment, would have been most unfortunate for the cause of truth and for humanity, because the attempt with all its experiences and lessons was a providential step in the march of human progress and a needful preparation for more wisely-planned and better-conditioned efforts yet to be put forth in behalf of the regeneration of society — efforts which, I believe, are some day to achieve a richly merited and glorious success.

No sooner had our Constitution and the accompanying Exposition reached the great public to which they were sent, than letters of inquiry, sympathy, and encouragement, as also of caution and admonition, poured in upon us from all directions. They were largely from persons of philanthropic spirit, who were ready to welcome and befriend any new method or movement which had in it the potency and promise of succor and redemption to mankind. The devotees and representatives of the churches, orthodox and heteradox alike, gave us little heed in their published journals, by correspondence, or otherwise. They were bound to a theoretical and dogmatical Christianity, not to a practical one; and held fast to traditional methods of saving men and bringing in the kingdom of heaven, caring little or nothing for any freshly devised schemes or plans whereby those devoutly-to-be-wished-for ends were to be achieved. In their judgment, there was no new light of this sort to break forth from the word of God.

There were, however, some very notable and gratifying exceptions to this generally prevailing indifference and silent disregard or contempt. Chiefest among these and pre-eminently important and valuable, was a communication from a no less distinguished scholar, philanthropist, and divine than Rev. William Ellery Channing, D. D., of Boston, to which I am moved to give a place in this connection. It appears in full in his "Memoirs," prepared by his nephew, William Henry Channing, pp. 119–122, Vol III. It was addressed to me personally and reads as follows :

"BOSTON, Feb. 27, 1841.

"*My Dear Sir:* I received your 'Constitution and Exposition' yesterday, and my early reply will prove my interest in your proposed 'Fraternal Community.'

"Your *ends, objects,* seem to me important. I see, I feel, the great evils of our present social state. The flesh predominates over the spirit, the animal over the intellectual and moral life. The consciousness of the worth of the human soul, of what man was made to be, is almost wholly lost; and in this ignorance all our social relations must be mournfully defective, and the highest claims of man very much overlooked. I earnestly desire to witness some change by which the mass of men may be released from their present anxious drudgery, may cease to be absorbed in cares and toils for the body, and may so combine labor with a system of improvement that they will find in it a help, not a degrading burden. I have for a very long time dreamed of an association, in which the members, instead of preying on one another and seeking to put one another down, after the fashion of this world, should live together as brothers, seeking one another's elevation and spiritual growth. But the materials for such a community I have not seen. Your ends, therefore, are very dear to me.

" How far you have adopted the best *means* of realizing them, and whether they can be realized in the present low condition of individual Christians, are different questions, and most men would give a negative answer. I do not, however, discourage any sincere efforts for social or individual improvement, but would say, God speed you! There is a tone of faith and sincerity in your document which gives me hope, and yet I cannot say that I am without fear. I have lived so much out of the world of business, I have had so few connections with society except those of a religious teacher, that I cannot judge of the obstructions you are to meet. The grand obstacle to success, however, I do understand, and you ought to look at it fully. It consists in the difficulty of reconciling so many wills, of bringing so many individuals to such a unity of feeling and judgment as is necessary to the management of an extensive common concern,—in the difficulty of preventing the interference, inter-meddling, harsh-judging, evil-speaking, self-will, jealousies, exactions, and love of sway, which scatter discord and woe through all our social relations. The Catholics have provided against these evils in their religious communities by establishing absolute power, and teaching the members that the first duty is obedience. Whether sufficient unity can be preserved in a free institution built on the foundation of brotherhood and equality, remains to be proved. I wish you to try it, and, in order to success, I wish you all to look the difficulty in the face and to feel that it is indeed a great one, —one to be overcome only by habitual self-denial, by the special culture of humility, meekness, and charity.

" There are undoubtedly dangers attending every social condition. These we are to understand that we may watch against them. The evils to be feared in a Community like yours are, the loss of individual energy in consequence of dependence on the Community, the increased facility given to the sluggish of throwing the burden of toil on their better-disposed brethren, the relaxation of domestic ties in consequence of the virtual adoption of the children by the Community, the diminution of free thought and free action in consequence of the necessity of conforming to the will of the majority or the intendant, the tendency to narrowness and exclusiveness, and the tendency to a dull monotony of mind and life in consequence of confinement to a few influences. These evils are not imaginary. There is danger of losing, in such establishments, individuality, animation, force, and enlarge-

ment of mind. Your security must be sought in carrying out
the principles of freedom and philanthropy to which you
attach so much importance.

"I am aware of the many economical advantages arising
from the gathering of the Community into one habitation; but
there are disadvantages. There is reason to fear that families
will not be sufficiently separate, and that the domestic feelings
may be thus impaired; and, perhaps, still more, that individuals
will lose that spirit of solitude, retirement, secret thought, and
secret piety, without which social relations are full of peril and
the character loses strength and dignity. These dangers seem
to me to require distinct guards.

"I should have been pleased to see in the articles some
recognition of the importance of courteous manners. The importance of these in keeping alive mutual respect and kindness
is great. In this country we suffer much from coarseness of
manner. Refinement, mutual deference, delicacy of intercourse, are among the fruits of Christianity, and very needful
in such a gathering as you propose. If I were to visit a
Community and see the floor defiled by spittle, I could not
easily believe that the members respected one another, or that,
with such violations of neatness and decorum, there could be
much aspiration for inward purity. Just in proportion as
Christians come to recognize in one another the spiritual, immortal children of God, an unaffected deference will mark the
tones of the voice and the manners, and the reaction of this
deference on the sentiment from which it springs is very great.
Where such deportment prevails, there will be no difficulty
about reproof. Kind, courteous reproof, which is seen and
felt to come from love, does not wound. Indeed, in such
a society there will be little to reprove.

"I trust that this letter will be a testimony of my sincere
interest in your movements. I pray God to bless you. I
should die in greater peace, could I see in any quarter the
promise of a happier organization of society. I am burdened
in spirit by what I see. May the dawn of something better
visit my eyes before they are closed in death!

"When you visit Boston I shall be glad to see you.

"Your Friend and Brother.

"P. S. I ought, perhaps, to say that I am not prepared to
subscribe to all the articles of your 'Declaration,' but I do not

blame those who hold them for making them the foundation of the Community. It should be understood, however, that you do not limit your *Christian communion* to those who agree with you on all these points. You can and ought to recognize as Christians very many with whom you have no desire to live on the same farm and in the same 'habitation.' "

How noble, elevated, wise, benevolent, and fraternal the utterances of this epistle! Dr. Channing was centuries in advance not only of the great mass of the nominal Christian church, but of the majority claiming to be *Liberal* Christians. What a confession he made in saying, "The materials for a such a Community I have not seen;" that is, one in which the members "should live together as brethren, seeking one another's elevation and spiritual growth." And yet he had known thousands of professed Christians in the course of his life. During his earlier years he must have been acquainted with large numbers of New England church members who claimed to have been "born again" and to have become "new creatures in Christ;" and later on he was intimate with the very flower of dissenters from the "orthodox" standards, who gloried in the sublime doctrines of the fatherhood of God and the brotherhood of man. Nevertheless, the materials of a truly fraternal Community composed of people honestly striving to live by the principles and precepts of the Gospel of Christ he had never beheld! What a commentary on the nominal Christianity of the world! !

That the counsels and admonitions which Dr. Channing by his sagacity and candor was prompted to offer us were well founded and appropriate, was demonstrated in our Hopedale experience at an early day. The very difficulties which he suggestively pointed out in his letter, we were obliged to encounter, spite of all our sanguine hopes and resolves, and they finally proved too much for our virtue and wisdom. Instead of rising above and overcoming them, we were in the end overcome by them.

It is proper to state that beside the sympathy and best wishes of the eminent and world-renowned clergyman mentioned, we had also those of Revs. Samuel J. May, Wm. P. Tilden, and a few others of the Unitarian ministry, but the mass of them probably regarded us as pitiable fanatics and gave us no heed. Much the same was true of the occupants of the Universalist pulpit: a few hoped for our success and bade us God speed, but the many were utterly skeptical in respect to our movement, even if they did not contemn it, and kept silent. The preachers among us had all belonged to the Massachusetts Association of Restorationists, and consequently were not in very good repute with the Universalist denomination from which most of them had aforetime seceded.

But we were in no better standing with the conservative wing of the Restorationist body, which actually outnumbered ours. We had outrun them in rigidly insisting upon the practical application of the principles of our liberal Christian faith, which they professed to hold in common with us, to all the activities and relations of life; not only espousing, as we had done, the Temperance, Anti-Slavery, and Peace reforms, but adopting the "Standard of Practical Christanity" against their emphatic protest, and finally enlisting in the cause of social reconstruction, thus severing the last ligament of the cord that bound us together. Our radicalism blasted the promise of building up a Restorationist sect, which was the ambition of some of the leaders, and this cooled the ardor of their friendship for us and sorely tried their patience. Honest in their intentions and convictions, they were not to be blamed for manifesting their repugnance toward us in a way not to be mistaken. Our worthy elder brother, Rev. Paul Dean of Boston, in August, 1841, addressed me a long letter expressive of his dissent from, and disrespect for, our whole Community scheme. It was not meant in unkindness, but it was in striking contrast with the communication of Dr. Channing, as to both its form and its spirit. It was tinged with sarcasm, and predicted, of course, with apparent glee, the ultimate utter failure of our vain-glorious undertaking. The result in our particular case may seem to justify his view. But the main question is not yet finally settled.

The second meeting of the new Community was held in connection with our Quarterly Conference, April 28th and 29th, 1841, at Boylston, Mass., the then parochial home of Br. George W. Stacy. The character and significance of it may be the better understood by giving a full report of its proceedings as found in the record book of the Secretary.

" Heard the document entitled 'Standard of Practical Christianity,' of which our test 'Declaration' is an epitome, read by Adin Ballou, with accompanying remarks.

" Heard sundry letters of friendly sympathy read, addressed by Wm. Ellery Channing, Edmund Quincy, Gerritt Smith, and others, to Adin Ballou, on the movements of our Community, much to the satisfaction and encouragement of the members present. Adjourned till 10 A. M. tomorrow.

" Met Thursday, April 29th, according to adjournment.

" Heard the report of the Provisional Committee as follows, viz.: That the Committee have procured four Record books for Community use: one for the General Proceedings of the Community; one for Subscriptions and Transfers of Stock; one for the Constitution and General Registry; and one for the Doings of the Executive Council: That they have received several subscriptions to the Constitution and to the Joint-Stock: That they have received no moneys into the treasury, having deemed it inexpedient to do so under existing circumstances: That they have prepared and published an Exposition of the Constitution as instructed: That they have collected some information touching the subjects referred to them by the visits of some of their number to the Lunatic Hospital at Worcester and to the Shaker Communities at Shirley and Harvard, Mass., and that such information is entirely favorable to the objects of the Community: That they have deemed it inexpedient to purchase books on Agriculture, Manufactures, and Education at present: That they have made inquiries about locations for this Community, and have partially examined several but are not prepared to recommend any one in particular, though it is their persuasion that a suitable one may be found and should be chosen in the neighborhood of Mendon, Mass.: That they have the means of defraying all expenses incident to their commission in their own and others' voluntary contributions, without charge to the Community itself: And that they have deemed it their duty to call the meeting here convened and report their doings. All of which they respectfully submit by their chairman.

"Report unanimously accepted and the Committee discharged.

"After admitting several new applicants it was unanimously

"*Resolved*, That the members of this Community individually will appropriate all the means they can reasonably command to the purchase of a farm for the same on or before the first day of March next.

"*Voted*, That this Community do now proceed to organize itself by the choice of its regular official servants. Whereupon the following named persons were chosen *viva voce*, to wit.:

"ADIN BALLOU, *President;* WILLIAM W. COOK, *Secretary and Auditor;* LEMUEL MUNYAN, *Intendant of Finance and Exchange;* EBENEZER D. DRAPER, *Intendant of Agriculture and Animals;* HENRY LILLIE, *Intendant of Manufactures and Mechanical Industry;* DAVID R. LAMSON, *Intendant of Health and Domestic Economy;* DANIEL S. WHITNEY, *Intendant of Education, Arts, and Sciences:* WILLIAM H. FISH, *Intendant of Religion, Morals, and Missions.*

"*Voted*, That the regular Annual Meeting of this Community be held on the first Wednesday of January in each year.

"*Voted*, That this meeting be now dissolved."

The Community was now fully organized and equipped for service whenever an opportunity for service, by the purchase and occupancy of a proper domain, should occur. Meanwhile the President and Intendants, both as a Board of Trustees and as Executive Council, were in frequent consultation by personal interview or by letter in regard to the general affairs of the body they represented, as well as in regard to the particular duties of the positions they respectively occupied. They were united in the determination to commence practical operations at the earliest possible date. The first thing to be done was of course to secure a location, and a large section of country was brought under consideration as the field from which a selection was ultimately to be made. This field was narrowed down very much by a critical examination, until the judgment of the Council settled upon a single farm, which seemed to offer more advantages and fewer disadvantages than any other and which was in due time made the site of the Community.

Much thinking and much planning was done subsequently to the meeting in April, of which the public knew nothing. It was regarded as good policy for us to keep our own counsels and noise our doings abroad as little as possible, until something definite was decided upon and we were prepared to go forward with our work in a well-ordered, systematic, effective way. The doings of our April meeting even were not published in *The Practical Christian*, and the fact of our organization was known only to those immediately concerned and a few of our more deeply interested and intimate friends. At length, just before our next meeting, on the 21st of August, Br. David R. Lamson, in the leading editorial of our little journal, discussed the subject of "Communities" in a general way, treating of the advantages to be derived from the mode of life which they provided for, and setting forth in a few particulars its superiority when compared to that existing under the established order of society. Only a few hints were thrown out in the article of what had been already done by us, or of what we had planned and were preparing to do at an early day.

The third meeting of the Community was held at Millville, Mass., where Bro. William H. Fish was pastor of the Restorationist Church, on Thursday, the 26th day

4

of August, 1841. The first business transacted was the consideration of a Report from the Executive Council relating to the purchase of a farm and the incipient steps taken toward a settlement of the members upon it. That Report gave a detailed statement concerning two estates that were for sale, both of which had been carefully examined and were deemed desirable. It said:

"They are both situated on Mill River in the westerly part of Milford adjacent to the Mendon line, about a mile distant from each other, and have respectable mill privileges. The most southerly of them had formerly been known as 'the Green Farm,' but latterly as 'the Grady place.' The other lies . . . higher up the stream and was formerly called the 'Jones Place,' but later the 'Hastings Daniels place.' The last contains over 258 acres in one body, inclusive of the old roads which run through it. Some 35 acres are woodland, 13 of which are said to contain well-grown wood; the rest is mostly sprout land of from three to six years growth and generally very thrifty. Large quantities of wood have been cut and sold off this farm within the past few years. There are from 10 to 20 acres of very young sprout land on another part of the farm. It has from 50 to 75 acres of mowing and probably cuts not less than forty tons of hay, much of it good English hay. It has been rented for the last thirty years, and its productions cannot be definitely stated, though always respectable. It keeps from sixteen to twenty head of cattle, and has an abundance of good pasturage. It has a large amount of orcharding and smaller fruitage. The land is naturally divided into sandy, ledgy, and gravelly loam. A fair proportion is tolerably smooth and free. It has great capabilities and advantages as a farm, and would, with good management, produce a large income. The buildings are old and in rather poor repair, though comfortable for the present. There is a dwelling-house two stories high, some 30 by 38 feet ground measurement, with back kitchen and other appurtenances. It has two barns of perhaps 30 by 40 feet in size, a cider house, and various outbuildings. There is no mill on the premises, and only the remains of an old dam. But the fall of the river is 24 feet, affording fine opportunities for applying it to various mechanical establishments. It was ascer-

tained that this property was in the market and could be bought
at the comparatively moderate price of $3800, less than $15 per
acre, to be paid on coming into possession of it, April 1, 1842.

"Taking into consideration the great capabilities and advantages of this estate, together with the price and the probability
that it might be purchased by some other party at an early
day, the President deemed it his duty to buy it in his own
name and assume the responsibility of securing it for the
Community. He accordingly entered into a contract for it with
Mr. Cyrus Ballou, who had recently bought it; which contract
was ratified by the proper writings being passed between them
on the 30th day of June last. This act has received the cordial approbation and sanction of the Council, who take pleasure
in declaring unanimously that it has greatly enhanced the prospects of the Community and opened the way for the successful
settlement in compact form and the industrial organization of
its now widely scattered members.

"It would be very desirable, if the Community had the pecuniary means, to purchase the 'Grady place' and other adjacent
lands immediately. But the Council cannot express any hope
that the necessary funds will be forthcoming at present. They
therefore recommend the abandonment of any attempt to make
further real estate purchases till the assurance of more capital
shall warrant it. They are confident that the Community will
be able to pay for the estate bought by the President and begin
improvements thereon in a few months. They therefore advise
that all its energies and resources be forthwith concentrated on
this estate; to pay for it, erect buildings and other works thereon, and cultivate the land. They are not without hopes that
some kind of a beginning may be made on the premises during
the ensuing autumn. If the property could be paid for and
improvements on it commenced this fall, it would be highly
auspicious and advantageous to the fraternity. It is, however,
recommended to proceed with all due caution, and to enter upon
no measures of expenditure not fully warranted by our resources
and all the circumstances of the case.

"The Council are happy to assure the Community that the
number of persons anxious to unite with them in this enterprise is rapidly increasing. One here and another there of the
pure and good, the honest and the oppressed, are eager to join
in one energetic, industrious brotherhood as soon as a home

and profitable employment can be furnished them. There are several individuals and families so situated that it is quite inconvenient for them to wait till we can provide for them. It is therefore suggested whether measures might not be taken to fit up and furnish the Community dwelling-house at the earliest possible day, with a view to locate such members and organize the industry of as many operatives as can be boarded on the estate. It is also suggested whether tenements in the surrounding neighborhood might not be secured for such families as cannot be sheltered there, and whether a school cannot be commenced at an early day. If the members could thus be approaching a centre, and be employed a part or all of the time in the service of the Community; if a school could be opened, a library founded, a printing office established, and other humble beginnings made, our social fabric would gradually rise to its intended height without conflicting effort or perceptible difficulty.

" Should the Community deem it proper to entrust the Council with discretionary power to act in accordance with their own judgment relative to all these matters, and guarantee the necessary appropriation of funds, it is believed that measures might be taken to accomplish much for the common interest.

" The Council would respectfully suggest that the time has now arrived when it is necessary for the Community to enact certain important By-Laws. They have accordingly appended to this Report the draft of a series of Resolves and By-Laws which they believe ought to be passed immediately.

"All which, being reported for consideration, they now respectfully submit to the disposal of their constituents.

" By order of the Council,

"ADIN BALLOU, *Pres't.*"

The report was unanimously accepted and its several recommendations and suggestions were taken up and freely discussed ; the discussion resulting in the adoption without dissent of the following

"RESOLVES AND BY–LAWS.
" RESOLVE TO RAISE FUNDS.

"*Resolved*, (1) That this Community will forthwith proceed to raise by subscription the sum of six thousand dollars, and as much more as possible.

"(2) That every member of this Community is called upon by the exigencies of our common cause to make the utmost reasonable exertions to advance money and other needful equivalents for the augmentation of our available funds.

"(3) That the Executive Council be instructed to urge forward all judicious measures for the increase of subscriptions to our Joint-Stock, and for the speedy collection of moneys thereon into the Treasury.

"(4) That the President and Secretary be instructed to furnish themselves at the common expense with the requisite books, printed blanks, and stationery, for the discharge of their official duty relative to subscriptions, and to issue certificates of title as occasion may offer.

"RESOLVE ACCEPTING THE FARM.

"*Resolved*, (1) That this Community do heartily approve of the late proceedings of their President, in purchasing, on his own responsibility, for the common advantage, the estate in Milford formerly called 'the Dale,' afterwards 'the Jones' farm,' and latterly 'the Hastings Daniels' place.'

"(2) That the said estate be cordially accepted by this Community for its future use and possession.

"(3) That this Community do guarantee the necesssary pecuniary means to pay for said estate and to fulfil all the obligations assumed by the President in his contract with Mr. Cyrus Ballou.

"(4) That the Executive Council be instructed to carry this Resolve into full effect, by ordering payment out of the Treasury at the proper time, and taking a Deed of the estate in their capacity of Trustees, according to Article II, Sec. 2, of our Constitution and agreeably to the laws of the land.

"RESOLVE ENTRUSTING CERTAIN DISCRETIONARY POWERS TO THE EXECUTIVE COUNCIL.

"*Resolved*, (1) That this Community do authorize and empower their Executive Council, if they shall judge the same to be warrantable in view of the resources at command, as follows, viz.:

"To make repairs on our dwelling-house and other buildings.

"To convert any of our frame buildings, by alterations and repairs, into temporary tenements, school-rooms or other necessary apartments.

"To provide ample furniture for the dwelling-house, with a view to the accommodation of as many boarders in commons as may healthfully occupy the same during the ensuing year and until other accommodations can be afforded.

"To provide oxen, horses, and other live stock, together with all necessary vehicles, implements, and conveniences, for carrying on the farming business or other labor on the estate.

"To commence improvements on the land, or the erection of a dam across Mill river, or the construction of trenches, or any other work whatever for the common benefit.

"To make arrangements for opening a school in accordance with our general design.

"To provide the foundation of a Library for the Community.

"To purchase a small printing establishment suitable for the publication of *The Practical Christian* and doing common job work.

"To engage tenements for members of the Community within two miles of the farm for the year 1842, if really necessary.

"Finally, to do or commence doing any other thing, work, or enterprise, constitutionally proper, as they may judge most conducive to the prosperity of the Community.

"(2) That this Community pledge all their available resources to the Executive Council, to sustain them in the discharge of their duties and for the accomplishment of all the undertakings authorized by this Resolve.

"(3) That the Executive Council be instructed to report to the Community from time to time the progress of their proceedings under this Resolve, as the general safety and satisfaction may in their opinion require.

"RESOLVE TO GIVE A NAME TO OUR LOCATION.

"Whereas it is convenient that the location of this Community should be known by some appropriate name; and whereas we have been hoping anxiously for a home suitable to our wants, which now our heavenly Father has providentially granted us; and whereas hope in His wisdom and goodness is the great support of our souls in beginning and carrying forward our glorious enterprise for the regeneration of human society amid the contempt of scorners and the fears of doubting philanthropists, — Therefore

"*Resolved*, (1) That our said location, formerly called 'the Dale,' afterwards 'the Jones' farm,' and latterly 'the Hastings

Daniels' place,' be hereafter called, known, and distinguished
by the name of HOPE DALE.

"(2) That we do humbly acknowledge our gratitude to
Almighty God for the success with which He has thus far
sped the cause of the Fraternal Communion; that we reconse-
crate our all to His service for the living out and extending
the principles of pure practical Christianity among mankind;
that our hearts are more than ever confirmed in these divine
principles, both as to their holy excellence and their final
triumph; and that we do unreservedly commend our bodies
and souls, our property and lives, our welfare and happiness,
to His guardianship, now and forevermore.

"BY-LAW TO PRESCRIBE THE MANNER OF ENACTING LAWS, ETC.

"Whereas it is proper that all our laws should be fitly
arranged into sections, and also that they should be authoritatively attested, *therefore* it is unanimously agreed and determined,

"SECTION 1. That in all cases where a law comprehends
several consecutive specifications or prescriptions, it shall be
divided into sections numerically designated.

"SEC. 2. That all By-Laws, Resolves, Rules, and Regulations, passed or ordained by this Community, shall be attested
by the signatures of the President and Secretary under date
of time and place, in form following, to wit: — Passed in regular meeting at —— —— 18—.

—— —— *Secretary.*   —— —— *President.*

"SEC. 3. That all such Laws, Resolves, Rules, and Regulations shall be duly published by the President and Secretary
in the official periodical of the Community or in some other
printed form, and all the members served with one copy each
at the common expense.

"BY-LAW PRESCRIBING THE MANNER OF CALLING, NOTIFYING, AND CONDUCTING BUSINESS MEETINGS.

SECTION 1. "All meetings of this Community for the transaction of regular business, whether annual, stated, or special, shall
hereafter be called by written notification of the Executive
Council, specifying the time and place of meeting with the

principal subject matters of business to be acted upon, signed by the President and countersigned by the Secretary.

"SEC. 2. Every notification of a meeting as aforesaid shall be published in the official periodical of the Community at least seven days previous to the time appointed for holding the same. Provided, nevertheless, that personal information given to each member by the President or Secretary, seven days previous to holding any meeting, shall be deemed sufficient.

"SEC. 3. The President or some one of the Intendants shall preside at all meetings. He shall call the members to order at the proper time, direct the Secretary to read the notification, and after a suitable season of prayer, silent or audible, declare the meeting duly opened for the dispatch of business.

"SEC. 4. Every important motion shall be reduced to writing and seconded by some member in the usual form; whereupon, after satisfactory deliberation, the question shall ordinarily be taken by *Ayes* and *Noes*. If there be doubt, it shall be taken by *Yeas* and *Nays*; also, when one-fourth of the members present demand it. And the choice of all official servants shall uniformly be by written or printed ballots.

"SEC. 5. Any meeting called and notified as aforesaid may be adjourned from time to time at the pleasure of the members present, until the business matter of the notification shall have been fully discharged.

"SEC. 6. Every meeting shall be closed with a brief season of prayer, audible or inaudible, as at the opening thereof.

"BY-LAW REGULATING THE ADMISSION OF MEMBERS.

"SEC. 1. All applications for membership in this Community shall hereafter be made in writing through some actual member thereof, whose duty it shall be faithfully to question the applicant in manner hereinafter prescribed — and upon obtaining satisfactory answers, to propose him or her as a candidate for admission substantially in the form following, to wit:

[It is not deemed advisable to insert the document here on account of its length, but refer those desirous of learning its contents to *The Practical Christian*, Vol. II, No. 11, in the Hopedale Public Library.—*Ed.*]

"SEC. 2. It shall be the duty of the President and Secretary of this Community to get printed and keep constantly on hand an adequate supply of the blank applications specified in the preceding section.

"SEC. 3. [*As subsequently amended.*] Upon presentation of any application for membership, the Community shall proceed to consider and determine, in the first place, whether they will entertain the same; next, whether they will receive the applicant as a candidate for probationary residence; next and finally, whether admission to full membership shall be granted. Persons received as candidates for probationary residence, if not already connected with some Inductive Conference, shall be invited to join one at Hopedale. And no person shall be admitted to full membership until he or she shall have actually resided in the Community one complete year, nor then without good evidence of worthiness, according to the true spirit and intent of the Constitution.

"SEC. 4. All applications for membership shall be carefully preserved on file in the Secretary's office for future reference and perpetual memorial.

"SEC. 5. Every candidate finally admitted into the membership of this Community, after having been put on probation, shall, upon settlement of accounts, be dealt with in all respects precisely as if actual membership had commenced on the first day of such probation. And in order that no misunderstanding or serious difficulty may arise in cases of *rejection*, the President, or some one of the Intendants, shall enter into special written contract with every probationer, attested by two competent witnesses, which contract shall clearly express, in as few words as the nature of the case will admit, the terms on which the probationer is to live and labor with the Community. And every such written contract shall be preserved on file in the Secretary's office.

"SEC. 6. Every present member of the Community, on being furnished with a copy of the blank application prescribed in this act, shall make answer to the questions therein contained, precisely as applicants are required to do; and the same shall be placed on file by the Secretary in his office in a distinct package marked, '*Memorials of Original Members.*'

"BY-LAW REGULATING THE ENUMERATION AND RECORD OF SHARES, ETC.

"All the shares of Joint-Stock, for which certificates are issued by the President and Secretary, shall be carefully num-

bered in the order of their issue. The number thereof shall
be specified somewhere in the margin of the certificate and
full record made accordingly. The certificate itself shall also
be numbered.

" BY-LAW TO REGULATE THE APPRAISAL OF PROPERTY, ETC.

"SEC. 1. Whenever any subscriber to the Joint-Stock shall
wish to turn in any kind of property instead of money, and
the Executive Council shall deem it expedient to receive the
same, they shall appoint three competent persons to act as
appraisers thereof.

"SEC. 2. Such persons shall carefully appraise every article,
item, or parcel of such property, make out an inventory thereof, duly certified under their hands, and lodge the same in
the Secretary's office for the use of the Council; who shall
thereupon, if all parties be satisfied, take a bill of sale of such
property and order the proper certificate to be issued.

"Passed in regular meeting at Millville, Mendon, Mass.,
Aug. 26, 1841."

It will throw some light upon the history of our movement in the constructive period of its existence, and perhaps interest the reader, to have some account given of
the success attending our efforts to raise the six thousand
dollars contemplated in the first of the foregoing Resolves.
When we left the place of meeting, the pledged subscriptions received from those present amounted to three
thousand dollars, just one-half of the desired sum. Sixteen persons had united in making them, no one of whom
promised more than five hundred dollars, and several only
fifty dollars each. None of us were rich, even in the
moderate, rural estimate of wealth; the majority were
comparatively poor. And those approaching what might
be termed under frugal management a competency were
so conditioned that they could not readily convert even a
small portion of their possessions into money. As to
people of means outside who might be reckoned among
our friends, they had too little faith in our untried
scheme to risk anything in it. They wished us well and

hoped we should succeed, but *at our own cost.* While the more unfriendly and worldly inclined used their influence to deter those who in their hearts were disposed to aid us, from doing so. All this was natural and to a certain extent excusable — at any rate, it was in accordance with the common course of the world. Wind and tide were against us in the matter of raising funds and we advanced slowly in that behalf, bringing us ere long to the conclusion, which was very repugnant to our feelings, that we should be obliged to resort to borrowing in order to realize the requisite amount. Fortunately my own personal credit was good for any ordinary emergency, as was that of others of our company; and, if worse came to worse, we could give a partial mortgage of the farm we had purchased as security for a loan, should circumstances compel us to obtain one. And this was what was finally done as a means of putting us upon our feet and getting us ready for effective work.

First Annual Meeting.

This took place at my residence in Mendon, Jan 5, 1842. The first business done was that of considering and acting upon applications for membership and for probationship in our body. As a result eight persons were received into full fellowship and three were placed on probation for the time being; their cases respectively to be finally adjusted at a future date.

The report of the Executive Council, which was a full exposé of the affairs, the standing, and the prospects of the Community as related both to its internal economy and to the public at large, was then presented. Only those portions which have a direct bearing upon the condition of things within the body, testifying to what had been accomplished and what was in process of accomplishment, are hereinafter given, the more discursive and hortatory passages being omitted.

"The Executive Council, at the close of their official term, respectfully submit the following report:

"They are happy to announce that the affairs and prospects of this infant Community, notwithstanding the many obstacles that impede its progress, are decidedly encouraging and demand acknowledgment of profound gratitude to the Author of all good. From the smallest possible beginning it has slowly advanced to its present hopeful stage. It is, indeed, but 'a little one' yet — creeping till it can walk. We trust, however, that the day is not far distant when it will stand erect in the full vigor of youth, master of its feet and able to provide for all its wants. Friendly inquiries continue to come in from different parts of the country, whither the report of our enterprise has been carried; new applications for membership are made by worthy men and women from time to time; and there is little reason to doubt that another year will witness large accessions to our numbers and resources. When operations shall have actually commenced at Hopedale by those intending to locate there in the spring, and it is seen that even the 'lazy ministers' are hard at work under a wise plan of operations, a powerful impression in our favor will be made on the public mind. Many will then know what they dare not now believe, that the projectors and wool-dyed friends of this cause are in earnest.

*   *   *   *   *   *   *

"We now turn our attention to the present and prospective financial condition of the Community — its internal affairs. Under the resolve of August last, 'entrusting certain discretionary powers to the Executive Council,' we bought out Cyrus Ballou, as lessee of the Hopedale farm, together with all the hay in the barns, 150 bushels of potatoes in the cellar, one yoke of oxen and ten cows. For the potatoes we paid him $37.50 in cash. For entire possession of the premises from December 1st to April 1st we are to pay him $554.00 on the first of April next, without interest. For this we have given him private security. The hay of all kinds was estimated at thirty to thirty-five tons. The oxen were reckoned at $60.00; six cows at $16.00 each, and four others at $13.50 each. Four head more of young cattle have been purchased for $50.00 cash. The whole cost of property bought amounts to $641.50. Besides this $9.00 have been paid for printing blank applications and certificates. Bro. Henry Lillie now resides upon the farm and takes the entire charge of the Community property.

"Having ascertained that it would be injudicious to begin any important improvements or outlays during the autumn, it was deemed unnecessary to urge the collection of funds; especially as most of our friends could use their money to advantage in their business. Therefore one subscription of two shares — $100.00 — is the only money yet received into the treasury. Nearly all this has been paid out for the items above mentioned.

"*The Practical Christian*, which may be now considered the property of the Community, will just about clear itself, leaving, perhaps, a little in fund. About five hundred copies are printed, most of which are in circulation. The paying subscribers must exceed four hundred without a close count. The whole expense of the first volume was $413.43, nothing being charged for editorial services. The present volume will cost about $366.00. The whole sum received by the Publishing Agent from the outset to Jan. 1, 1842, is $650.90. This leaves a balance on hand of $54.00, which, with what is due and collectable on subscriptions, will certainly defray the remaining expenses of the volume. It is hoped that new and successful efforts will be made another year for the increased circulation of this periodical.

"Setting *The Practical Christian* aside as balancing its own debit and credit, the Community finances will stand thus: Farm, as contracted for, $3800.00; hay and stock, $604.00; potatoes in cellar, $37.00; printed blanks, $9.00; making a total of $4450.00. Owing or due the first of next April, $4353.50. Cash actually received, $100.00; paid out, $96.50; on hand, $3.50. So that to meet our existing liabilities, according to contract, we must raise during the next quarter, $4350.00. Besides this, it is estimated that we shall need, to furnish our house, stock our farm completely, and provide for other indispensible wants, not less than $3000.00, in goods or cash; making, in all, about $7500.00. Much more than this is exceedingly necessary, and twice as much is desirable, for successful operations on even our small scale. But with less than $7500.00 we cannot get on to advantage and build what seems absolutely essential for the humblest commencement. We have

strong hopes that a much larger sum than this will come into
our treasury during the next nine months, and that the year
on which we are entering will see a substantial and respectable beginning of our Community life.

"Without anticipating the duties of the Council about to be
elected or recommending measures which will belong to them
to mature, we will only add, in conclusion, that we have
caused the survey of a *site* and a building *plat* for a Community village; a plan of which is herewith submitted, in the
hope that it will receive the general approbation. In executing
this survey, as on a former occasion of leveling the water
privilege, our friend, Newell Nelson, Esq., of Milford, practical surveyor, kindly made the Community welcome to his
services; for which he is entitled to their cordial thanks.

"And now, beloved associates, may the love of God continue
to animate us, his wisdom guide us, and his grace finally crown
us with eternal joy.

"In behalf of the Council,

ADIN BALLOU.

"After accepting the Report, it was *Voted*, to proceed to the
choice of our official servants for the year ensuing. This was
accordingly done with the following result, the brethren named
being declared unanimously elected:

"ADIN BALLOU, *President;* WM. W. COOK, *Secretary;* DAVID
R. LAMSON, *Auditor; Intendants:* LEMUEL MUNYAN, *Finance
and Exchange;* EBENEZER D. DRAPER, *Agriculture and Animals;*
HENRY LILLIE, *Manufactures and Mechanical Industry;* BUTLER
WILMARTH, *Health and Domestic Economy;* DANIEL S. WHITNEY,
Education, Arts, and Sciences; WM. H. FISH, *Religion, Morals,
and Missions.*

"The meeting then dissolved."

Settlement at Hopedale. No other meeting of the Community was held until after a substantial settlement had
been made on our Hopedale domain and practical operations effectively inaugurated. Br. Henry Lillie had already
gone thither with his family, having taken possession of
part of the ancient dwelling-house the previous October,
and assumed charge of the Community property on the
premises. He was our pioneer settler. On the 28th of

the same month a daughter was born to himself and wife, the first Hopedale child, who was named Lucy Ballou Lillie in honor of my wife. This made the family, parents and children, six in number. On the 20th of January, three weeks after the annual meeting just spoken of, the second family arrived, that of Br. Nathan Harris, consisting of himself, wife, and four children. Next appeared Br. Ebenezer D. Draper, his wife, Anna T. Draper, and Wm. T. Stacy, a lad they had taken to bring up, about the middle of March. A few days later, on the 22d, I removed my family there, four of us, and also Mrs. Charlotte P. Hooton, to whom I had sub-let a portion of my house in Mendon some months before in anticipation of locating at Hopedale about this time, with her children, four more. Br. Daniel S. Whitney, Br. Wm. W. Cook and wife, and Brother Reuben H. Brown and wife, soon followed; so that on the 1st of April, 1842, the Community family numbered twenty-eight persons.

Meanwhile myself and the more responsible members of the Executive Council had been moving under high pressure to raise the funds indispensably requisite to enable us to meet our obligations and set in order a multitude of preliminary appointments. We were disappointed by the failure of several fair promises on the score of Joint-Stock capital, and were notified that some hundreds of dollars actually paid into our treasury would have to be refunded in order to meet sundry unexpected contingencies in the private affairs of subscribers. Under these circumstances borrowing on mortgage of the farm became an absolute necessity. Accordingly, I, in behalf of the Council, negotiated a loan of two thousand dollars ($2000.00) with Mr. William Cargill of Cumberland, R. I. This loan, with considerable sums obtained from several of my personal friends as stock, but which I guaranteed, enabled us to meet all just claims against us

on the first of April and to enter upon some of our contemplated improvements. But our beginning was a hard
rub. Our reliable Joint-Stock capital uncontingently paid
in did not exceed four thousand dollars ($4,000.00) ;
what seemed a formidable debt had been imposed upon
our domain by the above-mentioned mortgage ; our time-
shattered dwelling-house could afford but stinted accommodations for our increasing Community family ; our
outbuildings needed substantial repairs ; our water privilege was yet without dam or mill-structure ; we had
a meagre amount of wood to be disposed of, or other
salable productions that could be converted into money ;
little profitable employment for those needing work was
immediately available ; consumers among us greatly outnumbered our producers ; — in fine, a host of disadvantages and hindrances beset us and taxed us sorely at
the very start. And I would forewarn and counsel all
who may hereafter propose to inaugurate kindred experiments to postpone them indefinitely rather than attempt
them under so many untoward and embarrassing conditions. Nevertheless, our Community pressed forward,
defying all hostile and discouraging circumstances and
triumphing for the time being over all hostile elements
and forces, though brought to disastrous failure at the
last, even in the midst of comparative prosperity, not so
much by reason of unpropitious external causes, as from
complex, subtle, internal ones : — all of which will be
made to appear in the sequel.

On Wednesday, March 23d, the day after I took up
my abode on the community domain, we began the work
of appraising the household furniture and other personal
property brought together by the several members already
located there, which it was deemed mutually advantageous
and desirable to have transferred to the ownership of the
Community ; crediting the amount of the valuation in
each case to the proper person as so much Joint-Stock

actually paid in and causing certificates for the same to be issued accordingly. On the evening of Thursday, the 24th, we held our first religious meeting — a social conference for devotional exercises, counsel, and exhortation — in the large front room on the west side of our ancient domicile, the very apartment in which what was afterward the First Church in Milford (Orthodox Congregational) was organized one hundred and one years and nine days before, that is, April 15, 1741. We were all weary with the labors and cares of removal to our new home, and with the difficulties attendant upon adjusting ourselves to our incommodious and crowded quarters; but mentally we were in a state of impassioned ecstacy — in the honeymoon of our new social life and our enthusiasm was at fever heat. We felt that we had entered the promised land, and our humble sanctuary, which was also our temporary abode, was better to us than the palaces and temples of Egypt. So we sang, prayed, exhorted, and glorified with all our heart. It was a melting and joyous occasion; none of us dreaming for a moment that any root of selfishness and discord would ever spring up among us to chill the ardor of our hope and zeal, or that daily familiar acquaintance with each other would ere long soil the gilt edges of the volume of our history we were just beginning to write. Thenceforth the Thursday evening *conference meeting* was an established community institution and an effective and much-prized instrumentality for promoting the moral and spiritual life of our people.

The Sunday following, March 27th, was my last as Pastor of the First Church and Congregation in Mendon, in the afternoon of which I delivered a written valedictory discourse to a large and deeply interested audience, from the text in II Corinthians, 13 : 11 : "Finally, brethren, farewell. Be perfect, be of good comfort, be of one mind, live in peace ; and the God of love and peace shall be with you." It was published in *The Practical Christian*,

5

June 25th following, Vol. III, No. 3. Most of our Hopedale adult residents were in attendance on the occasion. I
had preached in the pulpit occupied that day for the last
time as a settled minister for more than eleven years,
and had gathered about me many kind friends, who still
clung to me with a cordial attachment and earnest good
wishes as I left them to embark with my all upon a
strange, untraversed sea.

The next Sunday, April 3d, witnessed our first services
of public worship on our chosen territory. They were
held in the "Old House," a goodly number of interested
friends from the general vicinity joining our own little
company to make a respectable audience. I preached an
earnest discourse in the morning from Psalms 133 : 1 :
"Behold how good and how pleasant it is for brethren to
dwell together in unity." Br. Daniel S. Whitney delivered a sermon in the afternoon. These exercises were
accompanied by appropriate singing, praying, and exhortation, all being rendered under high inspiration from
above and with marked impression upon all present. It
was in its way a day of public and solemn dedication,
on which our community domain with all pertaining thereto was consecrated to God and Humanity. Three days
later I solemnized the first Hopedale marriage in the old-
fashioned "East Room," which for many months served
not only as our general reception room, but as our
Council Hall, our place of public convocation, and our
Sabbath sanctuary.

And now the Hopedale Community had become an
established fact — a *bona fide* institution — a practical
attempt to realize in individual and social life a grand
idea of fraternal unity, co-operation, harmony, peace, on
the broad Christian basis of "love to God and man."
It had passed beyond the theoretical stage of its development, beyond a mere existence upon paper and in the
speculations of its projectors, to the experimental stage,

to the actualization of its principles and promises in an undertaking which took its place in the great arena of human activity with other agencies designed to promote the well-being of mankind, challenging the attention of the world and ready to stand or to fall by what it might or might not accomplish in the broad field of human endeavor and attainment for human good and the upbuilding of the kingdom of God.

This Chapter I bring to a close by copying the last of a series of seven "Familiar Letters" written about the time of our locating at Hopedale to the members of the Community, for the purpose of awakening in them a sense of the grave responsibilities they had assumed by covenanting together, and of preparing them for their new position and the duties it imposed upon them. The one inserted below appeared under date of April 16, 1842, just after the settlement on our domain had been effected. It speaks for itself :

"*Beloved Associates:* Since my last I have gone through the bustle and fatigue of removal from Mendon to Hopedale in Milford, the selected home of our expected labors and enjoyments. There I have met a goodly number of dear brethren and sisters from the East, West, North, and South, and assisted them in organizing a Christian family and laying the foundation of our social fabric. We have been carried more pleasantly and quietly through the peculiar difficulties, toils and trials incident to the assembling of near thirty persons in *one old house*, than we had any reason to expect. Our heavenly Father has sustained us by his grace and strength; and now that we are getting settled in our chosen dwelling-place, I once more take my pen in hand to address you. A throng of emotions crowd upon my soul and retard utterance of thought. The great era*has actually commenced. We are no longer a Community on mere paper. Anticipation gives place to realization and theory to experimental practice. Poor and humble as our beginning is, do we not find it good to be here? Are our ills greater or our privileges less than we expected? Notwithstanding the unavoidable inconveniences, discomforts, and burdens of our pioneer service, who among us would go back to the Egypt of the old social state? Not one. We have been able to dissolve our former connections, to adjust our property affairs, to arrange our business, to spread a common table, to institute the true worship, and to make an auspicious beginning of the new moral world, without any of that selfishness, contention, and dissatisfaction which so many have always been predicting. Love, condescension, forbearance, patience, and the generous spirit of Christian self-sacrifice have gloriously reigned in our midst. We had faith that it would be so; and according to our faith hath it been unto us. Will it not be so in all time to come? Shall we not be and do all that with such a faith we strive for? Then let us not be weary nor faint in our minds. 'Time, patience, and perseverance accomplish all things.' What happy meetings, what holy communion of soul, what deep and thrilling religious feelings, have we thus far enjoyed! How applicable to our case have been the words of the Psalmist: 'Behold how good and how pleasant it is for brethren to dwell together in unity!' We may now reasonably look for a diminution of our temporary disadvantages and the increase of those conveniences which result from rational industry and wholesome domestic economy.

"But let us not feel that we are living and laboring wholly for ourselves. We are not of the world, even as Christ *was* and *is* not of the world. We have come out and separated ourselves from it. But we have done all this for the reformation and salvation of the world. Christ in us seeks as ever the redemption of poor self-destroyed man. May He live Himself out afresh in our thoughts, feelings, words, and actions. Let this great idea never depart from our minds, that the good we are toiling and suffering for is the good of all humanity. Thus we shall not only impart happiness of the purest kind to our fellow-creatures, but enjoy it in full measure, 'pressed down and running over,' in our own bosoms. Let the day never arrive when we become selfishly exclusive and affluently sordid. That day would be the funeral period of our holiest and sublimest purposes. 'The kingdom of God is at hand'; not that kingdom which some are looking for of personal display and physical observation, but the reign of God in men's souls and over all their interests; the spiritual dominion of the Word once made flesh; the kingdom of 'righteousness, peace,

and joy in the Holy Ghost.' It has already come within us
and it is our mission to proclaim its laws by precept and
example united to all around us. We are doing so with great
power and effect. What a change is there in the views, feelings,
and convictions of those who behold our onward movement since
we first announced our general design! What inquiry has been
awakened! What a press of souls towards the door through
which we have passed! What a Community spirit is breaking
out in different parts of our land! The bright morning star is
already beginning to lose its lustre in the growing brightness of
the dawning day. There are wonders before us—glorious events
—most salutary and sweeping revolutions in the moral world.
O, that we may be faithful to our light, true to our principles,
and worthy of our high calling in Christ Jesus! You that are
at Hopedale, you that are anxiously waiting for the first opportunity to come, and all who are intending to dwell together in
Fraternal Community, let your lamps be kept trimmed and burning and the loins of your minds be girded about with truth and
righteousness. Watch unto prayer and continue instant in good
works. Publish the glad tidings of the true gospel and perse-
vere with all patience unto the end in illustrating the divine
life. Thousands of eyes are upon you, to scrutinize your conduct and behold your progress. Walk as children of the light
and that Redeemer, who has led you by a way you know not,
will dissipate all darkness, make crooked things straight, and
spread out before you in due time the new heaven and new
earth to dwell in forevermore.

"Affectionately yours,

"A. B."

CHAPTER III.

1842.

A Beginning Made — Embarrassments — Discordant Notes — Passing a Crisis — Humbled but Undismayed.

IN the development of the family the incipient stages, collectively denominated courtship, culminate in marriage, which is followed by the so-called honeymoon, whose poetry ere long is transformed into sober prose. Similarly was it in our Community experience. Having entered upon the common-place realities of closely associated life and become familiar with the details and drudgery of daily activities, as well as with each other's personal peculiarities, many of our dreams vanished utterly while others lost not a few of their illusory charms. It was inevitable not only that our theories and hopes should be tested, but our own fitness or capability for realizing them. And there could be no severer test than the intimate and complex relationships of social, domestic, industrial, and financial economy into which we had entered. A hundred people can enjoy the society of each other occasionally under favorable conditions, without suspicion of inharmony or serious defects of character, where ten can live together in familiar intercourse a year undisturbed by feelings of mutual repulsion or perhaps disgust. This is true not only of common worldings but of the so-called refined classes, and even of professing Christians. Whoever can summer and winter each other without friction or alienation of feeling may be deemed reasonably fit for a practical Christian Community, such as we were attempting to inaugurate. And whoever cannot stand this test ought to be ashamed to profess either Christianity or true refinement of character. It has been said that ordinary civilized society with its partition walls, its class distinctions, its conventional barricades, and compulsory insularities, allows mankind quite as much unity and closeness of association as they will safely bear; and therefore that it is presumptuous to propose bringing them into more fraternal and harmonious affiliation and co-operation. And the incredulous cynic might upbraid me and my coadjutors for not knowing this before venturing upon our untoward and as it proved calamitous experiment. We did know it so far as respected the generality of our race who make no pretence to the ideals, the principles, the aspirations, or the moral and religious obligations of our distinctive form of Christian faith. But we did not know then, nor do I know now or believe, that sincere and high-minded persons, intelligently acknowledging such ideals, principles, aspirations, and obligations, ought not to associate and live together on a more elevated, Christlike plane than that of the existing order of civil society. If they ought not to do this — to transcend the prevailing civilization of the world, then I am confident, beyond all peradventure, that the religion of the New Testament is theoretically and practically false and worthy only of being ignored and reprobated.

I have stated that the number of those resident upon the Community domain April 1, 1842, was twenty-eight. These were all congregated and living together as a combined household in the old dwelling already mentioned, a portion of which had been standing about one hundred and forty years and the remainder more than a century. Several of them were entire strangers to each other and scarcely any of the families had been more intimately acquainted than as occasional visitors of one another, occupants of adjacent buildings, or worshipers together at the same house of public religious service. A few of us had enjoyed personal, domestic, social, and educational advantages open to the respectable middling classes of New England. But the larger number had lived and moved on a humbler, but in no wise dishonorable, level. There was, naturally, a corresponding diversity of manners, habits, and tastes, in addition to the varied personal peculiarities of each individual. These manifold dissimilarities, and sometimes incongruities, though all our adult population had confessed the same fundamental truths, objects, and duties, had to be harmonized and reconciled, so that all would work together with as little attrition or confusion as possible for the common good and the accomplishment of the great end we all nominally had in view. One third of our residents were children and youth from the very beginning onward, and many of the characteristics of these needed important modifications or transformations. Yet we were all domiciled under one roof, lived as one family, stocked a common larder, spread and sat at a common table, organized common industrial activities, placed our children under common regulations and restraints, and constituted to all intents and purposes a Community in fact as well as in name.

In addition to the several appointments to places of responsibility by popular vote, as already recorded, the Executive Council had commissioned Lucy H. Ballou Director of house-keeping for the current year, while I, by common consent, became the governing father of the younger members of the household. Some of these were rude and uncouth in their manners, and unused to self-regulation and self-discipline. Finding themselves massed suddenly together without the immediate oversight of their parents or guardians, they very naturally were disposed to have good times together, roaming the whole house over and making it ring with their clatter of feet and loud voices of merriment. Happily they all seemed to reverence and love me and to have respect for my wishes and requirements. I organized them into what was called *the silent band;* so that at a given signal from me their noise was instantly hushed, and their necessary movements up and down stairs or about the house were made with marked quietude and an almost inaudible tread. When I was at home I could always and with little effort secure their willing and orderly obedience.

But how limited were our accommodations and conveniences! They were none too ample for the needs of two middling-sized families of working people. We had only a single, old-fashioned, two-story house, with a time-beaten ell in the rear containing simply a kitchen, which possessed the most inadequate facilities for cooking, laundry work, and other ordinary domestic uses! Next to the kitchen, in the main building, was a long narrow apartment for our common table, and a pantry adjacent. The large west room in front we made a general sitting-room, while the corresponding east one served as a parlor, a council hall, and place of worship, as stated, and a guest chamber for visitors, having in it a folding bed of a rude sort and other conveniences. These, with a small entry and a few cupboards, were all that had place on the lower floor. The second story was partitioned off into as many lodging rooms as was practicable, and likewise the attic. The President, his wife, and little boy, occupied a small bed-chamber at the northeast corner of the house, which was crowded with their indispensable personal effects and which served as a study and office wherein to prepare editorials, records, documents, and memoranda of various kinds requisite to the satisfactory prosecution of his multiform labors. This, too, was his only indoor retreat and place of refuge from the general din.

Such were some of the difficulties and inconveniences under which our Community family started out in the house-keeping business. The case would have been sufficiently onerous and trying with our original smallness of numbers. But we could not be held to those limits. Every week almost from the outset fresh accessions pressed into our over-crowded camp, while plenty of transient callers and sojourners appeared among us all unawares, to occupy our room, take up our time, and tax our hospitality. Meanwhile, my wife, in her own quiet, unpretentious way, led off in the management of domestic affairs, with good Anna T. Draper for her faithful right-hand coadjutor, bringing order out of chaos, and putting the entire household machinery in running condition despite seeming impossibilities. As a matter of fact, our in-door family affairs were managed most efficiently and satisfactorily, and without the least friction or complaint. It had been confidently predicted by carping critics that however it might be with the men among us, our women would soon fall out with each other and come to open strife. Never were ill-omened prophecies proved more unfounded and misapplied, for through all the discouragements, privations, and misfortunes incident to those early days, no unkind word or grumbling wail was heard among our female associates; to their perpetual praise let this testimony be remembered. They bore their burdens, vexations, and trials with most exemplary patience and fortitude; though probably not without a frequently keen sense of unpleasantness if not of disgust. This must have been the case with the more sensitive and refined of them, who could but realize the striking and in some respects painful contrast between the pleasant, comfortable homes they had left behind and the multiform inconveniences and disagreeabilities of this to which they had come. But like most of their companions they calmly endured, as unavoidable, the temporary discomforts of this pioneer life for the sake of the cause of social reform and in hope of better times prospectively in sight. And when disquietudes and bickerings at length arose, it was the men and not the women who first proved weak, and wavered from the sacred standard of Christian amity and brotherhood. Nevertheless, during the early stages of our Community life, neither male nor female uttered a murmur of discontent or regret. All were genial, harmonious, and united; all were heroic and steadfastly persistent in their noble struggle for a better type of individual and social life.

To appreciate this fidelity to high ideals, their chivalric spirit, it must be remembered that several of us had left behind us prominent salaried positions, many professional advantages, alluring prospects of honorable success on the common plane of human affairs, and much of personal ease and enjoyment in our various relationships, dropping down voluntarily and cheerfully to a common fraternal level with those who had far less to share or hope for in the condition from which they had migrated. We were all here in one household, professionals, mechanics, farmers, ordinary laborers, male and female, agreeing alike to serve the Community if able, eight hours per day for fifty cents, and to pay for our board, lodging, etc., one dollar per week. Also to pay cost prices for clothing, livery, and other necessaries not included in the above. If ministers or others received any moneys from the outside world for special services rendered, all above incidental expenses went into the general treasury. Thus worldly and conventional superiority was abolished and the strong bore the infirmities of the weak. In these particulars the feeble and less productive classes among us were the only gainers by our peculiar arrangements, whilst the weight of responsibility and care must necessarily rest with intensified pressure upon those who elsewhere might have shared and profited by unusual worldly opportunities, preferments, and benefits. Yet many weeks passed by without faltering or murmur of dissatisfaction. Enthusiastic hope, ardor, and firmness of purpose reigned universal and supreme.

Perhaps I can best realize to the reader how we started out in our experiment at Hopedale by making a few extracts from the Community Journal and Record Book as they appear during the first month of our residence there. Having already spoken of the removal of myself and family to the place on the 22d of March, 1842, when our unitory life actually began, and of the appraisal of goods on the 23d, I proceed with my quotations from and after that date, as follows :

"The 24th was the day appointed by the Council to pay for the farm and take a Deed. But the money not coming in as expected, and there being an old mortgage to discharge by Claflin and Daniels (our grantors), the matter was postponed till Saturday the 26th. The President, however, paid John Claflin, Esq., $1900.00 and took receipt accordingly. A Mr. Howard came down from Leverett bringing $200.00 from Bros. Butler Wilmarth and Phineas Field. He was taken ill and had to be provided for to the best of our ability. On the 25th the President went to Woonsocket, R. I., *via* Mendon and Chestnut Hill, bought various articles, called on his friend, Carlisle W. Capron, to see about promised money, got meal of Kelley, etc. Saturday, 26th, he attended funeral of Noah Cole's wife in the forenoon. P. M., he completed payment for the farm to John Claflin, Esq., $3500.00 (excepting the $300.00 due Cyrus Ballou), received the Deed and went to Worcester to enter it for record. Agreeably to vote of Council the title was taken in the sole name of the President. As agreed with William Cargill of Cumberland, R. I., a mortgage was executed to secure the payment of $2000.00 borrowed of him for two years. This instrument was also put on record for the satisfaction of Cargill, who is to furnish the money next week. The President purchased sundry account books for the Community in Worcester before returning home, which he reached about midnight.

" Sunday, 27th. He preached his valedictory discourse in Mendon (as before stated). Monday, 28th. Mr. Howard, hav-

ing recovered from his illness, left for his home. Tuesday,
29th. A. B. went to Upton and married John C. Sweet and
Sarah Redfield. Afterwards gave a lecture in the school-house
near by on 'The Spirits in prison.' 30th. Mr. Cargill, a
brother of William, called on his way to Worcester to examine
Registry of Deeds and see that everything was safe. Next
day he returned, delivered to the President the $2000.00, and
went his way. Friday, April 1st, was spent by the President
in paying out money on contracts falling due: to Cyrus Ballou,
$854.00 — $300.00 to complete payment on farm, which had
been bought through him, and $554.00 for hay, cattle, etc.;
to Hiram Hunt and Co. for goods from store; to Millens Taft
for yoke of oxen, etc.; in all over $1000.00. We have some
confusion and many inconveniences, all of which we endure
like good soldiers for the sake of the great good we propose
and hope to accomplish. God blesses and sustains us, for which
all praise and thanksgiving be rendered to his holy name.

"Sunday, April 3d. Our first public meeting in the old
house (as described). Wednesday, 6th. A. B. married Amasa
Parkhurst and Hannah P. Brown of Milford in the common
parlor. Thursday, 7th. Annual Fast; Frederick Douglass, the
fugitive slave, with us. O, what a fast! A Fast indeed! Such
an one as we never observed before. All hearts were moved
and melted. The Father and the Son were with us by the
communion of their one Holy Spirit. p. m., A. B. went to
Mendon and married Micajah C. Gaskill and Hannah Taft at
the residence of her father, Leonard Taft. Sunday, 10th. A.
Ballou preached at Bellingham to a large audience, and lectured at 5 p. m. in E. Mendon school-house. Meeting at home,
small but good. Several brethren spoke to edification.

"From 10th to 17th much business done and good progress
made towards order and settlement of affairs. Preparations
were completed for erecting a building for school-room, printing office, etc., at the south-west extremity of Water St. The
frame is that of an old wood-shed to be vamped up. E. C.
Perham and Samuel Taft helped our workmen: Perham as
carpenter for several days, Taft as stonelayer for one day.
Wednesday the 13th. A. B. married a couple at H. Nelson's,
Milford, viz.: Daniel S. Chapin and Angeline P. Nelson. Sunday, 17th. Clother Gifford, a phrenologist, visits us. Good
meeting, a. m., A. Ballou and D. S. Whitney principal speak-

ers. P. M., A. Ballou went to Mendon to attend funeral of
widow Nabby Aldrich. Brief sermon in meeting-house. Br.
D. R. Lamsom preached at Mendon A. M., and was at Hopedale P. M. John Hawkins, the celebrated Washingtonian chief,
lectured at 4 P. M. in Mendon, most of our Hopedalians being
there. He came fully up to the highest expectations; had a
great audience and carried his hearers away like a flood, speaking two hours. Br. Whitney went to Millville in the evening,
partly to attend a meeting with the friends there but more
especially to marry a couple on the morrow.

"Monday, April 18th. A severe northeast storm. Not much
outside business done to-day. Bro. Gifford still here, and
Phrenology and Animal Magnetism occupied most of our time
and attention. He examined nearly all our heads and tried to
put Barbara Colburn into a magnetic sleep but failed. Discussion in the evening about the children. Settled it as a rule
that they should not take lights by themselves to their sleeping apartments at night, but be accompanied by some one of
proper age to attend to both them and their lights. 19th. Still
stormy. C. Gifford goes to Milford town to prosecute his
phrenological business. Our good friend, David Stearns God-
frey, called and informed us of the triumphant success of
Frederick Douglass last evening at his lecture in Milford
Academy Hall. Great excitement; the 'baser sort' active;
people turned out numerously; but they were wonderfully
overcome by his ingenuity and eloquence. The tide (which
was turbulent against him at first) turned strongly in his favor.
He lectured again this evening at Milford town-hall. Eleven
from Hopedale to hear him. A glorious lecture to a full
house. Package made up by A. B. for Whitmarsh, Boston
(our printer), with copy for *Practical Christian* and $15.00
enclosed. Wednesday the 20th. Stormy. Discussed at table
the matter of division of labor and settled it more definitely
so far as related to out-door work. Colburn takes care of the
cattle, Cook of the garden, Draper of the farming proper,
Whitney of the orcharding, while the carpenters confine themselves to their distinctive calling. A. B. lectured in the evening at the Orthodox Meetinghouse, Milford, on Temperance,
several of our people being present.

"Thursday, April 21. Bright and lovely. Business brisk.
P. M., raised the frame of the first new building at Hopedale.

Dr. Wm. P. Metcalf, who had dined with us, and friend Hiram A. Morse of Holliston were present. A. B. subsequently went into town with the farm wagon and after doing business at Hunt & Co.'s store bought a logging axle and pole of Perley Hunt, Esq., at a cost of three dollars, to be hereafter paid. All hands busy at their proper work except the little time spent in the aforesaid raising. Lamson has gone to Providence, R. I., to procure for himself a new wooden leg (he having lost one of his lower limbs). In the evening our neighbors, Daniel Scammell and wife, called upon us and as we had our weekly Conference meeting they remained through its exercises.

"Friday, 22d. Br. Draper was obliged to go to Blackstone on business in the morning. In the afternoon he and A. B. perambulated the farm, inspected the fences and pastures, and let off the cranberry swamp pond. Br. Lamson returns with his wife and children. Saturday, 23d. Pleasant. A. Ballou's 39th birthday. No ceremony; too much business in hand. Got home six bushels of potatoes from Eli Chapin's; paid $2.00. Charles Gladding, now with us, sends for his family to come here for a visit. An old acquaintance, Clark Jillson, calls with his son Orison, who look around and make inquiries. Br. Whitney off to Mendon in quest of materials for grafting purposes. Thos. J. Dunbar from Portsmouth, N. H., arrived to spend the Sabbath with us as an interested inquirer. Henry Chapin called to show us where we may cut birches on his land for pea-brush. President out with him noting the clumps and agreeing upon an estimated cord, for which we are to pay $2.00.

"Sunday, 24th. Pleasant. A. B. at home. Spoke at length A. M. and P. M. Brs. Gladding, Cook, and Brown followed. Preached in So. Milford school-house at 5 o'clock; Brs. Brown and Draper exhorted. Br. Whitney was at Millville with Br. Fish; Br. Lamson at Mendon. Monday, 25th. Rainy. T. J. Dunbar left by stage for Boston. Sent by him $150.00 to Jos. A. Whitmarsh in advance for printing-press, materials, etc., before bargained for. Also a letter, and copy for next No. of P. C. Br. John Wheeler, one of our non-resident members, called and paid into our Joint Stock $50.00. In the evening A. B. went to Hopkinton, nine miles, and married Adams Chapin to Polly R. Stone. Called at friend Perry Daniels on his way home, which he reached a little before midnight."

I will go no further with these quotations. What I have presented will furnish glimpses at the various activities of the Community during the first few weeks of its existence and thereby afford a clearer and more complete insight into its practical experiences than any number of general statements could possibly do. I now proceed to subsequent occurrences.

The next regular meeting of the Community was notified to be held in Gardner, May 5, and 6, during the sessions of the Quarterly Conference at the same dates; but failing of a quorum it adjourned to the 12th at Hopedale. It took place there accordingly and was continued by subsequent adjournments to numerous dates through the summer, as the exigencies of the case seemed to require. Only the more important items of business, those relating chiefly to the management of Community affairs and the general economy of the enterprise, will be noted in these pages, a multitude of minor incidental details being for obvious reasons omitted. And so far as the admission of new members and probationers is concerned, it is deemed sufficient to state once for all that this was continually going on at longer or shorter intervals through our entire history, without mentioning each individual instance as it transpired, with the name and date belonging thereto. At some one or another of the several adjourned sessions of the meeting of May 5th, the following Votes and Resolves were passed, to wit:

"*Voted*, That the communion of the Christian Supper be observed without the use of wine for the edification of all who deem the same a religious privilege, on the 4th Sunday of every month.

"*Voted*, That mothers, resident members of this Community, having nursing infants be regularly credited forty-eight hours per week; it being understood that they select certain portions of each day, amounting to eight hours, during which, if their health and the comfort of their children permit, they shall hold themselves in readiness to perform such labor as may reasonably be required of them.

"*Voted*, To defer the erection of a dwelling-house for the present, and proceed with all convenient dispatch to build a mechanic shop, 30 feet by 40, two stories above the basement, with dam and water-power sufficient to operate the more necessary labor-saving machinery usual in such establishments.

"*Voted*, To accept the right to use a patent shingle machine purchased by the President and Intendant of Manufactures, etc., for $100.00.

"*Voted*, That Tuesday evening of each week be devoted to improvement in singing; Thursday evening to religious conference; and Saturday evening to the reading of such public papers and periodicals as may be taken by the Community.

" RESOLVE RESPECTING THE ADMISSION OF MEMBERS TO RESIDENCE.

"*Resolved*, That no person shall hereafter be entitled to residence on the Community domain in mere virtue of having been received to membership; but the question of residence shall in all cases be determined by the Community at some regular meeting.

" BY-LAW REGULATING RECEPTION AND REPAYMENT OF MONEYS.

" Hereafter no moneys shall be received into the Treasury of this Community either on subscription to the Joint Stock or on special deposit for gratuitous use, except on condition that the same shall not be withdrawn without at least ninety days' notice for all sums under five hundred dollars, six months' notice for all sums over five hundred and less than two thousand dollars, and one year's notice for all sums exceeding two thousand dollars. And this condition shall be expressed in the body or on the back of all certificates and receipts issued for moneys so received.

" RESOLVE RESPECTING INDUCTIVE CONFERENCES.

" Whereas, no effectual measures have been taken to carry into effect the plan heretofore proposed for gathering our scattered friends into Inductive Conferences; and whereas the progress of our cause demands the immediate prosecution of that plan slightly modified; therefore

"*Resolved*, That wherever there are three or more persons seriously disposed to promote the principles of Practical Chris-

6

tianity as professed by the Fraternal Communion, they be advised
to form themselves forthwith into a religious class or conference inductive to this Community; and that to facilitate their
organization the following be recommended as a suitable *Constitution:*

"We, the undersigned, heartily desiring to promote in ourselves and others the growth of pure Christianity as professed
by the Fraternal Communion in their 'Declaration' of principles and duties, do form ourselves into a religious class, to be
called 'The —— Practical Christian Conference, inductive to
Fraternal Community No. 1.'

"1. Any serious person may become a member of this Conference by subscribing its Constitution. Any person may cease
to be a member by requesting his or her name erased. Any
unworthy member may be disowned after ineffectual admonition.

"2. This Conference may from time to time choose such
official servants as shall be found necessary to the orderly conduct of its affairs.

"3. The members of this Conference shall meet regularly
for Christian worship and edification at least once on the first
day of every week, and by agreement at such other times as
may be deemed proper.

"4. This Conference, by a vote of two-thirds of the members present at any regular meeting, may amend this Constitution or may establish such regulations not inconsistent with
its spirit and design as shall at any time be found necessary.

"In full ratification whereof we have hereunto severally subscribed our names under date of time and place of residence.

"*Resolved*, That whenever any Inductive Conference may be
organized in accordance with the advice and recommendation
herein given, the proper official servant thereof be requested to
report such organization immediately to the Secretary of this
Community, in order that our Missionaries may visit it and
a regular correspondence be maintained."

The foregoing Votes, Resolves, etc., are for the most
part self-explanatory and hence can be easily understood
by the reader. The one concerning Inductive Conferences,
however, may need some further elucidation in order to
be perfectly clear and comprehensible. It will have been

noticed that only a part of the members of Fraternal Community No. 1 were located on its central domain at Hopedale. Others of them, and for some time a majority, were scattered abroad here and there in general society, prevented from coming to us, either by our inability to accommodate them with suitable housing and remunerative employment or by their own condition and circumstances in life. Besides these there were also many other persons in different directions, sympathizing friends and interested inquirers, who believed and felt that our principles and aims were nearer the true Christian standard of faith and duty than those of the professing Christian world. They had lost confidence in the prevailing fashionable and conventional religion and morality. They were tired of the existing condition of things in church and state. They longed for something better. They desired and prayed for a higher, diviner type of individual, social, and civil life than was to be found in the world at large. They had heard of us and of our movement, and were inclined towards us and it. They would like to know more of both. They would be happy to become in some way associated with us and with kindred spirits for the purpose of learning more about us, about our views of truth and duty, about what we were doing and trying to do at Hopedale, and of improving themselves in the things that pertain to a noble character and a Christian life. And this they desired with an expectation of sometime actually joining us in our work, if, upon better acquaintance with us and it, they should feel bound in conscience to do so.

It was for such as these — detached members, special friends, and miscellaneous inquirers — that the system of Inductive Conferences was devised and in a few instances put into practical operation. Under that system, the several parties indicated, dwelling in the same town, village, or general neighborhood, could be associated with

each other and with us in an effective way for mutual
counsel, instruction, and encouragement, for nurturing in
themselves and each other the religious affections and
capabilities, and for building up ultimately a fraternal
order of human society among men and the kingdom of
God upon the earth. They would be helped by affilia-
ting with us, and we be strengthened and inspired by
having them as allied co-workers, as fellow-devotees of
a common faith and hope, and as possible members in
full fellowship of our own or some similar Community.
The Conferences thus formed were to be missionary stations, to be regularly visited by our ministerial brethren
and made candlesticks of truth and righteousness to
all the region round about. Members of them would
receive and distribute our writings, would assemble with
us on public occasions, would be living testimonies to
the excellence of our ideas and aims, and so help to
extend our influence in the world. They would, moreover,
be supplied with the means of educating their children
and youth in the doctrines and precepts of the unadulter-
ated Gospel of Christ, whereby they would be qualified to
enter upon and carry forward to a triumphant success
in years to come the work which we had inaugurated and
which was so full of promise for mankind. Under these
prepossessions and auspices was established the system of
Inductive Conferences, first announced to the public by
the Intendant of Religion, Morals, and Missions, Br. Wm.
H. Fish, in *The Practical Christian* of Oct. 2, 1841, but
modified, perfected, and finally adopted by the Community
as a part of its comprehensive polity, Aug. 8, 1842.

In order to show still further how we were getting on
as a Community during the first few months of our life
at Hopedale, more especially in the matter of our industrial activities, I will make a quotation from an article
which appeared in our little paper, June 11, 1842, entitled, " Community Affairs ":

"We have now on the Hopedale estate forty-four persons, all boarded in one general family; ten men, twelve women, and twenty-two children under fifteen years of age. We have 13 cows, 4 yokes of oxen and steers, 2 horses and 6 swine. We have planted with garden vegetables for market and our own use some 3 acres, with indian corn 4 or more, and with potatoes and beans 10 or more; in all from 17 to 20 acres. We have made numerous repairs in and upon our old buildings; erected a new one 32 by 14 feet, one and a half story above the basement, calculated for a printing office, school room, two sleeping apartments on the upper floor and two rooms for shops in the basement; all, of course, on a small scale. The brethren have just commenced a dam and the foundation of a mechanic shop, to be 30 by 40 feet in size, two stories high with a basement designed for various machines to be operated by water power. The erection and furnishing of this establishment will require all the labor and resources we can spare from other demands for several months to come. Our business is multiform and arduous. There is everything to do and small means with which to operate. Division of labor is also difficult to arrange properly; but we have got along better than most people might imagine and hope for better days ahead.

"Our school is now in running order. We might have many boarding pupils if we could accommodate them, but that is not possible at present. A few children in the neighborhood who can come from their homes will probably be taught in the school. The printing establishment was started during the last week in May. We print *The Practical Christian* every fortnight, and are prepared to do most kinds of job work, for which we already have several orders. Regular meetings for religious instruction and worship are kept up in our own house twice on Sunday, and a conference for social prayer, praise, and exhortation on Thursday evenings. These meetings are free for all our neighbors and friends to attend who choose. They are also free for all the attendants to speak as they feel impressed with a sense of duty.

"We are happy to say that the great body of the people in the region immediately around us evince a kind and friendly feeling toward us, and though the stand we have taken is new, strange, and doubtful to them, yet they seem to wish us nothing but success. And if there are others who feel hostile to us and would be glad to see us explode, may God enable us to live down their opposition by righteousness and to overcome all evil by the unwearied exercise of love and meekness. Thus far we rejoice to know that our influence is salutary on one another and those around us.

"Our internal affairs are getting along as well as could have been expected, especially when we consider the very great disadvantages under which we are placed for want of funds, house room, and other conveniences. We have found ourselves in close contact with each other, and of course had ample opportunities to find out each others weaknesses, failings, and besetting sins. It has been a most salutary school, in which the pupils have been unlearning old dispositions, habits, tastes, and manners, and acquiring new ones, as we trust for the better. We have found the great principles and well-defined duties of our declaratory test equal to every emergency — a bond of union and a correcting power for all errors of feeling and conduct. Our faith is therefore unwavering that by the help of God we shall one day realize our highest aspirations after a right social state. In the meantime our numbers and resources are gradually increasing, inquiries are becoming more frequent and urgent from all quarters, and we press forward to the fulfilment of our high mission."

As the days, weeks, and months of that first summer came and went, we extended our stakes and strained our cords to the utmost. We in due time learned that both internally and externally we had undertaken overmuch — that we were overtaxing our resources and our energies. But we could not turn back; we could not suspend our activities; we must go forward, but more cautiously, more deliberately, more wisely. We had learned that nothing was to be feared from abroad, from the surrounding world. Whatever threatened us in that direction at the outset had practically disappeared and all motives or incentives to unity and fidelity originating in an external pressure of hostility had been shorn of their strength. Our chief if not only danger was of an internal nature — from enemies within our own gates. Our prosperity, success, and happiness depended largely upon reconciling domestic incongruities and preserving a healthy social core. As we were all human, possessed of the frailties and imperfections, to say nothing of the follies and sins, of our common nature, we had within us the elements of unrest, disorder, confusion, in embryonic if not in nascent, active state. And it was not long under the trying circumstances of our lot before those elements began to effervesce. We had started out with too many raw recruits — with too many undisciplined minds, hearts, and wills. There were whims, fancies, crotchets, in the heads of some of our members, which, after becoming somewhat acquainted with their associates, they were ambitious to ventilate, and magnify. This they sought to do by questions or propositions involving them, calculated and probably designed to elicit a reply or provoke discussion. The hour of eating was their opportunity and they improved it, modestly and suasively at first, causing only light and dispassionate table talk, chaffing or repartee. But this soon grew into something more serious and earnest — into eager debate and sharp disputation. From the table conversation or discussion was transferred to regular Community meetings held for business and other important purposes. For awhile the themes of inquiry, remark, or controversy were chiefly dietetic, physiological, and economic, and though possessed of a certain intrinsic value and significance were not urged or maintained as of vital or even weighty import as related to the great problem of social reconstruction we were trying to solve. So long as this was the case — so long as the talk was novel and suggestive or inquisitive, no harm came of it and no one was disturbed by it or complained of it. But when, as was the case after a time, the topics were magnified into matters of indispensable concern, entitled to paramount consideration like that given to the primary principles of moral and social order and the divinely imposed duties of life, and were put forward in a dogmatic spirit and form, then the matter appeared in a new phase, assumed a more threatening aspect, and awakened apprehensions of coming ill to all concerned in the minds of our better and more responsible members. And when these, roused to a sense of impending danger, raised a firm but calm protest against the unwarrantable assumptions and claims that had been put forth, they were met, not with kindly and reasonable consideration, but rather with resentful petulance and with insinuations that after all the professions of fraternal equality made to the world, there was a smattering of aristocracy to be found even in that lowly old house. Under that pretence there were some attempts set in motion to draw our poorer and humbler members into a sort of democratic cabal for the maintenance of their proper rights under the Constitution. This movement, however, was of little avail, those thus appealed to realizing instinctively who were their real friends and under whose leadership they would be likely to fare best. Nevertheless, the uneasy elements, unwilling to yield or to be silenced, began to inveigh against our Joint-Stock system of finance and to glorify that of common property as much more to be preferred in founding a new social state. This proved a more serious matter in the end, as will ere long be made to appear.

Meantime a case of personal inharmony and unpleasantness arose between two of our original number from whom we never expected anything but the most amicable relations. These were our carpenters whose business it was to build our projected Mechanic Shop in mutual co-operation. All at once it transpired that they could not agree in their consultations and operations and that considerable unhappy feeling existed between them. I was most painfully surprised when informed of this, as I had a high regard for both of the men. But the trouble sprang very naturally from their dissimilar tem-

pers, tastes, and judgments. One of them, the official
head of the work, was a plain, unpolished, rustic sort of
man, extremely sensitive, retiring, and secretive; the
other was more fanciful and sanguine, blunt and sarcas-
tic in speech, and ambitious to direct withal, feeling no
doubt a little chagrined that his associate held a higher
position than he. The result was that they became
mutually disagreeable and repellant, drawing apart from
each other. This was the first palpable instance of discord among us and was most mortifying to my feelings
on the score of acknowledged principles, but no less so
to my Community ambition. The inharmony was mollified and quieted down somewhat by our pacific social
discipline, though never entirely healed.

As the tinsel of novelty wore off and the hard actuali-
ties of our uncomfortable domestic situation began to
overtax our nerves, we lost a portion of our spiritual
enthusiasm, firmness, and patience. Our religious natures
no less than our physical suffered for want of needed
solitude and repose, as they did for lack of wholesome
nurture and stimulus to holy aspiration and endeavor.
Social, secular, and financial matters engrossed so much
of our attention and energy that our higher faculties
were partially starved. We suffered in the very particular of which we were forewarned in the letter of
Doctor Channing. As a consequence, every temptation
that assailed us was less resistable than would otherwise
have been the case.

In such states of mind we were beset by those discussions referred to a few pages back, which, though
held somewhat in check by the controlling minds among
us or rendered partially nugatory, nevertheless, could not
be wholly suppressed or shorn of mischievous influence.
Indeed, on the whole, they rather increased, growing
from bad to worse, — from mere annoyances to threatening perils. So that when they were met on this

ground and when the points contended for by those leading off in them were repudiated by the better sentiment
of the Community, a crisis was brought on which resulted
in the withdrawal of four of our new members. Reuben H.
Brown and wife, Clother Gifford, and Lorenzo Smith; the
first secession that had occurred among us. They were
displeased with our general system, and when they left
avowed a determination to start a new movement, basing
it upon better principles and administering it in a more
fraternal spirit; a task, however, for which they had
neither the capacity, the character, nor the pecuniary
means. There was more rejoicing than sorrow at their
departure, and their promised El Dorado was never heard
of afterwards.

Unfortunately, the leaven which wrought their disaffection and separation from us was not all taken with them
when they went away. Enough of it remained to work
further trouble, and all the more trouble because it had
found a lodgment in better and more influential minds.
Even our ministering brother, David R. Lamson, from
whom only the best things had been anticipated, became
infected with it, causing him at length to follow on after
those who had gone before. In his case it manifested
itself in a resolute zeal in behalf of the poorer and more
dependent members, for whom he demanded in the name
of the Constitution greater privileges and more favors
than they were in the way of enjoying. His first open
demonstration in this direction was in the form of a
claim that his own wife who had a nursing child, and
other mothers similarly situated, should be allowed regular
wages for taking care of their little ones, on the ground
that a common nursery was guaranteed in our fundamental law, and that, notwithstanding it was as yet an
impossibility in form, its provisions should in substance
be insured to those they were designed to benefit. Upon
being questioned as to how many hours per day ought

to be credited to nursing mothers, he replied that in the case of his own wife sixteen would be no more than just. This would be twice as many as were allowed our common working men and women; that is, one dollar per day while they received only fifty cents. Some of us were hardly in a mood to accept such an interpretation of the principle of justice or to grant the claims based upon it. After long consideration of the matter and much tedious discussion, I proposed a compromise regulation, which was duly approved by the Community, to the effect that nursing mothers be regularly credited for eight hours' service a day, provided, that if the nature of the case reasonably admitted of it they should perform more common domestic labor occasionally.

Another manifestation of Brother Lamson's peculiar cast of mind or eccentricity of judgment appeared in his proposition, or perhaps suggestion, that such of our ministers as had occasion to go abroad to preach or lecture should offer rides to the mothers who were ordinarily confined and care-worn at home, especially when they went alone and when nothing would be added to the expense thereby. Brother Lamson seemed to have a special interest in and sympathy for the particular class of persons indicated, and to put himself forward as the guardian and champion of their rights and privileges, although, so far as ever came to the public ear, they never asked for or desired such interposition in their behalf. He even went so far as to admonish me directly in open Community meeting for calling on those referred to so seldom and paying them so little personal attention. This implication of neglect of duty and violation of solemn pledges of fraternal interest and regard was as unreasonable as it was humiliating, inasmuch as the multitude of my cares and labors, keeping me busily employed from early dawn till late at night — not infrequently till near midnight and sometimes after — together

with the wear and tear of my anxieties for the success
of our common cause, was taxing my energy and
strength to the utmost limit, as was obvious enough to
every reflecting observer. Still, I did not presume to
deny my sins of omission in the particular named; I
only offered what I felt to be sufficient excuses in vindication of my course. This little breeze presently subsided. It was sometimes hard to feel that the brother
who caused it was altogether disinterested and magnani-
mous in his action, since his own wife was one of the
few who were to be particularly favored by his scheme,
while other women there were among us, as worthy of
consideration as she, weighed down and worn to utter
exhaustion almost by the toil and drudgery of twelve or
fifteen hours per day imposed upon them by their position
in the administration of household affairs, for whom he
offered no method or proposition of recreation or relief.

Another exhibition of Brother Lamson's solicitude for
the well-being and protection of our humbler and more
dependent ones was far graver in both its nature and
results than those mentioned, and drew to his side several
members of good esteem. It was made in connection
with the discussions that were carried on respecting the
erection of new dwelling-houses for the general convenience and comfort, and their permanent occupancy. Incident to those discussions arose the question as to who
should be put in possession of the new habitations and
enjoy the many privileges they would offer when they
were completed. There were of necessity but few of
them at first and it was a foregone conclusion forced
upon us by our limited means, that a considerable number of us must for some time yet remain in the old
quarters and share still longer the discomforts existing
there, though the contemplated reduction of numbers
would afford partial relief. And the question referred to
elicited much difference of opinion and a sharp contro-

versy. Brother Lamson was foremost in the field, declaring that our principles and constitutional pledges bound us to give the poorest and least efficient the preference in the matter, and that the most talented and responsible should be the last to receive favors and advantages of any sort at the hands of the Community. His arguments were elaborated with much ingenuity on the basis of those divine precepts to which we all bowed, viz. : " He that is chief among you let him be the servant of all"; " It is more blessed to give than to receive"; " We then that are strong ought to bear the infirmities of the weak, and not to please ourselves," etc.

His plea was plausible and worn the endorsement of several of our most worthy associates. It would have been · deemed more conclusive by others had not a few glaring and significant facts been closely connected with it; facts too apparent to escape notice. (1) That Brother Lamson and his warm sympathizers were interested expectants of the preferments contended for; (2) That those of us who under his contention must endure yet longer indefinitely the existing discomforts were to furnish, either by subscription or personal credit, the capital requisite for the erection of the new structures and assume all the responsibility involved; (3) That some of us who would by his proposal be shut out of the prospective dwellings and deprived of the better accommodations they would offer, were in danger of sinking under the burdens we were voluntarily bearing for the good of all our members, and that our whole enterprise was likely to suffer great detriment, if not put in imminent peril, unless some relief could be furnished them like that which the new residences and the retirement and quiet of them would supply.

In reply to Brother Lamson's argument it was said that while the principles upon which it rested were sound, the application made of them was unwarrantable and

misleading; that we, who must take the heavy responsibilities of erecting the prospective dwellings claimed no
exclusive accommodations but were justly entitled to a
reasonable share of them; that we had made and should
continue to make willing sacrifices for the comfort and
happiness of all our associates; that there was no just
occasion for setting up class distinctions and preferences
in the matter under discussion; and finally, that it was
absolutely painful and disheartening to find that past
labors and sacrifices in behalf of our common cause and
our more dependent fellow-members inspired them with
so little confidence, love, and gratitude. Brother Lamson
took such umbrage at this last remark and its implied
censure of some of our numbers for lack of appreciation
of what had been done gratuitously and with no expectation of payment or reward, that he warmly denounced it
as contrary to our covenant obligations, and protested
that the word "gratitude" had no place in our Community vocabulary. We had come together as equals, to
enjoy co-ordinate rights, and to do what each could for
the other and for all concerned. And to talk of favors,
sacrifices, and above all of gratitude, was wholly out of
place and inexcusable. I as the mouthpiece of the
majority replied that our whole movement recognized the
primary right of the individual to whatever property,
talents, and gifts of any sort were justly his or her own,
and that the social fabric we were trying to build did
not presuppose or require the annihilation of the distinctive personality of its members; consequently, what was
put into the Community for the benefit of all concerned
and for the special benefit of the weaker and more needy
persons among us was so contributed under the law of
brotherhood and charity, not of arbitrary justice, and
should be so understood. Appreciation of and gratitude
for favors received imply no humiliation or degradation on
the part of those upon whom they are conferred and no

condescension of assumed superiority on the part of those
from whom they come ; but a reciprocal respect, affection,
and confidence. When, in urging the merits of our cause
before the public, I added, I have been met with the
objection that the more dependent and less responsible of
our number would claim every advantage extended to
them as a right, and be made by the generosity of
those able and willing to help them more discontented
and exacting, I have denied the statement as an imputation upon the better impulses of human nature and
upon the Christian spirit of brotherhood in the human
soul. And I am disappointed and made heartsick at
these contrary developments — by these indications that
our critics and detractors had a surer basis for their conclusions than I dreamed of.

And so the discussion went on for some time during
that first summer and the succeeding autumn of 1842.
There was nothing in it that could be deemed discourte-
ous, caustic, or bitter, at least that savored of hatred
and animosity, but it was earnest, determined, sharp at
times, and unpleasantly personal. The general tendency
and effect of it were to produce more or less of irritation,
unrest, alienation. To the better minds among us it was
a source of deep regret and discouragement. But it could
not be suppressed or avoided. There was such a radical
difference of views and feelings, convictions and judgments, between the two parties that had sprung into
being, and withal such strength of purpose and pertinac-
ity of will on both sides, that neither would or could in
conscience yield to the other and so end the controversy.
For the same reason no compromise could be made and
no harmonious combination or warmhearted co-operation
effected.

As will have been observed, the trend of Brother Lamson's mind and of his arguments as well as that of his
sympathizers, was in the direction of an absolute extinc-

tion of what may be termed individualism in the Community — a denial of all exclusive right to property, to privilege, to the use and voluntary disposal of one's time, talent, endowment of any sort, on the part of any of its members. His interpretations of the Constitution were in that interest and behalf, as were also his pleas for nursing mothers who could perform no remunerative labor for an equal distribution of wages without regard to competency, fidelity, or efficiency, and for the assignment of the newly built houses to those who had assumed no responsibility and contributed neither money nor work in the construction of them. But the Community was not established on any such foundation as that, and was never designed or calculated to foster, promote, and represent before the world such ideas, nor had its administration thus far been carried on in accordance with such principles and methods of operation. Moreover, the leading minds in our fellowship, with the exception of the brother named, were loyal to the original purpose of the movement and to the general system of Joint-Stock proprietorship and of personal rights, duties, and obligations which had thus far prevailed, and consequently averse to all theories or claims calculated to subvert them or in any way discredit or ignore them. And a large majority of our number were of the same way of thinking and acting.

At this juncture and crisis of affairs we were confronted with this alternative : either the Community must be dissolved or its Constitution must be amended on the points relating to the dead level of wages, board, etc., and to some of its extreme and indiscriminate guarantees ; for on these points had most of the discordant issues been raised. The only third course that could be suggested was to follow Brother Lamson's lead and transform our Joint-Stock Community into a Common-Stock Community, making all the other changes in our organization and polity which such a transformation would necessitate.

But that was out of the question — utterly impracticable, for various substantial reasons, and not to be considered for a moment. So we were thrown back upon the alternative mentioned. But what was to come of dissolution? Nothing but shame, blasting, disaster to all our avowed principles and most sacredly cherished hopes; a virtual denial of our much vaunted faith; a trampling in the dust of our blessed Standard of Practical Christianity. On the other hand, if the amendments of the Constitution necessary to save our little craft were made, several of our worthy, albeit mistaken members, as we thought, would be likely to secede, and that would impair our standing and lessen our influence with the outside public. Besides, in striving to escape the Scylla of threatening Communism, we might fall into the Charybdis of selfish, unscrupulous, and hard-hearted Individualism, which would be no less fatal to our highest purposes and noblest aims, — to all we were trying to stand for before God and men. We were in a critical and dangerous strait.

Nevertheless, after much painful reflection on my own part and numerous earnest conferences with several of my fellow-members, some of whom were also deeply exercised in regard to the matter, I addressed myself to the task of preparing such amendments of the Constitution as would meet the exigencies of the case and enable us to go on harmoniously and successfully with the work to, which we had sacredly pledged our lives, our fortunes, and our sacred honor. This was accomplished in due time and the result was submitted to the consideration, emendation, and final action of the Community in regular meeting assembled on the 16th day of November. The several changes made, approved, and adopted appear in the following form :

7

" AMENDMENTS.

" ARTICLE IV.

" Add one Section:

" SEC. 4. For the accommodation of such members as may prefer to build houses and transact business independently of the Joint-Stock Proprietorship, each Community shall select a Village Site, lay off house-lots and sell the same, as oppor. tunity may offer, to any members who will come under obligations that such lots with all their buildings and betterments shall revert to the Community at a fair appraisal whenever they shall cease to be owned within the pale of its membership, or whenever they shall be abused to purposes notoriously inconsistent with the principles of this Association.

" ARTICLE V.

" Strike out Secs. 3, 4, 5, and insert as follows:

" SEC. 3. All operatives of every description belonging to any Community, whether employed at home or abroad by the Community or by individual members on their own account, shall be allowed a fair compensation according to the nature and productiveness of the service rendered as may be mutually agreed on between the parties, never exceeding one dollar per day, six dollars per week, twenty-four dollars per month, or three hundred dollars per year.

" ARTICLE VI.

" Strike out at the end of Sec. 3 these words, ' its floating fund or ordinary resources,' and in lieu thereof insert the following: ' funds raised by voluntary contribution.'

" ARTICLE VII.

" Strike out the whole Article and insert the following:

" Every Community in this Association shall endeavor to grow, manufacture, purchase at wholesale, or otherwise provide, all articles of ordinary use and consumption, so as to supply the personal necessities of all its members and dependents. And every item furnished at a price for the supply of such necessities, whether by the Community or individual members, shall be afforded at cost as nearly as the same can be ascertained.

"ARTICLE VIII.

"*Strike out the whole Article and insert:*

"The clear profits of every Community in this Association not exceeding four per cent. per annum on capital for the whole time of its investment, shall be divided among the Stockholders according to the amount by them severally invested. And all excess of profits over the said four per cent. shall be devoted to such religious, educational, or charitable purposes as the Community may from time to time determine.

"ARTICLE IX.

"*Add the following words:*

"This article shall be carried into effect by voluntary contribution.

"ARTICLE X.

"Sec. 4, fourth line, strike out 'established' and insert 'highest.'"

The intent and practical effect of these Amendments had been stated in *The Practical Christian* of October 29, and were elaborated more fully at the meeting in which they were finally adopted. I copy them as they appeared in their more condensed form, as follows:

"1. They restore a large amount of individuality to the members of a Community and leave every one at liberty to associate his capital and labor in the Joint-Stock operations to such an extent from year to year as he may feel to be a duty and a pleasure; or, on the other hand, to dwell and transact business by himself, as he may prefer; in either case acknowledging himself bound to educate his children, trade, and assist his feeble brethren, on the same general principles as before.

"2. They enable a Community to combine all the privileges of a well-ordered village of free-minded, conscientious individuals and those of a close association of capital and labor without the disadvantages of either. They adapt the Community organization to the wants of all classes of Practical Christians without imposing excessive burdens or restraints upon any, and thus give association the vantage ground of a fair experiment on its own merits. If it prove to be as pleasant and economical as we have all hoped, it will tend to bring over the lovers of individuality and make them willing co-operators. If not, the same principles of justice and charity may be carried out in the other way.

"3. They break up all unreasonable dependence on the capital and industry of the provident part of a Community, quicken self-reliance, induce economy, and make a just distinction between alms and wages, gifts and debts.

"4. They place all the members of a Community, whether resident or non-resident, having much or little in the Joint-Stock, on a common level, under the same reciprocal obligations and responsibilities. Justice is done to all and charity is required of all. No one can hide behind the mass; none can screen themselves under constitutional prescriptions from voluntary contributions to support schools and relieve the needy. Every one will appear in his own true light.

"5. They will disencumber capital of its present great risks and dangerous liabilities, give it a moderate but sure profit, and at the same time secure to labor its just compensation.

"6. Finally, they simplify our whole social machinery, make the experiment perfectly safe on a large or small scale, and render the Community relationship more equitable, more pleasant, and more practicable to all free, honest, and unselfish minds."

The reader will naturally infer that such important changes as those specified could not have been consummated without serious opposition on the part of those whose unwarrantable claims under the original Constitution had jeopardized both our harmony and hopes, and thereby rendered them necessary. Such inference is correct. Long and earnest debates were carried on before the final decision was reached, but the requisite three-fourths majority was at length secured and the new policy was made imperative and obligatory. Whereupon, several of the opposition were so aggrieved as to immediately resign their membership and several others delayed doing so only for a short time; while a few, not ready to take such a step and abandon the cause altogether, still felt that the Community had backslidden lamentably from its primal virtue. About a dozen in all seceded by reason of the action taken, some of whom, however, upon further deliberation, rejoined us. But the larger portion left us to return no more, carrying with them an evil report which no doubt for a time affected unfavorably our standing and influence wherever we were known. Of these, the principal, Brother Lamson, soon after went to reside with the Shakers at Pittsfield, thinking to find in their midst that heaven upon earth which he had hoped for in Hopedale but had not realized. For a while all went happily with him there, so that at the end of six weeks he wrote a letter to Brother Stacy extolling the situation in which he was placed and the people with whom he had cast his fortunes to the highest degree. The letter was given a place in the columns of our little paper. It was and still is interesting reading. A few extracts will indicate its spirit and character. "They (the Shakers) are what they profess to be. And this I never could say of any other denomination of Christians. They are in a very eminent sense Practical Christians." "This people live under the divine government; and the greatest harmony and Christian affection prevail among them." "Their property is held in common; they do their own labor; a personal equality prevails throughout, except that the sick, the feeble, and the aged receive the utmost care and tenderness. The intercourse among them is like that of a well-regulated family of natural brothers and sisters." "In order to know them and appreciate their religion and its blessed influence upon the life it is necessary to live with them." And yet, after a more conclusive trial, Brother Lamson withdrew from these eminent Practical Christians, returned to general society, which he had professedly renounced and often denounced unsparingly for its unchristian character, purchased and settled upon a little farm in West Boylston, and was never heard from afterwards; — cer-

tainly not as a Social Reformer and an Apostle of
Human Brotherhood. He died July 2, 1886, aged 80
years. His wife, an estimable woman, shared his varied
fortunes sympathetically and devotedly while she lived,
passing to the world of spirits some years before him.

Our movement could but suffer more or less by the
trying experiences which have just been narrated. Not
only by loss of reputation and confidence in the public
mind, but by the saddening, depressing effect produced
upon those of us who had done so much for it, and who
were resolved to stand by it still and to spend and be
spent in its blessed behalf. As the prime mover in
starting it and the accepted leader in the administration
of its manifold activities, I was personally humiliated and
weakened by what had transpired. I felt less confidence
in my own moral competency for the work I had undertaken, less in the fitness of others for the kind of life
upon which we had entered, and less in our desired
speedy success. The more intelligent and conscientious
of my associates sympathized with me in this regard. We
were all of us shorn somewhat of our former strength.
Our principles were as true as ever and as obligatory,
our cause was as sacred, our standard of duty as high,
and our Heavenly Father as much our Friend and Helper
in time of need.

And so we tried to make the best of our adversities
and of our still imperfect conditions, and despite some
heart-heaviness girded up our loins for renewed effort
and an onward march. Though cast down we were not
destroyed. There was a silver lining to the cloud that
had cast its shadow upon us. Encouragements there
were as well as discouragements. Many of our interests
had been well fostered; many of our activities had been
fairly prosperous. Our field culture, gardening, haying,
etc., had gone on to general satisfaction. The harvest
had yielded us, if not abundant, yet satisfactory returns.

Our barns, our cellars, our larders, were by no means empty. Improvements upon our domain had been going on. The dam with its appurtenances was approaching completion. The basement of the mechanic shop had been finished and the frame of the superstructure was so far advanced as to admit raising on the 27th of October, which was followed immediately by the enclosing of the body of the structure and the putting on of the roof. The building designed for a school-house and printing office was considerably under way. A baker and a hatter had joined us and commenced operations in their respective callings, thus enlarging the field of our industrial activity. The general health of members and residents had been good, though some sickness had prevailed among the children but not of serious or alarming nature. No death had occurred on our premises since settlement. Winter set in at length finding us comfortably housed and provided for, all the more so that its inmates were somewhat reduced in numbers, — the withdrawals mentioned having sensibly depleted our population and removed the pressure in that respect. Soon came our reckoning day with its itemized account of the year's operations and their results. The Annual Meeting was held Jan. 4, 1843, at which the Executive Council submitted to their constituency the following

Annual Report.

"The Executive Council of Fraternal Community, No. 1, respectfully submit the following financial report: —

"The whole amount of property on hand is: Consolidated Fund, $4,300.00; Floating Fund, $2,504.40; Total, $6,804.40. Our debts to members, over dues is $1,298.85; leaving the present value, $5,505.55. The whole amount of Joint-Stock invested and for which Certificates have been issued is $5,600.00, showing an absolute loss of $94.45. But this loss would have been $597.54 had we not appraised our two new buildings $503.09 above their nomimal cost. We believed this to be a fair estimate and have therefore made it in the confidence that future years of ordinary success will justify us in doing so.

"The whole amount of labor employed has cost us $2,722.62, according to the following items: Agriculture and Animals, $739.47; Health and Domestic Economy, $999.00; Manufactures and Mechanical Industry, $577.00; Education, Arts, and Sciences, $31.92; Religion, Morals, and Missions, $78.00; Hatting, $74.39; Printing, $222.84.

"The profit and loss account in the several departments and branches is as follows: *Dr.* Incidental Expenses, $104.12; Education, etc., $45.77; Tailoring, $2.51; Health and Domestic Economy, $475.24; Agriculture and Animals, $231.38; Printing, $46.33; Total, $905.35. *Cr.* Hatting, $21.72; Manufactures and Mechanical Industry, $503.09; Donations, $111.90; Religion, Morals, and Missions, $45.27; Practical Christian, $50.82; Finance and Exchange, $36.00; Cash in Treasury, $42.10; making a total of $810.90. The balance shows the amount of loss as before stated, $94.45.

"All of which is respectfully submitted in behalf of Council.

"ADIN BALLOU, *Pres't.*

"Hopedale, Jan. 4, 1843."

This was a small showing for our much vaunted enterprise, exhibiting close calculation and leaving capital no dividend. But all things considered the loss was much less than might have been expected — much less than we actually feared. We therefore waived any discouragements the result of our year's operations was calculated to create and set our faces hopefully and steadfastly towards the future. When we considered how much we had to learn by dear experience and anxious vigils, the theoretic errors we had to correct, and the injudicious attempt to accommodate and employ from April to October so many persons at equal wages, we felt that we and all true friends of the Community had reason to be satisfied with what had been accomplished and with the condition in which we found ourselves at the opening of a new year.

The official servants chosen at this second Annual Meeting of the Community were : ADIN BALLOU, *President;* ABBY H. PRICE, *Secretary;* EDMUND PRICE, *Auditor;* EBENEZER D. DRAPER, *Intendant of Finance and Exchange;* AMOS J. BALLOU, *Intendant of Agriculture and Animals;* HENRY LILLIE, *Intendant of Manufactures and Mechanical Industry;* BUTLER WILMARTH, *Intendant of Health and Domestic Economy;* DANIEL S. WHITNEY, *Intendant of Education, Arts, and Sciences;* WM. H. FISH, *Intendant of Religion, Morals, and Missions.*

CHAPTER IV.

1843, 1844.

COMMENCING on the day following the Annual Meeting, which took place on the 4th of January, 1843, the present Chapter will outline the operations and progress of the Community under the provisions of its modified Constitution during the two succeeding years. This may be done more intelligibly and satisfactorily perhaps by a classified arrangement of the topics of chief interest indicated in convenient order by their respective titles.

1. *Domestic Economy.* Now that the opportunity was opened to such of our members as might desire it to establish and live in separate households, several families that preferred to do so and found it possible, at once began to form plans for leaving the hitherto unitary domestic mode of life and locating by themselves in the the usual order of the home. The facilities for doing this on the Community domain, however, were extremely meager and unsatisfactory. But almost anything was better than the incommodious and crowded condition which had been endured thus far by a severe tax upon human patience and fortitude, and the most contracted and unpropitious quarters were gladly accepted. Bros. E. D. Draper, D. S. Whitney, and Edmund Price, whose families were small, managed to set up their respective penates in the new building on Water Street, the school and printing press having been removed to the mechanic

shop then approaching completion. The Old House was divided into three tenements; one of which was occupied by Brother Lillie, another by Brother Harris, while the third, much the largest, sheltered the still existent Community family, which, though greatly depleted, was yet of considerable size. There I remained, as did also Bro. Amos J. Ballou, with our wives and children and such other members and dependents as were not provided for elsewhere. There, too, all new comers took up their abode, and there visiting friends, inquirers, etc., were received and entertained as time went on. Meanwhile two new dwelling-houses were projected and put in process of construction — my own humble cottage and a two-story double house belonging to A. J. Ballou and Edmund Price. They were able to move into their new quarters about mid-summer and I into mine early in September, where I and my family have ever since resided. Sr. C. P. Hooton was married to Elkanah Taft of Uxbridge, Feb. 27, and soon after left the premises with her children. Vacancies thus occurred from time to time in the common household, but only to be filled or more than filled by incoming members, probationers, and hired workmen needed to assist in the erection of the up-going buildings. All desired and aimed at a home of their own, and such as were able secured a half-acre house-lot in the Village Site to be built upon as soon as circumstances would permit Delays on the part of these were unavoidable, yet three were finished and taken possession of before winter set in. Besides those mentioned was one for Br. Geo. W. Stacy, in which he resided until his departure from Hopedale, his successor for many years being Br. Almon Thwing. Br. Dr. Wilmarth put up the ell part of his house, enabling him to occupy it during the succeeding winter or early spring in anticipation of the completion of the main structure. To answer the call of applicants, A. J. Ballou and Edmund Price fitted up a tenement each on the second floor of their spacious dwelling as soon as they were fairly settled in it. Such was the new order of domestic life with us — separate families in a compact neighborhood.

2. *Industrial Interests.* There was no general uniform system adopted concerning them. They were all provided for and supervised by the Community under the direction of the proper Intendant, and most of different kinds of business were carried on through his direct personal management. But exceptions were allowed in certain cases out of deference to individual enterprise and choice, abuses and dangers being guarded against by what were supposed to be adequate provisions and restrictions. Nathan Harris was permitted to engage in carpentry on his own account and in that capacity erected by contract the three dwellings heretofore mentioned. Printing was done by Brother Stacy, mainly at his own discretion, for several months; at first in the new Water street house and afterwards at his own home in Mendon; he being paid twelve dollars per number for bringing out *The Practical Christian.* Later, about the 1st of June, the press was located in an upper room of the mechanic shop, and thenceforth was run as a Community branch of industry. The department of Agriculture, which the previous year was managed under four heads, Farming, Gardening, Orcharding, and Stabling, was this year comprised in two divisions, Agriculture and Livery. A small amount of traffic was carried on by the Intendant of Finance and Exchange. The manufacture of hats was continued; the Boot and Shoe business started, also the making of boxes, Painting and Glazing, Tin and Sheet Iron working, all on a small scale and all under Community management. What was called "General Service" was regarded as a distinct industry and had a separate accounting. This covered my own official and miscellaneous labors as President of the Community, and also

those of others similarly employed for the common good.
The department of Religion, Morals, and Missions included all the professional labors of our ministers and
lecturers, whether rendered within or without our territorial boundaries. These brethren were active during
most of the year, on Sundays generally and occasionally
during the week, but their work brought in little pecuniary revenue. *The Practical Christian* with its accom-
paniments constituted an independent business enterprise
and had its own distinctive reckoning. Also the departments of Domestic Economy, the chief interest of which
was the maintenance of the combined household, and
Education, which concerned the proper schooling of our
children, of which little was done systematically during
the year under notice.

There was considerable complexity, as can be readily
seen, in our industrial management, and great skill and
care were requisite to the proper keeping of our account
books so as to render them at once intelligible and trustworthy. It was perhaps a mistake, it was certainly a
misfortune, that we felt ourselves obliged to establish or
authorize so many business undertakings, but' the skill,
capacity, taste, and previous training of our members
were so diversified, and our anxiety to give each and
every one remunerative employment at the earliest practicable date was so intense, that we did not feel at liberty
to limit the introduction of new industries as we ought
to have done. When a person apparently every way
qualified to become a worthy, useful member of our fraternity proposed to join us, and, having been accepted,
wished to establish a business for which he was well
equipped by natural aptitude and experience ; a business
that would enable himself and family to be self-supporting and furnish the opportunity of self-support to others,
we were quite ready to hear his plea and yield to his
solicitation, sometimes to our detriment and subsequent

regret and grief. It was chiefly in this way that our industries multiplied upon our hands and that we were made subject to many perplexing problems which under a more reserved and cautious regimen we should have escaped. Our desire to make as rapid progress as possible and to help as many as possible to a better life led us into many errors.

3. *Material Advancement.* The mechanic shop was completed in the early Spring, and the first story and basement were supplied with a considerable amount and variety of labor-saving machinery for facilitating work in carpentering, joinery, box-making, and kindred callings. The story above was so partitioned and fitted up as to afford tolerable accommodations in its southern part for the printing press and its accessories, while the northern was made convenient and comfortable for school purposes and for services of public worship; in which twofold capacity it met our needs, in a rude fashion to be sure, until we were in a condition to erect a building for the same purposes the following year. In the ways indicated the structure was at once put to use both above and below, and proved of great value to the Community in many respects. Nine half-acre lots were sold at an early day to individual members of our body, for which by common consent and mutual agreement they were to pay $100.00 each into the common treasury, without pausing to estimate their comparative natural worth. This was a good beginning in that direction and an augury of better days ahead.

During the season very considerable and important improvements were made upon what were collectively designated as the Community barns, though one of them was used up to the time of our occupancy of the premises as a cider house, the other two only having been devoted to the sheltering of cattle, horses, hay, grain, etc. They were somewhat remote from each other, inconveniently arranged, and in a considerably dilapidated condition. Their frames, however, were heavy, firm, and strong, rendering them capable of being moved without serious detriment to them or danger to the movers. A basement cellar for them was excavated at the southwest corner of Union and Water Streets, diagonally opposite the ancient farmhouse of the estate, and suitable foundations were laid, upon which they were in due time located in such proximity to and connection with each other as would best subserve the several purposes for which they were designed and needed. They were then put in respectable condition externally, and so fitted up internally as to contribute to the comfort and convenience of whomsoever might use them, and afford the proper protection and shelter for the animals and products of the earth that might thenceforth be housed in them. In their transformed condition they presented a somewhat straggling, unsymmetrical, inartistic, and withal unattractive appearance, but the change was a most desirable one, and one fully justified by the results secured. The conglomerate structure not only supplied the immediate needs of the Community, but has served important uses through all the intervening years down to the present time, and promises to do the same indefinitely in the time to come.

Mention should be made in this connection of what was done the same year towards the construction of our main thoroughfare through the village, now called *Hopedale Street*. It had been laid out in a northwesterly and southeasterly direction in the original survey of the residential portion of our territory without regard to any pre-existing highways, cutting across the old tortuous Magomiscock road near the junction of Hopedale and Union Streets, but little had been done towards making it passable. It ran over an uneven surface, rocky and considerably elevated in some places but low and marshy in others. Material excavated from the higher portions

of it was transferred to the more depressed and wet
localities, and before winter set in a tolerably good
wagon-way was opened and a promising beginning made
of a future excellent thoroughfare. People of the present generation little dream of the labors undergone in
those early days and afterward to make the rough places
of Hopedale smooth and its uncomely areas fair and
beautiful.

An enterprise of still greater significance was set on
foot early in the year and considerably advanced before
its close, viz. : the erection of a building which should
serve the purposes of a School-house and Chapel for our
immediate and prospective needs. As early as February
4th, the following editorial and prospectus appeared in
The Practical Christian, a copy of which will explain the
matter.

"SCHOOL-HOUSE AND CHAPEL.

"We are very much in need of a School-house and Chapel
at Hopedale. The establishment of a good permanent Seminary has always been a darling object with the founders of
this Community. Scarcely less necessary is a comfortable
room for our religious meetings, lectures, etc. The time has
arrived when these objects must be attempted. Many friends
have been advising us for months to this movement and have
assured us of their readiness to lend a helping hand. The
Community is too young and too poor to carry out any splen-
did design. We must be content for the present with a building which will answer the double purpose of School-house and
Chapel. Might not such a one be erected for $800 or $1000?
We think it might. And may we not confidently appeal to
our friends in this general region for handsome contributions
in money, materials, and labor towards the undertaking? There
are many who ardently desire to see a good school and convenient house of worship in this place. We have drawn up
a paper for the purpose of providing these, which we shall
circulate among those who, we believe, take a friendly interest
in our general cause. In the meantime we wish them to be
thinking upon the subject; and any friends at a distance, who

have the heart to aid us by donations, will lay us under great obligations by communicating their kind intentions to the editor immediately. Who will speak and act? Shall the suggestion be taken up and carried into effect?

"The following is a copy of the subscription prospectus drawn up for circulation:

"PROPOSALS

"For the Erection of a Chapel and School-house at Hopedale.

"In the name and behalf of Fraternal Community, No. 1, Adin Ballou proposes the erection of a decent and commodious building at Hopedale, to be used as a Chapel until a more suitable one shall be provided, and as a school-house permanently, to be under the general charge and regulation of said Community for preservation, proper use, and safe keeping. And the said Ballou, in said name and behalf, proposes and engages as follows, to wit:

"1. That the building to be erected shall be devoted to the purposes above specified, and to no others therewith inconsistent.

"2. That, as a Chapel, its seats shall be free to all persons of peaceable behavior who choose to attend religious meetings therein so far as its accommodations may extend.

"3. That a respectable and well ordered school or course of useful instruction and discipline, under Community regulations, shall be therein maintained for at least three-quarters of every year.

"Now, therefore, all persons friendly to the object herein proposed, and willing to promote the same by contribution of money, materials, or labor, are respectfully invited to subscribe their names with the amount of their several offerings. Said subscriptions shall be paid to the said Adin Ballou, to be applied economically in the name and behalf of said Community to the purpose herein specified."

In answer to this appeal about $200 were subscribed by outside friends, in sums of from $12 to 75 cents; individual members subscribed over $140 more, and the needful balance was guaranteed by the Community as such. So ground was broken, a basement with suitable

8

foundations for the superstructure prepared, and the frame of an edifice 26 feet square, exclusive of an appropriate vestibule portico in front, raised, the intention being to provide for immediate needs and add to the structure in the rear as future necessity, convenience, and ability might warrant. The portico was to be surmounted with a tasteful cupola and belfry. The project was well under way before severe weather came, and made ready for occupancy the ensuing spring.

Another interesting item worthy of mention comes properly under the present head. A warm and generous personal friend in Cincinnati, O., Andrew H. Ernst, Esq., who was engaged in the Nursery business at Spring Garden, on the outskirts of that city, being kindly disposed towards the Community, made us a valuable donation, the receipt of which was acknowledged in our fortnightly publication of June 10, as follows:

"The undersigned, in behalf of Fraternal Community, No. 1, gratefully acknowledges the receipt of 325 young apple trees, carefully packed in four boxes, comprising thirty choice varieties, sent as a donation by our kind friend and brother, A. H. Ernst of Cincinnati, Ohio. They arrived in good condition and promise to do well.

"ADIN BALLOU."

This much prized gift was heralded by a lengthy epistle from the donor and his estimable wife, expressing a most heartfelt interest in our endeavor to realize a true Christian order of society, promising future favors like that now shown us, and giving good practical advice in regard to setting out and caring for the trees. We were not in a condition to make the wisest use of them by reason of the unprepared state of the grounds where they were put and our want of skill in managing them, but those properly attended to did well and have been prolific of good fruit unto this day. We had ourselves started an infant nursery of our own, comprised of an

abundance of apple and pear sproutlings, and had put a
thousand or more peach and plum stones in the ground,
but as yet these were of no avail to us in planting
orchards or fitting up our little homesteads ; and hence
the kindly thoughtfulness of Mr. and Mrs. Ernst at that
date was all the more timely and acceptable.

4. *Relations with other Communities.* As already stated,
several Communities or Co-operative Associations besides
our own were founded about the time we located at
Hopedale. Others were in process of gestation merely.
They all differed from each other very considerably, either
in organization or method of administration, and they
were too unlike ours in both respects to admit of any
very close affiliation. Yet our principles and our polity
disposed us to maintain a friendly attitude towards them,
even towards those whose leading characteristics were
radically dissimilar to ours, and whose controlling spirits
were moved to criticize and denounce what we deemed
most fundamental in theory and most vital to ultimate
success.

Mention has already been made of the cordial feeling
that existed at Hopedale towards Brook-Farm, the
Northampton Community at Florence, both in this State,
and the North American Phalanx in Monmouth Co.,
N. J., and of the overtures looking towards a combination of interests and forces which were made and seriously
considered between us and the former. There were many
things that were common to us and to all these movements, and our intercommunication with each other was
always amicable and kindly. Other movements there were
mostly in the West, with which, though we were much
interested in them and wished them well, we were less in
sympathy, and of which we had less hope as agencies
for fraternizing and blessing mankind. With the projectors and apostles of some of these I was personally
brought into verbal collision, as will be seen, as will also

the occasion and ground of it, by a brief account of what was called a Property Convention, held in Chardon St. Chapel, Boston, on the evening of June 8. It was gotten up by John A. Collins, sometime General Agent of the Mass. Anti-Slavery Society, and a few friends who agreed with him in certain ideas which he entertained respecting the rights of property and the true basis of social reconstruction. I was invited to be present and participate in the debates, an invitation that I cheerfully accepted. I give a few extracts from my report of what transpired, published in *The Practical Christian:*

"Quite an audience convened. The meeting was addressed by John O. Wattles, Nathaniel Whiting, and John A. Collins. Friend Wattles, an amiable and benevolent man from the West, spoke in rather a poetic strain against the evils of the present social state as flowing from the assumed right of individual property, and painted in glowing colors the beauties of that proposed social state wherein no person should claim to own anything; where each individual should be a perfect community in himself and the congregated whole a heavenly communion of wisdom, goodness, and enjoyment. He took it for granted that the abolition of all individual property would certainly lead to these happy results, without any very careful analysis of facts or effort at argument. He was too indefinite in his speech to render an answer pertinent. Friend Whiting followed on the same side in a calm and candid style of address, yet with too little logical point to elicit an interesting debate. By this time it was 9 o'clock and the people began to think of going home. Friend Collins called on me to give my views, which I declined to do until he should state more definitely the positions he and his allies intended to maintain, with a few of the more important reasons therefor. He thought this had already been done but concluded to attempt a further explication. When he had closed, I took up the subject and attempted to show that individual property grew directly out of individual existence, was inseparably connected with it, and could never be wholly abolished so long as man had a stomach which must appropriate food exclusively to itself, and a body which must have raiment exclusively for itself, or so long as God and nature decreed the union of one man and one woman in marriage, devolving upon them the duty of nourishing and protecting their offspring through helpless infancy. That to perform these duties, mankind are endowed with faculties and furnished with means, in the right use of which by honest industry they may ordinarily avoid being burdensome to one another. That he who has produced food, or raiment, or any other good thing by such industry, has a natural right of property in such production. That he who *can* produce the necessaries and comforts of life and yet *will not*, has no right to consume the fruits of another's industry. That if he claims any such right he is virtually a robber; but that by the law of universal benevolence all men are bound to relieve the personal necessities of their fellow-men as the dictate of charity, whether there be any demand of justice or not. That the right of individual property being a natural, inherent, and necessary one to a greater or less extent, the question could not be, shall we abolish it? but rather, what are its proper limitations and uses? That we are not warranted in ascribing all the evils of society to individual property, nor in concluding that its abolition would necessarily do way with these evils; such not being the primary cause of social disease, nor such the remedy. The cause lies in the heart of individual man, and can never be removed but by enlightening the mind and subordinating the will to right moral principles. Individuals do as much to make society what it is, as society does to form the character of individuals. Any reorganization of society which will more directly, energetically, and certainly, discipline the individuals composing it into obedience to the dictates of right moral principle, is desirable and will prove successful. But any reorganization of society which starts with the assumption that man is a mere creature of circumstances, or that anything short of the enthronement of right moral principle in the individual mind will secure human happiness, is both undesirable and impracticable. And finally, I said, that as the kind of reorganization proposed by friend Collins and his coadjutors is of the latter description, its fundamental principles are essentially vicious, and all experiments for its practical illustration must inevitably fail."

The meeting adjourned to the next day. Imperative
duties prevented me from being present only at the morning session. The same general ground was again trav-
eled over by the different speakers, with about the same
variety of argument and conclusion. At one stage of the
discussion, friend Collins undertook to explain the doctrine of circumstances as he held it, that being a point
in his general theory of social reform scarcely less important and vital than that of common property. He affirmed
with great emphasis that the lazy and vicious in the world
at large were only what society made them, and that, if
surroundings were right, they would be the good and useful men and women which they ought to be and which we
all very much desired. As the talk was somewhat collo-
quial, I asked him if he was prepared to contend that no
man can behave better than he does under the present
condition of things in social life. His answer was that he
did not wish to be forced into the minutiæ of the question and be compelled by his argument to say that no one
could possibly behave better then he did in any respect,
yet he would maintain as a general affirmation that every
man is in the main just what society makes him and
there he would leave the matter. In this feature of his
system he had taken the position that man is a creature
of external circumstances, and he built his whole hope of
ameliorating the condition of the unfortunate and suffering classes of mankind and of bringing in the era of universal equality and fraternity on so reorganizing society
as to necessitate right action and consequent happiness;
on so ordering the externals of life, the environing circumstances of men, as that they could not help being
wise, good, and happy. I told him and his brethren to go
ahead and live out their theories, but I could not accom-
pany them though I wished them well. They heeded my
counsel, went out to Central New York, established the
Skaneatales Community, struggled along under great diffi-

culties for a few years, and at length yielded to fate and went to pieces, the victims of their own delusions.

A more congenial and gratifying occasion was enjoyed later in the season. It was a Convention called by George W. Benson and fourteen others to meet at Worcester on the second Tuesday and Wednesday of December, " to examine and discuss the propriety of reorganizing society into Associations or Communities in which all may have a *common interest* in whatever appertains to a physical, intellectual, and moral culture ; a common interest in all the advantages arising from the production and possession of property." Of this gathering *The Practical Christian* said :

"Quite a number of the members from the Northampton and Hopedale Communities were in attendance, besides volunteer friends from various quarters. We had hoped to meet delegates from West Roxbury also; but we believe none were present from that Association. The convention was animated by a good spirit and awakened an encouraging interest among the common people of the town. The evening sessions called out the best audiences, and we could but admire the very respectful, eager, and unfaltering attention of those present on the last evening. At the close notice was given that Mr. D. H. Barlow would deliver three lectures on the subject during the ensuing week. We hear that those lectures have been well attended and cannot doubt that they will leave a strong and salutary impression. Another convention was holden in Leominster the same week which we learn was an interesting meeting. None of our people were present."

A week later a meeting was held in Boston in response to " A Call to the Friends of Social Reform in New England " issued by David Mack, George W. Benson, James N. Buffum, Oliver Johnson, William C. Nell, H. C. Wright, William Bassett, and many others, " to aid the progress of the great cause of Social Reorganization "; " to cheer each other's hearts by taking note of the advance of the Social Scheme discovered by Charles

Fourier "; and to enable those " who believe that Association is to succeed the conflict and isolation of our present Social Order" and that through it "Man will achieve his destiny and our world be purified from vice, crime, and misery," "to concert means to actualize their idea and build a Home on the broad basis of Attractive Industry — a Home where all who love *Truth* and would live it may find a refuge."

As a further indication of the widespread interest in the cause of Social Reconstruction that had been awakened in the breasts of philanthropists and reformers and through them in the general public mind, it may be stated that during the year 1843 a new Quarterly Periodical, entitled *The Reformer, or Advocate of Industrial Association*, was started at Pittsburg, Penn., designed " to discuss the general principles which underlie the movement for a better order of Society, to suggest and consider different systems of organization and methods of administration, to report what was going on in the different localities where experiments had been undertaken, to note the signs of progress that were to be seen in various directions, and stimulate endeavor in behalf of the great uprising in all possible ways." During the same year another publication — *The Phalanx* — was launched upon the tide of American Journalism. It was intended to be the organ of the Fourier Associationists in the United States, — those who were either believers in or students of the plan of Social Reorganization devised or discovered by the distinguished French Philosopher and Reformer, Charles Fourier, of whom Horace Greeley and Parke Godwin of New York were noted disciples, and Albert Brisbane of Philadelphia a distinguished representative and interpreter. Rev. Wm. H. Channing of Boston, nephew of the renowned Rev. William Ellery Channing, D. D., was also a devoted follower of Fourier and an eloquent expounder of his system.

All these things were not only for our edification but for our encouragemeut, and we made the most we could of them in both particulars. We were desirous of learning all we could of other theorists and experimenters in order to make our progress more rapid and sure, and we certainly took heart and hope at every indication which we saw or thought we saw in any direction that the old order of human life was passing away and a new order was coming in — that the kingdom of righteousness, brotherhood, unity, peace, which is the kingdom of heaven, was at hand. So we girded the loins of our strength about us, became inspired with fresh zeal, and pressed forward toward the mark for the prize of our high calling.

5. *Religious and Missionary Matters.* Within the Community regular meetings for public worship on Sunday were maintained morning and afternoon, without intermission or relaxation of interest and fervor, in the northerly upper half of the mechanic shop. Likewise the established Thursday evening Conference, usually, for convenience and economy's sake, in the old house. If our ministerial brethren were engaged elsewhere, the exercises at both places were conducted by laymen and women, of whom we had several qualified to serve in that capacity efficiently and acceptably. In those days there were among us few stay-at-homes or indifferentists. It was the joy and the security of our people that they were dominated largely by the religious sentiment, — that the religious life had been awakened in their souls, that the religious motive influenced their conduct and shaped their character, and that religious exercises — singing, prayer, instruction, counsel, exhortation — were sources of satisfaction and enjoyment to them. Outside of our boundaries, our preachers and lecturers labored vigorously; seldom, however, going more than thirty or forty miles from home. Rarely did a Sunday pass by without an engagement in some church, hall, or school-house, and often

during the week were they in attendance upon some general public convocation or conducting the service in some gathering where they were the chief if not the only speakers respectively. Quarterly Conferences of sterling interest and of unquestioned profit continued to take place in various localities, as aforetime. The Anti-Slavery, Temperance, and Non-resistance reforms, enlisted much attention and effort on our part, and called us frequently into the general field throughout our vicinage and sometimes far away. Moreover, this was the year of the great Millerite excitement, under which many were looking for the speedy coming of Christ in the clouds of heaven and the accompanying end of the world, and I was personally drawn into several public discussions upon the subject as I was also led to prepare and publish a large leafed pamphlet of 32 pages, entitled *The True Scriptural Doctrine of the Second Advent, an Effectual Antidote to Millerism and all Kindred Errors*. It was issued from the Community press and was widely called for up to the time of the bursting of the bubble in October, when all concern and interest in the subject suddenly subsided. *The Practical Christian* went forth from the printing office regularly on its mission to its readers at home and abroad, its columns well filled with interesting articles upon topics it was wont to discuss, myself being *Editor-in-Chief*, with Bros. Stacy, Whitney, and Fish, *Assistants*.

6. *Other Incidents.* There was little sickness with no fatal or serious cases on the Community domain during the entire twelvemonth. A single death occurred among our non-resident members, that of Mrs. Barbara Colburn, wife of Samuel Colburn, at Dedham, where they were temporarily residing. Few new members joined us, owing largely to the doubt and distrust engendered by the withdrawals of the previous autumn. The places vacated at that time were slowly filled. Several probationers entered our precincts and three or four families of permitted residents.

The first and only depredation that for some years was
committed by lawless outsiders on Community property
occurred, if my memory is not at fault, during the
autumn of 1843. A gang of hen-roost robbers that had
prowled about Milford and vicinity for some months,
seizing poultry and carrying it away to some secluded
place for a nightly feast, visited us and took a turkey
and two chickens that they found on the branches of
one of our old apple trees. I think they dug a few hills
of potatoes to roast as a part of their surreptitious bill
of fare. It had been predicted by our enemies that, by
reason of our well-known Non-resistant principles and our
published pledge not to prosecute offenders and bring
them before the courts, we should be the victims of frequent burglaries and other offences ; in fact, that nothing
of ours would be safe from the ravages and spoliation of
the mischievous and criminal classes around us. Experience proved the reverse of this, as we had confidently
argued beforehand. We made no ado about this act of
petty larceny, but learned that two of the offenders were
overheard talking upon the matter not long afterward, the
gist of their conversation being that while they did not
care for those who kept dogs, set traps, and were ready
to send them to jail if they could be caught, it was too
bad to steal from the kind, peaceable people in the Dale,
and they should not do it again.

Two birthdays were celebrated during the year under
notice, some account of which will give a fairly intelligible idea of those festal occasions which were observed
from time to time among us, serving to relieve the tedium
and tiresome drudgery and nerve-strain of our common life.
They were not characterized by much display but were
full of good cheer and innocent pleasure. The first was
my own, and was described by Sr. Abby H. Price, who
wielded a facile pen and who was a sort of poet-laureate
to the Community for several years, in *The Practical
Christian* of April 29th. The article is subjoined :

"Sunday, April 23d, was Brother Ballou's 40th birthday. The evening celebration was a happy time for Hopedale. Not with the festival and dance, not with merriment and feasting, but with one spontaneous feeling of grateful and fervent congratulation did the friends and associates gather around him. The communion of soul that we enjoyed was sweet. It was a bright oasis in the desert of earth. The full feelings of affectionate confidence that gushed forth must have been as cheering as the union — the assurance we all realized that we were indeed of one heart and one mind — was to us. May our brother be spared to carry forward the enterprise so happily begun. May we be refreshed by many such birthday seasons, — the harp that is then tuned be ever as harmonious till its numbers swell on the eternal shore. The following hymn, written for the occasion, was sung with enthusiasm:

"Sing, Hopedale, sing ! your voices raise,
  Let every heart attuned to praise
    Sound forth the cheerful lay;
  Praise God who gave our brother dear —
  Who spares his life from year to year
    To cheer us on our way.

"United let our songs arise
  In grateful accents to the skies —
    To God's almighty love;
  He gave our friend the power to bless,
  He turned his heart to righteousness,
    And raised his hopes above.

"While passions raged and sin was rife,
  When earth was filled with war and strife,
    He sought a better way;
  His panting spirit sighed for peace,
  From all the crimes of earth release —
    Sighed for a perfect day.

"No flag was raised, no banner streamed,
  The light through fog and darkness gleamed —
    Weak were true souls and sad;
  In this sweet vale he found a place,
  The standard raised of truth and grace
    To make the nations glad.

*   *   *   *   *   *   *

" Now let these trees luxuriant grow,
    Let this sweet stream more sweetly flow;
      A work is here begun
    We trust will bless earth's distant shore
    Till war and sin are known no more,
      And Satan's work is done."

Another record of a similar event which occurred a few weeks later was from the same pen.

" Last Wednesday, June 14th, was Brother Draper's birthday. The meeting in the evening was pleasant and we trust profitable. How much it becomes us on such occasions to look back in solemn reflection upon our past lives; to let the bitter tears of penitence wash away every trace of our wandering from the straight path; and although shadows and fear may gather around us as we see our winding way through the wilderness, yet the kind encouragement of friends and new resolutions for the future may in a measure dispel our sorrow, and refreshed and invigorated we may begin anew the journey of life. The following was one of the hymns written for and sung on the occasion :

" How sweet our birthdays are
    When spent with those we love,
  Kind words like sunbeams fair
    Make all our gloom remove,
And love for friends so true and strong,
Will cheer our pathway all along.

" Then let us all unite
    To pray that this new year
  May shed a halo bright
    Around our brother dear;
That still in grace he may improve,
And ever onward humbly move.

" And when his days shall end,
    And he have done with time,
  Find God a smiling friend —
    Bliss in a holier clime;
Join with the bright celestial choirs
Where angels tune immortal lyres."

Financial Summary of 1843. Reaching the close of the year, the Community listened with much interest and satisfaction to the Report of the Council made at its Annual Meeting, Jan. 3, 1844. Without going into details as before and itemizing the several departments representing industrial and monetary interests it may be sufficient to state that the Joint-Stock property amounted, in the two funds representing it, to $6258.19 above all indebtedness; and that, besides cancelling the old deficit of $94.45 there had accrued net profits estimated at $658.19, making the entire gain arising from the year's operations, $752.64. The individual property of the members invested in house lots, dwellings, business, etc., on the domain, never appeared in the Summary of Community affairs, nor was any statement ever made of their gains or losses. The yearly exhibit included only what had been done by the Community as such in its strictly unitary character, and the results thereof.

Provision was made for the funds that might be required in carrying on the several departments of business for the year to come and for meeting all pecuniary obligations, by instructing the Executive Council to raise by an equitable method of taxation such sums of money as in their judgment would be required, and direct the expenditure of the same.

The following named official servants were chosen to fill the positions respectively indicated the ensuing year: ADIN BALLOU, *Pres.;* ABBY H. PRICE, *Sec.;* EBENEZER D. DRAPER, *Intendant of Finance and Exchange;* AMOS J. BALLOU, *of Agriculture and Animals;* EDMUND SOWARD, *of Manufactures and Mechanical Industries;* DR. BUTLER WILMARTH, *of Health and Domestic Economy;* D. S. WHITNEY, *of Education, Arts, and Sciences;* WM. H. FISH, *of Religion, Morals, and Missions.*

The meeting was a harmonious, enthusiastic, and highly gratifying one in all respects; far different from that of a year before, when a cloud of uncertainty and fear hung over our deliberations, and cast a dark and depressing shadow upon all our hearts. Now the skies were bright above us, the future seemed full of promise, and we were ready to press joyfully onward in our great and benefi-cent work. The prevailing feeling on the occasion found expression in a stirring hymn sung with much earnestness and exultant joy, a single verse of which will convey a good idea of the spirit animating the whole :

> " Where are the dangers and quicksands we feared?
>   All by his (God's) grace were removed;
> Where are the mountains our enemies reared?
>   Transient as mist they have proved.
> Now on the sky see the rainbow of hope,
>   Now let the brother desponding look up,
> Soon will our temple its pearly gates ope,
>   People come in and be glad."

Affairs in 1844. The general order and management of Community affairs during the year named continued substantially the same as they had been the twelvemonth before, though the tendency was to discountenance indi-vidualism in conducting business, and bring everything of that nature more and more within the sweep of Joint-Stock industrial operations. This policy was not univer-sally acceptable, and one of our early members, Nathan Harris, resigned his membership and erected himself a residence just outside the boundaries of our estate, on the northerly road to Milford. His wife, however, retained her connection with us, and our relations with him con-tinued cordial and friendly to the time of his death five years afterward. The Executive Council held weekly meetings with infrequent interruptions, being intrusted with large powers and weighty responsibilities as mana-gers of the industrial interests of the Association, the duties of which they discharged with untiring watch-fulness, diligence, and vigor. Measures beyond their authority, yet deemed essential to the common welfare, were recommended by them to their constituents, and, for the most part, promptly sanctioned agreeably to constitutional requirements, thus becoming an integral part of our established economy.

Principal Events. 1. The village site was more completely defined as to its boundaries, thoroughfares, public squares, etc. The names of streets and the designation of house-lots were determined upon, and a plan of the whole was drawn, properly representing the same, in accordance with which prescribed titles of conveyance should be made and recorded. This was done pursuant to a vote of the Council, passed March 18th, as follows:

"*Voted*, (1) To name the Streets of the Village Site preparatory to drafting a plan of the same. The following names were severally proposed and adopted, viz.: For the Street nearest the water privileges running from the horse-barn to the old dam, two rods wide, *Water Street*; for the next parallel Street east, running from Geo. W. Stacy's house by the school-house, three rods wide, *Main Street*; for the next parallel Street east, two rods wide, *High Street*; for the Street running from road to road across the old dam, or across the intended new dam, a little above the old one, *Freedom Street.* [The old road came down the hill from the northerly part of Mendon till it approached the river near the former dam, then by a sudden turn south swept downward around the front of the farm-house, thence northeasterly up the hill to the Scammell place on the Upton highway. Hence the phrase "from road to road" indicates a line forming a base to said bend.] For the next cross Street south, passing in front of the Chapel Site [where the public school-house now stands] and north of the intended square, *Chapel Street.* [This intended square was subsequently superseded by the one on which the Hopedale (Unitarian) House of Worship is now located.] For the next cross Street south, passing over the new dam by the mechanic shop and south of the square, *Social Street;* for the next cross Street south, passing in front of the old house and by A. J. Ballou's, *Union Street;* for the next cross Street south, passing by Adin Ballou's house, *Peace Street;* for the next cross Street south, passing by Geo. W. Stacy's house, *Hope Street.* [These cross streets were all two rods wide.]

"*Voted*, (2) That Adin Ballou be a Committee to number the lots and draft a Plan of the Village."

2. An important transaction of the year was the purchase, through authorized agents, of several parcels of land whereby the Community domain was very considerably enlarged in extent and enhanced in value. The first of these was mostly woodland adjoining the original Jones' farm on the northwest. It formerly belonged to Seth Davenport and was bought of his sons. It contained about nineteen acres for which we paid $362.38. The second piece was a detached lot of woodland containing six and a quarter acres lying on the westerly slope of Magomiscock Hill, purchased of Dana Perry for $270.00. The third and much the most important tract was the Amos Cook farm of 108 acres lying directly south of and contiguous to our territory with an outlying wood lot of twenty three and a half acres, for which we paid $3000. In order to make these new investments, more money had to be borrowed and secured by personal credit and mortgage. Our landed property was thus expanded more rapidly than our needs and pecuniary ability at the time would warrant.

3. Four new cottages were erected in 1844; those of E. D. Draper, Butler Wilmarth, Daniel S. Whitney, and Henry Fish. Several additional lots were taken up and preparation for building on them the next season was commenced. The School and Chapel building was completed, having one large room and two ante-rooms on the main floor with a basement suitable for a small store. The school and assemblies for worship were transferred to their new quarters in April, and soon after the room below was stocked with groceries and dry goods for the common convenience by the Community authorities. An old corn-house was removed to Water Street, extempo-

9

rized into a blacksmith shop, and supplied with the necessary equipment. A lead pipe aqueduct was laid from a reservoir on the northerly high land of our territory, a fourth of a mile away, into our young village, for sundry public and private uses. The streets were considerably improved and the general external condition of our little settlement assumed a more orderly, refined, and attractive appearance.

4. The School for several months of the year was in charge of Br. Daniel S. Whitney and during the remainder, of Sr. Mary Jackman, who became the wife of Br. Samuel Colburn on the 23d of June, their marriage being the first one solemnized in the new Chapel and hence a somewhat notable event. A committee of two, Butler Wilmarth and Edmund Soward, under the direction of the Intendant of Education, was appointed to have the general oversight of school affairs, furnish needed supplies, provide teachers, examine classes, see that proper discipline was exercised, etc. Some difficulty was experienced in adjusting the hours of juvenile labor, tuition, and recreation, as well as in maintaining salutary government over our heterogeneous brood. We might have sent our children and youth to the public district school of the town of Milford, for the support of which we were obliged to pay our due share by legal taxation. But we aspired to something better at our own additional expense; besides, the public school-house was too far away and too small for our accommodation. We petitioned the town to be set off as a new district, but satisfactory terms could not be arranged and the matter went over to a later day.

5. Our promulgatory and missionary operations went forward in all directions with unabated activity without in any wise restricting or neglecting the established means and facilities for moral and religious instruction and quickening within our own borders. *The Practical Chris-*

tian and our several preachers proclaimed their testimonies in all the old and in some new localities. The claims upon us of all the great moral reforms, as well as of our own distinctive Practical Christianity, summoned all our energies forth and put them to active and unremittant service. We had more irons in the fire than we were able to handle to advantage. And yet we were induced towards the close of the year to undertake the resuscitation of the suspended *Non-Resistant*, the organ of the New England Non-resistance Society. It was not a wise thing for us to do, as it increased to no little extent our burdens without contributing correspondingly to the advancement of the cause. The effort was in a line with much of our experience. Our ambition to disseminate the truth as it had been made known to us and to aid in emancipating our fellow-men from the evils and disabilities under which they suffered, was continually outrunning our ability and means of accomplishment. So we had to live and learn, and yet in this particular we learned but slowly.

6. Our interest in social reorganization and our friendly intercommunication with other laborers in the same field suffered no decline as the months went by. We watched what was going on in different localities under the direction of various experimenters with sleepless eye, studied their systems and methods in so far as they were at variance with ours, and occasionally met with those theoretically and practically engaged in attempts to solve the same great problem which was so dear to our hearts and was taxing so severely our mental, moral, and physical energies and resources. We were represented in two or three Conventions of Associationists during the year. Of one of them the following notice appeared in our paper:

"ASSOCIATIONAL CONFERENCE.

"In accordance with an arrangement made last winter in Boston a Conference consisting of two delegates from each of the three Associations in Mass., viz.: — Northampton, Brook Farm, and Hopedale, met at Hopedale on the 24th ult. (May). Present the following delegates: — Brook Farm, George Ripley and Ephraim Capen; Northampton, James Boyle and Josiah Hayward; Hopedale, Adin Ballou and Butler Wilmarth. The object of this Conference was the promotion of a friendly intercourse between the several Associations and a careful inquiry into the practical working of their respective internal economies with a view to mutual correction and improvement. These Associations differ widely in some respects and are perfectly independent of each other. It is not intended to bring them into any organic compact, but, by means of these friendly Conferences holden three times a year at each location in succession, to maintain a good understanding, and especially to enable all of them to profit by a mutual comparison of merits and defects. The delegates and volunteers met at 9 A. M. and proceeded to institute a close inquiry into the statistics, resources, industrial arrangements, methods of education, and particular operations of the three Associations, whereof minutes were taken for preservation and future use. Interesting statements and remarks were made by George Ripley, James Boyle, and others, unfolding the peculiar organization and workings of the Brook Farm and the Northampton Associations. The Conference throughout was very pleasant and profitable. Probably more solid practical instruction was interchanged than the inexperienced could acquire from a hundred theoretic lectures."

The next meeting of these three bodies was held at Broughton Meadows (now Florence), Northampton, Mass., on the 31st of August. The call for it was issued by the officers of the Community located there, the organic name of which was " Northampton Association of Education and Industry," and was addressed "*To the Friends of a Reorganization of Society that shall Substitute Fraternal Co-operation for Antagonistic Selfishness; a Religious Consecration of Life and Labor, Soul and Body, Time and Eternity, in Harmony with the Laws of God and of Life, instead of Fragmentary, Spasmodic Piety.*" This call was published widely in reformatory journals and brought together a large company of the friends of Truth and Humanity. A few extracts from the account of the meeting in *The Practical Christian* given under the heading of " Northampton Association " will indicate its character :

"Br. E. D. Draper and myself (Adin Ballou) as Delegates from Hopedale to the Associational Conference at that place, reached our destination about noon of Aug. 30th, and were most cordially welcomed by generous friends who did all in their power to render our visit refreshing and pleasant. We were conducted over the fields, meadows, and various industrial establishments of the Domain, which exhibited great natural capabilities and many creditable improvements." " They have much excellent land and a capital water privilege. We had small opportunity to get acquainted with the Associates individually, but we were abundantly confirmed in our previous opinion that they have among them many high-souled, pure principled, generous men and women. They have had many trials to encounter, and like other Associations no doubt have committed some errors by which to profit in the future. May they struggle through every difficulty and from the mount of ultimate triumph pour down abundant blessings on humanity." " The Convention of Saturday and Sunday abounded with most important and animated discussions. A Mr. Rykeman from Brook Farm ably represented and defended the Fourier system; Henry Clapp, Jr., of Lynn, the anti-organization and anti-moral-test doctrine; while Wm. Loyd Garrison and the writer of this notice earnestly contended that no Association could ultimately prosper without making the fundamental principles of practical Christianity the test of action, character and fellowship."

Individualism Checked. By the changes made in our Constitution near the close of 1842 much larger privileges were granted to members in the way of owning their own houses, carrying on business, and acting generally on their own account without being held amenable to Community authority, than were allowed previously under our original compact. The experiences of 1843 and 1844,

however, did not wholly justify our course at that time
and so a reaction came before the expiration of the last
named year. I was myself obliged to confess that in
trying to shun Scylla we had steered the ship dangerously
near Charybdis. The difficulty lay in the sad fact that too
many of us were insufficiently disciplined in our acknowledged principles of Practical Christian wisdom and righteousness. Hence if we communitized very strongly some
claimed too much at the expense of the whole, and if
we encouraged individualism beyond a certain point there
was presently an annoying and reprehensible manifestation of selfish egoism. Finding ourselves in this latter
condition we tried to get back to the center of the narrow strait in which we were obliged to sail. To effect
this we made such new alterations in our Constitution
and By-Laws as seemed necessary to save us from newly
threatened perils. The former remained much as it had
been for two years, and need not be reproduced at this
time; the most radical change being incorporated in a
By-Law which introduced an entirely new feature into our
industrial system. It is therefore inserted entire:

"BY-LAW RESPECTING INDUSTRIAL ORGANIZATION.

"SECTION 1. All the resident members of this Community
with their family dependents shall be organized as far as
practicable into Bands and Sections.

"SEC. 2. Each Band shall have charge of a particular interest and prosecute a definite subdivision of industry during a
specific portion of each day, week, or month, and shall elect
their Monitor once every fortnight.

"SEC. 3. Sections shall consist of several Bands engaged in
branches or sub-branches of the same general business, and
shall elect their Director once in two months, subject to a
negative of the Executive Council.

"SEC. 4. The Bands shall be formed as far as possible by
elective affinity; and no person over ten years of age shall be
a member of any Band by constraint or against the will of
a majority of the Band.

" SEC. 5. No Band shall be formed (except for a temporary service) or dissolved without the approbation of the Executive Council, who shall determine all questions in dispute not seasonably adjusted by the members of the Bands and Sections among themselves.

" SEC. 6. The average amount of time required of each individual for the service of the Community shall be forty-eight hours per week from the first of October to the first of April, and sixty hours per week during the other half of the year, abating for private use one day in each quarter.

" SEC. 7. The hours of service for the different Bands shall be so arranged as to insure proper attention to all the various interests of the Community, day and night, at home and abroad, throughout the year. Also in such a manner as to allcw each individual reasonable opportunities to go abroad and to entertain visiting friends. Also in such a manner as to allow each individual an equal participation, if possible, in all the social privileges of the Community.

" SEC. 8. The time pledged by individuals to the service of the Community covering certain specified portions of the day, week, or month, shall be held sacred to that purpose. If lost, except by severe sickness or unavoidable casuality, it shall be made up in labor or cash to the satisfaction of the Executive Council. If used for the transaction of private business whereby the individual receives money or acquires gain, the entire net profit of such business shall belong to the Community. But moneys received or profits acquired by business transacted in unpledged time shall belong to the individual.

" SEC. 9. The operatives shall ordinarily pledge their time and perform their services between 4 o'clock in the morning and 9 o'clock in the evening, according to the necessities of business and their individual inclination. But to meet extraordinary emergencies the Executive Council or any one of the Intendants may request and accept service at any hour of the day or night.

" SEC. 10. Each individual shall furnish him or herself with lodging, furniture, and all handicraft tools necessary to efficient industry, except such as general convenience may require the Community to furnish. And on the value of such furniture and tools the operative shall be allowed a fair per

cent. per annum. Otherwise the Community shall charge a
fair per cent. per annum for the use thereof.

Sec. 11. All who cheerfully concur in this organization
shall be insured, as a fair compensation for their services, the
following specified provisions, stipends, and contingent dividends, viz.:

"Each operative over sixteen years of age shall be allowed
for clothing and pocket money, payable in acceptable goods,
cash or credits, at the option of the individual, twenty-five
dollars per annum. Each operative under sixteen and over
eight years of age shall be allowed for the same purpose in
acceptable goods, cash or credits, fourteen dollars per annum.
Children under eight years of age shall be provided with suitable clothing to the value of eight dollars per annum. And
the making up of said clothing, so far as the same may be
done by Community operatives, shall be without charge.

"Each family and individual shall be provided with houseroom, fuel, light, food, washing and mending, medicine, medical and nursing attendance, and conveyance by horse and
carriage (reckoning only persons over sixteen years of age)
fifty miles each per annum.

"All State, County, Town, and School District taxes on
polls and on real estate situated within the limits of Hopedale, not exceeding in value one thousand dollars, shall be
paid by the Community. Also all governmental fines necessarily incurred by fidelity to the principles of our Declaration.

"Such individuals as own houses and lots in the village
which they intend to occupy and improve shall be allowed
four per cent. per annum on the just valuation thereof, not
exceeding one thousand dollars, and a reasonable amount of
team work, manure, and manual labor, for the cultivation of
their gardens. Provided, always, that they consume in their own
families whatever they may need of the production of their
lots, and, after making such friendly presents out of the same
as they may desire, deliver the surplus to the Community for
a fair equivalent; and provided also that they furnish their
houses and keep them in repair at their own expense.

"Each member shall receive of the net profits of the Community after the Joint-Stock shall have been paid its constitutional four per cent., an equal proportion with all the other
members not exceeding fifty cents for every ten hours of

service credited to him or her on the books of the Community. The services of dependents shall draw no dividend except by special vote of the Community.

"SEC. 12. The Monitor of each Band shall keep a correct account of the time spent by each individual in service appertaining to the province of his or her Band and report the same weekly to the Director of his or her Section, who shall make a monthly report of the whole to the Intendant of Finance and Exchange; and he shall prepare a quarterly abstract both of services rendered and of the pecuniary standing of the Community for the inspection of the Executive Council.

"SEC. 13. All children and youth under eighteen years of age connected with this Community shall be considered pupils, and after leaving the nursery shall be regularly instructed in the useful arts and sciences four hours per day through the year except on Saturdays and Sundays, and excepting also vacations of one week in each quarter. The infant class shall receive instruction two hours in the forenoon and two in the afternoon. The older pupils shall receive instruction wholly in the forenoon or in the afternoon so as to be regularly employed without interruption during the remaining half day in the industrial organization. No pupil shall be allowed to attempt more than three scholastic exercises in the same half day or to pursue more than four branches of study requiring recitation, analysis, or special instruction, during the same quarter. And it shall be the duty of the teachers to render every pupil as thoroughly proficient as possible in the studies attempted before permitted a transition to new or higher studies. It shall also be the duty of the teachers carefully to supervise the morals of the children and youth under their instruction, to check their vicious tendencies, refine their manners, oversee their recreations, and guard them against all evil habits.

"Passed in regular meeting at Hopedale, Dec. 17, 1844.

ADIN BALLOU, *Pres't.*

We now arrive at the Community's Fourth Annual Meeting held in their School-house Chapel, Jan. 8, 1845. At that time what was called the Consolidated Fund of the Community covered four hundred acres of land with valuable mill privileges, three dwelling-houses, one large mechanic shop, a School-house Chapel, barns, and other out-buildings. Besides this property, which was owned in Joint-Stock, individual members owned and occupied in the village seven dwelling-houses built within the previous two years. These dwelling-houses and their respective half acre lots, with all improvements and appurtenances, though under the general control of the Community and for all practical purposes a part of its serviceable capital, were not included in the report of the Executive Council as belonging to its proprietorship. That report related solely to what was strictly associated capital and operations carried on with it under the direction of Community officials. An abstract of that portion of it which pertained to financial matters is subjoined:

"Whole amount of cash received into the Treasury during the year, $9,094.38; disbursed, $9,109.57; due the Treasurer, $15.19. Amount paid for labor during the year, $5614.53. The amount of property in the Consolidated Fund, $12,364.68; deducting debts owing on mortgage, $5,300.00, leaves an unincumbered amount of $7,064.68. Amount of Floating Fund clear, $2,992.23; making the entire Joint-Stock property free of all indebtedness, $10,056.91. The amount of Joint-Stock covered by certificates, $9,600.00; giving a net profit on the year's operations $456.91.

"Considering all the unfavorable cirumstances under which the Community has hitherto labored," the report concludes, "the Council can but congratulate themselves and their associates on so cheering a result. They can not doubt that future operations going on under the present auspicious arrangements will realize, by the divine blessing, a constantly increasing prosperity.

"Per order of the Council.

"A. BALLOU, *Prest.*"

The official servants elected in due form for the ensuing year were: *President*, ADIN BALLOU; *Secretary*, LEMUEL MUNYAN; *Auditor*, HENRY FISH; *Intendants*:

Finance and Exchange, E. D. DRAPER; *Agriculture and Animals*, A. J. BALLOU; *Manufactures and Mechanical Industries*, HENRY LILLIE; *Health and Domestic Economy*, BUTLER WILMARTH; *Education, Arts, and Sciences*, WM. H. FISH; *Religion, Morals, and Missions*, GEORGE W. STACY.

An article in *The Practical Christian* of Feb. 1, 1845, written by the Editor-in-Chief, giving an account of this meeting, has the following passage:

"Nearly all the other Associations and Communities started off with more ample resources, operated on a larger scale, and of course put in stronger claims to the attention of the public than ours. Our object was grand, our aim high, our fundamental principles sublime. In these respects our Institution is second to no other. But in respect to numbers, pecuniary resources, and all that gives worldly distinction, it is comparatively a diminutive thing. Incited by deep religious convictions of duty, impelled by the ardor of enthusiasm, sustained by the energies of hope and crowned with the blessing of God, our members have surmounted all obstacles and laid the foundation of a social structure which promises, in compensation for the slowness of its growth, strength, durability, and ultimate importance. The undertaking was a great one. It was surrounded with a host of difficulties, more heterogenous and complex than could easily have been anticipated. They still array themselves in formidable groups along our pathway, but the achievements of the past assure us of future victory and are a presage of our final triumph. And what a triumph will that be when we can behold religion, talent, skill, capital, and industry combined in sufficient force, even in one single location, to insure domestic independence, and to diffuse around it the salutary influence of a truly Christian Commonwealth. We will hope on and labor ever for the results which illuminate the prospects of the future. Who can devote life to a nobler end? It is a pleasure to toil and struggle under the inspirations of so glorious an expectation. With our present convictions of duty and tone of feeling no worldly advantages or distinctions would reconcile us to the abandonment of this enterprise, though comparative insignificance and obscurity under the continuous pressure of anxious cares will in all probability be the lot of a life devoted to its support."

Remarkably good health prevailed at Hopedale throughout the entire year 1844, and no death occurred among either our resident or non-resident members. A former member, mentioned several times on the foregoing pages, Mrs. Charlotte P. (Hooton) Taft of Uxbridge, died by her own hand on the 5th of February. She had some months before fallen into a state of deep despondency, which ripened into partial insanity leading to the sad result. A great bereavement which befel my wife and her family connections, and indeed the public at large this year, must not be left unrecorded in these annals. It was the sudden decease of her honored and beloved father, Pearley Hunt, Esq., of Milford, who was fatally stricken with heart disease on the 29th of March in the 73d year of his age. He was a kind and devoted husband and father, a good friend to our Community, besides illustrating many excellent characteristics which entitled him to the distinguished respect so generally accorded him in the town where he had spent his life and the region round about.

CHAPTER V.

1845–1847.

VARYING FORTUNES — NOTABLE EVENTS — INCREASING ACTIVITY — NEW PERILS — A RECONSTRUCTED POLITY.

IT will have been noted by the thoughtful reader that the economical polity provided for in the By-Law which was given entire near the close of the last Chapter and soon after put into operation among us, indicated a swing again towards a more closely associated and also a more complex administration of Community affairs. To those at all familiar with the elaborate and somewhat mystical system of social reconstruction devised by the French philosopher, Charles Fourier, already adverted to, and urged upon the attention of philanthropists and reformers of the country by Albert Brisbane, Horace Greeley, Parke Godwin, and others, it will suggest our acquaintance with, and perhaps a distant imitation, after a bungling fashion, of some of his unique and fanciful methods. At any rate, it put the previously dominant individualism, with all its annoying and dangerous excesses of personal angularity, arrogance, and self-aggrandizement, for the time being under the ban, and made the idea of unitary interests and affiliated responsibilities—the idea of "each for all"—prominent and controlling. But this new arrangement we soon found to be beset by three difficulties which predetermined it to an early failure: First, smallness of numbers; second, lack of skillful, experienced leaders; third, a continual influx upon us of raw, undisciplined recruits. These were by no means novel with us. We had been encountering them from the outset, and they were our bane under whatever plan of operation we were tempted to act — all because we began to build without patient, adequate, pecuniary means and suitable materials. Yet, go on, awhile at least, in the way the change required, we must. We could not stop the momentum of our social movement now turned in that direction if we would, and we flattered ourselves that the wheel-horses of our omnibus had become way-wise and reliable — equal to all emergencies — and so pressed forward with our continually increasing freight. Nor were we altogether unsuccessful, though our burdens and hindrances were great.

The change of policy on our part seemed for a while to stimulate rather than check enterprise among us. Applications for membership or for probationship in our organization multiplied ; as also did applications for residence in our midst with a view of learning something of our ideas, objects, manner of life, etc., and of joining us if all proved satisfactory. Indeed, this feature of our experience was one of our trials — one of the burdens of responsibility that weighed upon us exceedingly.

A considerable number of house-lots were sold during the summer of 1845, upon some of which dwellings were erected before the year expired, wholly or in part, and other improvements made. Gardens were cultivated, fruit and other trees were planted, streets were extended, operations on the Community farm were carried on vigorously, new industries were introduced, and a growing appearance of thrift and contentment was manifest in all directions, in all departments of our widely diversified undertaking.

An interesting incident illustrative of the times and of the attitude of the Community towards a wronged and outcast race, is brought to notice in a vote passed the

28th of June, " to allow Rosetta Hall to reside at the
Community house for an indefinite length of time and
work for her board, education, etc." Rosetta was a
protégé of Frederick Douglass, the two having known
each other as slaves some years before she appeared in
our midst. On escaping from the house of bondage she
appealed to him for aid in her forlorn condition. He
kindly responded to her appeal and in due time brought
her to Hopedale, where she would be among friends who
would see that no harm came to her, and do all they
could to educate her and help her in other possible ways.
She was made welcome by our people, and treated with
all due consideration and kindness while she remained
within our borders. She proved herself a girl of most
amiable disposition, of engaging manners, and of refined
nature generally, winning the respect, confidence, and
love, as she won the compassionate pity of all who knew
her. Her stay with us was comparatively brief and she
left with the best wishes of all our people for her future
welfare and happiness.

The Hopedale Cemetery. Although no death had as
yet occurred on our territory, yet it was deemed advisable early in the year 1845 that a suitable tract of land
somewhere within our borders should be selected for
burial purposes and properly laid out for use when occasion should require, and a vote to that effect was passed
by the Community at a meeting held on the 8th day of
April. Pursuant to that vote several parcels of ground
that had previously been suggested were carefully
examined, but found by reason of the rocky nature of
the soil or an underlying ledge to be unfit for the purpose. These were located upon the original Jones farm
and were first spoken of before we had made any outlying additions thereto. But the recent purchase of the
Amos Cook estate had brought a more favorable site
into notice, to which the attention of the Council was in

due time directed. It commended itself to their best judgment and upon their recommendation the Community, on the 27th of September,

> "*Voted*, (1) That the lot of land situated on the Cook farm between the wood-lot of Henry Chapin on the west and the widow Amasa Parkhurst's meadow on the east, as the same is now fenced, be set apart, or so much thereof as may be deemed necessary, as a Cemetery for this Community.
>
> "(2) That the Executive Council be instructed to designate as soon as possible the particular part of said Cemetery ground on which it is proper to commence burying.
>
> "(3) That they cause a suitable portion of said ground to be surveyed and laid off into lots.
>
> "(4) That they enter a report of their doings, with a Plan of their survey designating all the avenues by name and the lots by number, in the Community Registry."

Thus was set apart and devoted to its proper uses the tract of land where as time went on all that was mortal of our dearly beloved was to be consigned "earth to earth and dust to dust," and where we ourselves, or so many of us as continued to reside in Hopedale to the end of our days, should finally, as to our material frames, sleep the last long sleep of earth and time. The location was happily chosen as not very far away and yet sufficiently removed from the bustle and toil of our common every-day life to insure that quiet which is becoming a place of sepulture and conducive to self-recollection, meditation, and communion with the spirits of those who are "not lost but gone before," and with the infinite Spirit, the heavenly Father of all mankind.

For some reason which does not now appear, but probably because there was no immediate need of a burial place for any of our people, no death occurring for some time after the above votes were passed, and because of the urgent demands made upon the time and energy of the members of the Council in other directions, the careful survey and laying out of lots, etc., with an accurate plan of the same were not completed for some two years after, as will be noted in its proper place.

By recurring to the records of Community action during the latter part of the year under notice, it is found that the industrial and economical policy inaugurated at its opening did not work so harmoniously and advantageously as was confidently anticipated. Like many other things, not only in Community life but in ordinary human affairs, it looked much better in theory than it proved to be in practice, its glowing promise not ripening into a happy fulfillment. In September the Executive Council was called upon "to make a special report of the financial state of the Community up to this date"; a very unusual occurrence, and one showing that an emergency had arisen demanding unusual action on the part of the members. Ten days later the required report was made through the Intendant of Finance and referred to a "select committee, who shall investigate the affairs of the Community in order to arrive at some method of obviating present difficulties." That committee after a brief interval reported, recommending certain modifications in the existing system of operations and the suspension of certain questionable methods of management till the following January. The report was accepted and the recommendations ordered to be carried into effect, a committee or board of direction being chosen to superintend the matter. From that time forward our social machinery ran smoothly and effectively, to the relief and satisfaction of most of those concerned, though one of our principal members had become so seriously disaffected that he soon after resigned and separated himself from us thenceforth, as will soon be seen.

Visit of Robert Owen. An event of great interest to us, and of considerable significance to the friends of Social Reform generally, was a two days' visit in the

10

month of November from the renowned English Socialist, Robert Owen. He was the author of several works on the subject with which his name is identified, the most important of which was entitled "The Book of the New Moral World," in which he promulgated an original system of Religion and Ethics, founded, as he claimed, on reason, and applicable to the needs of individual and social life. He was also the projector of an interesting and temporarily successful social experiment at New Lanark, Scotland, and also at New Harmony, Ind., where, in 1824, he purchased of the Rappites, a colony of German Socialists, their entire estate consisting of 30,000 acres of land and dwellings for 2,000 persons. This venture proved a failure and he returned to England after a few years to experiment still further though with no better success, and write and lecture upon his favorite theme. His system was a modified communism based upon an absolute equality of all human beings in rights and duties, and the abolition of all superiority even that of capital and intelligence. He had immense wealth, a large part of which he spent in proclaiming his views to the world and in putting them to the test of practical application.

At the time of his brief sojourn at Hopedale he was making a tour of the United States for the purpose of promulgating still further his views and of visiting the different Communities then recently started out in their varied and problematical career. Of him and his distinctive characteristics the editor of *The Practical Christian* spoke in the issue succeeding his call upon us, thus:

"He is a remarkable man. In years, nearly seventy-five; in knowledge and experience, superabundant; in benevolence of heart, transcendental; in honesty, without disguise; in philanthropy, unlimited; in religion, a skeptic; in theology, a Pantheist; in metaphysics, a necessarian circumstantialist; in morals, a universal excusionist; in general conduct, a philosophic non-resistant; in socialism, a communist; in hope, a terrestrial elysianist; in practical business, a methodist; in deportment, an unequivocal gentleman. We have enjoyed his visit, conversation, and public addresses much. We cannot sympathize with his Pantheism, skepticism, necessarianism, or universal excusionism, nor with all his hopes of speedily resolving this ignorant and wretched world into a Community Elysium. We expect as much good and as complete happiness as he does for the human race, but not so soon, nor through the same philosophy, nor by precisely the same practical arrangements and operations.

"And now for what we admire and sympathize with in the man. His benevolence and philanthrophy. He embraces the whole human race in ardent affection. He holds no human being an outlaw, an alien, a stranger, to be cast off, overlooked, or injured. He knows no enemies to hate, persecute, or punish. He loves all, seeks the good of all, labors for all, hopes for all. In this we admire him, agree with him, sympathize with him. We admire his frank, straight-forward honesty, coupled with tolerance, forbearance, courtesy, and kindness to opponents. He conceals nothing; he even dogmatises about his 'three errors' and their counter truths; he declares his abhorrence of the evils of existing society and denounces them; he proclaims himself the uncompromising apostle of his new dispensation, and declares that his whole life and substance are devoted to radical reform; and yet he is uniformly kind, calm, patient, conciliatory, and courteous in all his conversation, addresses and proceedings. This is noble, excellent.

"His knowledge of men and things; his extensive general reading and observation; his long and varied experience in the methods of conducting productive industry, manufactures, trade, education, and government; his accumulation and ready command of European statistics; his doctrines, schemes, and detailed plans for bringing mankind into a new social order;— these render him one of the most intelligent, instructive, and entertaining conversationists and lecturers with whom we have ever met. Notwithstanding all our differences about matters of religion, philosophy, ethics, etc.. we shall always be thankful for his visit to Hopedale and are sure of having derived much valuable practical information from his communications. These we hope to turn to good account in carrying forward the great enterprise to which we are devoted. One fact in his career will we mention which goes to confirm our confidence in the absolute practicability of Non-resistance. Mr. Owen testifies that he superintended at New Lanark in Scotland for thirty years a manufacturing establishment with 2500 population attached to it, originally from the dregs of the country. These he gradually rendered the best, the most orderly society of working people in Europe. Yet he never had one person, old or young, prosecuted at law, corporally punished, imprisoned, or fined in all that time. This means something and deserves to be taken note of and remembered.

"Mr. Owen has vast schemes to develop and vast hopes of speedy success in establishing a great model of a new social state which will almost instantaneously bring the race of man into a terrestrial paradise. He insists on obtaining a million dollars capital to be expended in lands, buildings, machinery, conveniences, and beautifications for his model Community; all to be finished and put in perfect order before he introduces into their new home the well-selected population who are to inhabit it. He flatters himself that he shall be able, by some means, to induce capitalists, or perhaps the U. S. Congress, to furnish the requisite means for attaining this object. We were obliged to shake an incredulous head and tell him frankly how groundless, in our judgment, all such anticipations must prove."

This nobly-endowed, great-hearted, sublimely enthusiastic lover of his kind, labored on, struggled on, for thirteen years after this visit to Hopedale, with all the ardor, courage, and zeal of an inspired prophet, for the actualization of his " New Moral World," but " died without the sight"; breathing his last in his native place, Newton, Montgomeryshire, England, Nov. 19, 1858, at the advanced age of 87 years.

Withdrawal of Bro. Geo. W. Stacy. Another but sadly interesting incident in the year's experience was the resignation of Bro. George W. Stacy from Community membership, followed not long afterward by his removal to the neighboring village of Milford. The domestic and industrial arrangements under which we were operating had become increasingly distasteful to him, and probably some features of their administration decidedly offensive. Moreover, there had arisen occasional friction between him and other brethren concerning the management of affairs, resulting at times in sharp disputes, and he with his temperament naturally began to sigh for a larger liberty and a more unchallenged exercise of his individual rights of thought, of speech, and of action. His wife had never formally united with us, having no real sympathy but rather an instinctive aversion to such close social relations and orderly methods of operation. This may have quickened his growing dislike of the existing policy, though he never pleaded it among the reasons for his course. Matters were brought to a crisis by certain articles, pro and con, in *The Practical Christian*, the first entitled "Devotion to Principle" appearing over his name in the issue of Nov. 29. It clearly indicated what some of us had more than suspected was the drift of his thought, as it did the loosening of the hold of the Community idea upon his mind and heart. A responsive article in the next number, from the pen of Clement O. Reed, reflected somewhat severely on Bro. Stacy's insinuations, and called for more specific statements of grievance, if grievance there really were, in the organization or administration of Community affairs. This brought out an immediate reply from the aggrieved brother, which contained such grave charges against the existing order of things, that I, though referred to by the author in a most fraternal manner and absolved from all blameworthiness, felt it to be my duty to meet the accusations with a deserved denial and refutation; and this I did in the same issue that contained Bro. Stacy's second article. A rejoinder on his part followed, with an accompanying "Omega" from me. All this was done in plain frankness on both sides, but without bitterness or personal reproach. It was, nevertheless, exceedingly unpleasant, nay, painful to me, as possibly it was to him. The newspaper controversy, which might as well have been omitted perhaps, no doubt hastened the final act of withdrawal though it could not under the circumstances have been long deferred. Thus the second of my brother ministers on whom I placed great dependence at the outset of the enterprise, abandoned it at a critical hour of its history and remained permanently alien to it, though on quite dissimilar grounds from those upon which the first left us. Whatever of ungenerous feeling or harshness of spirit was aroused in these cases at the time, has, I trust, long since been assuaged and overcome. Bro. Stacy has been our neighbor ever since he removed from our midst, and our relations to each other for these many years have been cordial and friendly.

The infelicities and disturbances that agitated us during the early autumn and awakened gloomy apprehensions in the minds of some of us, had for the most part passed by before the close of the year, and we came to our annual meeting in a calm and hopeful mood, with confidence restored and harmony prevailing throughout our entire membership. The report of the Executive Council for the year ending Dec. 31, 1845, presented an encouraging and satisfactory condition of the financial affairs of the Association, as the subjoined statement witnesseth:

"Property in the Consolidated Fund, $12,833.05; from which deduct mortgages, $5,300.00; leaving present value $7,533.05. Property in the Floating Fund is as follows, viz.: Stock on hand in the several departments, $7,664.64; due from individuals, $1,085.56; bills receivable, $884.03; profits on village site, $375.00; due from individuals on lost time, $193.72; making a total of $10,202.95. From this amount deduct debts owing to individuals, $3,772.91; bills payable, $1,396.23; Savings Institute, $24.48; interest on borrowed capital, $464.87; due individuals on gained time, $83.82; making a total to be deducted, $5,742.31; present worth, $4,460.64. Total property clear in the two funds, $11,993.69. Amount of Joint-Stock, $10,850.00; making the profits, $1,143.69."

A generous donation of $124.61 from E. D. Draper made the net gain for the year $1,268.30. This enabled the Community to pay a dividend of four per cent., agreeably to the provisions of the Constitution, on all the Joint-Stock for the entire time of its investment, and such dividend was accordingly declared; so that we started out on the year 1846 with no incumbrance of arrearage, debt, or deficit whatever, a financial condition never before attained and truly gratifying.

The official servants for the year ensuing were: ADIN BALLOU, *President;* EDMUND SOWARD, *Secretary;* HENRY FISH, *Auditor;* and the following *Intendants:* EBENEZER D. DRAPER, *Finance and Exchange;* ABNER ADAMS, *Agriculture and Animals;* CLEMENT O. REED, *Manufactures and Mechanical Industry;* BUTLER WILMARTH, *Health and Domestic Economy;* WILLIAM H. FISH, *Education, Arts, and Sciences;* DANIEL S. WHITNEY, *Religion, Morals, and Missions.*

A considerable portion of my annual address as President was devoted to a review of the preceeding four years' activities in the various departments of our undertaking, with a presentation of the grounds upon which those engaged in it could well rejoice together and gird up the lions of their strength, courage, hope, and zeal, for the continued efforts in behalf of the cause to which they were sacredly committed before God and their fellowmen. The more important passages may not be out of place in this connection:

"*Beloved Associates:* This is our fifth annual meeting; the fourth that has been held since our settlement on these premises. I congratulate you on its arrival. We welcome it amid blessings that ought to inspire our hearts with profound gladness, gratitude, confidence, and zeal. It comes to us replete with satisfactions and hopes. It is a green eminence in the progress of our enterprise from which we may survey complacently the past and the future. Never before were our affairs so prosperous, our foundations so firm, our prospects so cheering. This day's Financial Report will inform you that for the first time in our history we are prepared to declare a dividend of nearly or quite the constitutional four per cent. on all our Joint-Stock from the time of its investment. This will clear us of all our arrearages on that account and enable us to commence the new year with a fair probability of being able at its close to declare at least a moderate dividend on labor itself. Such a result is the more probable from the fact that under our present improved industrial organization, all branches of business are conducted with increasing efficiency, regularity, and order. And also from the fact that some important branches for which we have made considerable outlays are just beginning to render a profitable return.

"A brief review of the past will impress us with a just appreciation of our present highly auspicious circumstances. We commenced this great undertaking with less than four thousand dollars clear capital. We have now four times that amount, including, with our Joint-Stock, private property equally useful to the Community, besides our borrowed capital which we are prepared to employ to good advantage. We commenced with one time-shattered dwelling-house and two or three rickety old barns, without a single mill-dam, manufactory, or shop of any kind for mechanical business, or school-room for the comfortable accommodation of our children. We now have a thriving little village of a dozen dwellings, highly improved and comfortable barns, two valuable mill-dams, a commodious mechanic shop filled with useful tools, labor-saving machines, and various facilities for carrying on several branches of business; a convenient building for schools, religious and other public meetings, and numerous other fixtures and accommodations for the public advantage. The farm was completely run down, but is now in the way of material improvement, promising continually increasing returns for the labor bestowed on it.

"All this time we have had a large proportion of children to provide for and to educate, who till recently could not be employed to any tolerable advantage. Yet we have maintained schools for them from four to six hours per day, five days in the week, forty-eight weeks to the year, for at least three years out of the three years and nine months of our inhabitancy of this domain. And all this has been done entirely at our own expense, while we have been paying hundreds of dollars out of our hard earnings into the town treasury in the shape of taxes — not a cent having been refunded. Our direct and indirect taxes to the government of the old order of society to maintain its paupers, its prisons, its criminal code, its army and navy, its civil list, and its education (leaving its roads, which are directly beneficial to us, out of the account), you will perceive are of some consequence to us as items in the cost of living. But to that government, or rather to the old order of society which is taxing us, we are no expense whatever. But by precept and example we are promoting those salutary moral reforms which tend constantly to the diminution of its public expenses. So far as we are concerned we make no paupers, and can make none. We make no criminals to punish, nor put the public to any expense for punishing their criminals on our account. We bring no actions at law to be tried in their costly court-houses by liberally salaried judges, extravagantly feed lawyers, and well-paid officers and attendants. We educate our own children and youth. We govern ourselves by the divine law; and the Almighty, in whom we trust, protects us without the intervention of military and naval forces. Constables, sheriffs, magistrates, and prisons are rendered unnecessary by us. Our principles and our arrangements prevent all necessity for such appliances. The world cannot do without these things because it has no faith in any thing higher than its own standard, and no willingness to conform to the conditions on which alone it can ever be free from its present curses. We can do without them for the contrary reasons.

"During the nearly four years of these operations we have been able to meet our pecuniary liabilities to the satisfaction of all concerned, and to maintain an unsullied .credit. Our seceding members, to the number of nearly twenty in all, have been honorably settled with at their departure, and paid, either in cash or acceptable securities, every cent due them. This has been a draft upon our resources of several thousand dollars. But we have sustained it with firmness. And now we stand up in every possible respect better conditioned for future operations than at any former period. Without hard toil, incessant anxiety, and peculiarly favorable providences of God, it would have been impossible for us to reach our present hopeful position. Let us therefore humble ourselves in view of all our unworthiness and ascribe the glory, the whole glory to our Father in heaven.

"We really occupy an illustrious position. This now humble Hopedale is a Bethlehem of salvation to the glorious social future. If others despise it or protrude at us the lip of scorn because we thus esteem it, let them do so. It becomes us to stand erect in faith, firm in purpose, determined in zeal, immovable, uncompromising, intrenched behind our impregnable ramparts of divine strength, intent only on that sublime destiny which time will assuredly prove to have been decreed to our Community. Our only concern should be to do our duty, our whole duty, manfully, cheerfully, unfalteringly. God will take care of the rest."

On looking back thirty years on this fair exhibit of our Community affairs, the glowing hopefulness which animated my words, and the confident assurance of the divine favor, I cannot repress the sadness which subsequent reverses and ultimate failure on the eve of seeming triumph cast like a dark shadow over my life. I wonder at the enthusiastic rhetoric in which I arrayed my public addresses in the face of so many disappointments and drawbacks. The truth is, I was so certain I was right in principles and aims, so largely endowed with the organ of hope, and had such a persistent will, that I could not lie down in the furrow of weariness and disappointment, nor cease to paint my horizon with auroral hues, even when many clouds were flitting across my field of vision. But they all had a silver lining and would be soon dissipated by the rising sun. So holy and grand a cause must surely triumph. Therefore if one form of polity or mode of administration or set of coadjutors failed, I resorted to others and was fruitful of new expedients even to the last. And when the inevitable shipwreck came, I floated away on the last available plank of our shattered ark, and have been spared to tell the story of our unfortunate venture and blasted expectations to succeeding genera-

tions, and bequeath the fruits of our sorrowful experience
to a happier age. So I proceed with my narrative which
has many lights and shadows yet to be portrayed.

The Year 1846. It might amuse and surprise, if it did
not instruct, the curious reader of these pages were I to
open still further the casements of our social establishment and point out the movements of the complicated,
and, to an outside observer, perplexing mechanism con-
cealed therein —wheels succeeding wheels and wheels within
wheels in elaborate and manifold combination. But the
glimpses already permitted must suffice. They will convey
a reasonably correct idea of what existed and transpired,
so far as industrial organization and management were
concerned, for some time to come. Only that instead of
improving and running more smoothly, there seemed in
many directions to be more friction and more cause of
dissatisfaction with existing methods and arrangements.
Unforseen difficulties were developed requiring modification
of the prevailing policy or new expedients and modes of
operation. Instead of the hoped for increase of industrial
and financial prosperity, or at least continuance of the
previous year's success, there was serious decline, resulting in an actual loss of several hundred dollars on our
invested capital. Not only were we unable to pay dividends on labor as we had fondly anticipated but were
obliged to forego the four per cent. returns to our Joint-
Stock. This was a state of things exceedingly disheartening and led us to enter upon a rigid examination of
our affairs in order to determine the cause or causes of
our reduced revenues that we might remove or overcome
them and so be put upon the upward way again. Something must be done to render our industry more efficient
and remunerative. A careful inspection of the reports of
our managers revealed the fact that the actual production
of their several departments was not what reasonably
might have been expected — was not in average propor-

tion to the amount of time credited for labor. This demonstrated either that suitable employment had not been assigned to our operatives, or that the fruit of their labor had not been judiciously husbanded, or that the amount of time credited to them had not been productively employed. In whichever particular a defect might be found, or if it should appear that there existed some defect in all of them, it was evident that measures should be at once taken to remedy it. This was accordingly done as will soon be shown.

Another weak spot in our industrial management came to light upon careful examination, and that was, that the services of children and supernumeraries had not been made to accrue as they ought to the financial advantage of the Community. It was supposed that appropriate and remunerative employment of a sufficient amount had been provided for these, but for some reason or other it had not yielded satisfactory returns to the common treasury, and this called for some definite and wise action on the part of the proper authorities in the case.

Moreover, the year proved to be one of solicitude and trial—nay of bereavement and distress, by reason of much sickness within our borders. In the late summer, fever of a typhoid nature broke out in several of our families, causing great anxiety and much extra labor therein, and awakening more or less of apprehension and fear throughout our entire population. Three children and one adult died; and a number of other persons were confined to their beds for varying lengths of time, from which they arose mere shadows of their former selves, returning to their accustomed places and occupations after a lingering convalescence. This very naturally had a depressing effect upon the spirits of all of us, and taxed to an unusual degree our energies, our ambition, and our hope, as it did also our financial ability and resources.

But our numbers had suffered no diminution but rather increase, notwithstanding the four deaths and the removal of one family, which left us not from any disaffection, but at the call of duty to minister to an aged and infirm relative who was in great need of their varied help. We began the year with eighty-three members, dependents, and candidates; we closed it with one hundred and seven. Our Joint-Stock capital increased from less than twelve to more than fourteen thousand dollars and was soon to be augmented several thousand more by absorbing the credits due to individual members. Our private capital invested in dwelling houses, landed improvements, etc. had increased proportionally. We erected three new family habitations, a commodious shop for machinists and blacksmiths with a combined wash-house appended, and a saw-mill for the manufacture of lumber for home and outside consumption. Besides, some new branches of industry had been started, affording a wider scope for individual capability, taste, and choice, and a larger opportunity for remunerative employment. At the same time we had obtained an increasing run of custom from the immediate neighborhood and some recognized foothold in the markets of the general community. Our credit was deservedly sound and satisfactory in the entire region round about, and a growing confidence and friendliness toward us was manifest on every hand. Furthermore, the laying out of a much needed road to the southward of our village, to be built the following spring, opening communication with people and towns beyond, gave promise of advantage to our industrial interests, as did the approaching completion of the Providence and Worcester Railroad to Blackstone and Uxbridge, and of the branch line from So. Framingham to Milford. So with all our disappointments and adversities, we had our encouragements and persuasives to renewed diligence, steadfastness, and zeal in our chosen work, and we governed ourselves accordingly. We certainly had no occasion by what we had experienced of ill-fortune, pecuniary loss, or personal and domestic bereavement, to question our own motives and ambitions, to distrust our principles or the righteousness of our cause, or to doubt that doing our duty as we understood our duty, trusting in Him who had thus far, we believe, guided us on our way, we should in due time be crowned with triumphant success.

The spirit which animated and cheered us as we came to our Annual Meeting on the 13th of January, 1847, may be learned from the account of the proceedings given in our paper, which I quote entire.

"The Annual Meeting of this Community took place according to notification. It was an interesting, harmonious, profitable occasion. The President's address, several reports, choice of official servants, discussion of proposed measures, and business transactions occupied most of the afternoon and evening. Great unanimity and determination of mind prevailed throughout the proceedings, and important regulations for the improvement of our industrial, economical, educational, and moral affairs were adopted. The somewhat untoward results of last year's operations were contemplated without a murmur and seemed to serve only as a stimulus to more resolute and judicious efforts for the future. It was felt that it became us to bear with resignation the pecuniary losses of our great sickness, amounting, according to the best estimate of all the items that ought to be included in the reckoning, to at least a thousand dollars; especially as we had been so greatly favored in this respect during all our previous years of community life. And as to deficiencies arising from injudicious methods of operation, imperfect management, or individual short-comings, all seemed determined to enter vigorously on the work of reform and self-improvement. Whether we shall be able to give a more cheering account of ourselves at the commencement of another year remains among the uncertainties of the future. But we have the utmost confidence that the issue will be creditable to the Community. Time will show.

"The residents at Hopedale, unwilling that non-resident stockholders should fail of their four per cent. interest on capital, instantly raised by private subscription the requisite sum to pay them their full dividends. On our own capital we will be content to draw profits when the Joint-Stock operations shall have fairly produced them. We wish our stockholding friends residing outside of our domain, not to construe this eagerness to pay them their profits into any distrust of their generosity and confidence, but rather as a dictate of our own (perhaps excusable) pride, which prefers not to see their interests compromised by our misfortunes or ill management. Most of them have been uniformly patient, generous, and confiding towards us — friends indeed; and we have no reason to suppose them changed for the worse.

"The official servants for the current year are: ADIN BALLOU, *President and Auditor;* EDMUND SOWARD, *Secretary; Intendants:* E. D. DRAPER, *Finance and Exchange;* CLEMENT O. REED, *Manufactures and Mechanical Industry;* HORATIO EDSON, *Health and Domestic Economy;* D. S. WHITNEY, *Education, Arts, and Sciences;* WM. H. FISH, *Religion, Morals, and Missions.*

"These constitute the Executive Council. The election of an Intendant of Agriculture and Animals was postponed by general consent to a future meeting, and the Council were instructed to supply the temporary vacancy till regularly filled."

At this same meeting a By-Law was enacted making very radical changes in the organization and government of the industries of the Community. Under its provisions the operatives in each branch of business were constituted a co-operative association having a voice in the control of their own distinct affairs and in the arrangement of details, subject to the supervision of a Manager appointed by the Executive Council, who was himself responsible to the Council for the faithful discharge of the duties of his position as specifically set forth in one section of the enactment. There was also a set of Regulations, three in number, adopted, defining still futher the obligations and powers of the several Managers in their respective departments of official activity. And still further a Resolve was passed designed to regulate and make available to the profit of the Community, the family, and the individuals concerned, the labor of the women of each and every household, and all children under twelve years of age connected therewith, under a general system of what was termed Domestic Industry. As these acts of the Community were only tentative and of temporary service, it is not needful that they should have a place in these pages. They could in no proper sense be regarded as a part of the settled industrial policy of the undertaking. They were soon superseded, as will be presently seen, by others of more permanent value and use.

Incidents and Events of 1847. The Community started out upon this year's experiences, notwithstanding the resolute and somewhat elated tone of the annual meeting, under inauspicious skies and with wind and tide, so far as regarded its material interests, setting in the wrong direction. Despite the determination to go forward and meet all annoyances and obstructions with a courageous heart, despite the new expedients that were expected to serve a good purpose in the existing emergency, things went from bad to worse — from remote omens of coming disaster to imminent perils — requiring immediate attention and a most vigorous and effective stroke of public policy. The complexities and perplexities of the newly-devised industrial and economical system, though apparently judicious in itself, and though operated with as much consideration as seemed possible, interfered practically so much with individual tastes, feelings, and wills, that murmurs of dissatisfaction and even of revolt became at length so frequent and so bitter as to embarrass and obstruct the orderly and efficient management of our business activities. We still had among our workmen and operatives too many persons both unaccustomed and indisposed to methodical habits of industry and regularity of action in any direction — too many undisciplined recruits in our industrial army — persons unfitted by lack of sagacity and training, by their loose and heterogenous ways, to render service satisfactorily in decently managed establishments anywhere in the world. They failed to observe proper hours, to care for their tools or implements, to execute nice work, and in general to conform to the necessary conditions of success in their respective callings. In the matter of domestic supplies and culinary tastes, they were equally eccentric, fitful, and unreasonable. The most salutary rules, the most wisely arranged plans, the most indispensable requirements, with such, availed nothing. They were not respected and could not be enforced to any such extent as would make it pleasant in any voluntary, co-equal, fraternal association. Under such circumstances, both managers and managed were annoyed, irritated, disgusted. And though, for a time, most of them suppressed their real feelings and uttered no word of remonstrance or complaint, yet the trouble existed and was destined sooner or later to come out; at first occasionally and mildly perhaps, but afterwards more frequently and emphatically, and in time with displays of ill-will and bitterness.

This state of things was not calculated to increase the felicity of our Community paradise. And neither legislation nor official interposition could afford relief in the matter. The difficulty was not in the intention or purpose of those more immediately implicated. They meant no wrong and no harm. As a rule they were animated by worthy motives and exemplified many excellent traits of character. Else we could have summoned them to answer for their faults before the Community tribunal, and, if need be, cut them off from our fellowship. But their virtue saved them from such a fate. The preponderance of honesty, integrity, kindness of heart, honor, in them made us all slow to condemn them, slow to institute stern measures against them. And so the difficulty remained and increased, affecting more and more unfavorably those directly involved, and causing unrest and disquiet gen-

11

erally within our boundaries. Even the more unexceptionable in the respects indicated, the more orderly and carefully trained and thoroughly disciplined, could not but be affected and disturbed by the annoyances and vexations referred to. I myself walked miles upon miles and spent days and weeks in looking after things that were lost, in putting to rights things that were displaced, in bringing order out of confusion, by reason of the thoughtlessness, neglect, slovenly ways, and general lack of responsibility on the part of those whom I have portrayed. Under such circumstances, the more thoughtful and far-seeing must have realized that a crisis in our affairs could not be far away — that there must ere long be a recasting of our policy, a re-adjustment of industrial methods, and a new regime established. This in the very nature of things was a foregone conclusion. But before it was reached certain events occurred of considerable importance which were calculated to embarrass still more the situation and hasten the impending crisis.

The first of these, and the precursor or occasion of some of the others, was the voluntary retirement from our midst of our esteemed brother and efficient co-laborer, Joseph Kingman, who came to us from West Bridgewater and who proposed returning thither. He had not formally joined our membership nor was he even a probationer of the Community. But he had been from the outset an adherent of our distinctive ideas and principles and a sympathetic friend of our movement. So much interested was he in it and so much inclined to cast in his lot with us, that he had solicited and obtained the privilege of residence on our domain in order to become better acquainted with us and make trial of our polity and social status. When he came, he fully expected to become one of us, and very soon selected a house-lot for a permanent residence. He was a man of intelligence, sound practical judgment, high moral character, and con-

genial social qualities. He possessed a respectable prop-
perty and could be a much-to-be-desired help in that
respect. In short, he combined in himself every qualification almost that would render him a very useful and
influential coadjutor in our work. We reposed great
confidence in him, sought his counsel on many important
measures, and made him *pro tempore* Intendant of Agriculture and Animals. We had come to regard him and
his family as an extraordinarily desirable acquisition to
our fellowship. But he was not satisfied with the practical working of our industrial system and the condition
of things under it, and felt that he could not be contented
and happy in our midst — that he could do more good,
fill a wider sphere of usefulness in the world, exert a
more salutary influence, and find greater enjoyment, in
his native town and vicinity than he would if he remained
permanently with us. He therefore signified his intention
of leaving Hopedale in the month of February, and a few
weeks later bade us farewell. Our loss was great, and
our sorrow heartfelt.

This left our Agricultural department without a manager at the opening of the most busy season of the year.
The springtime was at hand. Work on the large Community farm was abundant and urgent. All the village
gardens had claims for plowing and enrichment. Several
cellars for new dwellings were to be dug and stoned.
Moreover, a contract had been made to fell and clear off
the wood and timber on a ten acre lot in the vicinity
before a certain day in early summer. These and many
incidental labors devolved upon this department and were
demanding immediate attention. And now by the removal of
Br. Kingman it had lost its executive head, and there was not
a man in all our subordinate ranks whom the Council could
appoint to fill the vacant place. What was to be done?

At this juncture of affairs I consented, as I had been
wont to do before in similar exigencies, to take the man-

agement of the interests involved into my own hands. This was more generous than wise, for I was already overtasked, loaded down with manifold labors of various sort, at home and abroad, by day and by night. But I addressed myself to the responsibilities of the position with all the ardor and zeal I could command, which, in addition to my other cares as preacher, lecturer, editor, and President of the Community, soon exhausted my physical energies, impaired my usual mental buoyancy, and seriously threatened an utter collapse of my entire system.

Meanwhile there was a gradual demoralization going on in all directions, among all grades of our Community forces. The unrest, irritation, and discontent, under our general industrial policy already adverted to, increased continually and assumed more menacing forms. Financial resources were running low. More money was needed than could be easily obtained. Our expenditures exceeded our income. To meet the demands made upon us, we had to fall back upon one of our more fortunate members, who was engaged in business outside of Community jurisdiction that yielded him a sufficient revenue to enable him to help us in every emergency by additional subscriptions to our Joint-Stock. He had already become the largest investor in such stock. While his kindness and generosity were duly appreciated as rendering us a most indispensable service, it was generally felt that it was by no means a healthy state of affairs which made it necessary for us to call for or receive the aid he was so willing to give.

And so in many a quarter the elements were fomenting and conspiring, unconsciously perhaps in some instances, to bring on a crisis — to compel a readjustment of the different parts of our social machinery — to necessitate the adoption of new and more harmonious, effective, and satisfactory methods of administration. Measures of relief, plans of action, devices of many a kind, were offered and discussed between individuals, in private circles, by the Executive Council, and at regular Community meetings. But nothing definite was done; no final conclusion for some time reached.

After much fruitless talk, and long deliberative sittings which accomplished nothing, it was at length felt by a sort of common instinct, and determined by common consent, that the elaborate, complicated, overgrown mechanism under which, with repeated modifications, eliminations, and additions, we had been living and operating from the very beginning should be abandoned altogether, and that we should build anew our social edifice from the bed-rock foundation of our Preamble and Declaration in a more simple, direct, laconic, unpretending, comprehensible fashion, and order all our activities and operations accordingly. And so with little more ado we proceeded to set aside the original Constitution of the Community, with all the By-Laws, Regulations, Rules, Resolves, and arrangements then in force, and to reconstruct the entire concern after a new and altogether untried model. On the 17th of July this work of reconstruction was inaugurated and put in process of practical development by the adoption of the following

"CONSTITUTION.

"In order to establish a state of society governed by divine moral principles, with as little as possible of mere human constraint, in which all the members may be perfectly free to associate or separate their secular interests according to inclination and congeniality, but in which no individual shall suffer the evils of oppression, poverty, ignorance, or vice, through the influence or neglect of others, we, whose names are hereunto subscribed, do unite in a voluntary association to be called

"THE HOPEDALE COMMUNITY.

"Article I.

"Section 1. No person shall be a member of this Community who does cordially assent to the following

"DECLARATION.

"I believe in the religion of Jesus Christ as he taught and exemplified it according to the Scriptures of the New Testament. I acknowledge myself a bounden subject of all its moral obligations. Especially do I hold myself bound by its holy requirements, never, under any pretext whatsoever, to kill, assault, beat, torture, enslave, rob, oppress, persecute, defraud, corrupt, slander, revile, injure, envy, or hate any human being—even my worst enemy; never in any manner to violate the dictates of pure chastity; never to take or administer an oath; never to manufacture, buy, sell, deal out, or use any intoxicating liquor *as a beverage;* never to serve in the army, navy, or militia of any Nation, State, or Chieftain; never to bring an action at law, hold office, vote, join in a legal posse, petition a legislature, or ask governmental interposition, *in any case involving a final authorized resort to physical violence;* never to indulge self-will, bigotry, love of pre-eminence, covetousness, deceit, profanity, idleness, or an unruly tongue; never to participate in lotteries, games of chance, betting, or pernicious amusements; never to resent reproof or justify myself in a known wrong; never to aid, abet, or approve others in anything sinful; but through divine assistance always to recommend and promote with my entire influence the holiness and happiness of all mankind.

" Sec. 2. Any person assenting to the foregoing Declaration and recommended in writing by seven members as sponsors, may be admitted into the membership of this Community by vote at any regular meeting, provided he or she shall thereupon subscribe this Constitution.

" Sec. 3. Any person may resign membership at discretion by entering a minute on the Records to that effect.

" Sec. 4. Any unworthy member may be discharged at any regular meeting by a vote requesting him or her to resign.

" Sec. 5. Any meeting reasonably notified in respect to time, place, and leading subjects of consideration, shall be deemed regular.

" Sec. 6. Every member shall have one and but one vote on all questions, and the concurrence of two-thirds of the members present and acting shall be necessary to the decision of every question.

" Sec. 7. Nine members shall constitute a quorum.

ARTICLE II.

"SECTION 1. The members of this Community shall own and manage such real and movable estate in the Joint-Stock Proprietorship as they may deem necessary to the maintenance of a neighborhood exclusively inhabited and controlled by persons honestly endeavoring to conform to the principles of the foregoing Declaration. And no person habitually setting at nought those principles shall permanently reside within the territorial limits of the Community by public consent.

"SEC. 2. This Joint-Stock property shall consist of shares of the value of fifty dollars each, for which the owner shall hold Certificates responsibly signed in the form following, to wit:

"For value received, A. B. or order is hereby entitled to —— shares in the Joint-Stock property of the Hopedale Community valued at —— dollars, together with such dividends as may from time to time be declared thereon.

"SEC. 3. The general management, safe keeping, and disposal of this Joint-Stock property shall be vested in a Board of Trustees consisting of not less than three nor more than five responsible members of the Community chosen for that purpose.

"SEC. 4. It shall be the duty of this Board of Trustees to sell off, rent out, or improve, under their official superintendence, the Joint-Stock property in such a manner as to afford, if possible, every individual belonging to the Community a fair opportunity to realize the objects of this Association, and at the same time to secure to the Stockholders unimpaired their capital, with a clear annual profit thereon of four per cent.

"SEC. 5. Any accidental excess of profits on the Joint-Stock capital over the said four per cent. shall be devoted to educational purposes for the benefit of the Community.

"SEC. 6. The Board of Trustees shall have power to lay out and improve the Village Site, to open and keep in order streets, commons, and cemeteries, and to sell house-lots to members who will come under obligations that such lots with all their buildings and betterments shall revert to the Joint-Stock Proprietorship at a fair appraisal whenever the same shall cease to be owned within the membership of this Community or be perverted to uses obviously repugnant to the principles of the foregoing Declaration.

"Sec. 7. It shall be the duty of the Board of Trustees to keep accurate accounts and permanent records of their official transactions, and to hold their books always subject to the inspection of any member or stockholder who may desire to examine them. And they shall present to the Community an explicit report of the Joint-Stock finances at least once every year.

Article III.

"Section 1. This Community shall elect a Recorder to serve during mutual satisfaction, and may from time to time appoint such other officers as occasion shall require.

"Sec. 2. Legislation and government shall be confined to matters of obvious public necessity and never be brought into conflict with the declared objects and fundamental principles of this Association.

Article IV.

"All the titles of property and all obligations entered into respecting the same under the Constitution and By-Laws of Fraternal Community No. 1, as may in any wise appear from records or documents, shall be held inviolate under this Constitution.

Article V.

"This Constitution may be altered or amended by two-thirds of the members present and acting at any regular meeting of the Community notified for that purpose."

This Constitution was published in *The Practical Christian* of August 7th, accompanied by a detailed statement of the reasons for the radical change in the disposition and management of our secular affairs which it was designed and calculated to effect, or at least to make possible. Experience had brought the more practically sagacious and responsible of our members to the conviction that it was impossible to attain the objects contemplated by our association and most ardently sought after by us under the former arrangement and mode of administration. We had tried to escape certain dangers that threatened us from different quarters by a variety of devices which involved us in others of equal or greater moment in an opposite direction. The more enterprising, reliable, and efficient among us, to whom was entrusted the conduct of manifold secular affairs were overloaded with care, anxiety, and excessive toil, and embarrassed by complex managemental machinery, multifarious counsel, adverse criticism, and tardy, half-hearted co-operation. While others less capable of planning, directing, and executing, were becoming less submissive to orderly methods, less contented and happy. The change was therefore not simply desirable or expedient, but indispensable — indispensable to our harmony and prosperity, and indispensable to our continued existence. Without it we should have gone to pieces.

As it was, the word went abroad and was heralded far and wide that the Community had virtually come to an end, been wrecked, exploded, disappeared altogether from among the things of earth and time. One well-meaning brother with strong leanings to the dead-level Communism of Robert Owen, who had come to us from New Brunswick expecting to enjoy here the beatitude of a renewed garden of Eden, gave vent to his ill-temper and disgust at what had transpired in a crisp notice of withdrawal from our no longer agreeable fellowship, of which the following is a copy :

"As the Fraternal Community, No. 1, of Hopedale, although a mongrel from the beginning, has ceased to be — is dead; but professes to be a Community, which is too bad — too barefaced to be thought of for a moment; — therefore I can have no fellowship with it, but call for what means I have here to be paid as soon as possible so that I can remove as soon as health will permit.

"Hopedale, Aug. 13, 1847.   JOHN HILL."

Similar ebullitions of a contemptuous spirit mingled with pride and exultation burst forth here and there in the outside world among the bigoted sectarists whose pseudo-piety and anti-Christianity were rebuked by an institution claiming to make the principles of the Gospel supreme in all human relations and concerns, as well as from the vulgar and godless crowd to whom the simple practical precepts of the sermon on the mount were as unintelligible and meaningless as the hieroglyphics of the Nile. To these carping critics of every grade and name, I made what I deemed a fitting response in our paper of October 2, under the ironical caption "Another Humbug Exploded," which, however, I coined from the current disparaging, captious, literature of our over-jubilant adversaries at the time. The article need not be quoted here as its contents are not essential to the purposes of this volume, but the interested and curious are referred to the issue of *The Practical Christian* named, to be found in the Hopedale Public Library.

It will have been observed that in the re-construction of our social edifice the name by which we had been designated as an independent body from the beginning, *Fraternal Community, No. 1*, was superseded by *The Hopedale Community*, which we were destined to bear ever afterward. This was done in the interest of greater directness and simplicity. Our original scheme, in its over-confident comprehensiveness, provided for an indefinite number of Communities, scattered far and wide throughout the land and world, which were to be co-ordinated and organically united in a great ecumenical federation styled "The Practical Christian Communion," of which each Community was an integral, subordinate part, with certain rights, privileges, and immunities distinctively its own. (See page 27.) We had now come to the conclusion that we had attempted to build on too large a scale; that it were the part of wisdom to be more modest in our pretensions and claims; that it were better for us with our limited resources of men and means, and with our none too large equipment of moral and spiritual

ammunition, to confine our ambition and our efforts for
the present to our own single experiment, and to address
ourselves chiefly if not wholly to the task of carrying that
forward to an ultimate triumphant and universally acknowledged success. And as a step — the first step perhaps
in the line of that policy — we deemed it advisable to
count ourselves no longer the initial or head of a vast
procession of regenerated social enterprises, placarding
that assumption on the very frontlet of our petty undertaking, but to stand in our own lot, independent and
unrelated, attending to our own duties, working out our
own destiny, under our own unpretentious, proper name,
"The Hopedale Community," leaving all succeeding movements in the same behalf to the efforts of other laborers
in the vineyard of the Lord, to the activities of a wiser
and better future, and to the beneficent providence of
Almighty God.

Under the newly adopted Constitution, a Board of
Trustees consisting of Adin Ballou, E. D. Draper, Horatio Edson, and Almon Thwing, was immediately elected
to take the place of the old Executive Council in the
general conduct of secular affairs, their term of service
expiring at the next Annual Meeting, Jan. 12, 1848.
Daniel S. Whitney was chosen Recorder for the same
period. The Trustees entered at once upon the discharge
of the difficult duties to which they were called. They
organized on the same day they were chosen by making
ADIN BALLOU, *President;* ALMON THWING, *Secretary;* and
E. D. DRAPER, *Treasurer;* and voted to appraise such
property of the Community as might be rented or sold
for the common benefit. They also decided that the new
industrial regime should go into operation on Monday,
the 26th inst., nine days afterward. Meanwhile they sold
outright the printing press, stock, and fixtures, to Adin
Ballou; the card-setting machines, stock, and appliances,
to Clement O. Read; the stock and tools of the boot

and shoe department, to David Beal; the transportation business, including horses, carriages, and appurtenances, to Charles H. Price; the painting and glazing department with its belongings, to Samuel S. Brown; the medical department with its dues, to Butler Wilmarth, M. D.; and *The Practical Christian* with its subscription list and what was owing thereon, also to Adin Ballou. The mechanic shop with its machinery and fixtures, they rented for a definite period to Horatio Edson; the saw-mill and fixtures, to E. D. Draper; the machine shop, etc., to Almon Thwing and Joseph B. Bancroft. The farm they retained for their own general management by the appointment of a proper agent or overseer, also the Community store. A few members or approved residents carried on business on their own account.

Soon afterward steps were taken to have the Community shops and other buildings with their contents insured, and Adin Ballou was chosen a committee to complete the laying out, plotting, and numbering of the cemetery lots, and to put everything pertaining thereto into proper and permanent form, agreeably to the orders passed some two years before. Certain new roads were laid out and submitted to the authorities of the town of Milford for acceptance as public highways; and some pieces of old road rendered needless thereby were discontinued.

Flowage Complaints. Two of our neighbors, Mr. Eli Chapin on the north and Mr. Nathaniel Bennett on the south, complained of the injury done to their lands by reason of the Community mills and the dams connected therewith, both of the parties placing the damages at what we deemed an unreasonably high figure. The contention of the former was that the water in our upper pond submerged a considerable tract of valuable meadow, killing out the grass and working harm to the growth of small wood along its borders. That of the latter was that the saw-dust, shavings, and other refuse matter, were floated down stream from our shops and lodged on his premises along the banks, to his serious annoyance and detriment. Adin Ballou and E. D. Draper were chosen a Committee to see the parties and effect if possible a settlement, either by the purchase of the lands or by satisfactory pecuniary indemnification. Friendly negotiations were opened with Mr. Chapin and an amicable arrangement was made with very little difficulty — the land in question, some ten acres, being purchased by us at a price mutually acceptable. We were less fortunate with our other neighbor, Mr. Bennett. We had some time before tried to buy his land but he was unwilling to sell. We had offered him peace-money, believing that he had suffered no real loss, but he refused to take it. We had then agreed to leave the matter to three referees, allowing him virtually the choice of persons. We now met the referees with him, each party presenting its side of the case. The decision was that he had no claim against us. Though in honor bound to accept it, he refused, and the difficulty remained a cause of irritation and vexation for several years afterward. Another reference and its award resulted in our obtaining possession of the territory involved.

Hopedale Juvenile Community. Early in the year now being reviewed there was effected at my suggestion and with my assistance an organization among our older and more mature boys bearing the above somewhat ostentatious designation. The occasion of this action was that considerable disquietude had arisen among this class of our population and some of their seniors, on account of their irregular employment when out of school, and frequent complaints of their lawless ways and growing disregard of proper authority. As they were always respectful toward me and ready to listen to my advice, I called them together for consultation upon the matter, proposing to them a scheme for employing themselves in some effective way when not otherwise engaged. They readily assented and an association was formed accordingly, duly officered, and put in working order. Several acres of land for gardening and tillage were set apart for their use and other facilities granted as an encouragement in their undertaking. The project worked well and happily for a few years, fulfilling all reasonable expectations and then passing away amid the fluctuations with which we were unescapably beset.

Hopedale School District. Two or three years after the settlement at Hopedale application was made to the town of Milford, to whose taxable property we were making substantial annual contribution, for some act on its part whereby we might receive a portion of the money we paid into its treasury to aid us in the education of our children under our own management, or be set off as a separate school district, with such restrictions as should be just and equitable in respect to all concerned. A vote was passed to return us three fourths of the amount of our taxes, as nearly as it could be ascertained. At a subsequent meeting the vote was rescinded on the ground that it was illegal to disburse school money in any way except to regularly constituted school districts. Several attempts were afterward made in the same behalf, but to no effective purpose. At length in the autumn of the year now in review a new petition was presented to the town, asking that the village of Hopedale and the surrounding territory within certain limits with the inhabitants dwelling thereon might be set off as a district by itself for educational purposes, agreeably to the established forms of law. The question of granting the request came up for consideration at a meeting held Nov. 22d, when, after a lengthy discussion in which I as representative of the Community took part, it was decided in the affirmative by a very large majority, thus consummating a long-delayed act of justice to a peaceable, law-abiding, and every way honorable portion of its population. Our entire Community truly appreciated this token of friendliness on the part of their fellow-townsmen and lost no favorable opportunity of reciprocating the same.

As a matter of personal interest to myself and for the general information of my readers, I may say that *The Practical Christian* and everything appertaining thereto, as before indicated, came with the new regime into my sole and individual possession, and that thereafter for a time I had the management, not only of the editorial department but of its publication and financial interests, entirely in my own hands. Yet I was always disposed and happy to give place in its columns to the contributions of my ministerial brethren and former associates on its staff of writers, as I was to other reputable correspondents at home or abroad, even though they played the part of critics and detractors of myself personally or of the cause which I felt myself called upon to uphold and defend. Having been relieved for the most part of those secular cares and labors which for some months had engaged so much of my time and attention and which came near crushing me utterly, I was in a position to devote myself more exclusively, as was my desire, to the general service of my fellow-men, by the proclamation of the great principles of Practical Christianity far and wide as possible through the press, the pulpit, and the lecture platform, and by urging their application to all the activities and relationships of human life. To the labors thus opened anew to me I addressed myself with all the diligence, single-mindness, and enthusiasm I could command.

The year 1847 was one of general health on our Community domain, although one of our number, Mrs. Abigail Draper Cook, wife of Br. Wm. W. Cook, who had never been vigorous and strong, fell into a confirmed decline in the spring which resulted fatally on the 22d of July.

She was but 27 years of age, a most estimable woman, of an amiable, devout, Christlike spirit, much beloved in life, and in death deeply lamented.

The sixth Annual Meeting of the Community was held on the 13th day of January, 1847. It passed off quietly, a somewhat subdued and undemonstrative tone characterizing its various proceedings. The experiences of the preceding year, though in no wise undermining or weakening our faith in the justice and intrinsic excellence of our cause or in its ultimate triumph in the world, did have a tendency to awaken no little distrust of ourselves, of our adaptation to and fitness for the sublime work in which we were engaged, and of the material at our command with which to build, upon the sure foundations laid in our "Declaration," the divine kingdom of "righteousness, peace, and joy." So we received and accepted the simple financial statement of the Board of Trustees, Reports of Committees, etc., in a calm, dispassionate state of mind, reserving our enthusiasm and manifestations of confidence and hope to a more auspicious day.

Our official servants under the new administration of affairs were few in number and their election was easily and quickly effected. On the first balloting, ADIN BALLOU, EBENEZER D. DRAPER, HORATIO EDSON, and ALMON THWING, who as members of the old *Board of Trustees* had inaugurated and directed thus far satisfactorily the existing system of operations, were unanimously chosen to fill the same position for the ensuing year, while DANIEL S. WHITNEY was re-elected *Recorder*. Thus equipped for active service the Community started out on the seventh year of its history.

CHAPTER VI.

1848–1850.

Education — Amusements — P. C. Ministry — Lyceum —
Industrial Army — Savings Bank — Water
Cure Infirmary, Etc.

UNDER the newly adopted Constitution, which was
much briefer and more general in its provisions
than the preceding one, the management of the secular
affairs of the Community was assigned almost exclusively
to a Board of Trustees, who were to account directly to
the whole body of their fellow-associates for the faithful
discharge of the duties pertaining to their official position.
Other interests were to be guarded, conserved, and promoted by such acts of special legislation in the form of
Resolves, By-Laws, Rules and Regulations, from time to
time, as the public and private need, determined by practical wisdom and experience, might seem to demand.
Some of these were held to be of primary and indispensable importance, requiring early attention, and they were
brought to notice, duly considered, and definitely acted
upon accordingly. It was not our intention or our habit,
at any period of our history, to allow any important
matter of whatever nature to suffer detriment by neglect
or default.

Pursuant to that policy, the Community at its Annual
Meeting spoken of at the close of the last chapter, in
consideration of the mutual obligations understood to be
imposed upon and voluntarily assumed by the members in
their organic relations to each other and to the whole

body, passed a declaratory resolve establishing that point of duty beyond all question, doubt, or peradventure. It affirmed that the Constitution in its essential spirit, character, and purpose, " is a mutual guaranty between all its members and a solemn pledge that they will never permit one of their number to suffer any serious evil for want of fairly compensated employment, or the necessaries of life when unable to earn them, or the decent education of children."

At the same meeting a special By-Law was enacted providing for the education of all the children resident on the Community domain and such others in the vicinity as might be received by the proper authorities under suitable restrictions, as a matter of public policy, at the public expense. The Preamble asserted the general duty enjoined upon the members in this regard by the Constitution, while the enactment proper prescribed " that a uniform and perpetual contribution of one per cent. should be levied annually on the net income of all the members and dependants over twenty-one years of age, for educational and kindred purposes." Also " that a Board of Education and Mental Improvement consisting of at least three responsible persons should be annually chosen to have charge of these matters." This Board was designed to supersede the " Intendant of Education, Arts, and Sciences " provided for in the original plan of the undertaking and holding office during the preceding years. Its first members consisted of Adin Ballou, Daniel S. Whitney, and Clement O. Read. The new regime served to distribute the responsibility pertaining to the educational department of the Community somewhat while placing it at the same time under more active and efficient supervision.

With the inauguration of the new system in the administration of our educational interests and instrumentalities, our public school was placed in the immediate tuitional charge of my daughter, Abbie S. Ballou, under whose direction it began at once to manifest signs of marked improvement, and ere long attained a rank second to none in all the region round about for efficiency of discipline, for thoroughness of instruction, and for arousing in the minds of the pupils an interest in study and an ambition to excel, not only in book knowledge and the essentials of intellectual culture, but no less in morals and manners, — in whatsoever pertained to an enlargement and ennoblement of character and life. The school, which had been in continuous operation from an early date in our history, had suffered somewhat from inexperienced and unskillful teachers, but more from frequent changes in the instructor's chair; such changes interfering with orderly methods of training in every department of school activity and indisposing the children to that regular, systematic, persevering, continuous application of the faculties concerned to the work in hand which is essential to success. The new teacher was fresh from the State Normal School at West Newton, since removed to Framingham, then in charge of one of the foremost educators of his time in Mass., Rev. Cyrus Pierce. To her natural fitness for the position and her previous attainments in scholarship she had added the results of a full course of instruction in the art of teaching at that admirable institution, the whole being reinforced by an enthusiasm which that renowned preceptor was wont to impart to or awaken in those who come under his inspiring influence. She remained at the head of the school not only during the entire period covered by this chapter but for several years thereafter, acquiring for herself in her chosen calling and for her school a reputation highly commendable and rarely equaled in those days. Both received the cordial approbation and praise of our own Board of Education from year to year, as they did of the Supervising Committee of the town of Milford, who were by no means predisposed to overestimate anything pertaining to Hopedale, educational or otherwise.

Amusements. The subject of amusements was introduced among us at an early day and became a somewhat frequent theme of private and public discussion, though at no time one of excited and sharp controversy. The necessity of some kind of recreation or merry-making, especially for our children and youth, was generally acknowledged, though we were inclined to regard many of the popular forms of entertainment and frolicry with suspicion and hesitancy — some of them with extreme aversion — on account of what was deemed their immoral tendency and effect. We felt that whatever practices of this sort were instituted or allowed within our jurisdiction must be at least innocent and morally heathful, and, if possible, conducive of elevating and salutary effects upon those engaging in them — in happy accordance with our professed standard of faith and righteousness. But we learned by experience that it was no easy task to realize our ideal in this respect. We found it difficult to devise modes of diversion and merriment wholly unobjectionable in themselves and satisfactory to the participants; still harder to regulate them and prevent them from running into reprehensible excesses and abuses; and almost impossible to thoroughly Christianize them in all their bearings. The great desideratum was to exclude all enervating frivolity, all unseemly vulgarity, all rough and brutal conduct, and to so combine physical, intellectual, and moral exercises and gratifications as to promote and not subvert the great ends of personal improvement and social order. We succeeded in this particular fairly well; not as perfectly as we wished, but about as we did in other departments of activity pertaining to our comprehensive undertaking.

By a sort of elective affinity or personal fitness for the position as well as by general consent, Br. Daniel S.

Whitney, while he remained with us, became a kind of
Purveyor of Amusements; providing ways and means of
interesting and pleasing both young and old, getting up
entertainments, festivals, and gala-days at irregular intervals as circumstances might permit or suggest, and arranging exercises of various kinds — sports, games, recitations,
tableaux, dramatics, singing, etc., to gratify and delight
whomsoever might be in attendance to participate in or
witness them. While most of these were of incidental or
casual occurrence, two of them had a more fixed and
institutional character, taking place on the first day of
May and at Christmas time annually, and hence called
our May Day and Christmas Festivals respectively. A
long account of one of the first of these, held May 1,
1848, was given in a letter from the then widely-known
reformer, Henry C. Wright, who was present, to his
friend and fellow-laborer in the cause of humanity, Philip
P. Carpenter of Warrenton, England, and published in
The Practical Christian of May 13. After detailing and
commenting upon what he sees and hears and feels, the
writer near the close says: "It is pleasant to witness
and enjoy the scene. Children and parents are here
sympathizing together in their amusements. How much
more rational, useful, and Christian these than others in
which men and women often indulge with the justification
of the orthodox world." "I believe this is as innocent
as any meeting and far more improving and Christianizing
than those in which a pro-war, pro-slavery, brutalizing
religion is instilled into men's minds and hearts. Scenes
like those of this occasion make us all better men and
women." "The Festival is about to close. It has been
a warm and kindly interchange of true, tried, and loving
hearts. They are blest in themselves, in each other, and
in God; and may they ever remain so."

The following hymn written for this particular occasion
by D. S. Whitney was sung with great enthusiasm and

glee, the children dressed in white with bouquets in their hands taking the principal part, while the congregation at large joined in the chorus.

" WILDWOOD FLOWERS.

" We've been in search of wildwood flowers
  In Hopedale glens and shady bowers,
      And gathered each a fair bouquet
      To celebrate this festal day.

"CHORUS:

" And why should we not love the flowers
  That grow about this Dale of ours;
      Sweet tokens they will ever prove
      Of our dear Father's precious love.

" How beautiful the flowers that spring !
  What rapture to our hearts they bring !
      And silent though their language be,
      It ever teaches purity.

" CHORUS: — And why should we, etc.

" We hope by patient toil to know
  Where each one dwells and when in blow,
      Its order and its class declare,
      And what its curious habits are.

" CHORUS: — And why should we, etc.

" We've twined these wreaths of flowers to be
  A symbol meet of unity;
      With cords of faith and bonds of love
      We're girt around and interwove.

" CHORUS: — And why should we, etc.

" The rose when crushed gives back perfume —
  To blossoms, fragrance follows soon;
      Fair rose, thou lovely Christian flower,
      Like thee we'd be in trial's hour.

" CHORUS: — Then why should we, etc."

Industrial Affairs. These were administered during the period now in review under a mixed but not altogether satisfactory policy, and various changes and modifications were made from time to time to meet some special exigency that had arisen, to promote the general harmony, and secure desirable financial results. A few branches of business were carried on in the name of the Community under the direction of managers appointed and supervised by the Trustees, but most of them by private parties or co-partnerships to which they had been rented or sold, as provided for by recent enactments. But human imperfection in its various forms and manifestations could not be suppressed or transcended by any legal or artificial devices, nor by any manipulation of social arrangements. The troubles that confronted us were generated, not by our general system or prescribed industrial polity; they were the spontaneous outcome of human nature itself, in its then existing stage of development, under the then existing circumstances amid which it was placed. There were so many interests to be guarded and conserved, so many wheels of activity to be kept in motion, all liable to more or less friction in some of their bearings, that abrasion, inharmony, and consequent difficulty, were sooner or later inevitable. Temptations from within one's own breast or from the prevailing social status round about us were likely to cause one to swerve, perhaps unintentionally and unconsciously, from that straight unwavering line of duty to which we had each and all of us pledged steadfast and unfaltering allegiance. Persons favored with the privilege of conducting business on their own account and entrusted with facilities for doing so were easily led to adopt the questionable customs of the outside world, seek profitable jobs without regard to their moral quality, employ objectionable help, and turn out defective work; or indulge in sharp practices with their brethren and employes. Com-

munity managers were sometimes thought to require too
much of their subordinates or to be too domineering and
ungracious towards them.   Members and probationers were
admitted to our fellowship from unworthy motives —
motives other than devotion to our test principles, love
for the cause we had espoused, and a desire to attain a
better life for themselves and for all mankind.   Moreover,
our lack of money to carry on business successfully, to
meet our obligations promptly, to relieve the burden of
debt we had injudiciously incurred, to introduce new and
promising industries, and to purchase desirable lands
offered us on the outskirts of our domain, was a cause
of embarrassment, sometimes of irritation and ill feeling.

These and other matters not needful to mention furnished
occasion for frequent comment, criticism, long-drawn-out
discussions, dissatisfactions, and even for withdrawals
from our membership.   There were connected with them
no open and flagrant wrongs to be rebuked and condemned, very few small ones, and scarcely any that could
be regarded as intentional and reprehensible.   In most
cases a little reasonable consideration, forbearance, and
patience would have obviated all difficulty and healed
every breach of confidence and good feeling.   A careful
and conscientious personal application and use of our test
principles would have smoothed many a rough place in
our Communiiy experience and carried us safely and
happily over many a turbulent and distressful tide.   It
was largely for the purpose of promoting such an application and use of our test principles and to secure a
greater self-control and a greater equipoise of character
that the Community voted, Oct. 28, 1848, to "hold
monthly meetings hereafter for Christian discipline and
improvement."   Unlike our regular gatherings for purposes
of public worship on Sunday, or our Thursday evening
conferences, these monthly convocations were designed to
consider and take action upon such instances of more or

less reprehensible conduct on the part of members as might have been made public, to correct existing abuses, to allay strife and bitterness, to reconcile alienated feeling, to restore harmony when broken or disturbed, and to apply the proper remedy to all known offences and misdemeanors; and also to talk over in an informal, friendly, and confidential way whatever was calculated to help repress and hold in check the lower tendencies of human nature, overcome bad habits, resist temptation, stimulate the better nature, and develop in all our souls the graces and powers of the Christian character and life. They were to be fraternal tribunals for obtaining judgment upon overt acts of folly and wrong, and at the same time schools for mutual discipline and culture in the things that pertain to the kingdom of God.

It was in the year 1848 that a Steward was elected for the first time, whose duty it was to provide for the proper accommodation and orderly convenience of our regularly established public meetings, and for all gatherings of a distinctively moral, religious, or philanthropic character. And to bring out whatever latent talent there might be among us, and especially if it was associated with religious conviction and aspiration, it was at the same time voted "that all members of this Community who feel it a privilege or a duty to deliver original or selected discourses in our Chapel on the first day of the week be invited to do so at their convenience, communicating a notice of their wishes to the Steward in season to have announcement of the same made two weeks in advance." This action resulted in securing a considerable amount of lay preaching to supplement and reinforce that of the regular ministry, as long as the Community continued to exist. It was also voted "that regular discourses, original or selected, not exceeding ordinarily thirty minutes in length, be delivered morning and afternoon every first day of the week" and that "all the members and dependants of the Community young and old not prevented by indispensable duties or otherwise justifiably excused ought to attend our religious meetings " regularly.

In order to secure systematic and effective methods of operation in the department of Religion, Morals, and Missions at home and abroad, and for the purpose of establishing a body to which young men and others sympathizing with our distinctive form of Christian faith and duty and desiring to become teachers and promulgators of its ideas, principles, and requirements, could attach themselves by appropriate formalities and so be legitimately inducted into the work of preaching the Gospel, our already ordained clergymen early this year formed an Association to be called *The Practical Christian Ministry*. Their position as religious, moral, and philanthropic propagandists was clearly set forth in the Preamble of a Constitution under which they organized for active service in their chosen field of labor, as follows :

" In establishing this Ministry we assume no spiritual supremacy, exclusive dignity or ecclesiastical authority whatsoever over others; disclaiming all right of forbidding them to teach or obliging them to hear us; and asking no other countenance in the prosecution of our mission than such as the reason and conscience of kindred minds shall freely accord. Nor in entering this Association and declaring our present convictions of truth, duty, and expediency, do we foreclose future progress or merge individual responsibility in the organization or make secession from us a sin."

The instrument then proceeds to state in detail the essential beliefs or doctrines which the Ministry was intended to represent and proclaim, its primary objects, its leading measures, and its order of membership, organization, and internal discipline. It also provided that a General Convention of the body should be held once a year during the week next preceeding the Autumnal Equinox and that its officers should be a General Directory,.

to consist of at least three persons, a Secretary, Treasurer, and such others as might from time to time be deemed necessary. At its original organization Adin Ballou, Wm. H. Fish, and Daniel S. Whitney were chosen as the Directory; Wm. H. Fish as Secretary; and Adin Ballou as Treasurer and General Agent.

Among the primal duties and paramount objects of this Ministry, next to that of promulgating the essential truths and insisting upon the practical exemplification of the absolute duties taught by Jesus Christ, was that of uniting in one general Practical Christian Communion all those in the community at large who should heartily embrace and be ready to make open confession of those truths and duties. In the practical development of this scheme, those members of the general Communion dwelling in any given town or neighborhood, and hence in convenient nearness to each other, formed a subordinate branch of the main body, called an Inductive Communion which was designated by the name of the locality where it existed. The Inductive Communion was a sort of primary school of personal religious culture and of Practical Christian Sociology, in which the several members formally enrolled expressed a desire to place themselves under social religious influences calculated to enlighten their minds, quicken their consciences, regenerate their hearts, and conform their moral characters to the divine requirements. They also accepted the statement of faith and duty embodied in the "Declaration" of the original Practical Christian Communion organized Jan. 27, 1841, (see page 28) with the following definite pledge appended, to wit:

"And, trusting that the work of spiritual regeneration has effectually commenced in my heart by the exercise of sincere repentance toward God and faith in his Son, Jesus Christ, I will earnestly endeavor to lead a true life according to the foregoing acknowledgement of duty; to walk in unity with all my fellow disciples of this Communion wherever I may have intercourse with them; to contribute liberally of my temporal goods toward the prevention of poverty, ignorance, and vice, and for the dissemination of the principles and spirit of Practical Christianity; and to co-operate cordially in establishing local Practical Christian Communities so constituted as to harmonize the interests and obligations of the members without destroying their proper individual freedom, enterprise, and responsibility."

Several organizations were formed under this general plan and entered at once upon the specific lines of activity respectively belonging to them. They flourished for several years or until the fatal collapse of the Community itself in 1856, and indeed for some time afterward, and wrought an excellent and most beneficent work, both within our own borders and throughout a wide extent of territory in the world outside, in behalf of a purer form of Christian doctrine and a grander type of a Christian life, personal and social, than had ever been proclaimed among men since the days of the great Teacher himself.

The Practical Christian Ministry, taking the place of the Intendant of Religion, Morals, and Missions, had charge of the various meetings and appliances established and employed at home for the quickening and nurture of the moral and spiritual energies of all classes of our population, while frequent and sometimes widely extended excursions abroad in the interest of the principles and cause for which it stood distinctively and of universal Reform, were planned and consummated under its general supervision. Our system of Quarterly Conferences passed into the hands of the General Communion, and was maintained with no falling away of numbers, of interest, and of enthusiasm. The convocations held under its auspices as aforetime were seasons of refreshing and of a renewed life to those attending them and to the communities where they were held; the preaching, the exhortation, the singing — all the exercises being " not with enticing words of man's wisdom, but in demonstration of the Spirit and of power; That our faith should not stand in the wisdom of men but in the power of God." The Inductive Communions which were instituted wrought effectually among young people, inquirers, novitiates, and sympathizing friends, in the way of indoctrinating them in the things of the divine kingdom and of qualifying them for efficient service in the work of building up that kingdom on the earth. The design of all these associations was highly useful and commendable, and their organic mechanism in our comprehensive scheme of human regeneration was well fitted to carry that design out to a full accomplishment. They only lacked the men and the means adequate to that humane and sublime result — a lack which a wiser and better future in the providence of God will no doubt supply.

At the Annual Meeting of the Community held Jan. 10, 1849, it appeared from the Financial Report of the Board of Trustees that the industrial operations for the year ending Dec. 31, 1848, had been fairly successful, furnishing no occasion on that score for lamentation or regret — no occasion to doubt that under wise and prudent management we were in the way of acquiring a well-earned and assured material success; indeed we had already acquired such a success, notwithstanding all the hindrances and drawbacks we had encountered. To be sure, the figures of the report as it was first presented did not give a sufficient balance of receipts over expenditures to enable us to pay our Joint-Stock capital the stipulated interest of four per cent. But no account had been taken of the considerable increase in value of our real estate by reason of the improvements made thereon, and when this had been duly estimated — an act that was justified by a sound financial policy and the facts in the case — the deficit was cancelled and the prescribed dividend was declared. The Community officials for the ensuing year were: ADIN BALLOU, *President;* LEMUEL MUNYAN, *Recorder;* ADIN BALLOU, EBENEZER D. DRAPER, HORATIO EDSON, ALMON THWING, and WILLIAM W. COOK, *Trustees;* ADIN BALLOU, CLEMENT O. REED, and EDMUND SOWARD, *Board of Education;* ASAPH G. SPALDING, *Steward.*

At an adjourned meeting held the second Wednesday in February it was " voted, that the order, prosperity and good faith of the Community demand that the rule adopted last year requiring monthly settlements be strictly adhered to in all business transactions." Also, " that the Trustees be requested to make arrangements for the regular transportation of the mail, and that letters and papers be taxed to pay the expense thereby incurred." The nearest U. S. Post Office was in the village of Milford, a mile and a half distant, and the plan hitherto adopted for the transmission of our mail matter to and fro having become inadequate and unsatisfactory it was deemed advisable to institute measures that would insure a more regular, definite, and acceptable administration of this department of the public service. A fixed Post Office pursuant to the foregoing vote was established, a Post Master appointed, and this important interest was thereafter cared for in a business-like way, though of course at the expense of those convenienced thereby, as before indicated.

In order to supplement the amount of money received from the town and other sources for educational purposes and extend the length of our school, as well as to supply it with greatly needed apparatus, the Trustees were instructed " to levy a tax of one and one-half per cent. instead of one per cent. as heretofore, upon the net income of members and probationers, to be expended under the direction and according to the best judgment of the Board of Education."

Steps were also taken at this time which shortly after resulted in the establishment of a Community Lyceum,—an institution that continued in active operation many years and proved to be an efficient and highly creditable educational force among all classes of our population. It was carried on under the auspices of the Community and by direction of the Board of Education, though it had its own independent organization, electing its own officers, and managing, within proper limits, its own distinctive affairs. The Board was authorized to furnish it with accommodations and facilities for carrying on its legitimate work, expending money in its behalf, if their judgment so dictated; but they were to see that it performed its legitimate functions, maintained a wholesome discipline, and so conducted its activities as to promote the real progress of its members in useful knowledge. Its meetings were held once a month from the first of April to the first of October, and once a week during the remainder of the year, the exercises of which were many and various, consisting of Lectures, Debates, Compositions, Readings, Recitations of Classes pursuing different branches of study, etc., interspersed with vocal and instrumental music. This institution was maintained for many years among us, received the encouragement and support of most of our people, and proved of great value as a means and stimulant of intellectual training and culture.

As a matter of permanent public policy and for the purpose of beautifying and rendering attractive our young and growing village, a Resolve was passed Feb. 20, 1849, requiring the owners of house-lots therein to set out and properly care for either forest or fruit trees along that portion of the street upon which their several estates respectively fronted. The same rule was observed by those having in charge lots belonging to the Community itself. As a result of this action our village in a few years became a gem among the rural boroughs of the

Commonwealth of Massachusetts, — its streets, well-graded avenues overarched with the outstretching branches of thickly planted maples, elms, etc., on either hand; its dwellings, embowered in the abundant foliage amid which they stood and thickly engirdled with shrubbery and flowers of multiform kind and coloring. The passing years lying between then and now, with the continued growth, culture, and improvement that have been going on, have only argumented and heightened the prevailing loveliness and fascination of the scene.

In the interest of morality, good manners and the truest culture it was enacted on 8th day of April " that the parents of children and those who have children from abroad residing in their families be required to see that those under their care refrain from all profanity, from all vulgarities in word or action, and from all obscene utterances or writings; that in their recreations they indulge in no habits of injuring, annoying or vexing their playmates; that they never leave the Community domain without the consent of their parents or guardians; that they retire from their sports to their respective homes by 8 o'clock P. M. " Parents and guardians were also enjoined " to have a watchful care over their children during hours of meeting both in and around the house where it is held, and to see that their conduct is such as becomes the place and occasion, — such at all times as will reflect honor upon themselves and the Community."

About this time incipient measures ripening into an early fulfilment were instituted for the formation of what was at first termed an *Industrial Army*, afterwards changed to *Industrial Union*, the nature and purpose of which may be understood by presenting a copy of the more important portions of the Enactment establishing the same, which reads as follows:

"Section 1. In order to promote the cheerful prosecution of public improvements and a generous assistance of persons needing occasional aid, all the members, probationers, and dependants of this Community capable of useful service, are hereby constituted a co-operative body to be called *The Hopedale Industrial Army.*

"Sec. 2. This Industrial Army shall be organized in two general Departments: a Male and Female Department. Each Department shall have power to determine and adjust its own roll of members, form such divisions, elect such officers and establish such rules as may from time to time be deemed promotive of its orderly, energetic, harmonious and successful operation. . . . .

"Sec. 3. Whenever the Male Department of this Army shall make requisition for the use of any working vehicles, teams, implements, or alien employees of the Community, such requisition shall be promptly complied with; provided, always, that at least three days' notice shall be given to the superintendent or manager in charge of such vehicles, etc.; and provided also that no serious detriment shall be done to the Community property by insisting on such requisition."

The agency thus created and empowered came to be of great service in developing plans promotive of the public welfare and in carrying into effect the stated or implied pledges of the Constitution. Its Female Department found much to do in caring for and helping individuals and families that, by reason of sickness, misfortune, or otherwise, were brought into circumstances of dependence and need, thus obviating the necessity in numerous cases of presenting demands upon the common treasury for means of relief or in any way making public the exigencies to which improvidence or adversity or injustice may have brought those who silently or openly appealed to our sympathy and friendliness for aid. While the Male Department was even more busy in projecting and executing improvements of one sort or another calculated to contribute to the convenience, comfort, pleasure, and happiness of all classes of our people. By this instrumentality most of our sidewalks were originally laid, numerous rough places about the village made smooth, and ugly features

13

of the landscape removed. Many trees on public grounds and in the streets were planted, and betterments multiplied on every hand. The most notable achievement of this arm of the public service was the laying out, grading, terracing, and adorning with trees and shrubbery, of Community Square, making it in most respects suitable and ready for the building of the then proposed house of worship upon it in 1860, some years afterward.

During the year now under review considerable addition was made to the Community Domain by the purchase of divers lands contiguous to our previous estate, amounting in the aggregate to about 130 acres, thus increasing our territorial possessions to more than 500 acres. The largest and by far the most important of these additions was that of the so-called "South Cook farm," containing with its outlying wood-lots some 65 acres. This lay directly south of our before acquired landed property, on the opposite side of the Mendon and Milford road, and was divided by the highway leading to South Milford, Bellingham, etc., and hence conveniently located for agricultural and horticultural purposes, to which it was admirably adapted by the nature of the soil and by careful husbandry in later years. We were now sole masters by legal title deeds of our little Mill River and nearly all the territory skirting it on both sides for about a mile in length, north and south, snugly ensconced between Magomiscock Hill in Milford on the east and Neck Hill along the border of Mendon on the west; as pleasant a location as could be reasonably desired for the purposes to which it was consecrated by us.

Another measure of public utility and of private thrift devised and put into practical operation this year was that comprised in an Enactment constituting the Community Treasury a Savings Bank "in which all persons residing on the general domain may deposit such parts of their earnings and income as they can conveniently lay aside for future use," subject to certain prescribed conditions and regulations, with a promised interest of four per cent. per annum. This was a wise and justly appreciated expedient, the beneficent results of which were equally apparent proportionally as are those of similar institutions in the financial economy of the world at large.

About the first of June there was issued from the Hopedale press a small volume of 224 pages, entitled *"The Hopedale Collection of Hymns and Songs for the use of Practical Christians."* It was compiled by myself and contained 316 devotional, moral, philanthropic, and reformatory pieces suitable for musical expression, arranged under eighteen different heads, and well adapted to further the great ends we were seeking to secure, and to fill an important place on all occasions of public convocation and in the more private circles of Christian nurture, instruction, and worship. The contents were mostly selections from the Hymnals and Psalmodies commonly used in the various branches of the Christian Church, though about fifty of them were written by different members of the Community, usually for some special occasion or to serve some special purpose. Some twenty of these were from my own pen and about a dozen each from the pens of Srs. Abby H. Price and Mary J. Colburn; the remaining six or eight coming from still other persons in our fellowship. Though urging no claims in their behalf to popular favor, on the ground of either poetical or literary merit, I yet deem it proper and fitting to put on record in these pages a few of these original productions, as illustrative of the spirit in which the work at Hopedale was carried on and of the means employed to nourish the better life in our own and each others souls, and to stimulate ourselves and others to a faithful discharge of the duties and obligations set forth and enjoined in the Gospel of Jesus Christ. I present them as they stand

in the volume from which they are taken, the number
in the collection, the meter, and name of the author
being prefixed.

"123. C. M. *Adin Ballou.*

"O Lord, our scanty faith we mourn,
  So languid weak and dim;
We scarce perceive the heavenly bourn,
  And faint in every limb.

"Far down thy holy mountain side,
  With Alps on Alps above,
Vast distances our tents divide
  From thy bright throne of love.

"How can we climb those rugged heights
  And gain those sinless skies,
Till grace our dormant will excites
  To grasp th' immortal prize.

"Rend off, O Lord, this sensual shroud
  That binds the torpid soul;
By faith eternal things uncloud
  And speed us to our goal.

"Then shall our darkness turn to light,
  Our rough ascent grow smooth,
And tottering weakness clothed with might
  At length triumphant prove."

"157. P. M. *A. Ballou.*

"God shall be all in all —
  And then shall marshalled warriors
  No more upon the plain
  Renew their battle fury
  To multiply the slain;
  Then shall the peaceful era
  By Zion's bards foretold,
  With all its promised glory,
  The ransomed world enfold.

"God shall be all in all —
  And then the horrid slaver
  Shall cross the waves no more,
  Defenceless men to ravish
  From Afric's injured shore;

And all the sable millions,
In bondage held abroad,
Present a grateful tribute
To their redeeming God.

" God shall be all in all —
The church long torn with faction
Will lay each quarrel by,
And all her jealous watchmen
See clearly eye to eye;
Attired in bridal garments
She'll take her Lord's right hand,
And, free from spot or wrinkle,
Fulfil his high command.

" God shall be all in all —
And then shall dark rebellion
Against his holy throne
Be hushed in endless silence
Where'er his name is known;
The all-prevailing Victor
Will make an end of sins,
And only yield the scepter
When perfect love begins."

" 212.   P. M.   O. Johnson.

" The bondmen are free in the isles of the main,
    The chains from their limbs they are flinging;
They stand up as men — never tyrants again
Their God-given rights in proud scorn shall profane —
    It is Liberty's song they are singing.
Hark, loud swells their strain o'er the foaming sea,
' Freedom! holy freedom! freedom, our joy is in thee.'

" That shout of the freed-men bursts sweet on our ears;
    Their hymn full of joy hear it swelling;
Their hearts throb with pleasure, their eyes fill with tears
As ends the hard bondage of many long years;
    Now exulant with pride they are telling,
' Free, free are we from the slave's hard yoke,
Freemen, faithful freemen — freemen, our fetters are broke.'

"Now praise to Jehovah, the might of his love
    At length o'er the foe is prevailing.
His truth was the weapon and by it we strove
In the light of his spirit sent down from above —
    Of his truth and his love never failing.
Thanks, thanks unto God! now the slave is free;
Freedom! holy freedom! Father, our thanks are to thee.

"O ye who are blest with fair Liberty's light,
    With courage and hope all abounding,
With weapons of love be ye bold for the right;
By the preaching of truth put oppression to flight;
    Then, your altars triumphant resounding,
Loud, loud let the anthem of joy ring out;
'Freedom! holy freedom!' let all the world hear the shout."

"254.   P. M.   *Mary J. Colburn.*

"Onward, though the world's impeding,
    Onward, every foe unheeding,
    Jesus now the cause is leading —
        He will be our guide;
    In his strength we'll conquer,
    In his strength we'll conquer,
    In his strength we'll conquer,
        For his truth is on our side.

"Not with earth's proud armor shielding,
    Not with carnal weapons wielding,
    These to mightier ones are yielding,
        Furnished from above;
    And we'll surely conquer,
        For our sword is truth and love.

"See the man of noble daring,
    Earth's proud laurels richly wearing,
    Leaving all and meekly sharing
        In this work of peace;
    Love will surely conquer,
        And all hate and war shall cease.

"Yes this earth though stained and gory,
    Filled with scenes of woe her story,
    Shall arise to former glory
        And God's light shall see;
    Light will surely conquer,
        Earth will have a Jubilee."

"262. 10's M. *Abby H. Price.*

"O thou blest Comforter! pure Spirit, hear!
  Bend we thy shrine before, trembling with fear;
    Hate like a shadow dark clouds all below,
    Love floats her shining bark o'er waves of woe.

"Spirit of Holy Power! give us thy light;
  And in the trial-hour — guide through the night;
    Gird us with strength and will, mighty to save,
    Striving with error still, valiant and brave.

"Keenly oppression's pain pierceth the weak;
  Help us the galling chains quickly to break;
    Earth's bitter founts of woe soon may we close,
    Making this world below bloom as the rose.

"Give thou thy Spirit free, Savior and Lord!
  Peace, love, and liberty follow thy word;
    While as a brother-band onward we move,
    Joy shall fill all the land gilded with love!"

The perplexities and disadvantages arising from the
great diversity of interests represented in the management
of business as it was carried on among us, causing more
or less friction between the several branches and the
different parties to whom they had been sold outright or
rented for a definite period, became so apparent towards
the close of the year and provoked so much criticism,
that, on the 28th of December, it was resolved that "it
is highly desirable that all kinds of business dependent
on Community facilities should as soon as practicable be
placed under Community management, and the Board of
Trustees are hereby instructed to govern themselves accordingly." It was exceeding difficult to find the exact mean
between too much and too little individual control in the
conduct of our leading industries, which would prove
pecuniarily advantageous to both the Community and the
employes, and whatever policy was at any time adopted,
despite all the reason, the persuasion, the diplomacy we
could bring to bear upon the matter, was likely to offend

the judgment, the taste, the idiosyncrasy, or perhaps the selfishness of some of the brethren and cause disaffection and loss of members. But this could not by any possibility be avoided, and we who were thoroughly and wholly committed to the cause of Social Reconstruction were obliged to submit with the best grace we could, though often to our great regret and sorrow. All this was illustrated in the case just spoken of, as will soon appear.

Another cause of trouble and anxiety was brought to notice about this time, requiring thoughtful consideration and decisive action on the part of the Community. The gradual multiplication and enlargement of our industrial activities on the farm, in the gardens, and in the shops, made it necessary to increase the number of workmen, who were often employed with too little regard to their moral character and the influence that they might exert upon our children and youth and even upon some of our adult population. It was found that in this way mischief was being done among us and that some of our most sacred interests were likely to suffer serious detriment unless a more careful and discriminating course was pursued in the matter. Whereupon, after due deliberation, the Community on the date last named

"*Resolved*, (1) That the protracted residence on the Community domain of persons who are not sympathetically interested in our objects, principles, and social order has a demoralizing tendency and ought not to be encouraged.

"*Resolved*, (2) That from and after the first day of April next no person, besides members, probationers, dependents, visiting friends, medical patients, nurses, or tenants holding under a contract prior to this date, shall be employed, boarded or harbored on the Community territory for a longer term of time than one month, unless by special vote of the Community.

"*Resolved*, (3) That the Recorder be instructed to open and keep a Book of Record with appropriate designations in which the names of all probationers and dependents (including all employes, whether engaged by the Community or individuals)

of this Community shall be duly entered, either by their own orders or those of their responsible friends, and also a minute of their discharge and the date when they ceased to sustain such relation."

Other less important resolves of the same nature aiming at the purification, homogeneity, harmony, and proper moral status of life within our borders were passed at the same meeting. We learned by repeated experience that in the new social order as in the old, "eternal vigilance is the price of liberty," especially of that "liberty wherewith Christ maketh free."

At the annual meeting held Jan. 9, 1850, the regular routine of business was followed with promptness and dispatch. Various reports of officers and special committees were read and accepted as conclusive and satisfactory. That of the Treasurer in behalf of the Board of Trustees represented our industrial affairs as in a healthful and promising condition, justifying existing methods of operation and inspiring confidence in the financial success of the movement. The old *President*, ADIN BALLOU, was re-elected, and ADIN BALLOU, E. D. DRAPER, and WM. H. HUMPHREY were chosen *Trustees;* WM. S. HEYWOOD was made *Recorder;* WM. H. FISH, C. O. REED, and EDMUND SOWARD constituted the new *Board of Education;* while A. G. SPALDING became *Steward* for another year. A Relief Committee was determined upon as a needed supplement to the pre-existing corps of official servants, and ADIN BALLOU, BUTLER WILMARTH, ALMIRA B. HUMPHREY, and ANNA T. DRAPER were elected to that position. At an adjourned meeting it was deemed advisable to have a Standing Community *Auditor*, "whose duty it should be to make frequent examination of the accounts of all branches of business carried on under Community auspices, keep himself informed concerning their actual and prospective condition, and once in three months report in detail to the Board of Trustees." Lemuel Munyan was chosen to the office.

In view of the increasing number of residents on our
Community domain as members, probationers, family
dependents, hired workmen, household servants, etc., and
therewith the increasing liability to the introduction among
us of some of the prevailing evils of ordinary human
society, whereby our children and youth would be con-
taminated, private and public virtue and happiness under-
minded, and our whole movement imperilled, it was about
this time deemed advisable to established a new Board
of officials, which should act as a kind of moral police
and judiciary in our social and civil economy. This was
accordingly done, the name of this Board being "The
Council of Religion, Conciliation, and Justice." It was
the prescribed duty of the Council to examine all applicants for membership and probationship in our body and
approve or disapprove them as they were deemed worthy
or unworthy, to recommend persons as permitted residents
on our territory, to maintain a scrupulous watchfulness
over the morals and manners of our entire population, to
apply proper restraints and correctives of existing wrongs
and misdemeanors, to hear and pass judgment upon
charges of ill-conduct of any sort, to arbitrate in cases
of controversy or serious disagreement, and in a general
way to exercise fraternal supervision and authority in all
matters pertaining to the moral and religious status and
welfare of all classes and conditions of people within our
borders. This official Board was accustomed to hold
monthly meetings for the proper discharge of the duties
assigned to it, and proved to be, while the Community
had a name to live and a power to exercise the functions
of a self-governing institution, an efficient and most helpful
arm of the public service. Its first members were Butler
Wilmarth, Lemuel Munyan, Wm. S. Heywood, Anna T.
Draper, and Phila O. Wilmarth.

In consequence of the new managemental policy adopted
the preceeding autumn as outlined a few pages back and

the modifications consequent thereon, six of our much
esteemed and highly useful members withdrew from our
membership and ere long removed from the place. The
ground of their action was not loss of faith in the distinctive principles on which our movement was based as
expressed in our "Declaration," nor in the Community
Idea as a solution of the great problem of Social Reform,
but, as one of them was pleased to phrase it, "too much
industrial consolidation, complexity and governmentalism."
Among those parting company with us at this time was
Bro. Daniel S. Whitney, the third of my original ministerial colleagues, and one upon whom I had relied with
great confidence as a man of intelligence, sterling recti-
tude, and honor, and as a reliable, trustworthy, unfaltering
co-worker in the cause of Practical Christian Socialism.
This step on the part of Bro. Whitney was the occasion
of profound regret, disappointment, and grief, on my part
and on the part of all his fellow-laborers, towards whom
he professed to cherish only sentiments of respect and
affection, charging none with any unfaithfulness to principle or duty as a reason for leaving them but ascribing
his act of retirement from Community membership to
"the industrial organization" which in his judgment was
productive of many evils and "cost more than it was
worth." Of the principles underlying the Hopedale movement he said, "I most thankfully accept them as the
truth of God. They are alike needful in their spirit and
power to redeem mankind, individually and socially."

And yet while he could not remain with the Community
in which those principles were acknowledged and made,
according to his own confession, the supreme law, by
reason of some real or supposed defect in their application and use, arising, not through any infidelity on the
part of his brethren but by error of judgment or lack of
insight into the bearing and tendency of things, which,
if it existed, they were most anxious to have remedied,

either by his superior wisdom and virtue or in some other way, — while he could not conscientiously remain with us under such circumstances, he could go back into existing society, where, as he had often asserted, they were systematically and persistently set at defiance and openly violated, engaging actively and without the least apparent scruple in the support or administration of a government whose fundamental law he had repeatedly declared to be hostile to and subversive of the government of God — "a covenant with death and an agreement with hell." His Hopedale brethren, kindly disposed as they were towards him, were hardly able to see the consistency, wisdom, or moral perspicuity of this, but he seemingly did, and acted accordingly. He continued much interested in special reform questions, became a frequent participant in local and general politics, was for a long time an earnest member of the Republican party, though for several of the last years of his life he affiliated as ally and adviser with the political Prohibitionists or Third Party men. He had the distinction of representing the town of Boylston, where he located about a year after leaving Hopedale, in the State constitutional convention of 1853, gaining therein considerable notoriety and honor for his manly and persistent advocacy of the claims of woman to the free exercise of the right of suffrage. Removing subsequently to Southborough, he was there a highly esteemed citizen, and held for many years the office of postmaster under the Republican supremacy at Washington. He died March 14, 1894, leaving a wife and two daughters, all of whom still survive.

The Hopedale Water Cure Establishment. The method of treating disease by a free and judicious use of pure water accompanied by a greatly diminished resort to drugs and medicines, usually termed Hydropathy, had a few adherents among us at an early day. Our genial, cautious, openminded, conscientious physician, Butler Wil-

marth, M. D., a skillful, successful practitioner of the
Allopathic school, quite incredulous at first of the new
system, was led to look carefully into its workings and
merits by witnessing the somewhat wonderful cure through
its agency of a little boy — the four year old son of
Bro. Wm. H. Fish — who had been stricken down with
a severe and alarming attack of scarlet fever. The result
of his investigation was a thorough conversion to and subsequent championship of its claims at home and abroad
wherever his voice could be heard. Having become fully
convinced of the essential efficacy of water as a remedial
agent, and the antidotes and restoratives employed in
connection therewith, he very soon started the project of
founding an Infirmary at Hopedale for the accommodation
and treatment of patients, however afflicted, according to
the principles and requirements of the Hydropathic system. The Community, to whose members he made an
appeal for approval and help as soon as his plans were
sufficiently mature, being favorably disposed towards the
undertaking, voted in April, 1850, "to appropriate $600.00
to establish a Water Cure Infirmary, provided new Joint-
Stock can be obtained" for that purpose. The funds
were forthcoming and the large double house built by
Amos J. Cook and Edmund Price, which had come into
the possession of the Community, was remodeled and
fitted up for the purpose indicated during the ensuing
summer. In the month of September it was opened to
the public agreeably to the terms stated in the following
advertisement :

"This Establishment is situated in the pleasant and peaceful village of Hopedale (Milford), Mass., and is under the care
of Dr. Butler Wilmarth, who, with his wife, will devote their
constant attention and services to restore to health all who
place themselves under their care as patients. *Terms:* $4 to $5
per week (payment weekly) exclusive of washing. Extra privi-

leges or attention will subject the patient to extra charges. Patients will furnish the usual articles for treatment.

B. WILMARTH, M. D.

Hopedale (Milford), Sept. 28, 1850.

This institution was something entirely new in this part of the country, as was its mode of treatment for the various ills which flesh is heir to, and hence failed of sufficient patronage to render it pecuniarily successful. It was therefore deemed expedient, after it had been open a few months, to close it and restore the building to its original uses. This decision was made with the entire approval of Dr. Wilmarth who had received a somewhat flattering offer to take charge of a similar establishment at New Graefenburg, N. Y., which had already acquired a good reputation and standing with the general public, and to that place he removed with his family in the spring of 1851, much to the regret of all of us, by whom he was held in sincere esteem as a truly Christian man and a physician of high degree.

Reconstruction of Land Titles. Early in the year now under notice it began to be feared by some of our number that the manner of transferring house-lots and other pieces of real estate in the Community was not altogether legal and sufficiently guarded to insure the holders against all possible future misunderstandings and complications. It was therefore deemed advisable to refer the whole matter to Ellis Gray Loring, Esq., of Boston, one of the most competent and experienced conveyancers in the Commonwealth of Massachusetts, and a good friend to all humanitary undertakings. This was accordingly done, and after a thorough investigation of the case in all its bearings, he gave it as his opinion that there was good reason for the growing disquietude in regard to it, and that there should be an entire recasting of our method of acquiring and transferring our landed property and its appurtenances. The titles by which I had come into

possession of the original Jones' farm were good beyond
all question, as were those by which I and others had
obtained additional territory by subsequent purchases.
There was no occasion for disturbing them or in any way
tampering with them. But all later action needed revision — needed to be put upon a new and invulnerable
basis. He therefore recommended that the Community
choose five of its most reliable members to be known as
Trustees of Real Estate, who, in their official capacity,
should execute a Declaration of Trust setting forth their
distinctive powers and obligations in due and lawful
form, and have it recorded in the Registry of Deeds for
the county of Worcester. These Trustees were to be the
legally constituted and recognized financial Agents of the
Community in all real estate transactions. He also recommended that all the members of the Community and others
concerned, whether nominal land owners or not, give a
quit-claim deed conveying all their right, title, and interest
in and to real estate within the limits of the town of
Milford, to some disinterested person, who should at once
quit-claim back again whatever of said property was outside of the Community to its respective and proper owners,
and all the rest pertaining to the Community domain to
the aforesaid Trustees, *as joint tenants and not as tenants
in common.* These Trustees should then distribute to the
previous purchasers of house-lots and other real property,
the pieces belonging to them, by regular legal conveyances, as they should whatever pieces might be disposed
of by regular sale in time to come. In this way each
land owner would be made secure in his title to his
estate, beyônd all doubt or peradventure. Before presenting this plan of obviating the existing difficulty to
the Community, Mr. Loring submitted it to the careful
examination and judgment of three other eminent conveyancers of Boston, who pronounced it adequate to the
exigencies to be provided for, and absolutely irrefragable.

These recommendations were gladly accepted and measures were at once taken to have them carried into effect. At a regular meeting of the Community, held May 1, the Board of Real Estate Trustees was chosen, consisting of ADIN BALLOU, E. D. DRAPER, WM. H. HUMPHREY, BUTLER WILMARTH, and ALMON THWING, who entered immediately upon the discharge of the duties assigned to them, and on June 1 the required instruments had been executed and transfers made and the entire real estate possessions pertaining to the Community were lodged in the hands of the legally constituted authorities, to be distributed, disposed of, and controlled, as equity and their best judgment might dictate. Thenceforward there was no trouble or anxiety on that score.

The service done to the Community in this matter by Mr. Loring was of great value and highly appreciated, but he rendered it gratuitously, out of a sincere friendship for us and our cause, refusing utterly the compensation we cheerfully proffered him. We could do no less than vote him an expression of heartfelt gratitude.

The establishing of a Trusteeship for the proper holding and management of real estate made it necessary for us to amend or change our Constitution and By-Laws somewhat, in order to have them conform to the new system and prevent all confusion and annoyance in respect to names of official Boards, etc. The most essential of these occurred in the third article of our fundamental basis of organization which was so modified as to read as follows :

ARTICLE III.

"SEC. 1. The Legislative powers of this Community shall be vested in the members thereof present and acting in regular Community meeting. The Executive powers not necessarily appertaining to the Trustees shall be vested in a President and Directory. The Directory shall consist of at least three members besides the President. The Judicial powers shall be vested in such tribunals as the Community may from time to time establish.

"Sec. 2. It shall be the duty of the Directory to conduct the prudential affairs, industrial operations and general interests of the Community in such a manner as to insure to every member, probationer and dependent, adequate employment, educational advantages and exemptions from the evils of poverty, ignorance and vice, and also at the same time, if possible, to secure to the Stockholders their capital unimpaired, with a clear annual profit thereon of four per cent."

Agreeably to the provisions of this Amendment the following named persons were on the 13th of July elected to serve in the official positions respectively indicated until their successors should be chosen at the next Annual Meeting in January, 1851, viz. : ADIN BALLOU, *President;* E. D. DRAPER, W. H. HUMPHREY, ALMON THWING, *Directors;* E. D. DRAPER, *Treasurer.*

Under the new auspices and methods of administration the Community became more homogeneous and consolidated than ever before, was more admirably and efficiently organized for the varied work it had in hand, and went forward on its mission with more substantial assurance of final success than had characterized any previous period of its history.

The Bennett Imbroglio Settled. One of the first acts of the new administration was to bring the long pending controversy with our neighbor, Nathaniel Bennett, already mentioned, to a successful termination. Time and reflection had mollified his temper considerably and led him to change his policy toward the Community. He had become willing to sell the so-claimed injured land to us, and to sell it for a sum, including the then present value of the property and past damages, to be determined by a Board of three Referees mutually agreed upon by both parties, their decision to be accepted and submitted to as final in the case. The Directory concurred in the proposition, and united heartily with Mr. Bennett in securing the end

14

in view at the earliest practicable date. The Referees
were Henry Chapin of Milford, Amariah Taft of Mendon,
and Wm. H. Cary of Medway. Pursuant to their award
of $272.67, rendered July 15, which included the
appraised value of four and a half acres of land, all
previous damages, and all possible future ones to adjoining property, we paid the sum named and received the
proper title deeds, and therewith exemption from any and
all contingent claims in time to come. The whole expense
to us, reckoning surveyor's fees, referees charges, and a
gratuity to Mrs. Bennett, was less than $280.00. The
conclusion of the matter was satisfactory to both parties
and was reached by a process much cheaper no doubt
for us, and probably for him, and better morally for all
concerned, than the world's stubborn, litigious method of
settling such controversies.

At the Annual Meeting of the Community, held Jan. 8,
1851, the opening exercises being concluded, the customary
required Reports were read and accepted. That of the
Treasurer, which was supplemented by statements from
the managers of the several branches of industry operated
under Community direction, represented the financial affairs
of the body as in a fairly prosperous condition, although
the profits accruing from the business activities of the
previous year were not sufficient to enable the Directory
to pay to Joint-Stock the contingently stipulated dividend
of four per cent. due for the past two years. The industrial and economical interests of the Community had been
well guarded and the several departments having them in
charge had worked harmoniously and efficiently, giving
promise of larger results and returns in the immediate
future. Good feeling prevailed and a hopeful spirit,
which were manifested by a cheerful readiness to adopt
measures for meeting all existing obligations and for
providing against possible deficits in years to come, as
will appear in the next chapter.

Officers elected at this meeting for the year 1851 were: ADIN BALLOU, *President;* E. D. DRAPER, W. H. HUMPHREY, A. THWING, D. B. CHAPMAN, *Directors;* E. D. DRAPER, *Treasurer;* WM. S. HEYWOOD, *Recorder;* ADIN BALLOU, WM. H. FISH, E. SOWARD, *Board of Education;* D. H. CARTER, *Steward;* W. W. COOK, HENRY FISH, LUCY H. BALLOU, B. WILMARTH, SYLVIA W. BANCROFT, *Council;* EDMUND SOWARD, ALMIRA B. HUMPHREY, S. S. BROWN, ABBIE J. SPALDING, *Relief Committee.*

CHAPTER VII.

1851–1853.

ICARIA — NEW LEGISLATION — EDUCATIONAL HOME —
RETIREMENT OF A. BALLOU — BEREAVE-
MENTS — FREE LOVE.

WHEN it was made to appear by the Report of the
Treasurer presented at the meeting referred to on
the last two pages that the proceeds of the industrial
operations for the year just closed were insufficient to
pay the dividends then due on the Joint-Stock of the
Community, it seemed to be the spontaneous and earnest
feeling of the members convened that some measures
should be devised and adopted, not only for the liquida-
tion of obligations of that sort, but also for the prevention
of similar emergencies thereafter. In order to provide
for the immediate and prospective need in this regard
and secure speedy, and efficient action, our faithful and
generous brother, Ebenezer D. Draper, submitted a proposition for the consideration of his associates, offering
to contribute a certain percentage of what was then
required to enable the Community to fulfil its promise to
the stockholders, on condition that the remainder should
be furnished by others of the brethren and that provision
should be made whereby no such exigency could possibly
arise in the years ahead. The proposition was favorably
and gratefully received, and a committee was appointed
to give it careful and thorough consideration, and report
at a future meeting some plan by which the conditions

specified could be met and the offered gift be rendered available.

The Committee in due time reported, submitting and recommending a plan deemed adequate to the accomplishment of the end in view, which plan was freely discussed and finally adopted. It was embodied in the following resolutions, to wit:

"*Resolved*, That the Treasurer of the Hopedale Community be instructed to assess 50 per cent. of the dividends due, on the Joint-Stock owned by members and others resident on the Community domain (the Stock of E. D. Draper, Matthew Sutcliffe and Charles May excepted), and a sum not exceeding 8 per cent. of the whole on all wages paid under the operations of said Stock for the past year to members, probationers and dependents, for the purpose of creating a fund to be devoted to the payment of the dividends now due on Stock; Provided that the Directory have power to make any abatement on said assessment that in their judgment may appear necessary and proper.

"*Resolved*, That the managers of the several branches of industry in the Community be hereby instructed to enter into such an agreement with the employes in their respective departments as that, from and after the first day of January, 1851, 10 per cent. of all wages agreed upon shall be retained in the hands of the Treasurer of the Community, for the purpose of establishing a contingent fund from which to liquidate any deficit that may exist in respect to the dividends due on Joint-Stock at the end of the year; with the understanding that the said employes have the right to demand whatever portion of the sum retained has not been used for the purpose specified, and nothing more."

These resolutions having been made a part of the economical policy of the Community, the Treasurer was then instructed " to declare a dividend on Joint-Stock of four per cent. per annum for the two years ending Dec. 31. 1850, payable in Stock or equivalent credits on account, subject to the reductions and offsets prescribed in the foregoing resolves."

In order to secure unity of action on the part of the several managers of business in respect to the carrying into effect the newly established policy towards employes, and gain the end sought with the least possible friction or cause of complaint, it was at an adjourned meeting ordered that they hold quarterly gatherings for mutual conference and counsel touching the condition and prospects of the particular branches of industry under their charge and the general monetary affairs of the Community.

It has already been indicated that we of the Hopedale Community were sympathetically disposed towards all the movements and enterprises of our day and time which contemplated a radical transformation of the social relations of men — a reconstruction of human society. Of these there were many, of many a kind and name. With some of them we were largely in agreement as to principles and methods, with others we were as largely in disagreement, though our ends were avowedly the same. Occasional correspondence was carried on between us and them, an instance of which may properly be given here as illustrative of the feeling of other workers in the same field with ourselves, though on quite different lines, towards us. It is in the form of a letter from M. Etienne Cabet, an eminent French Communist, who, about two years before it was written, with some three hundred others — men, women and children — had taken up his abode upon the vacated Morman estate at Nauvoo, Ills., and established there a Community according to his own distinctive ideal. The original was in the French language, a translation of which by Edmund Soward, one of our scholarly members, reads as follows :

"Nauvoo, March 31, 1851.
"To our Friends at Hopedale:

"Dear Brethren: — I have received . the letter which you wrote me last June; likewise your Constitution and the pamphlet accompanying it. I was desirous of answering it immediately but was so overwhelmed with business that it was not possible.

"I perceive with much satisfaction that the object of your Community is the same as ours, though our methods may be somewhat different; for you aim as we do at the improvement of mankind. Therefore we extend to you the hand of brotherly love and pray for your success.

"We publish an Icarian paper called the 'Popular Tribune,' ten numbers of which have appeared and been sent to you. The next number will contain the sketch of your history, your Declaration of Principles, forming the first article of your Constitution, and your letter of June last.

"As soon as we get one of our works translated into English we will send it to you. If you desire it, we will send you in French our two principal works, 'Travels in Icaria' and 'True Christianity.'

"Accept, I pray you, my fraternal salutations.

"CABET."

Nearly a year before this letter came to hand the author had written to Bro. A. G. Spalding acknowledging the receipt of several numbers of our little paper and giving some little account of himself and of his labors in behalf of a new social state. In that communication he says:

"I am a Communist. My doctrine is the same as that of Christianity in its primitive purity. Our fundamental principle is, 'The Fraternity of man and of nations,' the essential outcome of which is 'Equality, Liberty, Unity.' Our society is based upon Education and Labor, upon Marriage and the Family. We admit fully the epitome of your doctrines. According to our views, God, or the Supreme Being, or Nature, is Love, Goodness, Kindness, Justice, etc. . . .

"We call our society 'The Icarian Community,' or 'Icaria.' I have unfolded my system in a large work, entitled 'Travels in Icaria,' written in London during an exile of five years, and published in Paris in 1840. I have published forty other works for the purpose of developing and maintaining my theories, and a large volume, entitled 'True Christianity,' to prove that our

Communism is the same thing as Christianity at its origin. I
have published also a Journal under the name of ' Le Popu-
laire,' and a propagandism of ten years has procured me a
host of supporters in France and Europe. . . .

"We (at Nauvoo) are about 300 men, women, and children;
we expect many others in the autumn and we are told that a
very large number will follow later. . . . We live in community, having separate apartments, but eating, laboring, producing together. We have among us workmen in the principal
branches of business, and lands that we cultivate. We have
purchased the remains of the Mormon temple and intend to
reconstruct it for the purpose of establishing in it our schools,
our assembly rooms and debating hall, a great refectory for a
thousand persons, and sleeping apartments. Our government
is radically republican, founded on Fraternity, Equality, and
Liberty."

M. Cabet was a man of eminent ability, of high character, and of a broad, generous, humanitarian spirit.
He made great sacrifices for the sake of his principles,
and gained a large following as an advocate of social
reform.   His chief work, *Travels in Icaria*, passed through
five editions in about the same number of years, and
exerted a widely extended influence among his fellow-coun-
trymen. He gathered about him persons of exemplary
habits and noble instincts, and the colony he established
at Nauvoo was noted for the high moral tone that prevailed in it, and for the industry, purity, and honor of
its population. Nevertheless, differences of opinion in
regard to details of administration and matters of public
policy soon sprang up, which, fostered by persistent
discussion, at length produced such disaffection and
alienation of feeling as to embarrass, confuse, and work
injury to the whole undertaking, and finally cause its
dissolution. Cabet retired to St. Louis, Mo. where he
died in 1856, his disappointment, mortification, and grief
at the failure of his magnificent plans and ambitions,
hastening, it is said, the event.

During the year 1851 action was taken making the Community an Insurance Company for the protection of members, probationers, and others against loss or damage by fire and other casualties, and somewhat stringent regulations respecting the care of buildings and other property liable to loss or damage, the use of inflammatory articles and substances, the exercise of suitable precautions, etc., were adopted. Provision was also made for the appointment of three Wardens who should have sole charge of men and means employed to suppress any given conflagration or to rescue property at any time exposed to calamitous destruction. And all persons present on such occasions were admonished to yield cheerful and ready obedience to these Wardens.

An ordinance was also passed " Respecting Industry, Purveyance, and Trade," the purpose of which was " to distribute, define, and intensify, the oversight of business ; to encourage useful talent and skill ; to give every member of the Community, if possible, an appropriate sphere of enterprise ; to increase productive industry and income ; to facilitate the necessary purveyance and exchange ; and to establish a well-ordered system of trade." Under this enactment regulations were adopted calculated to afford every one so disposed and competent, either by himself or in company with others, an opportunity to set up and carry on any industry or handicraft pleasing to him ; to have all work in the several branches operated under Community auspices done by the piece, the quantity, the job, etc. ; to allow persons qualified to exercise greater skill or responsibility than they were ordinarily doing, the privilege of such exercise and furnish facilities therefor ; thus developing in all craftsmen and employes whatever latent capabilities they might possess and a deeper sense of personal accountability, thereby contributing to a more complete and self-respecting manhood and so to the great ends for which the Community was founded.

The regulations also provided for the establishment of what was called "The Hopedale Commercial Exchange," which was to act as a sort of Commission and Clearing House, for the distribution and sale of the various products of industry made ready for market on the Community domain and for the supply of material entering into the same, together with the multiform necessaries of human consumption; and also for the transaction of any other kind of business in the way of traffic, barter, or mercantile agency, conducive to the financial, economical, industrial prosperity and well-being of the Community and of all those connected with it.

The Hopedale Educational Home. The year now in review was especially memorable for the inauguration of a project, blasted, alas, in its very budding, which, in its nature, its constructive form, and contemplated results, was among the most important and ambitious ever generated under Community auspices and devised as a constituent part of our general system of social regeneration and of our ideal type of rightly-ordered human society. It was nothing less than the founding of a great Educational Establishment, the characteristic features and predominating purpose of which may be learned from the *Prospectus*, published and widely distributed among the friends of moral and social reform and philanthropists, wherever residing, the more essential and explanatory portions of which are herewith given to the reader.

"PROSPECTUS

OF

THE HOPEDALE EDUCATIONAL HOME.

"One great want of the age is an Educational Institution, in which the sons and daughters of the common people, especially those friendly to the great Reforms and to constructive Progress, may receive a comprehensive and well-balanced development of all their natural faculties. An Educational Home for children and youth is demanded — one pre-eminently worthy of the confidence of good parents and guardians; where they can trust their young without hesitation; where by day and night, in study, in active exercise, in recreation, in the parlor, in the dining-room, in the dormitory, in social intercourse, and in public places, they may be judiciously cared for with parental fidelity; where they may be trained to useful industry, provident economy and self-subsisting enterprise; where their moral principles and character will be regarded as of fundamental importance; where every requisite attention will be paid to their physical health, whether in the way of preservation or recovery; and where, by due processes, they may be inducted into a thorough knowledge of all the scholastic arts and sciences necessary to give them a reputable standing in the intellectual world. Such an institution was contemplated by the projectors of the Hopedale Community as an integral department of their operational system. It has been deferred only till the material interests and social arrangements of the Community should become sufficiently consolidated to insure it a good foundation. That time has at length arrived. Meanwhile the urgent inquiry has come in from every quarter, 'Can you receive into your charge for education, my son or daughter, my nephew, niece or grandchild, my brother, sister, or ward?' We have been obliged to reply, 'Not yet! We can do nothing like justice to your child. We have no suitable establishment, accommodations or means, but we will have the institution needed when our preliminary work shall have been performed.' . . . The thing is now to be undertaken in earnest; and by the favor of Heaven it shall be accomplished. We offer you our plan and solicit your pecuniary aid. Are you ready to give us a helping hand?

"To erect a suitable edifice and furnish the accompanying indispensables for two hundred pupils and students, we must raise *Twenty-five Thousand Dollars*. We are sure this can be done. Let every friend of the cause make ready accordingly. The practicability of this will be more credible to some when they understand the details of our plan. A responsible Association has been formed with the full sanction of The Hopedale Community, and lands assigned to our permanent use for the purposes of a building site, public grounds and cultivation. The Constitutional Compact of our Association is herewith

presented as explanatory of our grand aim and general method
of carrying forward the enterprise. Let it be carefully read
and considered.

CONSTITUTION.

"Under the auspices of the Hopedale Community and in
harmony with the various operative branches thereof, the
undersigned hereby unite in an Educational Association to be
called THE HOPEDALE EDUCATIONAL HOME. And we do
ordain for the organization and government of the said Association the following CONSTITUTION.

ARTICLE I.

"SECTION 1. The grand aim and work of this Association
shall be to educate the young who may be entrusted to its
care for that purpose; to develop properly, thoroughly, and
harmoniously all their natural faculties, moral, intellectual, and
physical; to give them, if possible, a high-toned moral character based on scrupulous conscientiousness and radical Christian principles — a sound mind, well cultivated, stored with
useful knowledge, and capable of inquiring, reasoning, and
judging for itself — a healthful, vigorous body, suitably fed,
exercised, clothed, lodged, and recreated — good domestic habits,
including personal cleanliness, order, propriety, agreeableness,
and generous social qualities — industrial executiveness and skill
in one or more of the avocations necessary to a comfortable
subsistence, and withal practical economy in pecuniary matters.
In fine, to qualify them, so far as a thorough and comprehensive education can do it, for solid usefulness and happiness in
all the rightful pursuits and relations of life.

"SEC. 2. Nothing shall be taught, encouraged, or allowed
within the province of this Association, obviously repugnant to
the Constitution, By-Laws, and Regulations of The Hopedale
Community.

"SEC. 3. This Association acknowledges its obligation as a
regularly organized branch of Community operations, to aid
equitably all the other branches in fulfilling the general guaranties respecting employment, education, moral order, and
succor to the needy."

Articles II, III, IV, and V, of this Constitution provide for the membership and organization of the Associa-

tion, the mode of raising and using money, of holding
and managing real estate and other kinds of property,
and for the proper ordering of the Institution which it
proposed to build and equip after it should have been
made ready for practical operation, the minutiæ of which
need not be recited here. The document closes with the
following appeal :

" Thus, friends, you have a full view of our general plan and
system of operations. We trust the undertaking commends
itself to your hearts and understandings as at once benevolent,
noble, and practicable. What more need be said? Pardon a
word from the General Agent (an office to which I was appointed
November 25, before the Prospectus was issued) on his own
individual responsibility. I make my appeal to all over whom
it is my good fortune to possess personal influence. My heavenly Father, the All-wise Lover of Humanity, has set my heart
on the accomplishment of this work. He has impressed on
my soul the assurance that He will open the way before me,
give me the favor of many willing patrons, guide me by His
suggestive wisdom in the adjustment of details, and crown the
enterprise with a glorious success. Therefore have I made it
the *next*, perhaps the *last*, leading object of my life. I shall
give myself to it with all the zeal and judgment of which I
am capable, — firmly persuaded that the Guardian Hand which
has hitherto sustained me in my labors for the good of mankind will carry me triumphantly through. Who, then, will
remember THE HOPEDALE EDUCATIONAL HOME in their wills?
Already liberal bequests have been made to it. Who will come
forward ungrudgingly to donate or loan it money? Already a
single friend has pledged it one tenth of the twenty-five thousand dollars asked for; . . . who will follow this example
of liberality? Who on visiting the Institution a few years
hence, admiring its edifice, passing through its well-ordered
apartments, beholding the cheerful faces of its youthful inmates
at their recitations, studies, or innocent recreations, and contemplating the blessings to follow, will have secured the heart-
thrilling satisfaction of saying, as he pronounces a fresh
benedication on the establishment, ' *I, also, was an original
and willing patron of* THE HOPEDALE EDUCATIONAL HOME.'

" ADIN BALLOU, *Gen'l Agent*."

It will be evident to all readers of these pages, that this enterprise, though crudely anticipated and dimly foreseen by my brethren in common with myself at the outset of our social experiment, and though projected under the favoring approval and assistance of our Community, many of whose members were profoundly interested in it and joined me in the endeavor to make it a notable feature of our general polity at Hopedale, was largely a child of my own begetting — a creation of my own forming hand. To me had fallen the lot of putting into definite form the, idea from which it had sprung — of devising the plan by which our original purpose in this behalf was to be at an early day realized. Long time had we waited for our Community to attain a position in which it could foster and promote so gigantic an undertaking, but the hour had now struck when it seemed as if a beginning should be made in the work of putting our long deferred purposes in the matter into execution. And this feeling was confirmed in my own mind as also in the minds of others by the fact that my dear son, Adin Augustus, was just entering upon active life, and that the founding of the proposed Educational Home at Hopedale, the principalship of which he was amply qualified to assume, would open to him a sphere of activity for coming years every way gratifying to his tastes and ambitions, pleasing to his parents and friends, and most inspiring in its promise of usefulness and happiness to the world. He was the only son of his mother and myself dwelling with us upon the shores of mortality. Upon him we had lavished the warmest affection of our hearts and built our fondest and sublimest hopes for the future. We had given him the best home training of which we were capable; we had furnished him with such opportunities for attending school as were at our command, and had rejoiced at the conscientious fidelity with which he had discharged the duties devolving upon him there and at the evidences of native

talent and thorough scholarship he had there displayed;
he had passed through the regular course of study at the
State Normal School at Bridgewater, Mass., graduating
with honor and winning for himself the confidence and
high regard of his instructors; he had taken a supplementary course of a single term under the same tuition
and had so commended himself to the authorities in
charge of the Institution as to have been invited to the
position of Junior Assistant Principal on the Board of
Instruction, the duties of which he had already taken up
and was discharging with praiseworthy ability and success.
What reason and occasion had we all, parents and friends,
to look forward with high expectation and exulting joy
to the near future, when his brilliant talents and scholarly
attainments would shine forth resplendent at the head of
an Academic Establishment in our very midst; an establishment in which he had already manifested a profound
personal interest, and to the development of which he
had lent a helping hand, and for the promotion of which
his last manual labor on earth was expended. Alas! how
little did any of us dream that two brief months, as
time is measured by us, would give his mortal body to
the grave, translate his spirit to immortal abodes, and
blast all our grand and noble schemes built on the
promise of his long-continued earthly career. Yet so it
was, as will be duly seen a few pages farther on.

The Community was at this time — near the close of
1851 — enjoying a season of unusual prosperity, and
those who were at the head of its affairs indulged once
more in emotions of exuberant self-gratulation and in
pæans of enthusiastic rejoicing. They felt that all serious obstacles to the final triumph of their cause had been
effectually overcome and that the future of their enterprise
at Hopedale was assured beyond all doubt or peradventure. With them, virtually, "Hope had changed to glad
fruition, faith to sight, and prayer to praise." It takes

many dark waves of adversity to drown the extravagant expectations of such people and suppress their surcharged aspirations. I was myself much elated at our condition and prospects, and deemed it a suitable time to retire from the Presidency, a position I had occupied from the beginning, feeling that I was no longer essential to the wise and safe management of affairs, and trusting that all would go well with another at the helm to direct our richly-freighted bark on a favoring tide to its destined haven of successful security and untroubled peace. I therefore signified to my brethren my determination not to allow my name to be used in the canvass for official servants of the Community at the approaching Annual Meeting in January, 1852, and prepared an elaborate Valedictory Address to be delivered on that occasion. An account of the meeting as it appeared in the columns of *The Practical Christian* is for obvious reasons given entire.

"ANNUAL COMMUNITY MEETING.

"The annual meeting of The Hopedale Community for 1852 took place on January 14th at the Chapel. An unprecedented attendance, interest, unanimity, and cheerfulness characterized the occasion. The proceedings commenced between nine and ten o'clock A. M. and continued, with a brief intermission, till late in the afternoon, when an adjournment was made to the 23d inst. for the completion of miscellaneous business. The general Financial Report, presented by Bro. E. D. Draper, the Treasurer, exhibited a more successful year's operations than ever before, and gave promising indications of increasing prosperity in the future. For the first time in the history of the Community it had handsomely sustained itself — compensated its operatives, cleared its incidental expenses, borne its losses, been able to declare the highest dividend allowed by its Constitution to Joint-Stock capital, viz., *four per cent.*, and secured a small excess of clear profits. We are permitted to make the following *Extracts from the Report.*

" '*Beloved Friends and Associates:* I have the pleasure of making a more favorable report of the Community's standing, financially, than ever before. That word, *Deficit*, which has been rung so much among us, and especially among the enemies of our enterprise, will not have to be used by me as applicable to the operations of the past year. It is true that the sale of house-lots has been a greater source of income than for some years before. But there has been decided improvement in several branches of business, which will be shown in the reports to be given by the managers. I think the gains made are attributable to several causes. The plan of jobbing, or piecing out the work has been one of the greatest of these; and in all cases has given better satisfaction to those who have done the work, and has taken much responsibility from the managers.

" 'Having stated the present financial standing of the Community, let me anticipate a little. I think it safe to prophesy that very few deficits will come hereafter, unless by fire or flood or some other casualty we suffer loss, and for several reasons: First and foremost are the new arrangements adopted by the Community in November last and now being put into operation, and also the formation of several new branches of industry. Among these, and not the least is *The Commercial Exchange*. This branch, I think, will greatly extend the business of the Community with a very small addition of capital, and furnish employment for many more operatives than we now have on our domain.

" 'The new arrangements will give a very decided improvement to the Agricultural branch which has now to stagger under a heavy load, viz.: its four per cent. and taxes amounting to about $850.00 per annum, with large tracts of land unimproved. The present policy separates it into several departments which will divide the responsibility very much, and it is hoped increase the profits. Heretofore one man had the whole to manage and all the accounts (which were legion) to keep, and this has left him but little time to perform manual labor with those employed or to prosecute the different improvements as ought to have been done and as will be done when the division is completed and several responsible persons are put in charge of the different departments. In consequence of having large tracts of land without men or means to cultivate them, we have run behindhand in this branch; and some of our brethren have sighed for a new location — a fatter estate.

15

But I contend that on our domain we have resources hitherto undeveloped and unused, which, with our proximity to good markets, will yet pay our landed investments well. We have from 75 to 100 acres of cranberry meadows, which, with small outlay, can be made to yield in a few years greater profits than we now realize from our entire territory, woodlands and all. "Wait a little longer," and with the blessing of heaven we will demonstrate to *all* that we have a good agricultural basis for our Community, and that agricultural activities will pay well, even here. Then the principal objection urged by some against our present location will have been done away.'

"Interesting Reports were made by many of the Managers of Branches, by the Board of Education, etc., all evincing the growing intelligence, business talent, order and consolidation of our social superstructure. Before proceeding to the choice of officers for the ensuing year, Adin Ballou, hitherto President of the Community, delivered a valedictory address, declining a re-election to any of the active executive stations heretofore occupied by him; which address, with the response thereto, is published below.

"Next followed the election of official servants for the year ending with the second Wednesday of January, 1853, viz.: EBEN-EZER D. DRAPER, *President;* ALMON THWING, WILLIAM H. HUM-PHREY, DUDLEY B. CHAPMAN, WILLIAM W. COOK, *Directory;* CATHARINE G. MUNYAN, *Recorder;* LEMUEL MUNYAN, *Treasurer;* WILLIAM H. FISH, CAROLINE M. MAY, EDMUND SOWARD, *Board of Education;* DANIEL H. CARTER, *Steward;* ABBY J. SPALDING. HENRY LILLIE, WM. G. COMSTOCK, EMELINE H. BEAL, ANNA T. DRAPER, *Council;* ALMIRA B. HUMPHREY, ALMON THWING, CATHARINE G. MUNYAN, EDMUND SOWARD, *Relief Committee.*

"VALEDICTORY ADDRESS.

" '*Beloved Associates*: Having presided for more than ten years over the affairs of this young Commonwealth as its chief executive servant, besides occupying sundry minor official stations therein, I now deem it my privilege to decline for the future these honors and responsibilities. I consent only to retain, during your convenience, the less changeable and active office of Trustee. In retiring from official authority and direction, I may be permitted to state the motives that actuate me, and to offer a few words of valedictory reflection and counsel.

" 'My first motive is a desire to promote your improvement
and solidity in self-government. As a local Community you no
longer need my personal superintendence or official services.
The difficulties of your experimental era have nearly passed
away. You are well organized under a polity of arrangements
at once judicious, practical and flexible to your further growth.
You have become accustomed somewhat to orderly methods of
procedure and you have a sufficiency of material in your
membership for all official purposes. It is best for you to
bring that material into use, to develop your own internal
capabilities and to exercise all your talents for self-government.
I stand out of your way that I may not be a hindrance to such
progress and consolidation.

" 'My second motive is a desire to witness results. I have
assisted in constructing and setting in motion a system of
social machinery which I feel confident will operate happily
for mankind under the superintendence of any fairly honest
and intelligent management. Some have predicted that it
must soon fall into disorder and become impracticable when
I shall have ceased to be at the head of it. I do not believe
them and I wish to see their predictions falsified by demonstration to the contrary. I wish to see the intrinsic merits of
our social system vindicated against all such suspicions.
Therefore let me stand aside and cease to exercise official
authority. Let me not even be called to interfere by counsel,
except in unusual emergencies. Let me become, as nearly as
the nature of the case admits, what I expect to be after death,
a silent spectator of your proceedings, though still a suggestive
guardian in the hour of danger. Go forward, then, and act
yourselves. Show forth the measure of your love and wisdom.
Prosecute your well-begun undertaking to a glorious consummation. Fall not out by the way. Disappoint not the hopes
that cluster around your social standard. Justify my confidence
in you; actualize my ideal; and by your fidelity realize to me
my cherished anticipations of a better day for humanity's
unfortunate and perishing classes.

" 'My third motive is a desire to devote my energies more
concentratively to important labors in other departments of our
great regenerative enterprise. Think not that I consign myself
to indolence or to the indulgence of a curious spectatorship. I
retire from one sphere of duty that I may enter the more

undistractedly on another. Our excellent social system is to be extended to the ends of the earth. Its great basilar principles are to be promulgated. The minds of men are to be enlightened and their hearts animated by the true faith, piety, philanthropy and morality of Jesus, as comprised in what we call *Practical Christianity*. The Word is to be preached, written and published abroad. A new order of Educational Institutions is to be founded. Other Communities, in close confederation with yours, are to be established, wherever practicable. The kingdom of God's righteousness and peace is to be developed on earth as never before. I am called to contribute my mite of instrumentality to the accomplishment of all this. I shall have no excuse for standing idle. I do not ungird myself from labor. I only obey the Master's orders to serve in other fields. Dismiss me then cheerfully from positions where I am no longer needed. Apply yourselves with renewed zeal to *your* duties and send me mantled with your blessing to the discharge of *mine*.

" ' A few reflections. The universal Father moved us to undertake the establishment of this Community. We were bondmen in the midst of the old social Egypt. He caused the light to shine through our heavy eyelids. He called us to seek a better land — to find the place of a more peaceful city. His Holy Spirit brought unto us the maturer things of Christ's Kingdom. He showed us the true social significance and bearings of Christianity. We beheld and appreciated the outlines of a divine government to be established on earth. We took our scanty substance in our hands and departed from the old church and state. We passed through the sea and the desert, led on by protecting angels. But like Israel of old we had much to learn by dear experience. We had many trials to endure, many difficulties to overcome, before we could plant ourselves in the goodly heritage which now is spread around us.

" ' The voice of the murmurer, the despiser and the prophet of failure pained the ears of the faithful and turned away from us the feet of the unstable. A new social birth had to take place, fraught with pangs and struggles and haltings between life and death. But the issue was one of grateful joy. By degrees the infant learned to breathe the vital air and evinced an assured existence. And now, grown robust by wholesome discipline, the child enters on its youthful stage, able to tell in triumph the story of its own precarious nativity. Yes, our Community proclaims itself established.

" ' Who hath watched over us all this while, wrought all these deliverances and secured to us all these blessings? Who hath led us by a way we knew not, smoothed the rough places, straightened every crookedness and turned darkness into light before us? Who hath sent the false prophet away ashamed, and silenced the croakings of the murmurer, and caused the scorner to withold his reproaches, and plucked up the roots of bitterness from our midst, and bruised the heel that lifted itself against the faithful, and saved us from ourselves when we unadvisedly fell into error and sin? It is the Lord our God, the Father of our Lord Jesus Christ, 'the Giver of every good and perfect gift.' To him alone be all praise, thanksgiving and glory. He hath not done all things for our sakes alone but for the sake of our common humanity. Not because of *our* worth or wisdom but of *his own* spontaneous love and wisdom. Our cause was not our own but His. His name was engraven as with steel on all the foundations of our social fabric. We were but instruments in His hand for the beginning of a superstructure in which He purposes to bless the world. Therefore for His own infinite love's sake towards our race hath He wrought out our success, and crowned us with all our prosperities. Let us re-echo the chant of the angels, ' Glory to God in the highest, and on earth peace, good will among men.'

" 'Accept, beloved associates, my grateful acknowledgments for the almost unanimous and uniform confidence, sympathy and co-operation which you have accorded me during these ten eventful years. As your elder brother and fellow servant, I have been with you from the beginning. I have participated with you in all your experiences of woe and weal. I have not coveted your silver or gold or goods; but have sincerely aimed always at your highest welfare as a Community. I have never sought to enrich or aggrandize myself at your expense. Thus far I have a conscience void of offence. But it was impossible that I should not sometimes betray the weaknesses and infirmities of a man possessing like passions with yourselves. I have done so many times. Yet you have borne with me; you have trusted me; you have respected and honored me. You have rallied at the sound of my voice and deferred to my counsels in every trying emergency. You have sustained my humble efforts with a fraternal constancy which I shall remember with affectionate gratitude forever. I thank you, I thank the Highest, for it. Whereinsoever I have wronged you, or neglected you, or aggrieved you in anything, let me feel that you have forgiven me, as God, I trust, has forgiven me my greatest sins, and as I desire to forgive all that have or ever shall have trespassed against me. If I have been instrumental of any good to you or to our common cause I demand no thanks for it. It has all come from Him of whom I received the ability to be useful. I have done only that which it was my duty to do and that but imperfectly. What have at the moment seemed hardships or sacrifices, all dwindle into nothingness when compared with those internal satisfactions which I feel in surveying the results of our common efforts, and in anticipating the thousand times greater ones yet to follow. To see what I daily behold in this orderly, tranquil, thriving, hopeful Dale — abounding in privileges and comforts and quiet dwelling-places — and to hear the whisperings of angels assuring me that this is but a single cluster of unripe grapes compared with the luxuriant vintage of numerous vineyards yet to be planted — surely this is a reward not to be estimated in dollars and cents. And my joy is, not that these lands and houses and good things are *mine*, to be bequeathed to my personal heirs, but that, without enriching myself, I have labored with you to render them blessings to many who else had been crushed under the huge car of that Juggernaut of selfishness which is continually rolling over the perishing classes of society. My portion is not with the world's successful adventurers who glory in fortunate battles, or in political triumphs, or in huge estates piled up at the cost of ten thousand ruined competitors, to be a curse to lazy and quarrelsome children. I fall back on those interior moral possessions which the world can neither give or take away; the untarnishable and indestructible treasures which I can carry with me through all the mutations of time and eternity. Give me these, O my God, and I can well afford to be laughed at for my *simplicity* by all the worshipers of Mars, Mercury and Mammon. Let me feel that I share, as a rightful partaker, in the inheritance of them that serve God by doing good to humanity, and it shall be enough. I shall lack nothing essential to true happiness. Be it then our common consciousness, beloved associates, whatever our incidental failures and shortcomings may have been, that in laboring together to build up this Community, we have not lived merely for self but withal to better the condition of the human race.

" 'It remains only that I offer a few words of valedictory counsel and fraternal admonition.

" '1. *Be true to your acknowledged Religion.* That is the beginning, middle and end of your welfare. Succeed in this, and all will be well. Fail in this, and you perish. Remember that this religion is the one taught and exemplified by Jesus Christ. It came from the bosom of the Infinite Father and there is nothing that can be substituted for it. Remember that it is an absolute religion, not a temporary contrivance inductive to a higher; that it is a religion of fundamental, immutable principles, not one of external ceremonies, nor of subtle, scholastic dogmas, nor of technical formulas, nor of philosophical niceties, nor of poetical sentimentalities, nor of carnal flexibility, nor of disfigured countenances, nor of solemn, cant phrases, nor one of exclusively holy places, times and seasons. It is a religion, not of the letter but of the spirit — not a religion for the soul only, nor for the body only, nor for the next world only, nor for this world only, nor for individuals only, nor for society only, nor for one people only, nor for one age only. But it is a religion for both soul and body, for the next world and for this world, for individuals as such and for society as such, for all peoples throughout all ages, for all the interests of mankind of whatsoever nature, world without end. It is a religion of faith and also of works, of the feelings and also of the reason, of piety and also of philanthropy, of truth and also of kindness, of justice and also of charity. It is a religion of divine truth, applicable by an enlightened conscience and understanding to all times, places, pursuits, occasions, and cases wherein man acts or suffers. Interpret this religion justly, truthfully, practically. Distinguish carefully between essentials and non-essentials, between fundamentals and incidentals, between what is possibly allowable to individuals on their own responsibility and what is absolutely prohibited to any and every human being. For the essentials of this religion be ready to sacrifice all earthly good, even life itself; in non-essentials be tolerant and accommodating to the last degree. Be a truly religious people in the highest and best sense; not superstitiously, formalistically, pharisaically, cantishly, heartlessly, laxly; but rather spiritually, cheerfully, artlessly, earnestly, piously, and humanely religious. This is your all-important concern. Make sure of this and all things else shall be added unto you.

" '2. *Make progress.* Be characteristically an advancing people. Do not crystalize, do not petrify. Great principles you will have no occasion to change. Those you have acknowledged are eternal and perfect as the divine attributes. Your grand object, the regeneration, holiness and happiness of all mankind, you can never change for a nobler. But applications of principles, particular arrangements, ways, means, forms, methods and minor details, may be susceptible of improvement *ad infinitum.* I would not have you unstable, fickle-minded and ready to be carried about by every wind of novelty. There is no need of this in order to progress. Your land-marks may be permanent as respects everything essential in religion, grand objects, and moral order. Only welcome new light; keep your minds open to conviction; cultivate knowledge; hail advancement; 'prove all things, and hold fast that which is good.' Never sacrifice the substance to the shadow of anything.

" '3. *Hold the Community in sacred regard.* Be reverently and devotedly attached to it. Consider every merely individual and ordinary interest as subordinate to the honor, the welfare and the prosperity of the Community. Never place anything but God, divine principle and conscience above it. Why do I say this? Because your Community is founded on divine principles, aims at divine objects, and solemnly forbids injury to any human being, even your worst enemy. You cannot uphold such an institution, nor promote its welfare, nor subserve its honor, by doing anything which insults God or injures man. Therefore have I enjoined you to reverence it so supremely. I have so felt and acted from the beginning. I have regarded him who respected, befriended, and upheld the Community, as respecting, befriending, and upholding me; him who despised it as despising me; him who forsook it as forsaking me; him who slandered it as slandering me; and him who injured it as injuring me. Bound by its blessed principles to love my own enemies and to forgive my own offenders, I have endeavored to do the same by those of the Community. Thus have I indentified myself with it at all times and held its welfare and honor as sacred as my own. I exhort you to do the same and never to leave its existence or any of its great interests in the hands of those who can justly be suspected of a readiness to betray or desert it in the hour of temptation. Be true to your Community until itself has ceased to be true to its fundamental ideas. Then you may and ought to abandon it. If at any time you feel that those who manage its affairs are unjust, or unwise, or unfaithful, seek friendly explanations, apply frank and fraternal correctives, and do all you can in honesty and kindness to restore matters to a healthy tone. But do not fly off in a tangent from a noble institution, nor punish the innocent for the offences of the guilty, nor stealthily plot faction, nor work by intrigue to break down influences which you dislike, nor be alienated from your allegiance by accidental interferences of Community enactments with your individual peculiarities. Consider always whether what you happen to be crossed in is really anything worth contending for against the general welfare. Be humble, self-denying, generous, public spirited. Be true, practical Christian Communitists, and you shall find yourselves unselfishly happy together.

" '4. *Maintain and cultivate order in all things.* This is the dictate of wisdom. All the love, good-will and kind intentions you can cherish will be insufficient, without method, system, regularity, order. Remember that Love must be married to Wisdom for the bringing forth of blessed offspring. Order is the eldest born of these parents. Therefore let there be order in your public assemblies, in your discussions, your deliberations, your legislation, your official proceedings, your public documents, your records, your accounts, and in all your organic transactions. Let there be order in your streets, your public grounds, your cemetery, your industrial operations, your workshops, fields and gardens. Let there be order in your families, your private affairs, and in your individual souls. Not an overstrained, unnatural, oppressive order; but a rational, beneficent, pleasant order, which shall commend itself to God, conscience and reason. Thus will you be happy in yourselves, happy in all your associate relations, and happy in commending your Community as a model one to the thousands that shall yet come from the east, west, north, and south, to learn its excellences. See that you do nothing in a loose, confused, disorderly manner, lest you bring reproach either on the Community or yourselves.

" '5. Finally, '*Endeavor to keep the unity of the spirit in the bonds of peace.*' Be of one mind; be conciliatory; be forbearing; be frank and forgiving; have compassion one of another; love as brethren; be pitiful; be courteous. And 'whatsoever things are true, whatsoever things are honest, whatsoever things are just, whatsover things are pure, whatsoever things are lovely, whatsoever things are of good report; if there be any virtue, if there be any praise, think on these things.' The things that ye have both learned, and received, and heard, and seen in me (always excepting what has been amiss), *do*; and the God of peace shall be with you and your children for-evermore.' "

At the conclusion of the above address a committee consisting of Bros. Wm. H. Fish and Edmund Soward was chosen to make an appropriate response to it, which was done at an adjourned meeting in form following, to wit:

"Dear Brother Ballou: — Though your resignation of the Presidency of The Hopedale Community tendered at our late Annual Meeting was not unexpected by any of our Fraternity, it was nevertheless received with much general reluctance and a most sincere wish that you might change your purpose, and still continue in the position which you have so long filled with great ability, fidelity and usefulness. But we know that the duties of the office have been many and arduous, absorbing so much of your time, your thought and your energies, that there was left to you little leisure for study and other pursuits in which you have a deep interest; and we did not feel, therefore, that we could justly insist upon your longer serving us in a capacity demanding so much labor. Whilst, then, we have submitted to your desire and decision, we have deemed it a duty and a pleasure to express the deep sense of obligation and gratitude which we feel towards you for your important services in our common cause. This we most cordially now do, as a Committee of the Community, and in accordance with the vote unanimously passed immediately after the hearing of your able, interesting and excellent farewell address. Of that address, though we were chosen partly for the purpose of

responding to it, we deem it unnecessary to say anything at
length, as it will go forth into the world to speak for itself.
You know that it was appreciated and heartily responded to
by all who heard it, and that they were prompted by its
impressiveness and intrinsic worth to call for the publication
of it. Such a response must be of far greater value than any
formal eulogy our feeble words could pronounce; and those not
of us will judge it by its own character, and therefore pass
upon it a sentence of approbation.

"We only add, that though you are succeeded in the Presidency by one competent and worthy to occupy the position,
being a pioneer and a constantly devoted and generous laborer
in the cause of Christian Socialism, we shall still regard you,
as you will naturally be regarded by the world, as really the
leader in our enterprise, to whom we shall constantly look
with fraternal sympathy, confidence and hope, certain of all
the aid you can render us whenever needed and called for.
We therefore take an affectionate leave of you as our nominal
head, wishing you continued health and prosperity both temporal and spiritual, and, what will be still better for you,
success in all your philanthropic and Christian labors; and
after this earthly life a still higher and broader mission of
love and usefulness, in association, under the Infinite Father,
with the good and faithful who have gone before us, and whose
rest is unwearied activity.

"WM. H. FISH,
EDMUND SOWARD,
Committee."

This response was unanimously adopted by the Community as expressive of the most earnest and sincere
sentiments of its members towards the retiring President.

LAMENTABLE BEREAVEMENTS.

Following closely upon these heartfelt, tender, impressive, jubilant exercises, were there occurrences of a far
different nature — scenes of trial, bereavement, calamity,
and distress, which cast a deep shadow over our happy
vale and pierced many of our bosoms with a sorrow that
left a scar never wholly obliterated. The first of these
occurrences was the decease, at Worcester, on the 21st of

January, of our excellent and much esteemed Sr., Susan
Fish, in the 63d year of her age. She was for some
years a resident member of the Community, of most
exemplary character and life, endearing herself to all who
knew her by her gentle and loving spirit, her devotion to
high things, her self-forgetting usefulness, her calm and
hopeful trust in her heavenly Father even to the last
hour of her mortal pilgrimage. She was ever loyal to
Hopedale, bequeathing a goodly portion of her worldly
possessions to the promotion of some of its most cherished interests, and requesting with her almost dying
breath that her body might have a final resting place in
its peaceful cemetery. A tender tribute to her name and
memory was written by our chief poet, Abby H. Price,
a few stanzas of which are subjoined:

> " Weep not for the sleeper — a gentle repose
>   Spread over her form as she yielded her breath;
> As calm as a summer day comes to its close
>   She laid her tired head on the pillow of death.

> " Her life like the sunbeam was radiant with love;
>   In the pathway of peace, her true feet ever trod;
> The joys that she sought were all born from above,
>   And the pleasure she asked was the smile of her God.

> " The cause we here cherish was dear to her heart;
>   Her prayer oft ascended that we might be blest;
> Though absent at last and dwelling apart,
>   She longed in the peace of our valley to rest.

> *   *   *   *   *   *   *

> " As we pass one by one through the fathomless wave,
>   Perhaps she will meet us with welcoming hand;
> With angels will come to the verge of the grave,
>   And lead us away to the bright Spirit-land."

The same number of *The Practical Christian* that contained the obituary of our departed friend just named,
conveyed to its readers the startling announcement of a
fresh and overwhelming affliction which had come to us

all in the sudden death of our own dear son. It was
from the pen of Bro. Wm. H. Fish, whose communication
is given entire :

"ADIN AUGUSTUS BALLOU IS DEAD.

"Our esteemed friend, Samuel May, Jr. writes to us under
date of the 10th inst. (Feb.), 'Is it possibly true as we see
announced in to-day's *Commonwealth* that Augustus Ballou is
dead?' and the answer to his question we have put at the
head of this article. He died at Bridgewater, where he was
connected with the Normal School as a teacher, on Sunday
last, February 8th. He was attacked very violently with typhoid
fever, of which disease he was sick only a little over a week.
His father and mother were summoned to his bedside in time
to be recognized by him, to exchange affectionate greetings
and minister to his expiring wants. He lived two days after
they reached him, when they returned home with his remains;
which was the first intimation any of us had received of his
departure. Our friend May exclaims, 'What a terrible blow
it must be to his father and mother! The shock must have
fallen upon them like a thunder-bolt from a clear sky!' And
indeed it is so. We are prompted to say, 'No grief can be
equal to their grief!' They are bowed in sorrow as never
before.

"Augustus — by this name we always called him — was a
young man of uncommon ability and excellence, and of great
promise; and he has gone down to his grave just as he was
passing, early developed, into the man, and entering upon public
life for himself. He had pure and high aspirations within
him and noble objects before him, for the realization of which
he had already marked out some of his life plans. He was only
in his nineteenth year and yet as mature as many at twenty-
five. But as he was, he has gone from us — not dead but still
living unto God, no doubt, and to great ends. He leaves a
revered father, a most devoted mother, and an ardently affectionate sister, to mourn in sadness his early departure and the
burial of many hopes garnered up in him, and without the
Christian faith and trust they would be inconsolable. But their
sorrow is not unto despair — deep, overwhelming as it is. They
have consolations not few nor small, and can rejoice even in
their tribulation — at least can be calmly, patiently, humbly sub-

missive. All the members of our Community are afflicted with them, as is also a wide circle of acquaintances here and elsewhere.

"The funeral was attended by as large an assembly of relatives and friends as could possibly be accommodated in our Chapel, and it surely was an impressive and affecting occasion. The writer of this delivered a discourse appropriate to the event, and was followed with interesting remarks of sympathy and consolation by Revs. Henry A. Eaton, Samuel H. Lloyd, and Geo. W. Stacy of Milford, and Bro. Wm. W. Cook of our Community; Bro. Ballou simply saying from a full heart and in a most impressive and touching manner as he took leave of the corpse, 'We bless the Lord God that He gave us such a son as this; we bless Him now that He has taken him away; and we bless Him that he liveth evermore.' "

The discourse of Brother Fish, with accompanying tributes, hymns, etc., was published in the next number of the *Christian* and did it seem proper in this work I should follow my own strong personal inclination to insert here a full account of our dear son's last sickness, death, funeral testimonials, and obituary eulogies. I, however, forbear, but warmly commend to my readers the little volume, entitled "Memoir of Adin Augustus Ballou." I prepared and published that work during the year 1853, and I have never seen the person who read it that did not profess to have done so with much satisfaction and profit. I pass to other scenes of the sad year now in review with one of the poetical tributes of the funeral occasion from the pen of Abby H. Price:

"As fair as the beams of the morning wert thou,
     As sweet as the fragrance of May:
 Love shone like a gem on thy frank, open, brow,
     And thy smile was as bright as the day.

"Oh yes, we loved thee, a treasure so dear,
     We were glad as we thought thee our own;
 But selfish a love that would fetter thee here;
     Let us smile that the prisoner hath flown.

"Not far will he leave us, his bright soul will bend
    To breathe the soft whisper of love;
As a guardian power he will gently attend
    To woo each grieved spirit above.

"Adieu, then, our fairest ones, pass ye away,
    Lest we love this poor earth-home to well;
Bereft of our jewels as longer we stay,
    It shall fit us with them yet to dwell."

The tragic event thus depicted not only had a most depressing effect upon my health and spirits, rendering me for months almost wholly incapable of active service in any department of usefulness, but it crushed many of my most sacred and ardent hopes to the earth, and brought some of my most carefully devised and strongly cherished plans to speedy destruction. This was especially true of "The Hopedale Educational Home" spoken of a few pages back, an enterprise "upon which I had lavished an incalculable amount of thought and labor, and in which centered so many glowing anticipations on my part and on the part of our ascended son." The proposition to found such an institution had met a hearty reception from the friends of progress and reform at home and abroad — had indeed been hailed with delight by many of these — and they could not well bear the thought of having so noble a project given up altogether, — come to naught in its very budding. They appreciated the situation in which I was placed by my bereavement in respect to it, and sympathized deeply with me, but had faith to believe and feel that with the aid that would be gladly furnished by those interested in the undertaking and the blessing of Heaven, the way would open to a grand success, if I and my immediate co-adjutors would press forward in the work that had been so auspiciously inaugurated and received so cordial a welcome from those seeking a higher education and a nobler life for themselves and for humanity. The feeling of such was fitly voiced in a resolution passed at the Quarterly Conference of the general Practical Christian Communion held at Hopedale on the 20th and 21st of March, and appended hereto.

"*Resolved*, That in this present day of darkness to 'The Hopedale Educational Home,' and particularly to the General Agent thereof, our beloved and revered Brother Ballou, we will pronounce upon it our holiest benedictions and express our most earnest desire that it may be carried forward with all the wisdom and efficiency that its immediate co-operators, under the direction of the Divine Wisdom, can bring to its aid; that so far as in us lies we will stay their hands and cheer their hearts, hoping, praying and believing that the Great and Good Father will never leave or forsake them, but will raise up true and faithful souls to fill the void that has been made in their expectations and plans, and by His overruling and fatherly Providence bring their and our eyes to see what we have so long desired to see, and our ears to hear what we have so long desired to hear; to the permanent good of our common brotherhood, to the honor of our cause — the cause of Christ, and to the glory of His ever-blessed name."

And yet, notwithstanding these and other expressions of sympathy and encouragement, of faith and confidence, with the accompanying assurances of kindly assistance, for which I am truly grateful, I had not the heart to go on with the undertaking. The "staff of accomplishment," so far as early practical results were concerned, was gone, and I knew not where to look for what was most needed to insure success. I therefore yielded, though with profound regret, to what seemed to me to be the inevitable, and with many a sigh and pang saw one of my most sacredly cherished schemes for benefiting my kind pass forever from my sight.

Of Community affairs in general much more might be said than seems to be required in a work like that now in hand, the more marked and notable occurrences only being of interest to historical readers. Some tolerable idea of the ordinary course of operations from month to month and from year to year must have been gleaned from what has been presented in the foregoing pages, and it is not desirable that further particulars be given. Suffice it to say that great activity prevailed in every department of our social economy during the period of which we are now writing — industrial, educational, religious, promulgatory; that there was a constant influx of new comers to our domain, with frequent accessions to our membership, and some withdrawals and departures; that our capital steadily increased and therewith business enterprise; and that there was, moreover, sufficient friction in our complex machinery to require untiring watchfulness with some disciplinary treatment, and to awaken in the minds of the more far-seeing and thoughtful more or less anxiety for the future, although in a constantly diminishing degree.

About this time there sprang up in and around the city of New York a new school of social philosophers under the leadership of one Stephen P. Andrews, a man of considerable ability and culture, of whom the present distinguished President of Brown University is a nephew, whose proposed system was denominated "Equitable Commerce," based upon two fundamental doctrines, "Individual Sovereignty" and "Cost the limit of price." These doctrines were originated by one Josiah Warren of Indiana, who started a Community in that state in illustration of them and also one at a place near Thompson's Station, L. I., some 40 miles from New York city, which was christened *Modern Times*. The primary idea of the movement, "Individual Soverignty," which made every man and women not only his own prophet, priest, and king, but virtually his own law-giver and law-maker — his own God in fact — captivated several of our Hopedale people and interested for a time quite a number of others. Two or three of the former falling into disrepute among

16

us, not by reason of their opinions but on moral grounds,
finally left us and went to join this new Elysium on Long
Island. The practical attempts to actualize that idea,
East and West, were of brief continuance, the fundamental postulate mentioned proving a rope of sand when
brought to a practical test and made subject to any
considerable weight or tension.

A movement with which we were more in sympathy was
projected in the autumn of 1852, at Raritan Bay, N. J.,
in which Rev. Wm. H. Channing, already spoken of, was
much interested, as a devoted apostle of social reform,
and of which our good brother, Clement O. Read, formerly of Hopedale, was one of the responsible originators.
It claimed to be simply an Industrial and Educational
enterprise, with no definite moral and religious standard
or test of membership, though it courted the co-operation
and support only of persons of high character and of
humanitary aims in life. A public meeting in its aid and
for the furtherance of its objects was held at Clinton
Hall, New York City, Dec. 8, at which Bro. E. D. Draper
and myself were present by invitation as delegates from
our Community, the North American Phalanx also being
represented on the occasion. The gathering was not large
but made up of choice spirits, desirous of helping any
and every effort calculated to improve the condition and
uplift the life of their fellowmen. The general plan and
purpose of "The Raritan Bay Union," as the Association
already formed to carry the project into execution was
called, were stated and commented upon by Mr. Channing,
and several others spoke words of sympathy and encouragement, even though in some instances the proposed
undertaking was not regarded as sufficiently radical and
comprehensive to insure the most far-reaching and desirable results. This was my own feeling, as I frankly
stated, but I had nevertheless only the best of wishes for
those engaged in it, who had already purchased lands,

etc., to the value of $27,000.00, and who were resolved to press forward to the accomplishment of the laudable ends they had in view. I am happy to be able to say that their labors were crowned with a good degree of success. They were never very large in numbers, but they built up a Community on its own plane of rare excellence, founded a school of superior standing in the educational world, at the head of which was that distinguished scholar and reformer, Theodore D. Weld, illustrated a high type of private and public morality and showed to all thoughtful observers " what might be done if men were wise " to make the world better and happier. It filled a place in the procession of human advancement, made an honorable record, and passed away.

At the Annual Meeting held Jan. 12, 1853, and by adjournment at several succeeding dates, it appeared from the report of the Treasurer that the total amount of Community property Dec. 31, 1852, was $58,264.18; and the entire liabilities, including the maximum dividend of four per cent. on the Joint-Stock, $58,553.07; showing a deficit on the operations of the preceeding year of $288.89. This sum was duly cancelled by individual contributions and the Community started out on its career for 1853 free of all incumbrances from the past and hopeful of success for the future. Its newly elected official servants were : EBENEZER D. DRAPER, *President;* WM. H. HUM-PHREY, ALMON THWING, WM. S. HEYWOOD, ALONZO A. COOK, *Directory;* MARY A. WALDEN, *Recorder;* LEMUEL MUNYAN, *Treasurer;* DUDLEY B. CHAPMAN, WM. G. COMSTOCK, ANN E. FISH, ANNA T. DRAPER, HENRY LILLIE, *Council;* WM. H. FISH, EDMUND SOWARD, CAROLINE MAY, *Board of Education;* ABNER ADAMS, *Steward;* EDMUND SOWARD, JOSEPH B. BANCROFT, ABBY H. PRICE, ALMIRA B. HUMPHREY, *Relief Committee.*

In the early part of this year a formal and definite proposition came to me, as representative of our Commu-

nity, from A. C. Church of Kingston, Lucerne Co. Pa.
contemplating the establishment of a Community similar
to our own, in the vicinity of his home. He had learned
of us through Horace Greeley of the N. Y. Tribune, and
was desirous of securing our co-operation in the projected
enterprise. A tract of land, 700 acres in extent, of
excellent quality, capable of producing all kinds of grain,
having upon it large areas of timber, with three saw-mills
and other improvements, admirably adapted, as he thought,
to Community purposes, could be had for a reasonable
sum, to the purchase and development and utilization of
which in the way indicated, he was willing to contribute one
thousand dollars. But we were not large enough to colo-
nize, still needing all the capital, talent, skill, and moral
vigor we could command for our own enlargement and
consolidation, and were obliged to decline the proffered
opportunity. We, however, commended it to the consideration of our friends scattered abroad but nothing came
of it.

This year like the preceeding one was marked by the
decease of two of our most estimable associates. The
first was that of Sally Borden, who passed on at Charlton
on the 15th of April, in the 44th year of her age. She
was one of the original members of the Community and
paid the first hundred dollars into its Joint-Stock Fund.
A noble-hearted, generous-spirited, outspoken friend of
human reform and progress, she was also characterized by
the affections and virtues that shine in the domestic circle,
and was deservedly dear to those who knew her best.
Her health gave way some ten or twelve years before,
and her active nervous system became sadly shattered and
deranged, producing insanity of a distressing and hopeless
type from which she found no relief till death severed
the chords that bound her to earth and time, and set her
imprisoned spirit free.

Early the following month a terrible bereavement befell us in the calamitous death of one of the oldest, best known, most distinguished, and most beloved of our number, Dr. Butler Wilmarth. It occurred in the memorable railroad catastrophe at Norwalk Bridge, Conn, on the 6th of May, when many valuable lives were lost and a multitude of fond and loving hearts were overwhelmed with the tide-beats of indescribable distress and anguish. An article in *The Practical Christian* from the pen of Bro. Wm. H. Fish, after announcing in appropriate terms the awful tragedy, due largely to reprehensible recklessness, speaks of our friend's death as follows :

" One of our own and earliest Community members, greatly respected and beloved by us all and by hundreds of others, was whelmed in that wreck of ruin, and brought to us a corpse to be buried in our peaceful cemetery! We knew he had gone to New York to attend a Water Cure convention of physicans, but thought it more than probable that at the close he had visited the new Community at Raritan Bay as he proposed, and would return to his home on Saturday evening. But, alas! to what disappointment and anguish of spirit were his family and friends destined! On the Monday following that tragic and memorable Friday, his lifeless remains were brought to Westboro' (where he was residing for a season and fitting up a Water Cure establishment) by Dr. Wellington of New York, who very kindly and humanely took upon himself the service, leaving his home on purpose to see if he could find, as he feared he might, our lamented brother among the dead. He did find him! And we must leave our readers to imagine the distress of his family and friends which followed the first intelligence received of him after his departure.

" On Tuesday, the body of Bro. Wilmarth was brought to Hopedale for interment, where the funeral was attended by a large concourse of people, many coming from adjoining towns to give expression to their respect, their sympathy and their sorrow. Brother Ballou gave the principal address which though brief was appropriate and impressive and worthy of the occasion. Remarks were also made by the writer of this, by a Mr. Campbell, a clergyman who had come from New York to put himself under the medical care of the deceased, and who was greatly affected by the event, and by Brother Stacy.

"Dr. Wilmarth was fifty-five years of age, and he died in the Christian faith which he had honored for thirty years at least, not only by profession but by practice. 'Blessed are the dead who die in the Lord.' 'Blessed are they that mourn, for they shall be comforted.' "

A memoir of this excellent man was prepared by Brother Fish and published not long afterward, and the interested reader is respectfully referred to that volume for further particulars of a character and career worthy of emulation.

A Free Love Episode. As we at Hopedale, wherever we were known, had a reputation for hospitality to new ideas and a friendliness towards everything calculated to benefit our fellowmen, we were frequently confronted with theories and doctrines, good, bad, and indifferent, claiming, through their apostles, consideration and acceptance on the ground that they were helps to human progress or panaceas for the maladies of mankind. Some of these were thoroughly false in principle and mischievous in tendency and effect. It was impossible to prevent the introduction of these pernicious theories and doctrines within our borders and the discussion of them among our people. It was no part of our policy to attempt to do this; but it was a part of our policy to prevent them from doing any of us harm; it was a part of our policy to be continually watchful concerning them, lest they get a foothold among us, captivating the unwary and causing injury to personal character and the social well-being.

Among these reprehensible speculations was that, which, under a plea for the broadest and largest liberty, contemplated the removal of all conventional restraints pertaining to the relation of the sexes to each other, and especially in the matter of marriage, and granting to each and every one the privilege of forming connubial alliances and dissolving them at will, as inclination, pleasure, convenience, or whatever else, might dictate, under the general name of *Free Love*. But notwithstanding our vigilance, and in utter contravention of our solemn declaration concerning chastity and of our well-known adherence to the principle of monogamic marriage, there arose in our midst during the year 1853, a case of marital infidelity and illicit intercourse that caused great unpleasantness, perplexity, and scandal, and that required, at length, Community intervention.

The story is simply this : One of our male members, the head of a family, became enamoured of a woman, also a member who had for sometime resided in his household, and proportionally estranged from his. faithful and worthy wife. Suspicions of something wrong arose among outsiders, causing considerable talk of a scurrilous nature, though nothing was absolutely known or could be proved to that effect. At length the unhappiness of the wife was revealed, and the cause of it, upon investigation, made public. The matter then very properly received attention from the Council, who summoned the delinquents before them for examination and discipline. Upon being questioned and confronted with proof of misconduct, they acknowledged culpability, professed regret, and penitence, and promised amendment. But these professions proved insincere, or at least, transient, and the parties were again called to account. They then did not deny or attempt to conceal their criminality, but rather justified it on the ground that it was consonant with the principles of the new philosophy touching personal liberty, sexual relations, and the conjugal bond, which they had embraced — in a word, they openly and unhesitatingly avowed themselves to be *Free Lovers*, from conviction and in practice also. Having taken that position they could not do otherwise than withdraw from Community membership and leave the locality where both their theory and their action were held in almost universal derision and abhorrence. They went from us to the settlement of kindred *Individual Sovereigns* on Long Island already adverted to — " Modern Times," where they undoubtedly found congenial companionship, and unbridled liberty to carry their doctrines out to the farthest possible limit, with no one to question or reproach them, or say them nay.   For, as one who had been unwittingly induced to take up his residence among that " peculiar people " for a time, and who knew them well — a man of ability and character, well qualified to judge and to judge wisely — said : " There is a lurking combination among the leaders to do away entirely with the name and essence of marriage and to introduce instead an open and respectful sanction of promiscuous co-habitation. They not only cut the bonds of legality and set at nought the proprieties of custom, but they also scout the idea of constancy in love, and ridicule the sensitiveness of one who refuses to barter connubialities.   Wife with them is synonymous with slave and monogamy is denounced as a *vicious monopoly of affection."*

This case of marital infidelity and contempt of the marriage covenant occurring in our very midst and at a time when the most lax, corrupting, and dangerous sentiments concerning the general subject to which they relate were bruited abroad and extolled throughout the general community under the specious and captivating guise of *Liberty* and *Reform*, led us at Hopedale to declare our views and make our position known to the world beyond all doubt or peradventure.   This we effected in a series of resolutions covering the whole ground involved in the divinely appointed distinction of sex, so far as it applies to the human race, which was passed in Community meeting held July 10, 1853.   The series culminated in the last one which records most unequivocally and emphatically our conviction concerning the pernicious assumption adverted to, as follows :

"*Resolved*, (10) That, with our views of Christian Chastity, we contemplate as utterly abhorrent the various 'Free Love' theories and practices insiduously propagated among susceptible minds under pretext of higher religious perfection, moral exaltation, social refinement, individual sovereignty, physiological research and philosophical progress; and we feel bound to bear our uncompromising testimony against all persons, communities, books and publications which inculcate such specious and subtle licentiousness."

The occurrence which has formed the subject of comment in the last few pages and which in justice to the truth of history could not have been omitted from the present volume was the only one of its kind that ever transpired during our entire existence — the only one in which the inculpated parties justified themselves and took refuge under the bewitching sophistries of "Free Love." In the other few cases of indiscretion, similar in nature though by no means in degree, that came to light, the erring ones, when called to account, bowed to their acknowledged standard of duty, made due confession of their wrong, and in Scripture phrase "brought forth fruits meet for repentance." But on the whole, and to the credit of our young men and women as well as of those of riper years, it is to be put on record and kept in lasting remembrance that we were singularly exempt not only from positive scandal touching matters pertaining to the sexes, but also from covert suspicion and innuendo. Great freedom there was between male and female in the home, in the social circle, and in all public places, but few instances of excess, undue liberty, or impropriety, calling for reproof and reprehension.

The Address of the President made at the end of the year 1853, which I have before me in the original manuscript, gave a comprehensive but succinct review of Community affairs for the preceeding twelvemonth. It bore a good moral and financial tone, affirming that progress

had been made in most if not in all departments of public
activity and service, and that the outlook for the future
was auspicious of good to all interests and concerns. It
would seem that a new basis of valuation of Community
property was established at this time, the former one
having been adjudged too high as compared with that
upon which the estimates of similar property similarly conditioned elsewhere were made. This statement will suggest
the reason why there is a reduction from the previous year's
figures in the financial report of the year under notice,
and how it happens that there is an appearance of financial decline when it is claimed that there has been continued advance in this no less than in other particulars.
It is simply due to the fact that inflated values — values
determined by regarding simply the relation of property
to business — what it is worth to use — gave place to
market values — what it would bring if offered for sale.

With these comments and explanations, a few interesting and suggestive extracts from the President's Annual
Report are introduced :

" Total present valuation of Community property $55,225.22 ;
present liabilities $54,236.45. Leaving towards paying dividends
on the Joint-Stock, $988.77. The operations of the year will
pay all expenses and 3 1-2 per cent. on Stock, being only 1-2
per cent. less than its constitutional claim. The 10 per cent.
reserve due from the several branches of business will amount
to about enough to make up the deficiency, so that there will
be little or no deficit.

" I find by referring to the Community books that its property has increased rapidly since Jan., 1844, a period of ten years.
The present valuation is $55,225.00; that of 1844, $8,658.00, omit-
ing the decimals. Increase in ten years, $46,567.00. Add to this
sum, the value of tools, machinery, etc., in the several branches
of business not now appearing in the Treaurer's statement,
which is $7,499.00 and the whole gain is $54,066.00.

" The property invested in houses owned by individuals clear
of debt Jan. 1, 1854, is $27,400.00; the same Jan. 1, 1844, was
$3,200.00. Gain in this particular in ten years, $24,200.00.

The gain therefore in Community property and in private real estate is $78,266.00. And the amount of property now in Hopedale according to these estimates is $90,124.00. [This, of course, did not include the personal property of members, probationers, and others, residing on the domain. Ed.]

"The following is an estimate of the increase of property in Community buildings and business equipments, during the year 1853. Houses and shops erected, $10,150.00; implements and fixtures in Machine Branch, $2,000.00; in Soap and Candle Branch, $800.00; in Printing and Publishing Branch, $1000.00; in Transportation Branch, $300.00; in Agricultural Branch, $850.00; in Boot and Shoe Branch, $1,600.00; in Division Store, $400.00; making a total of $17,100.00."

The following paragraphs are copied from the Report of the Council made at the same time :

"Of the thirty-one persons examined by the Council for probationship in the Community during the past year, twenty-three were approved; and of the nine persons examined for membership, seven were approved. Of the twenty-three approved by us as probationers, only eleven have been received by the Directory; while of the seven approved for membership, all have been received by the Community.

"One of our fellow-members has been removed by death during the year, three have withdrawn, and one has been discharged. The Community now numbers seventy-six resident and six non-resident members, twenty-two probationers, seventy-nine family dependents, and fifty-two permitted residents. So that the present population of Hopedale is two hundred and twenty-nine persons. Among these we are happy in expressing the belief that a good degree of harmony and fraternal feeling prevails. We do not think that the Community for a long time has exhibited a phase in which so much unity, kindliness and good feeling has existed as at the present time.

"We think it proper to remind you in this connection that we are not here in this Community as mere neighbors, dwelling together for no other reason than because it is mutually convenient. But we are here as a great family of brothers and sisters, bound together by a common interest, pursuing together a common end. And no one of us can suffer essentially unless all suffer, neither can one of us do a wrong without all in a greater or less degree feeling the effect of that wrong. And under these circumstances we ought always to feel free to advise, counsel and admonish one another as we would if bound together by the ties of consanguinity. Indeed, we are bound together by a far holier tie; even that bond of spiritual union that embraces the entire Church of the redeemed and unites them in the service of Him by whose name they aspire to be called.

"What we all need, is to be quickened in Spirit, and as an important means to the attainment of this end, we would recommend to your special favor our Conference Meetings and the Inductive Communion Meeting, together with all the opportunities of moral and religious improvement provided by the Community; and that beside these you should not forget to seek for divine illumination and strength by earnest prayers made in the recesses of your own closets."

Officers for the year 1854 : EBENEZER D. DRAPER, *President;* MARY A. WALDEN, *Recorder;* DUDLEY B. CHAPMAN, ANNA T. DRAPER, ANN E. FISH, WM. H. HUMPHREY, ELIJAH S. MULLIKEN, *Council;* WM. S. HEYWOOD, ALMON THWING, JOS. B. BANCROFT, ALONZO A. COOK, *Directory;* LEMUEL MUNYAN, *Treasurer;* WM. H. FISH, CAROLINE M. MAY, CATHARINE G. MUNYAN, NOYES S. WENTWORTH, JEROME WILMARTH, *Board of Education;* ALMIRA B. HUMPHREY, NANCY M. COOK, HENRY LILLIE, DAVID BEAL, *Relief Committee;* ABNER ADAMS, *Steward;* WM. S. HEYWOOD, DUDLEY B. CHAPMAN, WM. W. COOK, SARAH B. H. RICH, ANNA T. DRAPER, *Promulgation Committee.*

CHAPTER VIII.

1854–1856.

Signs of Promise — Practical Christian Republic —
New Communities — The Fatal Issue —
The Inevitable Accepted.

THE Hopedale Community was now, at the opening of
the year 1854, passing through the palmiest period of
its history. Nothing for a long time had transpired to
seriously disturb the on-flowing tide of its prosperous
career. Perplexing questions were, of course, continually
arising, to tax our mental energies and sometimes our
patience and our faith, as there were also differences of
opinion, personal grievances, clashing of interests, irrita-
tions of temper, outbursts of feeling, etc., showing that
we had not yet risen above the infirmities and faults of
our common human nature and were in no proper condition to boast, as individuals, of our superior, unexceptionable moral and spiritual attainment. But these we
regarded as purely incidental matters — as eddies in the
current — grievous enough and regretful, to be sure, yet
not of serious and threatening moment — not deep-seated
and virulent enough to worry or oppress us, or awaken
apprehensions of coming disaster and woe. We felt, too,
that they were sufficiently under the ban of both the
private and public conscience, were sufficiently held in
check, restricted, and watched by our Council and the
guardians of our virtue and peace generally, and sufficiently subordinated to our distinctive principles, to the
prevailing morality of the place, and to the influence of

our religious teachers, to be not only comparatively harmless for the time, but to be gradually disappearing from our borders. So, despite our minor imperfections and defects, we were hopeful as never before and more expectant than ever before of good and happiness to our kind through the movement of which we deemed ourselves the especial guardians, prophets, and apostles, called of God to the position we occupied and to the work we had undertaken to do. Of the thriving, perhaps I may say, felicitous condition of affairs with us at this time, no better idea can be given than by copying a few extracts from contemporaneous articles, entitled "Local Intelligence," appearing in our organ over the signature of W. S. H. (William S. Heywood).

"The condition and prospects of the Community in all outward concerns is as favorable and promising as has been the case at any former period of its history. There have been no recent withdrawals from our membership. Quite a number of probationers are residing on our domain, some of whom are nearly or wholly ready to be presented for admission to our fraternity, and will no doubt ere long be welcomed there. Besides, numerous families now abroad in the world are waiting with expectant hearts for an opportunity to locate in our midst and unite their energies and resources with ours in the endeavor to realize a new and divine social order. There is no lack of numbers, here and elsewhere, who profess to be prepared to help on by their means, efforts, and personal influence, our work. There is nothing to fear on that account. The occasion for apprehension has been and is, not that the Community will die or suffer from want of men and women to unite with and support it, but rather for want of those of the *right kind* to be co-laborers in it. And special care, watchfulness and anxiety are now and will always be needed in respect to that matter."

"The general external appearance of the village is improving from year to year. New dwellings are going up; new streets being opened; new sidewalks laid; new house-lots taken up and cultivated; fruit and ornamental trees appear along the public ways, in private gardens, and on the general domain;

shrubbery and flowers are constantly increasing in amount and beauty around family residences; the public square is gradually assuming a more pleasing aspect, preparatory to the erection of a more commodious and imposing Chapel than we now have and the laying out of lawns, walks, avenues, terraces, etc.,— all these things, contributing to the loveliness and charm of our beloved Dale, are receiving a due share of attention. Cellars are already dug and foundations are going in for two new cottages, while plans are in preparation for two others to be erected this season."

"Aside from these, which are the work of individuals, the Community is about building a large barn, eighty feet long by forty wide with twenty-two feet posts, mainly for the use of the department of Agriculture. When it shall be ready for occupancy, the old barns will be devoted exclusively to the needs of the Transportation, Livery, Horticultural, and other Branches that can profitably use them." "In addition to this, it is determined to enlarge the building hitherto assigned to school, chapel, and other purposes of a public nature. An extension of some twenty feet is proposed, to be so arranged internally as to have two rooms for schools, with folding doors between that can be thrown open when occasion requires, making a commodious auditorium for larger gatherings."

"The various Industrial Departments are prosecuting their several distinctive activities with a good degree of attention and vigor. In many of them the demands are even greater than can be answered without overtasking the employes. The Agricultural Branch is in a remarkably prosperous and hopeful state. The Orcharding Branch has had a good run of business in its nursery, which is stocked with a large number and variety of fruit, shade, and ornamental trees, shrubbery, etc., including an extensive assortment of flowers and foliage plants. Horticulture has some eight acres in garden vegetables, and will soon be running a wagon to the neighboring town of Milford, where a ready market can be found for all it can produce. The Machine Branch, which manufactures hatchets, picks and similar implements, together with power-loom temples, boot lasting apparatus, etc., though not so well supplied with advance orders as last season has thus far kept all its operatives employed. The Soap-making business is brisk, and Hopedale is getting quite a reputation for this kind of manufacture. Boot and Shoe making is dull, but fortunately those formerly engaged in this calling are able to find and execute other kinds of employment. The Box, Cabinet, and other Branches belonging to the Community, are flourishing, and promise a fair compensation to labor, above rents, expenses, etc., besides an equitable return to the capital invested in them."

"Notwithstanding the general industry of the Hopedalians, and a devotion to business running almost to excess, there is unusual attention given to Education, General Culture, Correspondence, Moral and Religious Training, and the Nurture of the Spiritual Life among us. I doubt whether any neighborhood of the same population in the world furnishes so many subscribers to newspapers, magazines, etc., as ours. Besides, the *P. C.* exchanges, to the number of forty or fifty per week, mostly of a religious or reformatory character, are distributed among our different households. Nearly every family has a liberal supply of books of its own, supplemented by the Public Library containing six or seven hundred volumes, which is opened every week to applicants, and well patronized. Our regular School Year is of forty weeks' duration, while, during the Fall and Winter seasons, classes are formed by those not in the school for the acquisition of useful knowledge or for private instruction in some special lines of study. Our Lyceum, which is required by the enactment establishing it to meet every Tuesday evening for six months in the year and once a month for the remainder, has, for awhile past, given way to a Singing School, under the direction of one of our probationers. For moral and religious edification and nurture we have two regular meetings on the first day of the week, at each of which a discourse is usually delivered, with accompanying exercises of devotion and praise, perfect freedom of utterance being maintained for all present, whether agreeing with or dissenting from the regular speaker. Also, a Thursday evening Conference for mutual improvement in spiritual things, a Monday evening meeting for young people presided over by Brother Ballou, and a monthly Sunday evening meeting for admonitory and disciplinary purposes, under the supervision of the Council of Religion, Conciliation, and Justice."

So much for the state of things within our own borders in relation to the special work in which we were engaged

and to the cause of Christian Socialism. Nor was the
wider outlook upon the world around, and especially upon
the world of general Reform and Moral Progress, less
auspicious and inspiring. To be sure, a considerable
number of social experiments which commenced operations
about the time of our locating at Hopedale or soon afterward had come to irretrievable disaster, so that the
places that once knew them knew them no more; to be
sure, there was still abroad the same deep-seated and
contumelious distrust of all forms of Associationism —
the same indifference or hostility to all radical, uncompromising, high-principled methods of bringing the kingdom of God into the world among the dignitaries and
acknowledged leaders in both Church and State; and yet
there were on all sides signs of promise to the friends of
Social Reform, and from diverse directions light streamed
in through the dark, chronic conservatism of the day.
A few particulars warranting such a statement may be
noted.

In the *New York Independent* of Feb. 16, 1854, an
Orthodox Congregationalist paper of distinctively progressive tendencies and aspirations, appeared an article under
the caption of "Christian Colonies in the West," in which
the essential principles of Christian Socialism were stated
and urged much in the same fashion and for the same
reasons that we had stated and urged them from the
beginning. After descanting upon the kind of persons
needed in those portions of our common country lying
mostly beyond the Mississippi River to restore to their
former allegiance "thousands of families lost to the
Church by removal," to save "the once fair and flourishing professor who is seen relapsing in his principles, and
with perverted taste conforming to the irreligious habits
of frontier life," to stay the tide of demoralization sweeping over that fair and fertile region, and build up on
sure foundations a Christian civilization there — after

17

affirming that a high-minded, noble-hearted, consecrated class of people should emigrate to those far-off latitudes, the question of the manner of their going was considered at considerable length, indicating the extent to which the socialistic idea had taken possession of the author's mind and heart. Mark his words :

"How then should such persons (as he had described) go West? Observation in the West, and a careful study of the whole question prompts this answer: In companies, with persons of congenial, moral, and religious sentiments, embracing mechanics and others of pecuniary ability to make the school and the church paramount institutions from the outset. To name the reasons for this opinion is enough. It will contribute to the protection of those emigrating." "If it be said that the Christian should be a light everywhere and as leaven among the ungodly, the position will not be denied; but the facts are, the few yield to the many, and a single Christian family or a few poor families can effect little in a community where there is a strong pre-organized irreligious sentiment. A weak society may be formed with the best of principles, but, from its pecuniary dependence, only be led and perverted by designing men to the dishonor of religion, thus, as numerous localities evidence, inflicting a blow on a given denomination from which it will require years to recover."

"Organized emigration becomes a Christian duty if a new home is sought." "Fitful, chance lights on the shore will not suffice in the nights of darkness and storm; no more will single Christians, mostly poor, and of necessity secular in their pursuits, scattered through the West, effect that which requires to be done by a combination of influence. If Christians, then, would unite to this end, 'the solitary place would be glad for them,' and the report would go out through the land, 'there are profits of godliness and conquests for Christ.' "

"There are social and material bearings of this question which deserve a brief mention. We are made for society; but society is not 'got up to order' like a military company for an emergency. Persons of the same faith, with a common aim and a free will, embarking together, will find a variety of pleasing correspondences in a new home where all are called to the same trials and inspired by kindred hopes. Construct-

ing a social and religious fabric, and not complaining over
that which cannot be remedied, is the proper employment, and
contributes to real affinity, happiness and strength of character." "The *economies* of the question are evident."

These passages are but samples of what was appearing
with increasing frequency at that time in the more progressive and reformatory publications of the land. They
indicated a growing conviction in many directions of the
insufficiency of the hitherto employed methods of alleviating
the woes of mankind and bringing in the reign of righteousness, and of the need of a radical change in that
regard — of some more comprehensive and unitary movement for human elevation and happiness than either the
church or reformers generally had yet devised — of something indeed quite like what we were endeavoring to make
a factor in the affairs of men at Hopedale. To our
minds they were proofs that the drift of the better thought
of the age — of the deepening humanitarian spirit that
was abroad — was towards a reorganization of the entire
social fabric, and we rejoiced and took courage, and
pressed forward with new heart and hope in our work.

Nor were these the only tokens of a widely growing
interest in the cause we held so dear — the only gleams
of light shining out through the rifts of selfishness and
sin to illumine our pathway and give us good cheer. The
pulpit in certain directions began to utter itself in the
same behalf, and to bear testimony to the glaring defects
of the existing social system, though it rarely proposed
any remedy save that of a slow outgrowth, produced by
a wider diffusion and application of the principles and
spirit of the Gospel to human life through individual
responsibility and agency, like leaven, leavening, in the
process of time, the whole lump of humanity. Nevertheless, there were a few instances of clergymen who, penetrating more deeply into the causes of human ill and
comprehending more fully the remedy, openly and boldly

announced and defended the essential principles of Social
Reform, or commended the efforts and sacrifices of those
engaged in applying those principles practically to the
manifold relations and activities of life. One of these,
Rev. J. S. Dennis, a Universalist minister, in a sermon
upon " The State of the Times," after depicting the disabilities, the evils, and miseries pertaining to the existing
order of society, proceeded to affirm that the only sure
remedy for such a state of things " lies in the adoption
of such social and industrial arrangements as will do forever away our fierce competitions and strifes, and secure
to the laborer the certain and full reward of his toil;
such arrangements as will preclude the possibility of any
becoming immensely rich while multitudes are held in
degrading poverty; such arrangements as will cause the
wealth that industry produces to flow equally to all and
secure to all a certain and never-failing abundance."
He then adds :

"Do not let it be said that this state of things cannot be
realized and that most easily. Above all let it not be said by
any one who has studied the sublime principles of the Christian Religion. When the lofty meaning of these principles
is understood, there will be no doubt of what I have been
asserting. When Christianity shall have been made practical,
in the manner in which a noble Christian man whose name I
delight to mention here to-day is endeavoring to make it
practical, then truly the ills of our present social life will be
removed.

> "'And poverty and wealth, the thirst of fame,
> The fear of infamy, disease, and woe,
> War, with its million horrors and fierce wrong,
> Shall live but in the memory of time.'

"I refer to Rev. Adin Ballou, who, with a few kindred
spirits, is working out at their Community at Hopedale the
problem of unity and harmony in labor, by which man is to
be led from want and misery to the blessings of abundance
and to happiness."

In closing his discourse the preacher exhorted his
hearers to give the subject he had discussed serious
consideration, for "in it," he said, "is contained the
wisdom that hereafter shall work our social regeneration
and restore the lost Eden." In calling the attention of
the readers of *The Practical Christian* to this sermon
which was published in its columns I said: "I hope
we shall hear from him (the author) often. It greatly
encourages us to see the flower of the progressive ministry in various religious denominations advancing into
the field of Christian Socialism. There is an elect host
of them gradually ripening for the advocacy of this great,
comprehensive and crowning reform."

Facts like these, continually occurring, could not but
make a very decided impression upon the minds and
hearts of all our more thoughtful and aspiring members,
and the friends of Social Reform generally. Moreover,
letters from far and near were multiplying expressing
faith in our distinctive principles and methods of uplifting, harmonizing, and blessing in many respects, our
fellowmen; and repeated offers of lands and moneys were
made to us in aid of movements kindred to our own that
we or others might be moved to inaugurate. I have
already referred to a proposition coming from the state
of Pennsylvania, in which the writer was willing to put
a thousand dollars into a Community enterprise and
furnish seven hundred acres of land possessing unusual
capabilities and resources at a merely nominal price.
Another from the fertile areas of Wisconsin tendered the
gift of a hundred acres and personal co-operation for the
same purpose. A third interested party in Ohio would
invest his entire property — lands, mills, etc., worth some
eight or ten thousand dollars — in a Community if one
could be started where he resided.

These and other considerations, added to my own never-
tiring ambition and desire and the prevailing prosperity

of Hopedale affairs, induced me to undertake the elaboration and consummation of a scheme which I had for a long time contemplated. This was nothing less than the formation of a plan for a communal confederacy — for the development of a grand system of society, which should bring the various kinds of Community that might be established agreeably to its provisions into close affiliation and helpful co-operation with each other, as agencies in promoting the economical, industrial, domestic, social, moral, and spiritual well-being of the children of men. This I was able to bring to a satisfactory conclusion during the spring of 1854, in the production of a form of organization and government for such a union or confederacy under the title of *A Constitution of The Practical Christian Republic*. The Document was submitted to my brethren for examination, criticism, emendation, and perfecting, at a meeting held for that purpose May 7, and, after long and patient consideration resulting in sundry alterations and amendments, was approved and adopted by a practically unanimous vote.

By this action of the Community a well-defined public policy and the line of confidently expected progress for the future were clearly sketched and authoritatively prescribed. The accepted Constitution was formed on the most comprehensive and inclusive plan, making provision for a wide diversity of methods and activities in the direction of social reconstruction. It granted the right and privilege of forming, as conviction, inclination, or circumstances might suggest and allow, four different kinds of Fraternal Associations under the same general head and as co-equal constituent parts of the same great system, to be denominated, respectively, Parochial, Rural, Joint-Stock, and Common-Stock Communities. All the needful details of organization and administration pertaining to each of these were set forth in due form according to the light I then had and to the best of my ability.

An unabridged copy of this document will appear in the Appendix of this volume, and to that the reader is referred for further knowledge of its nature and purpose.

Another important and laborious achievement of the year 1854 in the interest of the cause with which our Hopedale undertaking was identified and for the further- ance of which we were devoting time, effort, money, energy, — all we had of executive power and skill, — is briefly delineated on pages 391, 392 of my *Autobiography*, from which I venture to copy herein a single paragraph as serving sufficiently the ends I have now in view.

" This (the framing and adoption of the Constitution of the Practical Christian Republic) being accomplished, I felt the importance, as it was sent out into the world, of having it accompanied with some explanation or elucidation of its dis- tinctive characteristics and methods of operation; and this feeling grew upon me until I resolved upon preparing and having published a complete exposition of what I deemed the true system of human society, comparing it carefully with the prevailing system and with certain proposed new ones that were claiming the attention of philanthropists and reformers in both our own and foreign lands. I then addressed myself to the assigned task, devoting my time and strength, so far as they were not demanded by more urgent duties, for several months to the preparation of such a work. As a result there issued from our Community press towards the end of 1854, an octavo volume of six hundred and fifty-five pages, entitled, PRACTICAL CHRISTIAN SOCIALISM: *A Conversational Exposition of the True System of Human Society. In Three Parts, viz. : I. Fundamental Principles; II. Constitutional Polity; III. Supe- riority to Other Systems.*"

Under the circumstances indicated on the foregoing pages it was most natural and legitimate that the spirit of propagandism — a determination to enlarge the field of our missionary operations — a purpose to expand our work even to the extent of taking possession of new localities and of founding therein new communities, should be engendered among us and prompt us to definite action in regard thereto. After the adoption of the Constitution of the Practical Christian Republic by the Community and subsequently by our Quarterly Conference at West Wrentham on the 25th of June, a leading subject of discussion among us was, What shall we now do to carry forward this Social Reform movement in the world at large; to make its merits known and to give it increased power as an effective means of redemption to mankind? At a meeting of the Conference held at Hopedale Sept. 16 and 17, it was

"*Resolved*, That the time *has now come* for this Conference to institute and put in operation an efficient system of promulgation, and the Executive Council are hereby instructed to prepare and present to the next Quarterly Meeting of this body a draft of some definite plan for consideration and action."

At the same meeting Wm. S. Heywood delivered a " Discourse suggestive of efficient measures for proclaiming The Practical Christian Republic, disseminating its principles, and promoting its expansion," and Adin Ballou one in exposition of the said Republic, in its objects, principles, and polity, and of its claims upon all who accept the Religion of the New Testament.

Pursuant to the action of the Conference and in illustration of the spirit that animated it, one thousand dollars were pledged to the prosecution of the proposed work for the coming year, provided an efficient system of missionary operations could be established as contemplated. At the next meeting the Executive Council reported that several tracts relating to the work in hand had been published and were ready for distribution, but that endeavors to put lecturers into the field had not been crowned with success.

Meanwhile, under the inspiration of the times, I had made announcement that I intended to devote myself thereafter (so far as domestic duties, health, strength, opportunity, and Divine Providence permit) to the Expansion and Consolidation of The Practical Christian Republic, entering the field as a determined advocate of the New Order of Society, my plans and methods of operation being in a general way outlined.

Under the same inspiration the subject of Western Colonization began to be agitated in our borders, as it was being agitated in other localities, near and far away. Bro. Wm. H. Fish became deeply interested in the matter as one that commended itself to our people on the ground that it opened to us a way in which we could advance our peculiar work and make our influence felt more widely for good among our fellowmen. In several articles published in *The Practical Christian* during the autumn of 1854 and afterward, he enumerated the advantages to be derived from such colonization to those engaging in it, and the benefits that might accrue to humanity thereby. He made a special appeal to those interested in the cause of Social Reform and besought a favorable response. In the issue of our paper for November 4, he states the case and urges his plea thus :

"It has long been a favorite idea of mine, and I think of the leading members of the Hopedale Community, to have some of God's acres in the far West redeemed from the curses of present civilization and devoted to the purpose of realizing upon them a more fraternal and Christian order of social life. And it would gladden my heart to know that something was being done to secure permanently that result. If I could aid such an undertaking in no other way, it should have my good will and my word of encouragement and hope. I doubt not that the right sort of persons, with right principles, though with moderate means, might in a few years attain to such a position of prosperity, excellence, harmony and happiness, as to receive the respect and commendation of all decently worthy beholders, and to teach by a living example and with powerful effect a more excellent way of life in its various relations. The time, I believe, is not far distant when this Community or the Hopedale Quarterly Conference will take specific action in this direction."

The subject discussed in the foregoing paragraph was kept before the readers of our paper and the public at large by successive articles from the same pen and from the pen of others during the following two years. Unprecedented interest was awakened in different directions and meetings of friends of the Western movement were held for the purpose of urging its claims, enlisting recruits for its service, and devising ways and means of securing its actualization. At one held in Millville early in 1855, which was largely attended, an advance was determined upon, an organization effected, a Constitution adopted, and two agents appointed to visit the West for the purpose of selecting a location and making needful preparations for occupying it. Iowa, Minnesota, and perhaps Kansas and other states were to be visited in the search for the most desirable section in which to make a beginning. Some twenty or thirty families were said to be ready for immediate emigration, while letters from friends in the West itself gave assurances that goodly numbers there would gladly join the movement as soon as it should begin practical operations, and aid in carrying it forward to a successful issue. The outcome of all this agitation and action will be reported on a succeeding page.

Celebration of West India Emancipation. It was our custom at Hopedale, as radical Abolitionists, to celebrate from year to year the Anniversary of the Emancipation of 800,000 slaves in the British West Indies; an event which took place by a decree of the English Government on the 1st of August, 1834. This was done on the year in review in a pleasant grove near the southerly borders of our domain, half a mile from the central part of our village. It was estimated that an audience of about eight hundred persons was in regular attendance upon the exercises and that not less than a thousand visited the grounds during the day. Besides speakers of our own, Adin Ballou, Wm. H. Fish, and Wm. S. Heywood, there were present from outside, Rev. James T. Woodbury of Milford, Rev. Robert Hassell of Mendon, Rev. John Boyden of Woonsocket, R. I., Rev. Geo. S. Ball of Upton, Rev. Daniel S. Whitney of Southboro', and those well-known redoubtable champions of Impartial Liberty, Henry C. Wright and Charles C. Burleigh. There was also with us a remarkable colored woman, once a slave in the State of New York, Sojourner Truth, whose impassioned utterances on the occasion were like the fiery outbursts of some ancient prophet of God "lifting up his voice like a trumpet and showing the people their transgressions and the house of Jacob their sins." The general tone of the meeting and the nature of the testimonies given may be inferred from one of the seven resolutions passed, which, in view of what afterward transpired, seems like a veritable prophecy written by inspiration from on high, as evidenced by its reproduction here :

"*Resolved*, That the celebration of this day naturally turns our eyes to the horrible abominations of American slavery and inspires us with fearful forebodings of the tremendous retribution which our professedly Republican nation is treasuring up for itself by obstinately persisting in the perpetration of its unparalleled crimes against God and humanity; that we abhor and deplore the brazen impudence with which its government justifies the wickedness of enslaving millions of beings confessedly endowed with unalienable human rights; that we behold in its merciless Fugitive Slave Laws, in its insatiable ambition to extend the ravages of slavery into new territories, in its daily declension from all its former professed love of liberty, in its utter contempt of British emancipation, in the recklessness of its aspiring politicians, in the subserviency of all its departments to the dictation of slaveholders, in its constitutional, inherent, habitual, confirmed, and inveterate

pro-slavery tendencies, unmistakable evidence that it is ripening for some terrible convulsion — some overwhelming visitation of calamity, in which the whole nation must inevitably
share."

Hopedale Home School. During this year 1854 plans
were elaborated and put into execution for the establishment within our borders of a private Boarding and Day
School which should provide tuition in all the various
branches of study that range from the first lessons for
juveniles to those requisite for admission to the college
and other educational institutions of equal grade. It was
also designed that in connection with this scholastic training the pupil should be taught the laws of health, in order
that a symmetrical development of the body be secured;
also the conditions and laws of moral and spiritual life,
so that the roots of selfishness and sin should be elimi-
nated from the nature of the child, and all the higher
faculties of the soul be nurtured and inspired, to the end
that he become amiable, kind, and loving to his fellow-
creatures and grateful and obedient to our Father in
heaven. And this was to be accomplished under influences and amid surroundings which would in no wise
hinder but help the attainment of the contemplated object.
The active agents in this new and praiseworthy enterprise
were Mr. and Mrs. Morgan L. Bloom, a young couple
from New York City, well-fitted for the work by native
endowment, scholastic training, refined manners, and a
restless ambition to make themselves useful in the world
and help bring a better kingdom in.

The institution opened as a juvenile and rudimental
Seminary in October, 1854, furnishing instruction only of
an elementary character, but taking on its higher phases
and more complete form the following spring,— its curricu-
lum including not only the studies usually belonging to a
regular academic course, but also the Elements of Agriculture, Book-keeping, Vocal and Instrumental Music, Drawing

and Painting, etc. It was the initiative of what afterward became a somewhat notable educational instrumentality in Hopedale and vicinity and throughout the reformatory public under the superintendency of Wm. S. and Abbie B. Heywood, continuing in operation about eight years, acquiring for itself an enviable reputation for scholarship, effective service, and moral standing, and leaving behind it, when by reason of the breaking out of the Civil War it was finally given up, a grateful and enduring memory.

FOURTEENTH ANNUAL MEETING.

The Fourteenth Annual Meeting of the Community was held at the Chapel Jan. 10, 1855. Wm. S. Heywood was chosen Moderator, and Helen L. Mulliken, Secretary *pro tem.* After an invocation of the divine blessing and the transaction of a few items of incidental business, the President, Ebenezer D. Draper, delivered an address embodying a general statement of the moral, social, and industrial standing of the Community, with such supplementary suggestions and recommendations as seemed to him wise and necessary to healthful progress and permanent prosperity.

The Annual Report of the Treasurer was presented, accompanied by corroborative and explanatory statements from the Managers of the several branches of industry in the order named : Post Office, Livery, Transportation, Agriculture, Box-Making, Soap and Candle Factory, Boot and Shoe Manufacture, Painting, Machine Business, Horticulture, Orcharding, Printing, Grist Mill, Cabinet Shop. From that Report it appeared that the whole amount of Community property, Dec. 31, 1854, was $60,441.08 ; of liabilities $59,090.87. There was, therefore, left to pay dividends, $1,350.21. Adding to this the sum of the deficits ·for 1852 and 1853, $471.23, which had been cancelled during the last year, and it made the net profits on the operations of 1854, $1,821.44. Deducting the amount of dividends on the Joint-Stock, $1,574.00 and there remained a final net gain over all expenses and obligations of $247.44 — a sum which, though small, was larger than ever existed before.

From the statements of the Managers it appeared that the amount paid for labor within the jurisdiction of the Community was $18,341.68. Of this, residents on our territory received $15,090.50; non-residents, $3,251.18. The amount paid for labor on individual account was $3,039.00. Of this sum, there went to residents, $1,320.00; to non-residents, $1,719.00. The entire amount therefore, paid for labor within our proper boundaries was $21,380.68; to residents, $16,410.50; to non-residents, $4,970.18. By this showing it was made evident that from a financial point of view the year 1854 had been advantageous to all concerned — to the employed, who had received satisfactory compensation for their services, and to the Community, which, out of the proceeds of its industrial activities, had paid all its expenses, met all its obligations, returned the stipulated four per cent. to its stockholders, and was ready to start out on another year owing no man anything but love and goodwill.

The several Boards of Official Servants, the personnel of which differed little from year to year, were filled at this meeting as detailed: E. D. DRAPER, *President;* ABBIE J. SPALDING, *Recorder;* ALMON THWING, WM. S. HEYWOOD, JOSEPH B. BANCROFT, STEPHEN ALBEE, *Directory;* WM. H. HUMPHREY, ANN E. FISH, E. S. MULLIKEN, LUCY H. BALLOU, SARAH B. HOLBROOK, JOHN LOWELL HEYWOOD, *Council;* LEMUEL MUNYAN, *Treasurer;* WM. H. FISH, NOYES S. WENTWORTH, CATHARINE G. MUNYAN, *Board of Education;* ALMIRA B. HUMPHREY, WM. W. COOK, ANNA T. DRAPER, HENRY LILLIE, *Relief Committee;* WM. S. HEYWOOD, ANNA T. DRAPER, WM. H. FISH, HELEN L. MULLIKEN, SYLVIA W. BANCROFT, *Committee of Promulgation;* ABNER ADAMS, *Steward.*

A few extracts from the Address of the President may not be out of place in this connection. It is significant as showing how unreservedly he at the time felt himself committed to the cause which the Community represented, and how unwavering was his faith in the ultimate triumph of that cause as a regenerating agency in the world of mankind.

"*Beloved Associates:* We come together to-day, all things considered, under favorable circumstances. I think we are as united and harmonious in our various relations as ever before and that there is a growing interest in the welfare and success of our holy enterprise. I have reason to believe that on the whole selfishness is decreasing, and that the experience we have had is drawing us nearer and nearer to each other in the bonds of a true Christian Fraternity, where brotherly love shall more and more abound. Still we have many imperfections to outgrow and great progress to make before reaching that condition of individual and social excellence which our divine principles are capable of superinducing in our hearts and lives. May we now and ever seek the aid of our Heavenly Father — the aid which we *must* have in order to fulfill the duties incumbent upon us as members of this Community."

"The present crisis in financial affairs around us, compelling business men and men of wealth to pay 18, 20 and even 30 per cent. for money, suspending industrial operations, throwing hundreds into bankruptcy and thousands out of employment, suggests to us the importance of looking about us and of ascertaining, if possible, the causes of this state of things. And especially are we reminded of the necessity of looking *at home*, to see if we cannot improve our condition by more labor, more economy, and by more knowledge of the things in which the financial success of an individual and of a Community consists. I think the meetings held of late to discuss matters relating to expenditures and modes of living, and to consider the obligations of the Community to the individual and of the individual to the Community, have been and will be productive of much good. I am glad to see the improvement there is in the spirit which prevails at such meetings; that it is more fraternal and Christian. When we can come together and talk plainly concerning what we shall eat, drink, and wear — talk of economizing in a way that shall be understood by those at fault, and all preserve a loving disposition and maintain a proper self-control, I think it speaks much for our good. May we ever be wise in what we say and in what we hear."

"May we learn wisdom by the experiences we are passing through as we labor together here in the great cause of Social Reform. May we be faithful to our high calling. As for me and my house, *we have enlisted for life*, and I thank God that he called me so early into the work and that he has blessed me with means to help it forward. That I may be more worthy of it and more worthy of your love and confidence, is the prayer of your friend and brother.

"E. D. DRAPER."

Brief extracts from the Report of the Board of Education are introduced to show what provision was made by us during those busy, responsible years for the proper intellectual and scholastic training and nurture of our children and youth, such training and nurture being always accompanied by sedulous care for their moral and spiritual well-being.

"Our school has not been open as many months the past year as it ordinarily is, in consequence of the remodeling of the building in which it has been kept; but it has, nevertheless, been making a commendable and encouraging improvement, both in education and deportment. It has been divided within the year into two departments, Mrs. Abbie S. Heywood having charge of the older and more advanced pupils, and Mrs. Helen L. Mulliken, the care of the younger ones. The former has been the teacher for several years and stands deservedly high among us for her varied qualifications for her work; and the latter though comparatively a new teacher is doing remarkably well and giving general satisfaction. They receive their remuneration from the school appropriation of the town of Milford for a part of the year, and from the Community for the remainder; the town and town's committee always seeming to be disposed to do full justice to us."

"There was a brief season when we did not get back any of our taxes in this way; but now that an understanding is established between us, we anticipate only satisfaction and harmony."

" The division of our school before referred to has worked well and has fully compensated for the extra cost consequent upon it. Our educational facilities and prospects were never before so good. And with our greatly improved accommodations, with two such teachers as we have, — teachers who are well qualified for their chosen mission and deeply interested in it — it cannot be otherwise than that a more manifest improvement than heretofore will be constantly made. We shall be justified in expecting much and if *visible* progress is not realized during the year upon which we have entered we shall have sufficient cause for complaint. But whoever visits these schools will, we confidently believe, find them speaking for themselves and reflecting deserved honor upon the teachers, the pupils and the Community."

"If parents and guardians do their duty, as we do not doubt they will do according to their knowledge and ability, then there will be nothing in the way of our yet having a 'model' school — a school in which each pupil will be able to receive the elements at least of that kind of education adapted to the peculiar calling in life which he or she may select, whether that of scholar, artist, mechanic, teacher, farmer, or whatever other employment a man or woman can honorably engage in. And gradually to create such a model school is our aim and ambition, and we shall ultimately accomplish our object."

Under such flattering auspices as are indicated in the foregoing pages, the Community once more entered upon its annual career. All things conspired to invigorate our purposes and aims, to fill our hearts with gladness and gratitude, and to make us feel that our great humanitarian venture had reached the "full tide of successful experiment." Our activities, industrially and otherwise, as well as our ambitious hopes, were multiplied and intensified, and we pressed forward in our course with renewed and unquestioning courage and zeal. Our faith seemed changing rapidly to sight; our victory drew near.

At a meeting held on the 7th of February, an Enactment was passed providing for the creation of a Contingent

18

Fund by increased subscriptions to the Joint-Stock, the design of which was to insure the more prompt, effective and satisfactory conduct of the financial affairs of the Community and of individuals connected with it, in the carrying on of business, the payment of debts, and the meeting of all claims of a pecuniary nature. It was virtually the establishment of a sort of Bank of Exchange, to be in charge of the Directory and Treasurer, from which both the managers of Community industries and private parties could draw, in any case of emergency or special demand, for money with which to serve their temporary needs and relieve them of anxieties and perplexities to which under ordinary circumstances they would not only be liable but frequently subjected. It was believed that this arrangement would contribute both to business efficiency and ease, and to the general harmony and contentment.

An industrial enterprise of the early part of the year was the starting of a Book-bindery and Blank Book Manufactory under Community auspices and with the sanction of Community authorities. This establishment was equipped with the best modern machinery and other appliances for prosecuting the work to be done, and men competent to use the same. Our faithful and trustworthy brother, Lemuel Munyan, was chosen General Agent of the company interested in it.

Our missionary operations, carried on with special reference to Community expansion, were considerably enlarged and distributed over a continually widening area. I was myself busy in the general neighborhood of Hopedale, going hither and thither over a territory having a radius of some forty or fifty miles, with occasional visits to more distant localities, proclaiming the principles and polity of the Practical Christian Republic, and preparing, as I thought and believed, the way for its speedy upbuilding on the earth. Rarely a Sunday passed, when I was not by permanent arrangement at home, that I did not hold two and frequently three services elsewhere, while many week-day evenings were employed in lecturing, either upon my distinctive chosen theme or subjects tributary to it. As all roads in the ancient time led to Rome, so in my philosophy and in my practice all specific moral reforms were suggestive and helpful of Social Reform — pointed to and culminated in a new and divine order of society.

At the same time Bro. Wm. H. Fish was laboring diligently and conscientiously in the same blessed behalf. For a while we both occupied the same general field — the region round about home. But in the month of April, he went out on a preaching and lecturing tour to the central part of the state of New York, in execution of a plan previously arranged and announced through the columns of *The Practical Christian*. The paper had many subscribers scattered here and there through that general region, and these gave him, as he journeyed from place to place, most hearty welcome, and provided facilities whereby he was enabled to deliver his message to large numbers of people interested in whatever proposed to ameliorate the condition of mankind and bring in a better future to the world. He spent the greater part of the remainder of the year in the section of country named, and his letters to our organ bore abundant testimony to the unwavering fidelity and tireless industry with which he proclaimed the gospel of the new era to the children of men. He was occasionally welcomed to Unitarian and Universalist pulpits, as he was to those of congregations which had seceded from some of the more popular denominations on account of their complicity with American slave-holding and were maintaining the institutions of religion under the name of *Christian Unionists* — the distinguished philanthropist and statesman, Gerritt Smith, being prominent in the movement. But much of his labor was performed in public

halls or school-houses, and in the homes of people hospitable to progressive and reformatory ideas.

Just how life at Hopedale in those days appeared to
an outside observer may be gleaned from an editorial
published in *The Woonsocket Patriot* in the month of
May, which reads as follows:

"*Hopedale Community.* On Tuesday we made a flying visit
to this home of Associated Industry located in the neighboring town of Milford. The village is one of the pleasantest in
this section of country, presenting an inviting, homelike aspect.
The pretty dwellings and their surroundings give evidence of
order and neatness; while the inhabitants looked like pictures
of happy content. All were busy; we saw not an idler in the
village, notwithstanding the Community suffers, in common
with all of us, by the general dullness of the times. There
are sixteen branches of business carried on under Community
auspices, among them a printing office and three occupied mill
privileges. Of dwelling-houses there are forty-one, including
three concrete octagons. The presiding genius of this 'Happy
Valley' is Adin Ballou, who has spent the prime of his manhood in efforts to practically demonstrate the advantages of
associated labor. He is a man of enlarged, philanthropic
views, guided by a clear head, and governed by principle. We
think he is not fully appreciated by the great world — and
perhaps this is consequent upon his being shut up in his *little
world* of 'Hopedale.'"

The matter of emigration to the West was kept constantly in mind, forming a theme of frequent conversation
and discussion with us and our friends at home and
abroad, and entering more or less into the addresses of
our ministers and lecturers. It had come to be taken
for granted that new Communities were to be started
at an early day, under which assumption some of our
brethren who had the time and means visited the states
of Minnesota, Iowa, etc., in quest of a suitable location
for the same, though without any immediate definite
results. At a Conference held in Hopedale on June 9,

our President, E. D. Draper, who had recently returned from such an expedition, stated that while his search had not, for various reasons, been as successful as he and others had hoped, yet he felt that the time was near at hand when a site for a settlement should be secured. Through the columns of *The Practical Christian* its readers and the interested public were kept advised in regard to what was taking place respecting this contemplated forward step of our general cause. In its issue of June 30, one of our editors, over the signature of " H.," referring to it, says : " As yet, but little has been accomplished, either in the way of securing territory or of bringing forward persons suitable in responsibility or numbers for the undertaking. Nevertheless, it is quite certain that another year will not roll round before a domain will be obtained, either in Wisconsin or Iowa, and consecrated to the Divine Kingdom." In that of August 11, " W. H. F." says : " The project is not given up and its prospects seem to us better than ever. Our esteemed friend, David Campbell, of the New Lebanon Springs Hydropathic Establishment, has taken great interest in the matter, and, having three sons in Minnesota, has given us such information respecting that territory that we are now thinking seriously of going there, at least to explore. Let not our friends, therefore, whose faces are westward, despair, but be patient and hopeful awhile longer. And let those who are in earnest to go send us their names to record as prospective pioneers."

Six weeks later, the same writer, who believed thoroughly in the movement and was its most active promoter, was authorized to announce that " a Community in Minnesota is a probable fact in the not distant future. Two of our enterprising and excellent brothers, George O. Hatch and Elijah S. Mulliken, young men, both carpenters, are to start from Hopedale for the above-named territory on the first day of October with a

view of spying out the land and finding a good place to
locate upon. They will probably spend the winter there
and therefore be able to give us accurate information
respecting that most dreaded season of so northern a
latitude. Some other friends will probably join them on
the way or follow them."

The immediate result of this initiative step was reported
November 17 as follows:

"It is with great satisfaction that we announce to our
friends abroad the success attending the explorations of Bros.
Hatch and Mulliken, who left Hopedale some weeks since for
the purpose of procuring and settling a domain for a new
Community in the great West. Recent letters from them
inform us that they have succeeded in finding a location possessing almost every conceivable natural advantage desirable
for such an undertaking. Operations are to be commenced
immediately. They are providing themselves with equipments
for a winter's campaign in an entirely new territory twenty-
five or thirty miles away from any human settlement or habitation. They are full of hope and zeal. Heaven prosper them.

"The place selected is now government land and not yet in
the market. It can be obtained only under the U. S. Preemption Law — every actual settler claiming and holding 160
acres and no more. It is desirable, therefore, that a goodly
number of persons join our friends as soon as practicable in
order to secure a large tract for the purposes in view. They
have accordingly called upon us for recruits. Several persons
will leave Hopedale on the 19th inst. in response, and it is
hoped that if there are any friends abroad favorable to this
new movement they will do what they can to aid it. It would
give all concerned great pleasure to have ten, fifteen, twenty,
or more good men — true Reformers — go out at this time and
take up "claims" with those from this place, holding them
for the general purposes of the enterprise, at least until they
can be secured by title deeds. What say you, friends? Those
who go should be willing to enter into a mutual obligation
whereby any certain portion or the whole of the land taken
up shall be hereafter devoted to Community uses if a majority
so decide, each individual being guaranteed a fair compensa-

tion for all improvements made by him previous to such appropriation. Will any come to our aid? Now is the time for action."

The party referred to in the above quotation as in preparation for leaving Hopedale November 19 to join the one which went before, bade farewell to friends there as proposed, and hastened on their way as fast as rail-car and steamer could carry them. It consisted of four persons, thoroughly in earnest, looking forward with fond expectation to meeting those who had preceded them, and uniting with them in founding a new home for themselves and their dependants on the virgin soil of the Minnesota prairies, so full of promise to the industrious and skillful husbandman. They hoped to reach their place of destination before cold weather should impede transportation or hinder them seriously in getting established in comfortable winter quarters. They confidently expected that their forerunners would have at least one cabin erected, a supply of provisions on hand, and other necessaries for their protection and sustenance until they should be able to make ample provision in these regards for themselves. But all phases of human life have their difficulties, disappointments, and reverses, and a pioneer experience, beyond the sound of human habitation, in an unexplored region, with a bitter winter coming on, is not without its full share of them, as the sequel in this case fully showed.

It is sufficient for the present to state that the plans and efforts of these resolute, high-purposed emigrants, going forth from their pleasant, cheerful, well-furnished homes, seeking what they believed would ultimately be to them a better inheritance, were destined to a complete temporary failure. The first party in their attempt to reach their chosen location a second time with teams purchased at St. Paul and loaded with lumber, household goods, provisions, and the like for immediate use, were obliged, by reason of the severity of the weather, the impassableness of the country across which their journey ran, and their ignorance of the proper or best route for reaching their chosen place of settlement, to make a retreat and defer all further efforts till the coming spring. Seeking employment at different localities for the interim and failing to find it, they disposed of their team, goods and chattels, and the principals, Messrs. Hatch and Mulliken, returned very soon after to Hopedale.

Meanwhile the second party, of which J. Lowell Heywood and Lyman Allen were the responsible leaders, knowing nothing of their predecessors' discomfiture, hurried along their way with many hindrances and vexations, reaching Monticello, forty miles above St. Paul, some days after the others had turned their faces eastward, and learning there for the first time of the actual status of affairs and of the consequent dilemma in which they themselves were placed. After reviewing thoughtfully the situation and taking counsel of friends at Hopedale and elsewhere, they decided to remain where they were, get what they could of employment during the intervening months, and prepare for active preparations in the early spring. What they finally did will be detailed hereafter.

In the undoubting expectation that these brethren and friends would be successful in their laudable venture, and that an offshoot of the Hopedale Community was to be planted in the western soil without further delay, I spent much time and thought during the summer and early autumn in devising and putting in proper form a Constitution suited to the needs of a Community formed and operating under circumstances like those amid which the one contemplated would be placed. It was published in full in *The Practical Christian*, and thereby submitted to the considerate judgment of whomsoever it might concern. But the progress of events and the convulsion that even then was hastening us on to irretrievable disaster rendered such service on my part, and many of my other labors, null and void.

Ignorant as I was of the drift of things and inapprehensive of approaching doom, I later in the season conceived and elaborated into a definite plan a new idea concerning the constitutional structure and working policy of the general Community system. It was that provision should be made for the organization of subordinate associations among the members — wheels within the main wheel — to be called Communes, composed of persons of similar tastes, inclinations, and pursuits, drawn together by elective affinity and acting under a simple compact or bond of agreement for the accomplishment of an object or of objects mutually agreeable and satisfactory, responsible to the parent Community only in matters pertaining to fundamental principles, interests of universal concern, and the common organic polity which it had established. It seemed to me that such Communes, properly related to each other, would strengthen the Community itself and secure several very important results : 1. Variety in unity ; 2. Freedom from undue centralization of power and from prescribed uniformity of rules, formalities, and methods, in matters really unessential and extrinsic ; 3. Congenial companionship in business affairs and in other cherished interests common to those associated together.

To give this new feature of Community life the benefit and test of practical experimentation and to meet certain existing needs among our people, I myself led off in the formation of an association thus provided for, partly for the purpose of carrying on certain industries that had recently been introduced within our borders by some of our incoming members, and that were in rudimental and semi-chaotic condition, and partly to aid some of my fellow-associates in acquiring the means of independent and honorable self-support — said association to be called,

as it was called during the brief period of its existence,
Hopedale Commune No. 1, similar co-partnerships being
expected to follow and to be designated by numerals
in their proper order. An Act was passed by the Community December 14 authorizing this new departure in
our general polity, signatures were obtained to a Special
Compact or Bond of Union, an organization was effected,
and operations shortly after began. The body started
with some six or eight members, myself included, and in
order that the venture might be wisely inaugurated, I
consented to act as its President and virtually to father
its financial obligations. Several kinds of business were
established by us, the principal of which was the manufacture of a tackle-block, or device for lifting in a perfectly safe way heavy bodies in warehouses, on board
vessels, and elsewhere — a contrivance invented and
patented by one of our number. The required monetary investment exceeded our calculations and available
resources, and we found ourselves at the outset heavily
burdened with debt. Our chief article of production did
not secure the market we anticipated, which, with the
crisis that not long after came in Community affairs,
produced confusion in our ranks and plans, the result of
which was the dissolution of the Commune ere its importance and value as a factor in our general movement
had been fairly tested.

And so the year 1855 was brought to its close — a
year of unusual activity in every department of our complex and comprehensive undertaking — a year in which all
our leading and most responsible members were taxed to
the utmost; in which great expectations were raised and
great plans laid for the future; in which we were reaching
out into new territory whereon to build new outposts for
the prosecution of the work; in which our labors and
prayers, our aspirations and self-denials, our faith and
our hope seemed nearing their consummation, and our

cause its triumph and its crown;— but a year alas! whose weeks and months were hurrying us on as fast as time could carry us, to the end of our communal career. For the day of reckoning was at hand — the day that sealed our fate as a Community, and visited us with disastrous overthrow!

The fifteenth Annual Meeting of the Community was held in our Chapel, Jan. 9, 1856, its sessions continuing through the day and evening. The President, E. D. Draper, presented his customary Address, embodying, in a general way, from his point of view, a summary of Community operations during the preceding year in its several departments, its then present condition, and its prospects for the time to come. The Treasurer, for reasons that were satisfactory at the time, asked leave to defer his yearly statement of the public finances for a month, and his request was granted. The Board of Education through Wm. S. Heywood (the Chairman, Wm. H. Fish, being absent), made their Report, which was accepted. The Relief Committee also made a statement of the amount expended by them during the year, the names of beneficiaries and the sums received by them being, as was our custom, withheld. The balloting for Community Officers for the ensuing year, including that of Vice President, which had been added to the list by recent Enactment, resulted in the election of the following-named persons, viz.: E. D. DRAPER, *President;* WM. S. HEYWOOD, *Vice President;* CYRUS BRADBURY, *Recorder;* WM. H. HUMPHREY, ANN E. FISH, LUCY H. BALLOU, GEORGE GAY, ANNA T. DRAPER, *Council;* JOSEPH B. BANCROFT, STEPHEN ALBEE, WM. W. COOK, *Directory;* LEMUEL MUNYAN, *Treasurer;* WM. S. HEYWOOD, ANN E. FISH, CATHARINE G. MUNYAN, MELISSA M. INMAN, GEORGE GAY, *Board of Education;* ALMIRA B. HUMPHREY, PHILA O. WILMARTH, RICHARD WALKER, DANIEL H. CARTER, *Relief Committee;* WM. S. HEYWOOD, ANNA T. DRAPER, GEORGE

O. HATCH, ELIJAH S. MULLIKEN, PHILA O. WILMARTH, *Committee of Promulgation.*

The meeting passed off harmoniously and quietly, no one even suspecting that any peril to our organization and its interests was impending — much less that we were on the brink of a precipice from which we were soon to be hurled to our doom. The reports generally were enlivened by a tone of cheerfulness, and that of the President was especially encouraging in its closing passages and calculated to allay any apprehension of coming ill that might have arisen in the minds of any of us. The more important portions of it are subjoined:

"Beloved Associates: I have but a very brief and somewhat imperfect statement to make to you of the affairs and operations of the Community in its various departments and dependencies during the past year. The Treasurer has not had time and assistance sufficient to render it possible for him to so audit his accounts as to make his usual statement with any degree of confidence and certainty, and proposes to ask your indulgence for a short time to enable him to finish up his work with due care and to his own satisfaction. The reports of the several branches of business operating under the auspices of the Community are made up, and will be read to you in their proper time and place.

"The Directory acting concurrently with the Trustees have just obtained of each member, probationer, and responsible dependant, a detailed and definite statement of his or her financial standing, which they design to repeat in years to come. This plan will, I think, be of great advantage, if judiciously managed, to all parties concerned — to the persons themselves and to the Community. It will enable the Directory to know how each and all are getting along from year to year, to make their assessments justly, to favor and relieve those whose conditions and circumstances demand it, and to accept or require responsibilities and risks of those, and only those, who are able to take them without endangering the stability of their own or the Community's financial affairs. I think that this plan will be of especial service to the individual. It will help all to know for themselves — every family to know for itself — just where they stand in respect to the means and resources of subsistence, and to their worldly possessions. They will ascertain how much their income is and how much are their outgoes. They will then be able to tell definitely whether they live within their means or not, and be led thereby to institute such inquiries in regard to industry, economy, and the like, as cannot be otherwise than salutary upon themselves and upon the whole body. I hold it to be the duty of every one to know his or her pecuniary standing, and whether their income is sufficient to cover their expenditures or not, and it seems to me that this new and more precise method than any heretofore pursued will aid much in the way of discharging that duty.

"From the statements obtained from individuals under this new method we find the whole amount of individual property to be $146,386; the whole amount of individual indebtedness, $53,479; making the individual property free of debt, $92,907. Amount of gains in the Community, $2,144; in business abroad, $6,574; total gains for the year of $8,718. Amount of losses for the year, $1,416; showing a net gain of $7,302. . . . . The whole amount paid for labor for the year past in the general operations of the Community, aside from what individuals may have expended on their own account, was $18,114.46; of which foreigners received about $2,400.00."

* * * * * * * *

"We may rejoice together in considering the degree of harmony that exists at the present time in the Community; greater I think than ever before. And I hope and believe that with our past experiences and present advantages we shall continue to increase in love and wisdom, and so become more and more a light to those around us, proving to the world that Christian Socialism opens a more excellent way in which men may live together, and that it gives us, as it will all who yield to its saving power, 'peace and good will' to one another and the whole human race. May the good God prosper and bless us all.

"E. D. DRAPER."

In listening to these utterances one could hardly anticipate that in less than two months it would be deemed necessary to abandon the Joint-Stock Proprietorship and

Industrial System of the Community, and so virtually give up the ship in which our hopes our fortunes and our destinies were launched. And yet to that inexorable conclusion were we brought and by processes not difficult of apprehension, as will be presently seen.

It is to be observed that the cheering picture of the condition of property affairs presented in the President's address and of the gains made during the year 1855 did not relate to *Community* affairs at all, but to those of individuals. And it should be understood that at least three fourths of the $7,302.00 net gain were made by himself and his brother George, in profitable business operations carried on entirely outside of our associated industries, in which neither the Community nor other individuals had any direct interest whatever. It was a piece of good fortune for the brothers named and every way honorable on their part, but it concerned the rest of us no further, and was no further encouraging to us, than that it would enable them, out of their generosity and regard for the Community, to render it substantial aid in any unprovided for emergency or time of special need.

At an adjournment of the Annual Meeting, held February 5, the Treasurer, Lemuel Munyan, submitted his deferred report, a summary of which is given to our present readers.

"The amount of property on hand (Dec. 31, 1855) is as follows, to wit: Dues from branches including lands charged to Horticulture, Orcharding, and Agriculture, $25,117.92; Real Estate, including wood-land and buildings, $24,471.98; Sundry Book Accounts, $6,010.40; Bills Receivable, $8,053.41; Box Branch Tools, $290.25; Dues to Transportation and Saw Mill, $741.56; Interest on Bills Receivable, $469.57; Ten per cent. on Machine Branch gains, $120.00; total, $35,275.09. The liabilities of the Community are: Joint-Stock, $41,300.00; Bills payable, $14,792.14; Sundry Book Accounts, $8,042.40; Interest due, $990.67; Transportation Debts, $60.00; Taxes unpaid, $235.03; Total, $65,420.24. Deducting the Assets, $65,275.09, shows a deficit of $145.15."

This statement was no doubt correct so far as it went, but it made no mention of what was required to meet the four per cent. dividends due on Joint-Stock, amounting to $1,652.00; nor is there in it any allowance or estimate for depreciation in the value of buildings, machinery, tools, etc., which had taken place during the twelvemonth preceding, but which had not been cancelled by repairs, purchases, or improvements.

The upshot of the whole matter, which could no longer be disguised or kept out of sight, was, that the Community had been running seriously behindhand in its industrial departments — and that its financial condition was sadly demoralized. A shrewd business man or an expert in finance could easily see by looking over the situation, that the Community liabilities actually exceeded its assets by several thousand dollars, and that under our peculiar circumstances we were pecuniarily in a very bad way. Of this fact, I presume, Bro. George Draper was abundantly satisfied, or, at least, was convinced that as things were going, either the Community would ere long become bankrupt or be obliged to draw upon him and his brother Ebenezer for a greater sum to extricate it from its difficulties and meet its obligations than he was disposed to give it. At any rate it soon transpired that he was becoming weary of Community financiering, especially when his capital was involved and when it blocked the way of his money-making ambition.

Nevertheless, when the situation was made apparent to us and it was seen that something must be done to meet the emergency, we set ourselves about devising some expedient by which that end could be gained. The one that finally obtained favor and secured adoption was that of assessing the members of the Community to an extent sufficient to liquidate the four per cent. dividends and cancel the nominal losses that had been experienced, and this was carried into effect, so far as outside parties were concerned — all such being paid their rightful claims in full.

In accomplishing this result and therewith arranging many kindred matters, there were, as may be supposed, protracted and drastic discussions both inside and outside of our public meetings, which, on the whole, had no tendency to promote harmony and confidence but rather distrust and ill-feeling. If there were blame in the management of business, as many believed to be the case, it was difficult to locate it, although the head of one branch openly confessed to what was at least a semi-betrayal of the trust reposed in him, practiced for several years and causing a considerable percentage of the existing losses; as an idemnity for which he surrended his private property — house, lot, furniture, tools, etc.,— to the Community.

Failing to discover definitely, save in this instance, where the fault was, it was natural and easy to attribute it to the system, and this was the culminating accusation. In making it the lead was taken by George Draper, before-named, who had been with us but a short time, and who probably never had more than a half-faith in Community life or in the fundamental principles which constituted the basis of our movement. He was a man thoroughly honest in his opinions, upright in his dealings, and of undoubted integrity and honor. A man, however, of inflexible will, and one not to be turned from his purpose if its attainment were within the realm of possibility. Hence, when he came to feel that our socialistic undertaking was financially impracticable, that it stood in the way of his success as a business man of the world, and that therefore it must be abandoned, so far at least as he was concerned, all his energies were directed to the accomplishment of that result. Inasmuch as he and his brother were intimately associated in an important industry, and must act concurrently in all matters affecting that industry, it was his first concern, in taking measures to gain the end he had in view, to win his brother to his own way of thinking and secure his co-operation in withdrawing their joint capital from the Community treasury. It was some time before he succeeded in doing this, but at length by argument and appeal urged with unrelenting persistency, his point was gained, and this point gained the destiny of the Community was sealed. The two owned three-fourths of its Joint-Stock and the withdrawal of that from our working capital would cripple us beyond power of recovery.

This I saw clearly as soon as I learned that these two men had decided to take the position indicated, and a deathlike chill settled upon and almost froze my heart. What I then and for months afterward suffered of disappointment, mortification, and grief, it would be alike difficult and useless to describe. But I was able finally to rise above it and am now not only reconciled to my seeming calamity but rejoice in it. Regarding things as I do at present. I would not lift a finger to save such a Community from its legitimate, predetermined fate. It served as a school of valuable experience to its members and others connected with it, and as an instructive lesson to those who looked upon it and knew of its varied fortunes, and to coming generations. Such, in the Providence of the all-wise, all-loving Father, was its mission, and that mission it fulfilled.

I have stated that the decision of the Brothers Draper to withdraw their proportion of stock from the available funds of the Community was the culmination of the tragedy — the verdict which pronounced the Community's doom. The rest of us, with our limited resources, were practically powerless. We were in no condition to purchase their interest in the property, except by using our credit, as we might have done, and raising the requisite means among our outside sympathizing friends or the

19

money-lending public. Some of our number were desirous
of pursuing this course, and urged it with considerable
persistency and zeal — with a determination born of their
faith in the underlying principles of our cause and
worthy of the devotion with which they had ever sustained and defended it. But to have done this would
have been alike fool-hardy and perilous — would have
loaded ourselves with a burden of debt, which, in all
probability, would sooner or later not only have crushed
the life out of us, but would have defrauded those who
might yield to our appeal and befriend and help us.
The proposition therefore was not to be entertained for
a moment longer than was necessary to see its bearings
and reject it. The only thing for us to do was to yield
to the inevitable and make the best of it.

Forced to this conclusion we at once set about arranging the conditions and details of a transfer of the Community property to the Draper brothers, agreeably to their
wishes, and of adjusting all our financial and industrial
affairs in a manner every way equitable and honorable.
My position in respect to our movement from the beginning, among my associates and before the world, was
such as to make me specially interested and responsible
in this matter, and I determined that in the final settlement the Drapers should obligate themselves to take the
entire Joint-Stock property at an appraisal that would
enable them to cancel all the liabilities of the Community,
which they were to assume, so that no further assessments should be made, or further losses fall, on any of
our members or our friends and creditors outside. ·To
this they willingly agreed and entered into written bonds
for the execution of the contract; and these they in due
time discharged to the satisfaction of all concerned.

The many preliminaries to this final arrangement of
affairs were gone through with and decided upon in regular Community meetings, held at frequent intervals during

the month of February, and by the agency of Committees chosen to aid in the work. When everything was at length settled in these regards, it became necessary to take further definite Community action, in order to complete the revolutionary process and establish the changed regime in the History of Hopedale.

These things were required: 1. To decide by Constitutional vote that the change verbally provided for and agreed upon should be made. 2. To alter and amend the Constitution, By-Laws, and several Enactments of the Community, so as to conform them in all respects to the new order of things respecting property-holding, business management, and other secular interests and concerns. 3. To institute measures for the appraisal of the property that was to pass into the possession of the Drapers, for its proper legal conveyance to the same, and for protecting the rights of each and every one in any way involved in the transactions that were taking place. All this was accomplished at a meeting held on the evening of Saturday, March 8, and before the month closed everything pursuant thereto was adjusted and permanently settled. So that on the 1st of April, 1856, the new industrial and economical system in our village was fully established, and The Hopedale Community, as the type of a regenerated form of human society, and an attempt to realize the Kingdom of God on earth, for which so many of us had prayed and toiled and sacrificed for so many years, had become a thing of the past—had been transformed into a mere religious, moral reform, and mutual guaranty association. Its glory had departed; its sun had set forever.

From that time forward our beloved Hopedale village became gradually secularized and conformed to the habits, customs, and usages of similar boroughs elsewhere, losing that distinctive character and the well-earned reputation which its founders and responsible guardians always felt

was "rather to be chosen than great riches." Business
enterprise and management, having now assumed the
scepter and the control of the fortunes of the place,
returned to the methods and maxims of the unregenerate
world, no longer subject, except as individual conscience
might suggest and demand, to the principles of Practical
Christianity dominant there from the beginning. Employes
were engaged or discharged, as interest or convenience
dictated with little regard to higher considerations. Old
residents, whose services for any reason were not wanted,
or who could do better elsewhere, departed, and new
comers multiplied, not always of a moral type agreeable
to the tastes and convictions of previous settlers. All
that was left to the Community, as such, was *moral
power*.

This, to be sure, was very considerable at the outset,
and, although it perceptibly waned from year to year,
somewhat of it has remained for good unto the present
day. How long it will last and be availing to any
appreciable extent, I cannot foresee. But from the moment
that Community control over the general domain, over
property, industry, labor, inhabitancy, etc., was surrendered, it could, in the nature of things, be only a question of time when the last vestige of our undertaking must
be obliterated, and when all its distinguishing ideas and
principles so precious to many of us would be deemed of
little account, even if they were not looked upon as an
impertinence and an offence in the very places where they
were once exalted and glorified. Some of our members did
not see that such would be the ultimate result of what had
transpired, and were disposed to hold on to our organization, to struggle on, and labor on, and pray on, in the hope
that we should be able after a few years to regain what
we had lost, take up once more the work that had been
laid down, and go forward to a long deferred victory.
I was myself inclined at first to take this view of the

situation; but I soon came to understand from the revolutionary character of the change, from the spirit and ambition of those to whose demands we had yielded and in whose hands we were as potter's clay, and from many other considerations, that this could not be — that all such hope was illusory and vain. I saw that if The Hopedale Community was ever to be resuscitated — that if ever the truth it stood for, the principles it represented and held sacred and inviolable, were ever to be made the basis of a similar endeavor to set up the kingdom of righteousness, brotherhood, and peace on the earth, it must be in some new locality; not on the ruins of our former venture, not where all our purposes, and plans, and expectations had gone down in disastrous overthrow, but on virgin soil, beneath more favoring skies, amid better surroundings, and with material better fitted by nature, by culture, by consecration, to the sublime, divinely appointed work. God in his great mercy grant that in his own good time that place may be found and that work be done. So shall The Hopedale Community have a glorious resurrection, — an apotheosis, of which its earlier manifestation was but the harbinger and prototype.

With the decadence of the Community, as an exponent and practical illustration of Christian Socialism, passed into oblivion or into a state of arrested development, many plans and schemes dependent upon or supplementary to it, while our whole system of propagandism received a shock and a set back from which it has never been able to recover. If our missionaries went abroad to proclaim the gospel previously represented by it, their words were shorn of much of their pertinency and power by the failure of our efforts to actualize that gospel in the manifold relations of life at home. As a moral and religious teacher, called of God, as I believed, to fill that office, I could not wholly cease from my ministrations in behalf of what, notwithstanding all disappointments and failures, I still believed to be true and right, and, as a consequence, essential to the enlightenment, regeneration, and happiness of mankind; yet I felt that I was seriously handicapped by what had transpired and that my utterances had lost much of the vitality and effectiveness which formerly characterized them and made them acceptable and profitable to my fellowmen. Nevertheless, I must go forward in the same general way as before, following the same lines of thought and discourse, though obliged by the circumstances of the case to deal more with the theoretical than with the practical aspects of divine truth, save in its application to individuals in their more immediate personal relations to God and man, and to treat of it in its larger phases and applications, as a means of building up the divine kingdom *on the earth*, and of the obligations it imposed upon men in that regard, ideally and prophetically rather than otherwise — as something to aspire after and to be realized in the sometime future, but not in the living present of the world's history.

My brethren in the ministry felt much as I did in this matter, and were impelled to adopt essentially the same ministerial policy and pursue the same lines of ministerial service. To be sure, there was enough for us to do in the way of seeking to " turn men from darkness to light and from the power of Satan unto God "; enough to do in warring against the great evils of social and civil life, Slavery, War, Intemperance, Licentiousness, Commercial Fraud, Political Corruption, etc., and in urging forward the specific reforms that were calculated to overcome these iniquities and banish them from the world; but at the same time we still believed that pure Christianity meant more than these things, more than individual enlightenment and sanctification, more than the abolition of social abuses and abominations and the triumph of great and good causes; we believed it meant *a Redeemed Order of Human Society, the Kingdom of God on the Earth*. And

this belief must still come in to shape more or less our
testimonies, to give direction to our endeavors, to fill the
measure of our heart's desire for humanity and keep alive
in our souls a sense of God's presence and providence in
the world and of his beneficent purpose touching the
children of men. So we wrought on as best we could in
the places that opened to us here and there, trusting that
though our fondest expectations were not to be realized
by us or perhaps by any in the near future, our efforts,
put forth in all sincerity and earnestness, would yet be
to some extent efficacious in urging forward the cause of
human progress and redemption and would contribute in
some humble degree to the bringing in of that long
prophesied era when the blessed doctrine of human brotherhood should animate all hearts and bind men and
nations together in amity, concord, and peace; when
they should "beat their swords into ploughshares and
their spears into pruning-hooks and learn war no more";
and when God, even in this world, should be "all and
in all."

As a result of the changed conditions and circumstances under which we were placed at Hopedale, the
enthusiasm that had been growing among us for a year
or two in favor of colonization rapidly subsided, and the
so-called "Western Movement" which seemed so near its
culmination in the establishment of a branch Community
in the state of Minnesota at the very moment of the fatal
collapse, was postponed forever. If anything of the kind
contemplated should be undertaken in the indefinite future,
as I still believe, it will be substantially a *new* experiment,
wholly independent organically of that at Hopedale, though
it would undoubtedly derive some important lessons for
its guidance from Hopedale's experience and history, —
from its failure as well as from its temporary success.
It may be proper to state that our brethren who went out
from us in the autumn of 1855 and who through divers

difficulties and disappointments were obliged to suspend their labors and spend the succeeding winter at Monticello, as noted a few pages back, resumed them again at the opening of the spring. They soon found a satisfactory locality on the open rolling prairie about forty miles due west from Monticello, some eight hundred acres of which they immediately took measures to secure under the U. S. Preemption Act, and proceeded to erect dwellings for the shelter, convenience, and comfort of themselves and their dependents. These they completed in the early summer, when, joined by the other members of their households, they re-established their home-life, and went on in the discharge of those duties and the performance of those labors, incident to pioneer experience in that then almost wholly uninhabited region. There they remained but a few years, one of the number dying meanwhile, when they left — some of them on economic grounds, the others because driven away by Indian invasion — returning to the East, and taking up their abode once more in the old Bay State. They christened their little settlement *Union Grove*, from the fact that their habitations stood within the precincts of a sparsely wooded tract of land which skirted one end of their otherwise unshaded farms, which name it bears to the present day. It constitutes the northwest portion of Meeker County.

It is needless to go into further details of what took place within our borders during the year 1856. It may be readily inferred from the delineations and intimations contained in the last few pages.

CHAPTER IX.

1857–1876.

DISMANTLED CONDITION — INCREASING PARALYSIS — IN WAR
TIME — RELIGIOUS ASPECTS — THE HOPEDALE
PARISH — CONCLUSION.

BEFORE proceeding to sketch the last act of the
drama which this volume is designed to present to
the reader, or, in other words, to recall and record the
principal features of that process of deterioration which
terminated at length in the utter extinction of The
Hopedale Community, it seems fitting and desirable to
set forth the exact status of its affairs at the opening of
the year of 1857 — to show, with considerable degree of
precision, what was taken away from its original powers,
rights, immunities and obligations by the revolution of
the previous year, and what was left as an equipment
for further service in the cause of Christian Socialism.
It has already been stated that thereby the enterprise
had cast off many of its former cardinal characteristics
and become a merely religious, moral reform, and mutual
guaranty society. This was in a certain way and in a
large measure true. But something more specific and
positive is requisite to a clear comprehension, on the
part of the average reader, of the condition of things
with us at that date. And hence a few paragraphs at
the beginning of the present chapter are properly devoted
to the elucidation of the matter.

It must be obvious to the thoughtful mind that the
abandonment of the united proprietorship of the Commu-

nity capital, including lands, buildings, machinery, money,
and other forms of real and movable estate, together with
the surrender of the supervision and management of its
multiform branches of industry and the operations they
represented, was the obliteration of one of the most
essential and distinguishing features of our movement,
as it was of other movements of that period contemplating the radical reconstruction of the existing order of
human society. It was indeed so. The great watchwords
of all Social Reformers then before the world, from
Fourier to Robert Owen, were "Co-operation," "Combined Industry," "The Harmonization of Capital and
Labor"; some of them making the thing these terms
stand for the leading, if not the only, object and end of
their efforts. With us, this was not the only or the main
desideratum, and yet it was a very important and vital
one — so important and vital, indeed, that when it was
given up with us our whole structure was weakened and
imperilled from foundation stone to topmost spire. Taken
in connection with other things that went with it, its
relinquishment was, as the sequel showed, the virtual
overthrow and demolition of our entire system; at least
the precursor and occasion of such overthrow and demolition in those respects that differentiated it from the
prevailing civilization of the world. For with it went
the control over residents on our domain, the regulation
of trade and of the contraction and payment of debts,
most of the restrictions upon the sale and uses of lands,
the Community Post Office, Savings Bank, Fire Insurance
Company, The Industrial Union, Enactments relating to
the Employment and Supervision of Children, etc., etc.
In all these things the Community, as such and in its governmental capacity, was rendered practically powerless.
All these things, which had cost us infinite study, labor,
care, and which constituted some of the most salutary
and valuable characteristics of our undertaking, were gone,
and gone beyond the possibility of recovery.

On the other hand, what had we saved? What was left as a foundation upon which to build anything promising and durable for the [future? What, to prize, to conserve, to use, as agencies or working forces wherewith to promote the great objects for which we had toiled so hard and sacrificed so much in the past — for the furtherance of which we still felt ourselves bound in conscience and in fealty to our Practical Christian principles to labor and to pray, notwithstanding our disappointment and discomfiture? We had

1. Our organic fraternity and pledged fidelity to each other and to our common cause. A few of our associates left us soon after the great change took place, and the number increased as time went on, but yet at the date named there had been but few withdrawals; the great majority remained, a loyal band of brothers and sisters, animated by a common spirit and ambition, cherishing a common faith and hope, and seeking by united effort the attainment for ourselves and for humanity common laudable and beneficent ends.

2. Our name — The Hopedale Community; which was very dear to us by reason of the circumstances under which we first assumed it; by reason of what it represented to us of truth, of righteousness, of a broad worldwide humanity, of what is noblest and best in individual and social life; and because it stood in our thought and affections as a type — an imperfect one, to be sure — and yet a *type* of the kingdom of God.

3. Our distinctive ideas, principles, purposes, and aims, with dependent duties, as announced and avowed by us in the Preamble and Declaration of Article I of our Constitution. These were as true, as sacred, as obligatory upon us as when we first acknowledged them. By the change that had taken place we had in no proper sense disowned, renounced, or abandoned them. We still stood by them and were still bound to be governed by

them in all the interests and relations of life. We had only given up certain applications of them to certain economical concerns, holding them in abeyance for the time being as impracticable in such applications in the present moral and spiritual stage of human development.

4. Authority and control over certain kinds of property that were retained in our possession when the bulk of our estate passed into other hands. Of these there were several dwelling-houses, the School-house and Chapel, the village site, the public squares and other common lands, our Cemetery, etc.

5. Our religious meetings and their exclusive management; the care of all our means and appliances for moral and spiritual culture, missionary operations, promulgatory agencies, etc.

6. A restricted supervision of our educational interests and institutions, subject, so far as our legally established School District was concerned, to the management of the general Committee of the town of Milford. All instruction in excess of that provided for by them, and all extra apparatus, appliances, etc., were in our own hands.

7. Our Community Lyceum, which for several years was an important educational agency among our people, with its lectures, discussions, recitations, essays, classes, and other activities, established and maintained by Community enactment, and provided for by special Community action from year to year. Also the Public Library, already well established and supplied with six or eight hundred volumes of well chosen books, representing every department of literature and a wide field of knowledge.

8. Our general Constitutional Guaranty against the evils of poverty, which made us organically a Mutual Aid Society for the help of one another, pecuniarily or otherwise, in times of misfortune, need, or distress. For the proper fulfillment of this Guaranty a Relief Committee was chosen from year to year, and money was ap-

propriated and placed in their hands, to be used as their wisdom and sympathy should direct.

9. Certain funds, coming to us by donation or bequest and held in trust for the promotion of definitely specified objects; said trust to be honestly administered and honorably discharged according to the best of our judgment and ability.

10. Our reputation, which, by fair dealing, regard for the rights and welfare of our fellowmen, interest in good causes, promptness and cheerfulness in meeting our obligations, and an exemplification in good degree of manly and womanly worth, secured us the confidence of the public and a host of faithful devoted friends through all the exigencies, transmutations, and diversified fortunes of our checkered and finally disastrous career.

Such, in detail, was what was left to us and for us as a Community after the crisis of 1856; what was saved from the wreck of our ill-fated bark, which had been laden with most precious freightage, launched amid great hope and rejoicing, and been borne bravely along upon a now prosperous and now adverse tide for fourteen eventful years, only to founder at last on the shallows of worldly ambition and desire. In view of this condition of things — in view of what remained of our former possessions, and of the opportunity still open to us at home and abroad for effective service of God and men, we all, with few exceptions, resolved to stand by each other and by our unfortunate experiment, making the most and the best of what we had at our command, and using it, as Providence should direct us, for our own and each other's good and for the good of the world. "We were perplexed, but not in despair"; "cast down, but not destroyed." Our Vice-President, Bro. Wm. S. Heywood, who, in place of the President, made an address at the Annual Meeting held Jan. 14, 1857, voiced the general feeling of his associates and awakened a ready response

in all their hearts, when, after recapitulating the blessings
we still enjoyed and the means of uplifting and benefiting
our fellowmen still at our command, he concluded his
counsels and exhortations as follows:

"Is it not certain that whatever is lovely and of good
report among us, whatever is wise and advantageous, whatever
is beneficent and salutary, can be sustained and perpetuated
altogether better by union, by mutual co-operation, by the
maintenance of our organization, than in any other way? In
my judgment, if our organic connection, the bond that unites
us in Community relationship, be given up, all is sooner or
later gone; while, by continuing it and being faithful to its
obligations, we shall accomplish much for ourselves, for each
other, and for the world in the way of preserving the things
that are desirable and good, and do it far more freely, effectually, heartily, and happily, than could be done in any other
way.

"In conclusion, then, I would most earnestly call upon you
who still love our great and good cause, who still reverence
the everlasting principles which it embodies, to stand by each
other, and co-operate cheerfully and unitedly for the promotion of our declared objects, here and in the world. Failing in
certain things, we have not lost all. What we need is a
quickened sense of our individual and social obligations — the
mind and the heart to *do*. With a united purpose, a determined resolution, and a reliant faith, we can realize to ourselves and to each other much of divine good, and make our
Community still a light to them that sit in darkness. Shall
it be done? God still lives; there is to us all the same
inspiring presence as of yore; the loving angels bend down
yet to bless us; our aspirations for a better state continue
quick within us; the eternal truth is even now held out to
us; humanity, as in days that are past, cries for help and
salvation with her ten times ten thousand voices; the cause of
Non-resistance, almost abandoned by her professed friends,
urges us to renewed effort and to faithful service. In the
name of all these I exhort you to a revival of hope, to union,
to vigorous, manly, Christian exertion, to self-sacrificing fidelity
in the work of Practical Christian Socialism. In their name
I pledge my influence, my means, myself, anew to you, to the

Community, to our common cause. Let no mistakes entirely overcome us; let no disappointment drive us to despair; let no failures make us apostates; but, rising above all these, may we still do our duty, still cherish our sublime faith and hope, which are to us an earnest of the blessed era when "the kingdoms of this world shall have become the kingdom of our Lord Jesus Christ."

In much the same strain and to the same general effect did I myself write a few weeks afterward, and publish in our organ, the brief article which follows, under the caption, "*Our Cause — What Is It?*"

"Do any ask what is proposed to be done? I answer, to establish the Practical Christian Republic — at least to prepare the way for its establishment. Friends and fellow-laborers, calmly re-examine its objects, principles, polity. What noble aspiration of the immortal spirit does it not encourage! What grand truth does it not recognize! What cardinal duty does it not magnify! What needed reform does it not include and urge! What fundamental idea or measure of human regeneration does it not embrace! Shall we abandon it? Where are we to look for anything better — anything half so worthy of our undying devotion? To what sect or anti-sect in religion shall we go? To what party or anti-party in politics? To what progressive, reformatory, or socialistic enterprise in the wide world? Where can we find higher aims, diviner principles, or a wiser polity? We can find fragments of wisdom and goodness in all sects, parties, societies, and coteries; but where else so much of truth and good mixed with so little evil and falsity.

"What if we cannot at present organize the higher kind of Communities! Are not *Rural* and especially *Parochial* Communities practicable? What if we cannot do much toward founding and multiplying even these? We can at least hold fast what we have already gained; we can foster true education; we can elevate individuals and families; we can discipline and purify our membership; we can be making new converts and steadily enlighten the public mind. All this must be done in order to ultimate success. It is our duty and privilege to labor faithfully in these ways; which, if done, the stones and cedars will have been prepared for a glorious Social Temple that will at length rise in symmetrical majesty 'without the sound of axe, hammer, or any tool of iron.' "

With such words as these did I and my ministerial brethren strive to cheer the hearts and keep alive the faith and stimulate the fidelity and zeal of our fellow-associates, prompted by the earnest desire to preserve, as far as possible, whatever of good pertaining to the Community we had at our command, and by the lingering hope that such good might be used, as a means or motive for renewing at some not-far-distant day the struggle for a lost cause; or as a basis for a new enterprise in some more favorable locality and under circumstances that would give us greater promise of success. But no efforts in that behalf seemed to be of any permanent value or practical use. The decree seemed to have gone forth that I and my generation should never enter the promised land; our eyes being merely privileged to look upon it from the mount Nebo of faith as it lay outspread in the dim distance beyond Jordan. For, do what we could to stay its progress, the work of disintegration and spoilation went on around us as the years swept by — one stone after another of our social structure being thrown down until now scarcely one is left resting upon another — the last vestige almost of what was once · so beautiful and fair having either been carried away or defaced beyond recognition.

The remaining portion of this History, which is the narrative of the Community in its dismantled condition, shorn of many of its most prominent and praiseworthy features — shorn too of much of its power for good both at home and abroad — of the Community in its " decline and fall," requires but little attention to details or to the regular methodical flow of its outgoing but never-returning tide. It might perhaps have been brought to a close with a recital of the incidents and resultants of the crisis of 1856, since that was virtually and practically the end of its existence as an experiment in the science of a divine order of society, or an attempt to actualize in an organic form the kingdom of God on the earth. But certain things transpired in its subsequent career which in my judgment possess moral and spiritual value of their own and are calculated to throw some additional light upon the great problem we endeavored to solve. Even in its decline and disappearance from the face of the earth, the Community had some important lessons for individual souls and for students of the great questions that relate to the progress of the race and to the final enfranchisement and harmonization of the world. What is to follow will be presented topically rather than chronologically, as a matter of convenience and as serving equally well the ends just indicated and the general purposes of historical literature.

Membership. The membership of the Community was at about its maximum when the change of 1856 was made, numbering some one hundred and ten persons. But for obvious reasons it at once began to decrease, the process of disintegration and excision going on by slow degrees until at the expiration of a dozen years scarcely more than forty remained, of whom not more than half were residents of Hopedale. The organization was preserved intact for that period, and such common interests and responsibilities as it represented were carefully and systematically guarded and provided for by those of our number who continued to dwell on the original Community domain. In process of time, however, the last hour of organic existence came to the body, and membership in it ceased forever.

Business Meetings, Official Servants, etc. Annual Meetings of the Community were held regularly on the second Wednesday of January from year to year until the 8th of that month, 1868, when the last one on record occurred.

20

Others also took place occasionally for several years, for the transaction of such special business as required attention. At the former, reports from the several Boards of Officers — the Directory, Treasurer, Council, Board of Education, Relief Committee, and Promulgation Committee — were presented, considered, and acted upon, in due order. Official servants were also elected for the ensuing year and business matters of interest and importance were formally introduced, discussed, and settled. Of these nothing requires notice in this connection, and only the more prominent officers elected subsequently to 1856 need be enumerated. E. D. Draper remained in the Presidency till Nov. 14, 1859, when he resigned and was succeeded by Wm. S. Heywood, who held the position till 1863, declining re-election at that date as he was making arrangements for removing from the village. Wm. H. Humphrey was chosen in his stead, and served by successive re-elections to the end. The Vice-Presidents in their order were Wm. S. Heywood, from 1856 to 1859; Wm. H. Humphrey, from 1860 to 1863; and Wm. W. Cook, from 1863 to 1868. The Recorders were Cyrus Bradbury till 1863 and J. Lowell Heywood thenceforth. Cyrus Bradbury was Treasurer after the retirement of Lemuel Munyan in 1856 until the office was rendered needless and abandoned. The original Real Estate Trustees, appointed May 1, 1850, were Adin Ballou, Ebenezer D. Draper, Wm. H. Humphrey, Butler Wilmarth, and Almon Thwing. The first three continued in office to the last. In 1853 Stephen Albee took the place of Butler Wilmarth, deceased, and was succeeded, upon his resignation in 1858, by J. Lowell Heywood. Almon Thwing relinquished his place on the Board in 1861, and the vacancy was filled by Jerome Wilmarth. A few years later the last two removed to other localities, the remaining three, who had been on the Board from the beginning and who constituted a legal majority, discharging the required duties of the office as long as there were such duties to discharge.

Landed Property, Buildings, etc. At the time of the dissolution of the Joint-Stock Proprietorship in March, 1856, and the consequent settlement of affairs pertaining thereto, nearly the entire bulk of our Real Estate possessions, including lands, mill-sites, streets, shops, barns, and other buildings, was transferred by legal conveyance to the firm of E. D. & G. Draper, for their sole use, behoof, and disposal forever. The Community, however, retained the ownership of several parcels of similar property, as before stated, the aggregate appraisal of which was about $10,000. It consisted of three dwelling-houses and the lots on which they stood, the School-house and Chapel, the village site, Community Square (so called), and the Hopedale Cemetery. The dwelling-houses were not long after disposed of to individual purchasers, the School-house and lot (the use of the building as a place of worship having been relinquished) to the town of Milford at a later date, and the village site was in process of time surrendered to the proper authorities of the resident population. The final act of transfer was executed on the 15th of December, 1873, when the Trustees of the Community conveyed to the Trustees of the Hopedale Parish, a religious body formed a few years before, " all right, title, interest and control in, unto and over Community Square, the Meeting-house standing thereon and the Hopedale Cemetery." This transaction virtually concluded the real-estate operations of the Community and cancelled the last claim it had upon that once widely extended domain, which, more than thirty years before, we, in devout thanksgiving to the giver of all good and with abounding faith and hope, consecrated to God and humanity.

The Practical Christian. The publication of this semi-monthly sheet, which commenced May 1, 1840, was continued with varying fortunes and to little pecuniary advantage through manifold vicissitudes for twenty years, or until May 1, 1860. I had always been its leading editor, though receiving substantial assistance from my clerical brethren at home, and from valued contributors and correspondents abroad. From an early date it had been printed at our own Community printing office, which, for my special convenience, was attached to my own little cottage at the corner of Main and Peace Streets. For some years its business interests were cared for by Asaph G. Spalding and Wm. S. Heywood successively as Publishing Agents; the latter holding that position at the time of the great change and through the then current and succeeding volume. But on the 1st of May, 1857, I, by definite arrangement with the Community, became sole proprietor and manager of all its interests and virtually the sole occupant of its editorial columns, except as I still welcomed to them acceptable articles from correspondents, of which there were not a few, especially at at the time of the "John Brown Raid" and subsequently thereto. With the decadence of the Community and the waning, at home and abroad, of interest in or care for the principles and objects to the furtherance of which the paper had always been devoted, there was a correspondingly diminishing inducement to continue its issue. The growing unrest of the country touching the great question of American Slavery, which was already assuming most menacing forms, and the concentration of the thoughts and energies of the people at large upon the impending crisis in national affairs, attended by an intensified arousal in all directions of the war spirit, to whose unhallowed sway many professed Non-resistants seemed to be giving way, led me to see that there must be a decided falling off from the subscription list at an early day and an utter failure thereby of pecuniary support; — led me to see furthermore that the ideas and principles which it was commissioned to disseminate among men, though constituting the very essence of the Gospel of Christ, were likely to become ere long the scoff and the scorn of men and to fail of a hearing even among the great masses of the people, and that consequently the continued publication of the *Christian* was largely a work of supererogation, and therefore, all things considered, inadvisable. Moreover, it appeared to me that whatever was demanded or warranted in the way of disseminating the truth we stood for could be accomplished satisfactorily through the agency of occasional tracts, which would impose but a light burden upon us, and one that could be assumed or laid aside at pleasure. So, after thoroughly canvassing the whole matter and coming to an intelligent conclusion concerning it, I recommended the discontinuance of the paper at the close of the 20th volume and the formation of a Promulgation Society, the work of which should be the preparation, printing, and distribution of such treatises, essays, dissertations, expositions, lectures, and sermons, in the form of leaflets and pamphlets, as might at any time be deemed needful or desirable. My recommendation was accepted by the brethren upon whom I had relied for financial support, the suggested Promulgation Society was organized, and *The Practical Christian* became a thing of the past with No. 26, Vol. XX, April 14, 1860.

The suspension of the paper, which was born out of an overmastering love for the truth and for humanity on the part of myself and my brethren, gave me not a little pain, and was an occasion of regret to a large number of subscribers, personal friends, and friends of radical reform scattered up and down the land. Many letters were received from these, expressing a grateful appreciation of the high character and salutary influence which the periodical had maintained, with sentiments of sincere esteem for the editor. The press also, especially the

progressive journals, philanthropic and religious, added
testimonials equally kind and commendatory. To one of
these, from the pen of Rev. Thomas Whittemore, D. D.,
editor of *The Trumpet and Universalist Magazine* — a
redoubtable dialectician and former antagonist of mine in
the Restorationist controversy, — was appended the following encomium upon our movement and its representatives :

"One word as to the Hopedale Community. So far as we
know they are a band of brothers and sisters who seek to
honor God by good lives. They are good citizens: they live
quietly and peaceably, and the Lord blesses them. Often when
we have been in Milford, we have desired to visit their houses,
but we felt (perhaps more than we ought) that in their sight
we were a heretic, and they would not receive us. Never
have we had an unkind word from them, however. Perhaps
it was a mere suspicion on our part. We will yet go to
Hopedale. We should love to live where Practical Christianity
reigns."

In War Times. The position of the Hopedale Community as the great War of the Rebellion came rushing
on and during its continuance, was unique and trying —
crucial even, to the utmost extent. We were tested by
it as to our faith as never before, and some of us were
found wanting. From the beginning we had been avowed,
uncompromising Abolitionists, doing what we could to
overthrow the system of American Slavery and hailing
with gratitude and joy every indication that the day was
drawing near when the last shackle should be riven from
the limbs of the bondmen and when "liberty should be
proclaimed throughout all the land to all the inhabitants
thereof." We had hoped and prayed that this great
consummation might be reached by peaceable means and
without violence and war, by the proclamation of the
principles of freedom and equity, and the consequent
enlightenment of the understanding and awakening of the
conscience of the people. But as time passed on and

the animus of the slave power became more and more rampant and diabolic, we were gradually brought to the conviction that this could not be; that the only way the gigantic iniquity would ever be brought to an end was by the effusion of blood — by the avenging judgment rather than the tender mercy of Almighty God. The nation had sinned away its day of grace. Its crime and guilt had become too virulent, too deep-seated, too much a part of its very life, to be expiated and put away except by commotions and upheavals involving immense sacrifice of men and treasure, and imperiling, in fact, the very existence of the Republic.

Even under these circumstances and with such a prospect before us, we could but rejoice in what we felt assured would be the outcome of the increasing disturbance — Emancipation — though it was to be accomplished by means which we could not in conscience approve and through agencies against which we were pledged by the most sacred of vows. Yet it was not without more or less of apprehension and solicitude that we watched the gathering storm and awaited the unfolding of events whose progress we had no power to withstand or direct. We could do little more than keep silence and possess our souls in patience, trusting that He who hath all destinies in His keeping, who bringeth light out of darkness and good out of evil, would overrule the threatened clash of arms to the ultimate deliverance of the oppressed and to the honor of His most holy name.

The question of American Slavery, which, in its primary and most radical aspects was of a moral and religious character, had for years obtruded itself into the political arena and affected to a continually increasing extent the organization and the policy of all political parties. With the growing aggressions of the Slave Power the agitation of it had increased in strength and in determination, until the time had come when the opposing forces were taking on a distinctively belligerent aspect and assuming a decidedly warlike attitude. The ill-advised raid of John Brown served to intensify the existing feeling in that respect, inflaming the war-spirit in all directions, and hastening the bloody outbreak, which, under any circumstances, could not long have been held in check. One after another of the old line Abolitionists seemed to be carried away from their moorings by the growing excitement, either renouncing outright their long professed Nonresistant principles or holding them in abeyance to such an extent as to enable them to eulogize and glorify the promoters of bloodshed and slaughter, and even the war system itself when employed for the emancipation of the slave. I was myself impelled to raise my voice in protest against and condemnation of such action on the part of my old friends and coadjutors, deeming it a violation of plighted faith and a practical adoption of the so-called Jesuitical maxim, "The end sanctifies the means." Nevertheless, the tide was against me, not only in the world at large but among Anti-Slavery Reformers, including some of my Hopedale brethren, and my favorite doctrine of Non-resistance, with its scruples against voting "in any case involving a final authorized resort to physical violence," was almost wholly swept away and submerged by the rising tide of brutality and blood. So that when the insane wrath of slave-holding secessionists lighted the flames of rebellion on Carolina's soil and "let slip the dogs of war" against the Federal Government, and the cry of military patriotism went through all the land calling men to arms in the support of *the Union*, several of our members, struck by the fell contagion, resigned their positions in our fellowship, thus honorably relieving themselves of their former acknowledged obligations "never under any pretext whatsoever to kill, assault or injure any human being, even their worst enemy," and also of the inconsistency of professing principles which they deemed impracticable and of no account in the existing crisis.

What now, in such a crisis, could the still adhering Community members do,— those who were still loyal to the Declaration which was the corner-stone of their structure and the summary of their religious faith? Their movement was wrecked — at least stranded on the shallows of time's outstretching sea — and mid the thickening gloom they could see little to hope for in its behalf within the sweep of their vision. They could scarcely keep their standing as the tempest raged around. Their only safety consisted in being true to their principles and true to each other, bearing aloft the white banner of " Peace and Good Will " while battle-flags were fluttering on every hand, and pledging themselves anew to each other and to the cause which they had in good conscience espoused, not for the passing hour or for peaceable and prosperous times alone, but for life. And so to keep their own record clean and their escutcheon immaculate ; to bear a united testimony for their avowed principles to their fellowmen, and protect themselves against any charge of treason to their native land or of indifference to its enduring welfare ; to make known in unmistakable terms their utter abhorrence of the Rebellion and of any and every measure, open or covert, North or South, which was seeking by force and arms to undermine and overthrow the Federal Government ; and to have their exact position in respect to the suppression of the Rebellion, as was attempted on the part of said Government, duly understood, the faithful remnant of our number, in regular meeting assembled on the 16th of Sept., 1861, passed a series of resolutions, seven in number, the first, second, and last of which, with the preamble, contain the gist of the whole and hence are given herein entire, to the exclusion of the others.

"Declaratory Resolutions.

"Whereas, a great and deplorable civil war has broken out between the Northern and Southern sections of the United States of America, the people of the latter being in organized revolutionary insurrection against the constitutional government of the Federal Union; and, whereas, we, the members of The Hopedale Community, are peaceable subjects of said constitutional government, though for reasons of conscience not active participants therein, nor martial combatants in any behalf; and, whereas, in the present momentous crisis our peculiar principles and position ought to be distinctly understood; therefore we the members of said Community, in regular meeting assembled, do adopt and publish the following Resolutions, viz.:

"1. *Resolved*, That we unanimously adhere with unwavering firmness to our fundamental religious principles as originally set forth by solemn Declaration in the year 1841 in the published Constitution of our Community, and as again set forth with some enlargement by a like solemn Declaration in the year 1854 in the published Constitution of *The Practical Christian Republic*, whereof we are also members.

"2. *Resolved*, That we unanimously adhere with unwavering firmness to the declared fundamental objects, positions, and policy set forth in the two said Constitutions, and especially in respect to the governments under which we live as peaceable subjects thereof yet non-participants therein, being conscientiously scrupulous against all chattel slavery, death penalties, injurious force, war, and dernier resorts to carnal weapons.

*   *   *   *   *   *   *

"7. *Resolved*, That in the light of the foregoing Resolutions our first and highest allegiance is due to the sovereignty of divine principles as taught by Jesus Christ:

"That our first and highest attachment must be to the glorious white banner of His kingdom, with the cross of self-sacrifice in the center, radiating a benignant halo in all directions, with a dove surmounting that cross, spreading her wings and bearing in her mouth an olive branch, and with a wolf and a lamb at its foot harmlessly resting together:

"That we cannot aid the best existing government on earth in destroying human life though our refusal should subject us to the bitterest martyrdom:

"That we are bound by our religious principles to be orderly, peaceable subjects of the governments under which we live, and to relieve the sufferings of our fellow-creatures around us to the utmost extent of a reasonable charity:

"That we can neither excite nor encourage any mob, riot, rebellion, insurrection or war-like revolution even for an ostensibly good object — much less such an abhorent insurrection as the one now raging at the South for the extension and perpetuation of human slavery:

"That while we deeply deplore the war itself now in process, we deplore still more the sinful causes which have rendered this great calamity inevitable under the eternal laws of divine order, as a just retribution for national transgressions, to wit: lust of wealth, lust of power, and lust of sensual pleasures, all culminating in the persistent upholding, by law and by force, of the gigantic institution of Africo-chattel slavery:

"That though we have no moral sympathy whatever with the insurrectionists, but much with the Federal Government and its loyal adherents, and though we see that the loyalists on their own worldly plane of action must conquer the rebels by overwhelming deadly force or ignominiously abandon their constitutional government and falsify their solemn obligations of allegience; yet we feel none the less bound to abide with Christ on his high plane of peaceful righteousness, and thereby endeavor, however gradually, to leaven the minds of mankind with those benignant principles which alone can put an end to all disorder and violence:

"That in the meantime we should be unfaithful to our convictions of truth and duty if we recognized this as a war for the emancipation of our down-trodden American bondmen, whatever may chance to be its actual results, and if we did not unequivocally reiterate our testimony against the aforementioned great national sins, especially the upholding of the slave system by both the North and South, which has brought on our country this calamitous scourge; and if, also, we did not earnestly entreat the people of all parties concerned to hasten their repentance and make all possible reparation to the injured millions whose cries are still going up to the infinite Father for redress:

"That we do not deem ourselves in any wise responsible for this terrible conflict, having done what we could in our humble way, by warning and example, to prevent it, and to avert the storm of retributive sufferings with which it comes down on the nation; so that nothing now remains for us in relation to it but to abstain from all complicity with it, to bear patiently our portion of its ills, to relieve where we can the distresses of its victims, and to look forward with unwavering confidence in the all wise providence of God to better days, when He shall have overruled all its wrath and woe for ultimate good:

"And, finally, that we deem it our proper mission under Jesus Christ to bear such testimonies and lead such lives as will tend to regenerate mankind, elevate them to the true Christian plane of personal and national righteousness, conform all human governments to the divine, abolish all dernier resorts to carnal weapons, supersede all deadly forces by beneficent ones, and thus consummate the reign of universal love and peace.

"Wm. S. Heywood, *President.*
"Cyrus Bradbury, *Recorder.*"

These resolutions were printed in tract form and distributed extensively among our friends and in the general community, serving no doubt a good purpose in making our attitude respecting the conflict that was already being vigorously waged and those engaged in it on both sides better understood than it could possibly have been before. And yet, however truthful, just, and meritorious the pronunciamento was, it was but a pebble thrown against the rushing tide of popular militant patriotism deluging the Union-loving but not yet slavery-hating North. And its effect was still less potent and salutary because it was cast by a palsied hand — by the remnant of a Community which had confessed itself incapable of putting into practice its own much vaunted principles of equity, brotherhood, and peace; especially in their application to the ownership and use of property, the management of business, the organization and right ordering of industry, and the maintenance of a miniature Christian commonwealth on its own proper domain. It served to appease the conscience of a few devotees of an ideal, to which, notwithstanding the violence of the storm — the wrath and scorn of men, they still could not be restrained from clinging, and to satisfy a small number of those who, although they were in full sympathy with the loyal North and saw no way out of the trouble but that of the battle-field, could yet appreciate the motives and respect the moral and religious scruples of devout and sincere men and women striving to be faithful followers of the great Prince of Peace; but it did not save those issuing it from the reproaches of the unthinking minions of the war-god, nor from the machinations of the agents of inexorable military power, than which no usurpation or despotism of autocrat or czar is more imperious, insolent, heartless, and unrelenting. This will appear from the following occurrence, which took place among us during the continuance of hostilities.

Case of Conscription. In the summer of 1863 one of our faithful and worthy members, J. Lowell Heywood, was drafted into the military service of the United (?) States under the Conscription Act of March 3 in the same year. This was a sore trial and a cause of much anxiety to himself and family, and scarcely less so to all the rest of us. That he could not enter the army and serve as a soldier there, was a foregone conclusion. The only question was whether he should pay the prescribed $300.00 commutation money, as the law allowed him to do, or submit to such military penalties as might be pronounced against him, however severe they might be. Public opinion among us was divided upon that question. A strong feeling prevailed that absolute consistency required that he should suffer a heroic personal

martyrdom, and thus bear the most effective testimony
to his religious principles; but it was also thought that
the commutation money might be paid by himself and
friends in good conscience and without blame, if it were
done under protest, thus saving him from indefinite incar-
ceration in fortress or prison, or from possible death,
should military infatuation or madness, as might be the
case, carry the matter to such an extreme. My personal
sympathies for his family in their distress overruled my
sterner convictions, and I gave my adhesion to the latter
view, drawing up a paper in remonstrance for presentation at martial headquarters, which, at the time, I persuaded myself met the moral demands of the case. This
course was finally approved by a majority of our members and carried into effect. As a further token of our
position at that great crisis of our national history, and
of our adherence to our standard of faith under perplexing circumstances, the document is herewith submitted:

" *To the Governmental Authorities of the United States and
their Constituents:* The undersigned, John Lowell Heywood of
Hopedale, in the town of Milford, in the eighth Congressional
District of Massachusetts, respectfully maketh solemn declaration, remonstrance and protest as follows, to wit:

" That he has been enrolled, drafted and notified to report
himself as a soldier of the United States, pursuant to an Act
of Congress, approved March 3, 1863, commonly called the
Conscription Law:

" That he holds in utter abhorrence the Rebellion which
the said law was designed to aid in suppressing, and would
devotedly fight unto death against it if he could conscientiously
resort to the use of deadly weapons in any case whatsoever:

" That he has been for nearly nine years a member in good
and regular standing of a Christian Community whose religious
confession of faith and practice pledges its adherents never
to kill, injure or harm any human being under any pretext,
even their worst enemy:

"That, in accordance with his highest convictions of duty and his sacred pledge, as a member of said Community, he has scrupulously and uniformly abstained from participating in the State and National governments under which he has lived — not only foregoing the franchises, preferments, emoluments and advantages of a constituent co-governing citizen but also the privilege of righting his wrongs by commencing suits at law and of calling on the government for personal protection against threatened violence, in order thereby not to make himself morally responsible for their constitutional dernier resorts to war, capital punishment and other kindred acts, and also in order to commend to mankind by a consistent example those divine principles which prepare the way for a higher order of society and government on the earth:

"That, nevertheless, it is one of his cardinal Christian principles to respect existing human government, however imperfect, as a natural outgrowth and necessity of society for the time being, subordinate to the providential overruling of the supreme divine government, and therefore to be an orderly, submissive, peaceable, tribute-paying subject thereof; to be no detriment or hindrance to any good thereby subserved; to countenance no rebellion, sedition, riot or other disorderly demonstration against its authorities; to oppose its greatest abuses and wrongs only by truthful testimony and firm moral remonstrance; and in the last resort, when obliged for conscience sake to non-comply with its requirements, to submit meekly to whatever penalties it may impose:

"That, with such principles, scruples, and views of duty, he cannot conscientiously comply with the demands of this Conscription Law, either by serving as a soldier or by procuring a substitute. Nor can he pay the prescribed three hundred dollars commutation money, which the law declaratively appropriates to the hiring of a substitute, except under explicit *remonstrance* and *protest* that the same is virtually taken from him by compulsion for a purpose and use to which he could never voluntarily contribute it and for which he holds himself in no wise morally responsible:

"And he hereby solemnly *protests*, not only for himself but also in behalf of his Christian associates and all other orderly, peaceable, tax-paying, non-juring subjects of the government, of whatever denomination or class, that their conscientious scruples against war and human life-taking ought in justice and honor to be respected by the legislators and administrators of a professedly Republican government; and that, aside from general taxation for the support thereof, no person of harmless and exemplary life, who is conscientiously opposed to war and deadly force between human beings, and especially no person who for conscience sake foregoes the franchises, preferments, privileges and advantages of a constituent citizen ought ever to be conscripted as a soldier either in person or property.

" Now, therefore, I, the said John Lowell Heywood, do pay the three hundred dollars commutation money to the government of the United States under military constraint and in respectful submission to the powers that be, but earnestly protesting against the exaction as an infraction of my natural and indefeasible rights as a conscientious, peaceable subject. And for the final vindication of my cause, motives and intentions, I appeal to the moral sense of all just men, and above all to the inerrible judgment of the Supreme Father and Ruler of the universe.

"Subscribed with my hand at Hopedale, Milford, Mass., this eighteenth day of August, 1863.

"JOHN LOWELL HEYWOOD."

Upon more deliberate and dispassionate examination of this whole matter, I had serious misgivings as to the rightfulness of the course that was pursued. The Protest, though inherently just and good, was too weak to meet the moral exigency of the case and produce salutary results. The spirit of conscienceless domination which tramples on such sacred scruples and rights as the document enumerates, seems to require a more stringent moral resistance in order to be made to feel its culpability and be brought to repentance — in order to be regenerated. It is sheer extortion and persecution; an outrage unwarranted, save in the ethics of brutal despotism, to conscript a man of such principles, character, and life as our victimized associate. And when committed, it should be met with unflinching moral heroism and personal martyrdom, even unto death, if need be, in order to

arouse public attention to the enormity of the offence
and induce a radical and most necessary reform in the
practical administration, not alone of military affairs but
of the concerns of states and nations. At least this is
my present persuasion.

Educational Interests. As Hopedale was a School District, legally established by the town of Milford as a
part of its general educational system, our common public
school was properly under the care and supervision of
the town's Committee. Nevertheless, we annually elected
a Board of Education, which acted in concurrence with
said Committee in public school matters, and exerted a
positive and salutary influence over the nurture and culture of our children and youth. Moreover, the Community appropriated money from year to year for the
purpose of extending the time of operating the school
beyond that provided for by the town, and of procuring
extra apparatus and supplies that might be deemed desirable for the more successful prosecution of school work.
Over this local appropriation and its expenditure, our
Board of course, had entire control. This practice was
followed down to the year 1861, our appropriations gradually decreasing meanwhile, until at that date they ceased
entirely; although our School Board was continued and
acted on substantially the same footing as before for some
years afterward. Our original Chapel-School-house served,
with sundry additions and improvements, though with
decreasing comfort and convenience, till the year 1868,
when it was superseded by the present commodious and
better arranged establishment erected on the same square.
This was built by the town, into whose hands the old
public school property had previously passed. While the
Community had a voice in the management of the schools
they maintained a high standing, and I am not aware
that they have in any essential respect degenerated since
that time.

21

The Hopedale Home School, under the successful management of Wm. S. and Abbie B. Heywood as joint
Principals, was closed soon after the breaking out of
the Rebellion, the troubled, uncertain state of things in
the country at large contributing chiefly to that result.
A private school at a later date was started and put in
charge of Miss Lucy Patrick, an accomplished and efficient teacher resident among us. It continued some two
years and was then given up.

Missionary Activities. The Practical Christian Communion, the organization which representated our cause in
the general region covered by our missionary labors,
continued to exist for some years after the opening of
the period reviewed in the present chapter, and held its
Conferences in different localities, though less frequently
than before. The local Inductive Communions subordinate to it very naturally declined in interest at the several points where they had been established, and at
length were given up altogether. The reasons for this
have already been indicated. There was a continually
diminishing call for the particular Gospel which our
ministers and lecturers deemed themselves commissioned
to proclaim and commend to the world, as there was
an equally diminishing opportunity to obtain a hearing
by any aggressive measures which we ourselves might be
disposed to inaugurate. The increasing disturbance in
the political world growing out of the multiplying usurpations and more desperate intrigues of the myrmidons
of oppression, unfitted the popular mind and heart for
the serious consideration of any great moral question or
theme of reform — of any weighty subject indeed, save
what related in one way or another to the essential cause
of the existing trouble and to the evidently approaching
crisis in the affairs of the nation. All else seemed out
of place and could get no hearing. The usual popular
ministrations of religion in all denominations were sensi-

bly affected by the prevailing excitement, and became
to a very large extent charged with a politico-military
spirit. The Old Testament rather than the New furnished
texts for sermons and maxims for human conduct. The
Jewish God of battles was the Deity to whom worship
was rendered rather than the Christian Father of all
mankind. And Joshua, leading the armies of the Lord
against the Canaanites, was deemed more worthy of emulation and imitation than Jesus, going about doing good
and teaching his disciples and all men to "*love their enemies, bless those that cursed them, etc.*" What were we
who were left of *The Hopedale Community* to do at such a
time as that with our Practical Christianity and message of
"Peace on earth and Good Will" to all mankind? What
could we do but wait until the storm had passed by, till
calmer days should come again and men were in a fitter
frame of mind and in a better temper to receive and profit
by the pure Gospel of the Son of God? To have attempted
anything else — to have kept up our missionary activities,
the instrumentalities of former days — would have been
as unwise as ineffectual — an utter waste of energy and
strength, of time and effort, on our part. And so our
Conferences were given up, our Inductive Communions
ceased to be, and our Promulgation Society, formed after
the suspension of *The Practical Christian* for the purpose
of issuing tracts and pamphlets when deemed advisable,
soon fell into dreamless inactivity. Whoever of us was
moved to go abroad, proclaiming the truth as he had
received it and applying it to human life as he thought
it wise and productive of good, did so on his own personal account, but the missionary feature of our socialistic
movement — our Community propagandism, with its various
appliances for service in the field of Humanity, was dead,
without hope of resurrection.

Religious Interests and Institutions. As was clearly indicated in the earlier chapters of this volume, The Hopedale

Community had a distinctively religious origin, and was
from the beginning to all intents and purposes a Christian
Church. So it was understood to be by its founders, and
so it was represented to the outside world. Its real basis
was an acknowledged Declaration of Faith, and its characteristic features and multiform activities were shaped
and directed by fundamental religious principles. Its
members all regarded themselves as pledged to loyalty to
Jesus of Nazareth, and to an earnest endeavor to lead a
life conformed to his precepts and example. They regarded
its various secular interests — educational, industrial, financial, social, civil, all its administrative functions, as subordinate to the dictates of divine and everlasting truth.
Its crowning purpose was to institute an order of society
conformed in all respects to the requirements of the Gospel of Christ.

One of its first concerns, therefore, after securing a
" local habitation and a name," was to provide for the
religious culture and nurture of all classes of our people.
As noted in its proper place, we established regular meetings on the first day of the week at the very outset for
purposes of worship and instruction in the things of the
spiritual life, and these were kept up during the entire
period of our history. An active and highly prosperous
Sunday School was opened early and became one of our
cherished and permanent institutions and an effective
instrumentality for good to our children and youth. The
Thursday evening Conference was a source of refreshing
and inspiration to considerable numbers of our population,
outside as well as inside our membership. The Monday
evening Meeting, designed more particularly for young
people but hospitable to all comers, prospered for many
years under my personal superintendence, and wrought a
most excellent work in the way of imparting to those
attending it a knowledge of religious truth and of nourishing the divine life in many souls. Even after the

change of 1856, although the more secular affairs of our people were subjected to a system of management radically different from what existed before, the religious activities remained virtually the same. And they continued much the same until circumstances and justice to all parties concerned seemed to warrant a readjustment in this respect, as will soon be made to appear.

In our early days nothing was paid as a pecuniary remuneration for preaching or otherwise conducting the services of public worship. There was a goodly number of professional clergymen, exhorters, and free-meeting talkers, in our home ranks, besides wayfaring public speakers from abroad, ready to serve us, both on Sundays and on other religious occasions. At a later day the Community adopted a more systematic method and selected certain responsible persons to take charge more particularly of our Sunday gatherings, an allowance of $1.25 being appropriated for each discourse delivered, the sum being afterwards increased to $3.00 per Sunday. Until the year 1856, the duties of the position were performed by the several ministers whose names have been repeatedly mentioned in the foregoing pages, although there was always provision made for such speakers from outside as might be acceptable to those having the matter in charge. Subsequently to that date, Bros. George Gay, a regularly ordained clergyman of the Universalist denomination, and Byran J. Butts, a graduate of the Meadville (Unitarian) Divinity School, both recent comers to our fellowship, shared the responsibilities of public religious teachers with Bros. Fish, Heywood, and myself. Bro. Fish soon after removed from the place, Bro. Gay later, and subsequently Bro. Butts retired from active ministerial service. This left Bro. Heywood and myself occupants of the field for several years, when, the former having gone from Hopedale and entered upon the work of the ministry elsewhere, I became the only approved

preacher of the Community and continued so to the end
of its days. The amount appropriated for the support of
preaching rose from $150.00 a year in 1856, or about
$3.00 each Sunday, to $6.00 dollars per Sunday in 1860,
$8.00 in 1864, and $12.00 in 1866. Two years later the
Community was virtually submerged in what has since
been known as "The Hopedale Parish," and its agency
in the management of the religious affairs of the village
came to an end.

The original school-house and Chapel building, completed in 1844, was made by enlargement and improvement to serve the public need as a place of worship and
general religious convocation until the year 1860, when
it was supplanted by the neat and commodious structure
which was erected on a commanding eminence at the rear
of Community Square, so called, near the center of our
growing village. The plot of land upon which it stood,
consisting of about two acres of rough wild pasture to
begin with, had been in process of improvement for several years, chiefly by the labors of our Industrial Union,
and of being made ready for the completed edifice by
grading, terracing, the planting of trees, etc. The building was provided for by subscription, a paper circulated
for the purpose of raising the requisite funds receiving
signatures and pledges of money varying from $1,800.00
appended to the names of E. D. and Anna T. Draper,
to $4.00 donated by one of our humbler members, the
whole amounting to $4,423.00. Its entire cost, including
slips and furnishings, was somewhat over $6,000.00 — the
excess above the subscription pledges being generously
supplied by the brothers, E. D. and George Draper.
The structure was in rectangular form, according to the
type of ecclesiastical architecture in vogue at that date,
measuring 58 feet in length by 44 feet in width with 30
feet posts, the front being surmounted by an appropriate
bell-tower. The Building Committee consisted of Wm.

H. Humphrey, E. D. Draper, and Wm. S. Heywood. Mr Lewis Fales of Milford was the architect; and Mr. Lowell Fales, the superintending carpenter until near completion; Bro. Wm. H. Humphrey succeeding him. The enterprise was brought to a fortunate conclusion in the autumn of the year named, and dedicatory services were held in the new sanctuary on the 15th of November. An account of what transpired on the occasion from the pen of Rev. Samuel May of Leicester, who was present, was published in *The Anti-Slavery Standard* of New York, from which the following extracts are copied:

"*To the Editor, etc.:* It is not often in this slavery-ridden country that the dedication of a new church building can have any special interest for the true anti-slavery reformer, or for the lover of Christianity in its genuine and incorrupt form. Very rarely would one of these receive an invitation to attend such an occasion and participate in its exercises. But the dedication of the new church edifice at Hopedale (Milford, Mass.) forms an exception to the rule on this subject; and as the Community there established is of a character to interest all true lovers of their kind, and all Abolitionists in an especial manner, a notice of the occasion becomes appropriate to your columns and may also prove interesting to your readers."
"Your correspondent was one of the numerous friends present and believes that all true Anti-slavery reformers may have a word of congratulation and God-speed for the Hopedale friends at this time."
"A particular description of the house will not be attempted. In a basement story, but entirely above ground, is a large and commodious room for vestry purposes; over that, the entire second story of the building (with the exception of two ante-rooms at the sides of the platform and from which there is communication with the vestry ante-rooms below), is devoted to the meeting-house proper. This is large enough to seat comfortably five hundred persons. It is neatly carpeted and the seats are cushioned uniformly throughout the house. The walls are simply but tastefully painted in fresco, and the entire interior has a very pleasing effect. It proves to be as favorable for the purposes of speaking and of musical expression as could be desired.

"On Thursday the 15th inst., at 10 o'clock A. M., an audience was collected from Hopedale and vicinity, which, with friends from greater distances, well filled the house. After an anthem by a choir of about twenty persons, the Building Committee delivered to the chosen Trustees the title deed and the keys of the house. The statement therewith made by Wm. S. Heywood was a very interesting one. The house had been built by voluntary subscription and donation; there had been no resort to a compulsory tax; there had been entire harmony and cheerful co-operation in the work; no accident to life or limb had occurred; and the completed building stood unencumbered by any debt. The pews were to be free to all without distinction — to old and young, to rich and poor, to black and white — and their occupancy would be entirely free of tax or charge; the house to be, in the first place, devoted to the uses of The Hopedale Community and of The Practical Christian Church there, and when not needed by them to be free to any person of good moral character who might desire to utter therein his or her convictions of truth and duty. Adin Ballou (the original mover and guiding spirit of the Community) then, on behalf of the Trustees, accepted the trust on the conditions named, adding that persons not connected with the Community were invited to come and take seats and share privileges in the house on the same terms with the members themselves, their contributions towards its expenses being wholly voluntary. After another anthem, an appropriate prayer was offered by Samuel May, and this was followed by the chanting of a hymn written for the occasion.

"The morning sermon of dedication was then delivered by W. S. Heywood, Principal of the Hopedale Home School, one of the stated preachers of the place. He essayed to define and illustrate religion. No better definition or classification of the duties of religion, he said, could be given than the old one — Love to God and love to man. The former of these two great heads he took as the subject of his discourse, the latter being reserved for the afternoon topic. The preacher proceeded in a manner clear, free and reverent, to set forth the being and character of God, the true nature of love to him and the ways of manifesting that love." "The hymn 'Nearer, my God, to Thee' was then sung very beautifully. The musical exercises throughout the day were under the direction of Mr. Joshua

Hutchinson of Milford, N. H., and were admirably arranged, forming a most attractive and impressive feature of the occasion.

"In the afternoon the numbers of the audience were perceptibly enlarged — the house being filled to the utmost extent. After a voluntary by the choir. Rev. John Boyden of Woonsocket, R. I., read well-chosen selections from the Scriptures most impressively. Another original hymn, beginning

'What house can we rear for the Infinite Mind,'

was sung, when Mr. Ballou offered the dedicatory prayer. Mr. Heywood read a summary of the principles held by the Community as sovereign and divine, and was followed by a song entitled 'What I live for,' from Mr. Hutchinson.

"The second part of the dedication sermon was then given by Rev. Mr. Ballou. It was an admirable exposition of the Apostolic doctrine that 'he who loveth not his brother whom he hath seen cannot love God whom he hath not seen.' Rev. Mr. Boyden and Rev. Mr. May made congratulatory remarks, each enlarging somewhat on the topics treated during the day.

"The house was then declared to be properly dedicated and set apart to the uses of religion as it had been defined and to the promulgation of those great principles relating to God and man and social life which had been set forth and enforced.

"In the evening the house was again well filled. Rev. Mr. Boyden offered prayer. A truly good original hymn by Miss Lucy Whitney (of Westminster) was sung; and Mr. Ballou said the meeting was free for addresses and remarks from any friends present, each speaker to be followed by some musical selection from the choir. Rev. Mr. Hassell of Haverhill was the first speaker, touching upon several interesting points in addition to the subjects presented in the day's discourses, opening a discussion in which Messrs. Ballou, Heywood, Hill of Milford, and May took part.

"Thus closed a series of uncommonly interesting and encouraging meetings." "And thus was set apart to the best of human uses — thereby best honoring the great and good Father of all — the new Hopedale Church wherein we trust and believe that many a meeting shall yet be held promotive of human freedom, growth and happiness; many a faithful Anti-slavery meeting, before whose penetrating light and earnest rebuke the hideous darkness of oppression shall be scattered and its apologists and defenders be put to shame and converted to a

better mind; many a Temperance meeting, which shall break
the soul-bondage of degrading habits and bring him who was
dead to be alive again, him who was lost to be found and
restored to virtue and peace; many a Woman's Rights meeting, where the shackles which tyrannical customs and laws
have imposed upon woman's just and rightful action shall be
weakened, until, at length, they fall entirely away; many a
Christian meeting, in short, where with all boldness the truths
of the kingdom of God shall be unfolded and multitudes be
brought by the beauty of holiness to lead lives of uprightness,
peace and good-will to man; thus rendering to God the highest glory.

> " 'My soul shall pray again,
>   Peace with this house remain,
> For here my friends and brethren dwell;
>   And since my Father here
>   Draws to his children near,
> My soul shall ever love thee well.' "

Although the Community in its organic capacity was
still in charge of the moral and religious activities of the
place, and although the formalities of worship and the
means of instruction and culture in the things pertaining
to the divine kingdom were scrupulously provided for and
maintained from year to year, yet, as time went on, there
was a manifest falling away from the high plane of
thought and conduct formerly occupied by the population
of Hopedale, and an unmistakably increasing conformity
to the spirit, maxims, customs, and general features of
that old social order from which we had been so long
striving to be emancipated. Plainly as some of us saw this
and deeply as we deplored it we were utterly unable to
prevent it. The gradually diminishing number of our
own members, the continual influx among us of individuals and families indifferent if not averse to our professed
principles and objects, the dominant spirit of secularism
and commercialism in our midst, and the spirit of politico-
military patriotism that prevailed in the community at

large, combined to relax and weaken the bonds that held
the masses of our people to lofty and noble ideals and
to cause a decline of the personally religious life on every
hand. A realizing sense of this state of things and an
ardent desire to stem the downward current, led a few
of the more devout and earnest of our remaining associates to propose the formation of a church, distinctively
so called, to include those outside our fellowship as well
as inside — all residents on our former domain who might
feel the embers of the divine life burning in their bosoms
and be disposed by a formal consecration to God, by
mutual pledges and confessions, and by whatever help
could be derived from associating together, to have these
embers fanned into a vigorous and perpetual flame. The
proposition met with considerable favor and measures
were taken to have it carried into effect. I hoped less
from this movement than some of my brethren but lent
it my encouragement, being in no wise disposed to throw
cold water upon any scheme which had in it the least
promise of promoting the Christian culture of any of
those resident within our borders, and especially of our
young people who were passing through the formative
period of their character and life. On the 29th of January, 1860, a church was organized, the nature, purpose,
and general tenor of which may be inferred from the
following extracts from its adopted

"Compact."

"In order more effectually to promote our own progress in
the Christian life as well as the extension of Practical Christianity among men, we, whose names are hereunto subscribed, do
unite in a Religious Association, to be called

The Practical Christian Church of Hopedale.

"And we do hereby pledge ourselves to care tenderly for
each other's welfare, both temporal and spiritual, and to
endeavor in all things to be to each other true and faithful
brothers and sisters in Christ Jesus our Lord.

" Any person may become a member of this body by a hearty acknowledgment of the following Declaration, and by conforming to such regulations as may be established from time to time for purposes of orderly edification and discipline.

" DECLARATION.

" We believe that there is one God, the Father, who is the author of all beings and things; who is infinite in Love, Wisdom, Justice and Power; and who is everywhere present both to will and to do as a self-conscious Spirit.

" We believe that Jesus Christ is the son of God; that the Father ordained him to be the saviour of the world; that he must reign till all things be subdued unto him; and that no soul can be saved without becoming personally Christlike in spirit, conduct and character.

" Therefore we acknowledge ourselves imperatively bound to reverence the teachings, obey the precepts, imitate the example, and cherish the spirit of Jesus Christ, according to our highest light and ability, in all the relations of life. And we further acknowledge ourselves imperatively bound by the precepts, example and spirit of Jesus Christ never intentionally to kill, oppress or harm any human being even our worst enemy.

" This Church shall from time to time establish or permit such ordinances as may be deemed promotive of personal holiness among its members. Such ordinances, however, shall never be considered as *ends* to be attained, but as, at best, only means of improvement and tokens of discipleship; and therefore their observance can never be required of any one who does not feel that it would be a privilege; nor can their administration be denied to those, whether in or out of our membership, who may sincerely desire it."

This movement started out promisingly and seemed to prosper for a year or two, attaining a membership, if my memory serves me, of fifty or sixty persons. But predominating influences were against it, the animus of the place being rather to acquire wealth and worldly distinction than to seek the kingdom of God and his righteousness. Under such untoward circumstances, *The Practical Christian Church of Hopedale* languished ere long into oblivion.

The last struggling effort to revive the Community cause and turn back the tide of events towards those objects and aims which inspired us at the beginning of our career and prompted the labors and sacrifices of those early days, was the formation of what was known as *The Hopedale Inductive Conference.* This was fashioned somewhat after the plan heretofore outlined and adopted many years before by our friends in certain favorable localities elsewhere. It was organized Sept. 26, 1861, and entered at once upon the work of indoctrination, unification, and consolidation it was designed to accomplish. It held regular weekly meetings, the exercises of which were conducted agreeably to a definite and carefully arranged system, devised and elaborated by me, and published the following year under the general title of "MONITORIAL GUIDE; *For the use of Inductive Conferences, Communities, etc.*" It was of a liturgical character, and was designed, as may be inferred, to aid in the intellectual, moral, and spiritual quickening and culture of both youth and adults in the principles and objects of The Practical Christian Republic, preparatory to practical efforts in behalf of the system of society represented by that comprehensive name. Its merits were satisfactorily tested by several years' experience in our Inductive Conference, which, running well during that period, was at length, for want of interested, hearty, persistent co-operation, indefinitely suspended at the close of the year 1867.

The end of the Community was now at hand. That consummation was hastened by the formation of what was called *The Hopedale Parish;* a name which the organization still bears. The reason for this new movement can be briefly stated and easily apprehended. With the advance of time the disproportion between the number of Community members resident at Hopedale and non-members had so greatly increased that the latter were largely in the majority. And yet they had no voice what-

ever in the management of matters pertaining to the
activities and institutions of religion, in which they took
more or less interest, and for the maintenance of which
they were year by year asked to contribute. There was
an inequality in this which arrested attention — a wrong
which the common moral judgment recognized and affirmed
ought to be righted.

Measures were therefore initiated looking to some
change in the administration of religious affairs whereby
all the people of the village — at least all who had any
care or concern in regard to such affairs — should have
the right and opportunity of co-operating on equal terms
with each other in the superintendence and control of
them. These, after due deliberation and consultation with
all parties interested, resulted in the organization on the
27th of October, 1867, of an association bearing the
before mentioned name, under a Constitution setting forth
its origin, its relations to the Community, its functions,
and general mode of administration. This instrument,
though quite unlike that upon which our movement was
based, had in it nothing essentially hostile to its spirit or
prescriptive requirements, and could therefore be approved
and supported by our remaining members without falsify-
ing any of their previous professions or avowals. It had
a flavor of religion about it, but contained no creed,
confession of faith, or declaration of principles, required
no promises from those subscribing it, and imposed upon
them no moral and religious obligations — not even the
obligation to lead an orderly, upright, humane, Christian
life ; every one being left free to think, believe, and act
according to the dictates of his or her own individual
reason and conscience. It simply claimed to establish a
Liberal Christian Society, to be called *The Hopedale
Parish*, composed of those resident in the village who
were willing " to co-operate, to a greater or less extent,
in supporting public worship, religious meetings, a Sunday

school, sacred music and other instrumentalities for the promotion of moral order in the neighborhood." This new body, which three months later, with myself as Pastor, was admitted to "The Worcester Conference of Congregational (Unitarian) and other Christian Societies," entered directly upon the execution of its proper work, the responsibilities and duties of which were cheerfully transmitted to it by the Community, and as cheerfully assumed on its part. The formal act of transmission took place at the Annual Community Meeting held Jan. 8, 1868, the record of which reads thus:

"Whereas, the inhabitants of Hopedale have recently formed a Liberal Christian Society, entitled *The Hopedale Parish*, under a Constitution which declares the same to be in general harmony with this Community, particularly in respect to 'supporting public worship, religious meetings, the Sunday School, sacred music, and other instrumentalities for the promotion of moral order in the neighborhood'; and whereas, said Constitution pledges said Parish to exercise all its powers, rights and privileges in friendly concurrence and co-operation with this Community in the respects aforesaid, and never to make any Constitutional changes unfriendly to our organization; and whereas, with the general consent of our resident members, who are also members of the said Parish, it has accepted the responsibility of managing the principal parochial affairs heretofore in charge of this Community— all of which fully appears in the Parish records: —

"Now, therefore, be it Resolved and Declared by the Hopedale Community in regular meeting assembled, that we fully assent to, approve of, and sanction the formation, organization, proceedings and measures thus far of the said Hopedale Parish.

"And be it further Resolved and Declared that, so long as The Hopedale Parish shall discharge the parochial responsibilities it has accepted in general harmony with the fundamental principles of this Community and according to its constitutional pledges, this Community will not interfere with its management of parochial affairs but quietly acquiesce in the same. Provided, nevertheless, that nothing herein contained shall in any way debar the Community from exercising its

right to advise or remonstrate, as a co-ordinate body with said
Parish, in respect to any future measure which may seem to
require Community intervention.

"Passed in regular Community meeting this 8th day of
January, 1868.

"Attest: E. D. DRAPER, *Moderator.*
                "J. L. HEYWOOD, *Recorder.*"

This was the last recorded act of The Hopedale Community in regular meeting assembled, and with it the
Community may be regarded as passing into a state of
innocuous desuetude and becoming only a memory of bygone
times. There had been chosen at a previous stage of
this same meeting the usual official servants, but all occasion for action on their part had ceased and they had no
successors. The Community, as such, now became utterly
and forever extinct. Some six years afterward, Dec. 15,
1873, its Real Estate Trustees, a permanent Board of
Officers and the only surviving representative of the parent
body, transferred, as stated on page 307, all right, title,
interest, and control in, unto, and over its remaining
territorial posessions to the Trustees of The Hopedale
Parish; and two years later, Dec. 7, 1875, passed into
the same hands the balance of the so-called Soward Fund,
which many years before had been donated by our esteemed
and faithful brother, Edmund Soward, for the purpose of
promoting the mental and moral improvement of the children and youth of the Community and village through the
agency of the Sunday School Library. According to the
conditions upon which this gift was made, only the income
derived from it could be expended from year to year,
and it had been held in trust subject to that restriction;
it was put into the keeping of its new custodians charged
with the same inhibition. Thus all transactions pertaining
to the affairs of the Community were brought to an end,
and the very name of our Hopedale movement became
thenceforth only a historical designation.

CHAPTER X.

THE opening paragraphs of this, the last Chapter of
the History of the Hopedale Community, will briefly
recount the more notable facts and features of our diversified experience in the new order of society we undertook
to establish, as a prelude to an exposition of the defects
and weaknesses of the enterprise, and especially of the
cause or causes of its ultimate failure. During the twenty
years that have transpired since it suffered the fatal blow
that sealed its doom, I have had time to review the whole
matter with painstaking and prayerful deliberation, which
has resulted in the recasting of some of my previous
hastily formed opinions, and in reaching conclusions that
I desire to put on record for posterity as my final verdict
in the case. A rapid survey of the field whereon we
toiled and suffered, won victories and sustained defeats,
rejoiced and lamented, will aid me in carrying my purpose
in this regard into effect.

The founders of The Hopedale Community, as has been
already shown, were so-called Independent Restorationists
in speculative theology, and universal moral Reformers in
respect to the application of religious truth to human life
in its various departments, relations, and manifestations.
They believed in the Fatherhood of God and the Brotherhood of Man, and in the principles and precepts of the

22

New Testament as taught and exemplified by Jesus Christ. They were animated by a rational and devout ambition to hold their faith, not merely as a dogmatic statement, or an intellectual conception, or a passional sentiment or emotion, but as the rule and the inspiration of life — as the power of a renewed personal character and the incentive to, and basis for, a divinely ordered form of human society. To their apprehension theory ought to be exemplified in practice, and the principles and spirit of Christianity should have illustration in, as they were deemed applicable to, all human interests and concerns; social and civil as well as individual. This view characterized their thought and directed their career. Their premises and conclusion were to their minds indissolubly related and invulnerable to just criticism. If God were their Father, they were to live before him and with each other as reverent, dutiful, trusting children. If all men were their brethren, they were under sacred obligations to love them and do them good; nay, more, all injustice, hatred, vindictiveness, cruelty, oppression, violence, wrath, and war was wrong and ought to be overcome and put forever away; and they were in duty bound to pray and labor to secure that important consummation. They ought, moreover, to espouse and do what they could to advance every good cause, to aid every movement calculated to benefit and bless mankind. If Christianity were a divine religion, charged with that truth and grace which are commissioned of God to redeem the world from sin and bring in the reign of universal righteousness, then it should control all human action; and the habits, practices, and customs of men — their institutions, laws, and systems, whatever their name and by whomsoever maintained, repugnant to it, should be renounced and abandoned, and the whole complex order of society, in its unfraternal and unchristian features, should be reconstructed and made to conform to and represent its holy requirements. In case this could not be done, by reason of the ignorance, moral incompetency, or unchristianized will of those by whose agency these things were practised, upheld, and perpetuated, under the existing social system, then it became the true followers of the Nazarene to join hands, hearts, and all possible active efforts for the work of building a *new* system from the foundations upward, which should be in harmony with the Master's teachings and stand before men and angels as the type and imperfect, because human, realization of that kingdom of heaven which he came to establish upon the earth.   Under the power and inspiration of such logic, which to them was incontrovertible, the founders of The Hopedale Community entered upon their work; under the same power and inspiration did they and their later associates and successors prosecute it to the end.

The membership of the Community during its entire existence was composed of men and women belonging to the more substantial, self-respecting middle class of American society — the rank and file of the American people. It included, first and last, six or eight ordained ministers of the Gospel, two experienced and skillful physicians, several well-equipped and competent teachers in the various branches of useful knowledge, writers for religious and reformatory journals, platform speakers, conference room exhorters, together with numerous farmers, gardeners, carpenters, machinists and a goodly number of other handicraftsmen — a plain, common sense, intelligent, high-minded population. As a whole, we were in no proper sense such a set of visionary dreamers, deluded fanatics, restless impracticables, and thriftless incompetents, needing a guardian or some master spirit to take pity on us and save us from our own folly and imbecility, as has sometimes been represented by certain orators and authors, who seemed more desirious of depreciating us and our labors, sacrifices and achievements,

than of telling the truth about us and doing exact justice
to us and our cause. To be sure, there were now and
then persons who came to us from selfish and unworthy
motives, seeking an easy place for themselves and a
supply for their own and their family's needs which they
were too indolent and shiftless to earn elsewhere. To be
sure, we were beset by a great variety of visitors, good,
bad, and indifferent, hailing from far and near, professing a friendship for us and our movement; not infrequently claiming to be philanthropists and reformers *par
excellence*, and bringing with them, it may be, some special
device for bettering the condition of world — some new
panacea for one or more of the manifold ills which humanity is heir to, — the crudest follies or impracticabilities
perhaps. But few of either class ever gained an entrance
within the pale of our organic fellowship; or, if they did,
were soon convinced that they were out of place and voluntarily retired, never attaining any appreciable influence
in shaping our polity or in the systematic management of
any of our affairs. Follies no doubt we had and defects,
whereof we had reason to be ashamed and repentant, but
they were not of the sort alleged. If we were in any sense
dreamers and visionaries, an imputation we were never
disposed to take offence at or deny, we were only such
as Jesus Christ and his Apostles were and taught us to
be, when they pictured to us a kingdom of righteousness,
peace and joy for which we should pray, a coming reign
of equity and brotherhood which we should seek to inaugurate, under whose benignant sway

> "All crime shall cease and ancient fraud shall fail,
>   Returning justice lift aloft her scale;
>   Peace o'er the world her olive wand extend,
>   And white-robed innocence from heaven descend."

As a matter of fact, no one who knew us and was
disposed to be just towards us could deny that, with the
rare exceptions alluded to, we were a most practical,

self-supporting company, industrious, ecomomical, hus-
banding well our resources, and putting our means to
good uses. Not a dollar was expended by us for intoxicating liquor, for enervating pleasure, or pernicious
amusement. Bad habits, always more or less costly,
were under proscription, and for the most part absolutely
prohibited. Even tobacco, when previously used, was
laid aside by those entering our membership, one person
only continuing the indulgence, and that after repeated
ineffectual attempts to overcome the appetite. We spent
nothing on military trappings or displays; nothing on
spectacular and boisterous demonstrations of any sort;
nothing on political manœuvreing or masquerade; nothing
on police supervision or litigation — no occasion for the
former ever existing and all differences or controversies
among ourselves or with our neighbors being settled by
amicable conference or peaceful arbitration. As to constables, sheriffs, criminal prosecutions, or court proceedings outside of simple probate concerns, we had no use
for them.

But it was not our chief ambition or desire to earn
and save money for our own necessity, comfort, enrichment, or exaltation, with no thought or regard for the
acquisition of those riches of the heart and soul which
are an eternal possession, or for the contribution we
could make for the promotion of the welfare of our
fellowmen. Our *chief* labor was "not for the meat that
perisheth but for that which endureth unto everlasting
life." We sought first "the kingdom of God and his
righteousnes." We were, I repeat, a sincerely and earnestly religious people: not on the ground of escaping
the merciless inflictions of an Almighty avenger after
death, or of gaining some exceeding great reward in a
future endless heaven; but in order to escape the evils
and consequences of sin both in this world and in the
world to come, and to secure by right-doing the benefits

and blessings of a heavenly inheritance here as well as hereafter; and not only for ourselves but for others, to the utmost extent possible. Pursuant to this predominating purpose, we maintained the institutions and appliances of moral and spiritual culture and inspiration with scrupulous fidelity at home; we sent missionaries out into the surrounding world to preach the Gospel of Chirst as we understood and applied it, calling men to repentance for their follies and sins and to the new life of love to God and man which that Gospel required; we also created a literature of our own, expository of our interpretations and applications of divine truth, and distributed it far and wide in all directions, as an effective instrumentality of human enlightenment and redemption. All this cost time, thought, effort, money—was a continual draft upon the varied resources at our command.

Nor were these the only contributions we made for the good and happiness of our kind. As Abolitionists we were not only called upon for financial aid in carrying on the general warfare against the giant iniquity of American slavery, but had frequent occasion to extend our hospitality to the apostles and champions of freedom going up and down the land preaching deliverance to the bondmen, and to furnish food, clothing, and shelter to some poor fellow-human being fleeing as for his very life from the clutch of the oppressor and making an appeal to us for help. As Temperance people we not only gave to the treasury of that movement, but received again and again to our care, protection, and uplifting influence the broken-down victims of the inebriating bowl, sent us by friends or coming of their own accord to find within our borders a refuge from temptation, as also encouragement and aid to reformation. Other good causes in their time and turn made their appeals to us for money or other means of promotion, nor ever made them in vain. Our reputation for kindness and charity in the general neighborhood about us brought us many a supplicant for alms, no one of whom was turned coldly away. We had advertised our Community extensively and were visited by professed inquirers, friends of social reconstruction, and others, from different parts of the country, to all of whom we offered entertainment for days and weeks sometimes, usually without pecuniary return — occasionally with sharp criticism and cheap advice as a recompense. Taking all things into account, it may be reasonably questioned whether any equal population in the country of corresponding pecuniary means gave, during the period of our Community's existence, a tithe of what we did for religious, philanthropic, and reformatory purposes and objects, outside of its own distinctive boundaries.

Moreover, for several years we educated our children at our own expense, never receiving a dollar from the town of Milford though we paid taxes continually into its treasury; and through all our history the amount thus contributed to its resources year by year was hundreds and thousands of dollars in excess of what was returned to us under any and every form of expenditure in our behalf or re-imbursement whatsoever. And yet we never made a single pauper or criminal whereby the town was put to the least trouble or cost, or caused it to use any of its funds for the relief of any of our own poor, for police surveillance and protection, or for municipal interposition and action of any sort. The Community was composed of not simply a busy, thrifty, self-subsisting class of people, but one eminently large-hearted and benevolent, their frequent and generous donations and their open-handed, ungrudging hospitality testifying to their enterprise, practicality, and power of production.

Further testimony to the same effect may be found in a brief statement of what was actually accomplished by The Hopedale Community during the fourteen years in which it was master of the situation and exercised supreme and undivided control over all industrial and business affairs within its recognized jurisdiction. It was organized under the name of *Fraternal Community No. 1* at Mendon, Mass., Jan. 28, 1841. The number of original members was 32, to which there were added by subsequent admissions and at indeterminate intervals, 165, making the entire membership, 196. Of these there are left nominally associated together at this time of writing (1876), about 35, only 14 of whom continue to reside on its former domain; the others who are still living being scattered far and wide over the country. The first purchase of lands at Hopedale for its occupancy and use was effected June 30, 1841, and consisted of what was known as " The Jones' Farm," containing 258 acres. Later additions from time to time, which included two adjacent farms and other contiguous territory, increased the aggregate extent of its domain to nearly or quite 600 acres, comprising the village site, horticultural grounds, orchards, farming fields, wood and meadow lots, mill-ponds, thoroughfares, etc. The earliest settlement on our territory was made sometime in October, 1841, by a family of five persons. In the latter part of the following March, at which date operations actually began, there was a colony of seven families on the premises, numbering twenty-eight persons. The population, including members, probationers, dependents, employes, and permitted residents, multiplied by gradual accessions until at the time of the surrender in 1856, it aggregated some three hundred.

The first Joint-Stock property of the Association actually in hand was $100.00; at the time of settlement in the spring of 1842, it was $4,000.00. It increased from year to year until it exceeded $40,000.00. The property of individual members of the Community was estimated to begin with at about $10,000.00; it was not less than $90,000.00 when the dissolution took place.

The Community entered upon its career on a much run
down estate, in a single ancient farm-house, with two
dilapidated barns and several outbuildings in similar condition; access to and egress from which were obtained
over narrow, crooked, uneven, wretchedly built highways; — it left that estate and the accessions to it in
excellent condition for agricultural and horticultural purposes, and made the center of its population and activities
a neat village of some fifty pleasant dwellings, located
amid gardens, orchards, shade-trees, shrubbery, and flowers, upon carefully laid out and well-constructed streets,
with substantial manufacturing establishments along its
western border — one of the neatest, most quiet, beautiful,
charming little hamlets in the Commonwealth of Massachusetts. A most desirable, highly prized, promising
possession it was to us, purchased for and consecrated
to disinterested, philanthropic, noble uses and objects,
preserved, enriched, embellished by us, as the seat and
center of a great movement for the bettering of the world;
but which, by force of adverse circumstances and conditions, we were compelled to convey to our successors,
to become under their skillful management the theatre and
vantage ground whereon to gain wealth, social distinction,
political honor, and other like emoluments and rewards.
The story of its varied experiences, joyous and sad, of its
struggles and attainments, of its victories and defeats, the
Community now bequeaths to coming generations, that the
wise and good and true belonging to them may be instructed
by its lessons, and peradventure helped to achieve, on
kindred but not necessarily identical lines of effort, far
larger, nobler, and more enduring results in the same
beneficent and blessed behalf.

Yes, we failed. Failed just as we had attained an
apparently praiseworthy and permanent success; just as
we were feeling assured that we had overcome our most
serious difficulties, surmounted our greatest obstacles, van-

quished our most obdurate foes, and were beyond the reach of peril; just as we had planned and were beginning to put into execution schemes of colonization and programmes for founding new communities — offshoots of ours — in some of the more attractive and promising sections of our great country. And our failure being a confessed fact, it is both desirable and important to understand the nature of that failure — the causes that led to it and the reasons why it transpired. To the solution of that problem the concluding pages of this volume will be chiefly devoted.

And the point which first demands consideration is that involved in the inquiry whether or not our discomfiture — the defeat of all our plans and hopes is to be regarded in any proper sense as a financial or business disaster; or in other words whether or not it was primarily and essentially due to a lack of business capacity on our part and to the special pecuniary straits in which we found ourselves at the opening of the year 1856. Had the Community become bankrupt, as the saying is, and was it compelled to stop operations in order to meet its pecuniary obligations and satisfy its creditors? By no means. No one who knew the exact status of our several industries, the condition of our treasury, and our standing in the business world at the time, would decide the question affirmatively. Nor would any one familiar with our industrial and financial history from the beginning as it has been outlined on the preceding pages. Notable facts of that history having a definite bearing upon the matter may be formally recapitulated. 1. Our Joint-Stock investment at the time of the suspension of our consolidated activities was, as stated, more than $40,000.00, while our individual property was about $90,000.00; nearly all of which had been produced on our own territory since we first occupied it. 2. The Joint-Stock had never depreciated in value but remained at par from the beginning;

not a share having ever been sold, transferred, or surrendered for one cent less. The final disposal of it was on that basis, and not a single person ever suffered loss by having it in his possession. 3. For the greater part of the time the entire list of stockholders received the stipulated four per cent. interest on their money, and outside parties always. 4. Every dollar of the Community indebtedness from first to last was honorably paid and our credit wherever we were known was never impeached or questioned. 5. The members, probationers, and dependents of the Community were able to secure under its management or by industries which it established or sanctioned upon its territory, a comfortable home, means of subsistence, and an adequate supply for all the material needs of themselves and families; with money besides for intellectual, moral, and religious culture and for benevolent uses, while most of them realized an increase of individual property; the whole of such increase amounting to $80,000.00; or an average of about $2,000.00 for every household in our membership. 6. The reported deficit at the time of suspension was less than $2,000.00; reckoning actual depreciation of property, losses incurred, etc., it might have amounted to $10,000.00 or $12,000.00. But what was that compared with the average losses of the business world, where, as carefully prepared statistics prove, more than 90 per cent. of the enterprises and ventures result in bankruptcy? The deficits incurred by an equal population with ours engaged in similar kinds of industry for the same length of time, under ordinary circumstances, are far greater than we experienced. Several persons once in our membership and living comfortably, with gradually accumulating means while with us, sunk more in ten years after leaving than we all together did in fourteen, and in one instance six or eight times as much. 7. Again, the great majority of our people, both managers and common workmen, gained under our

regime such habits of industry and frugality, such lessons
in handicraft and financiering, such development of productive ability, as enabled them to become more independent and successful from a secular point of view
after Community administration was given up than they
were before or probably would subsequently have been
without that experience. They were therefore on this
ground gainers rather than losers by the Community, to
say nothing of the superior intellectual, moral, social, and
religious advantages which, under its wise and generous
provision, they were privileged to share. 8. Finally, it
is to be noted that the successors of the Community in
the ownership and management of business affairs, on
the foundation which the Community laid and with the
facilities which the Community had provided and passed
over to them, proceeded at once, without disaster or
serious hindrance, to build up a fortune that in a few
years far exceeded the wildest fancies of any of our
dreamers in that direction and would have been deemed
collossal by all of us — would, in fact, have placed us
on sure foundations and beyond all danger in that particular. Taking all these things into account it is made
to appear that our failure was not like that which so
often occurs in business circles — not like that of most
of our contemporary social experiments, a financial one —
was not caused by a lack of business capacity among us,
or by the pecuniary exigencies and embarrassments to
which we had been brought in the conduct of our affairs.

What then did produce the fatal crisis? Why was it
deemed necessary to suspend the operations of our combined industry, surrender our Joint-Stock holdings, and
dissolve our peculiar associated relations, going back to
the assumption of strictly individual interests and responsibilities, to the old competitive, unfraternal, unchristian
business methods and to the long-established usages, maxims, customs, and institutions of the world at large? It

was because, as a whole, we lacked the Christlike wisdom
and virtue necessary to the successful prosecution and final
triumph of such an undertaking, — those qualities of mind,
heart, and character, without which any comprehensive,
all-sided movement for the individual and social uplifting
of humanity — any organized attempt to realize the divine
kingdom on the earth in a radical form, must, in the nature
of the case, prove abortive. Our experiment was born
out of due time. It was scores and perhaps hundreds of
years ahead of the age in which it was put on trial.
The world, even the best part of the world, was not
ready for it — was not at the stage of moral and spiritual
development in which it could understand, appreciate and
supply the appropriate atmosphere for a work so thorough,
so all-embracing, so superior to all the ordinary aspirations
and ambitions of men, so antagonistic to the selfishness,
pride, arrogance, contention, belligerancy, and barbarism
that characterize existing society ;— to say nothing of its
indisposition and lack of desire to enter into, sustain,
and carry such a work forward to triumphant issues.
And not only was the world, or the best part of the
world, notwithstanding all its professions of intelligence,
virtue, philanthropy, piety — of Christian love and loyalty — not ready for such an undertaking, but we ourselves, who had assumed to enter upon it, were not ready.
We had too many of the infirmities of the carnal nature
about us, we were too much under the dominion of the
worldly mind, we entered too little into the Spirit of the
Master, and were entangled with too large a number of
the errors and follies of the prevailing religion of the
church to win the success of which our cause was intrinsically worthy. We lacked the wisdom, the grace, the
large-mindedness, the generosity, the nobility of soul, in
a single word, the Christlikeness that was requisite to the
end we sought, that qualified us to be the builders of a
temple on every stone of which was to be inscribed

" Holiness to the Lord." Probably the best of us lacked these qualities in too great a degree, and it may be that those most wanting in them were as true to their light and capability as their more favored brethren. I judge no one in this matter but refer all judgment, whether of approval or condemnation, to Him who cannot err and whose verdict is righteous and irreversible.

Some have been disposed to censure severely and blame without reserve the Brothers Draper for their course in the matter — for their agency in bringing on the fatal crisis, charging them with treachery to the cause they had espoused and with infidelity to their brethren. I have never sympathized with such imputations. To be sure, these men unitedly owned three-fourths of the Joint-Stock of the Community and had a constantly increasing income from their own .private business, which was carried on outside of Community superintendence, though in accord with its established polity. To be sure, it was their decision to withdraw their portion of the common funds from the treasury that precipitated our overthrow. And it is also true that they were enabled to erect upon the foundation which had been laid by us with much study, labor, self-denial, and prayer, an enterprise that yielded them personally an ample fortune and enabled their successors to rise to a commanding place among the opulent capitalists of their day and generation. But I could never yield assent to any charges, open or implied, of infidelity or betrayal of trust that may have been preferred against them, usually from outsiders; certainly not of perfidy or injustice towards their brethren; nor could I count them sinners above all others in the competitive, money-making, self-seeking world. For the reason, that neither of them ever sought to enrich himself at the Community's expense, or took advantage of its necessities, or shirked his share of its burdens, or tried to absolve himself from any of its obligations. On the contrary, both helped it in many a time of need, by augmenting its capital, by enhancing its credit, by co-operating cheerfully with their brethren in maintaining its honor, and not infrequently, especially in the case of the elder, by making it important and gratefully-received donations.

I did at the time greatly deplore the decisive step on their part by which our associated endeavors were brought to an end. I longed to have them and all my associates prize the cause as I did, see the matter as I saw it, feel as I felt, and be willing and happy to do with their means as I should have done had I been favored as they were — use them for the good of our body and for the continuance and advancement of the work to which we were all sacredly pledged. And I then had, as I have now, no doubt, that if these two brothers had been so minded, the Community would have gone on prospering and to prosper for many years after its career was terminated.

But as the movement rested wholly on the basis of the inherent and indefeasible individual rights of its members — rights of conscience, of private judgment, of personal possession of property, and of voluntary action in the management of our common affairs, I always held these sacred, and never attempted or desired to dictate, coerce, overrule, or over-persuade any one, even to save the Community from dissolution. I never could respect or love or have confidence in any social experiment that was not undertaken by intelligent, free-minded, willing-hearted men and women — persons sincerely and reverently obedient to divine moral principles, and not blindly subservient to mere human authority of any sort whatsoever. Much as I desire and pray for a true Community, I want none for the sake of merely temporal and worldly advantage, and none in which the individual member loses his identity in the general mass and is made less a man or woman by socialistic organization or polity. Perish all plans of social reform — all devices, expedients, schemes, systems, that destroy or dwarf the human personality, that limit or enthrall any of the capabilities or possibilities of the children of the infinite Father of all mankind. I do, however, sincerely believe in the practicability and coming actualization of a social order, or system of communal life, under which those capabilities and possibilities shall be exercised, unfolded, and enjoyed illimitably. Only that attainment is far more difficult and demands a far higher development of character and a far fuller and richer experience of the life of God in the soul of man than I formerly conceived.

Moreover, I am now able to see from my present point of observation, that, if the Brothers Draper had been of the same mind as myself — had been willing to devote their rapidly accumulating property to the further development, growth, and prosperity of the Hopedale Community, it would have sooner or later failed; and for the same general reason already given; on account of the same lack of moral qualification which existed at the time of its suspension, and which, I repeat, will forever prove fatal to any enterprise of like character and purpose at any period of the world's history. I at present see no ground for believing that, with the prevailing currents of society setting so strongly in the direction of the accumulation of wealth, of political preferment, of fashionable display, of easy-going morality, and of a religion still studiously careful not to offend too seriously the popular taste, or habits of the multitude by arraigning and condemning giant wrongs and unchristian practices in social, civil, and national life, — I see no ground for believing under these circumstances that the menbership of the Community would up to this moment have been raised to a higher moral and spiritual level than it occupied at that time, even had it been possible for it to have maintained its then existing integrity and standing before the divine law and in the presence of Him who is of purer eyes than to look upon iniquity with favor, and whose kingdom in this and all possible worlds is righteousness and peace and joy. No Community can be a success except its membership consist of persons the like of which the world even now possesses very few.

For it is my profound conviction, formed at the time and confirmed by long and careful observation, experience, and reflection since, that, notwithstanding the weaknesses, faults, and shortcomings of our Hopedale fraternity, it was composed of men and women as well equipped, intellectually, morally, and spiritually, for the realization of their ideal of what human life and human society upon the earth ought to be, as any equal number that could have been brought together from any quarter or portion of the habitable globe. I sincerely believe that if we had gathered our numbers from the rank and file of any church, philanthropic organization, moral reform society, or philosophical club in or out of Christendom, organized them, and put them to the work of social reconstruction under circumstances like those amid which we were placed at Hopedale, we should have met with a no less disastrous defeat than we encountered, and very likely at an earlier date. The religion, ethics, philanthrophy, culture of general society, or of any particular class of reformers or moralists, impose too little self-discipline, self-denial, self-restraint, upon individuals and families to fit them for a voluntary, close intimacy, and union of the manifold secular interests and business activities of life. They leave their subjects too egoistic, angular, self-opinionated, mercenary, combative, belligerent, revengeful; too crude, inconsiderate, capricious, fastidious, undrilled, in their tastes, tempers, wills, judgments, to live with each other or with any number of their fellowmen on terms of equality, fraternal co-operation, and mutual good feeling. The great mass of people, even of reputed good people, find it somewhat

23

difficult to get on harmoniously and happily together in existing society for a great length of time, notwithstanding all the bars, prohibitions, and restraints imposed upon them there. They can meet as neighbors and acquaintances, as persons interested in certain common pleasures, pursuits, objects in life, and continue permanently in sweet and joyous accord. They can commingle and act together on occasions and for a brief period, in order to promote some cherished intellectual, literary, charitable, scientific, æsthetic, moral, or religious enterprise or aim — they can maintain a conventional round of friendly visitation, of mutual conference, of amusement seeking, of lecture hearing, or of church going, without jeopardizing their good opinion of each other or the general harmony and happiness. Whereas, too frequent intercourse, daily contact, seeing each other in all moods, in all costumes, in all habitudes of thought and feeling, and, above all, working side by side, holding property in common, managing business together — this is quite another matter; this is leaving the poetry for the prose of life; it is an ordeal which few can patiently submit to or endure. The intimacy of the relation which must necessarily exist in any form of Community life, whereby the weaknesses, follies, foibles, idiosyncracies, disagreeabilities, and offensive characteristics of each and every individual are disclosed, requires a consideration, a forbearance, a kindly and forgiving disposition, a measure of the true Christ-like spirit, rarely possessed by any considerable number, much less by any associated body of persons, whatever their profession or the name by which they are designated. In taking this view of the matter I can but have brought forcibly to mind a passage from the letter of Dr. Wm. E. Channing to me in the early days of our movement, as it appears on page 42 of this work: "I have for a very long time dreamed of an association, in which the members, instead of preying on one another and seeking to put one another down, after the fashion of this world, should live together as brothers, seeking one another's elevation and spiritual growth. *But the materials for such a community I have not seen.*"

Such materials as a matter of fact do not exist at the present stage of human development, save in rare instances, even within the pale of the nominal Christian Church, the more liberal and progressive branches of the Christian Church not excepted. And there are good and sufficient reasons for this. The mass of professing Christians of all schools have no definite and adequate conception of a divine order of society *among men* — no lofty, sublime, inspiring ideal of the reign of righteousness, brotherhood, love, peace, and joy *on the earth.* If they have any conception or idea at all of such an order or reign, it pertains, not to the present but to a future state of existence, — not to this world but to the world to come. Christianity is generally preached and believed as culminating in so-called civilization; in civilization improved, it may be, lifted to a somewhat higher plane of thought and conduct perhaps, but yet a civilization or order of human life in which the essential maxims, usages, customs, institutions of the world *as it is* shall continue to exercise predominating sway in the affairs of men; in which the existing relations between man and man, between different classes of people, between the great interests of society, shall remain virtually the same as they now are, especially in the more advanced portions of the globe. The notion of a radical change in these regards; of a social regeneration corresponding to a regeneration of personal character and life, is quite foreign to the thought, the aspiration, and the specific aim of the average church-member of this age. The notion of a dynasty of right principles — of justice, mercy, truth, and love, under which self-seeking, mammonism, love of display, scramble for preferment and power, the gross inequalities of social condition, tyranny, national jealously and ambition, and above all, injurious force, vindictive punishment, and the barbarous war system, shall have no place, seems to be quite above and beyond the apprehension of the common religious teacher of divine truth, save as a beautiful theory, as it is of the great majority of the so-called Christian world. Such notions are deemed fanciful, impracticable, Utopian; the speculations and vagaries of visionaries and eccentric enthusiasts, not the conclusions of judicious, level-headed, practical, common sense men and women.

And yet there is all about us a most solemn professed and conventional reverence for Christ and his teachings, and a constant Sabbath-day iteration and reiteration of his injunctions against every type of human selfishness, every form of harmful violence, every degree of cruelty and revenge, every manifestation of the spirit of wrath and war, and a corresponding repetition of his requirements concerning those kindly sentiments and duties calculated to promote gentleness, compassion, unity, peace, and good will among men. Familiar as household words to all bible readers and church-going people are the passages: "Blessed are the merciful for they shall obtain mercy"; "Blessed are the peace-makers for they shall be called the children of God"; "Ye have heard that it hath been said 'An eye for an eye and a tooth for a tooth,' but I say unto you, Resist not evil; but whosoever shall smite thee on the right cheek turn to him the other also, etc." "Ye have heard that it hath been said, 'Thou shalt love thy neighbor and hate thine enemy,' but I say unto you, Love your enemies, bless them that curse you, do good to them that hate you, and pray for them that despitefully use you and persecute you; That ye may be the children of your Father who is in heaven; For he maketh his sun to shine upon the evil and the

good and sendeth rain upon the just and the unjust."
"All things whatsoever ye would that men should do
unto you do ye also unto them." "Put up thy sword
into its place, for all they that take the sword shall
perish with the sword." "The princes of the Gentiles
exercise dominion over them and they that are great
exercise authority over them. But it shall not be so
among you, but whosoever will be great among you let
him be your minister, and whosoever will be chief among
you let him be your servant." "My kingdom is not of
this world, else would my servants fight." "A new com-
mandment I give unto you that ye love one another."

And all this is done with an air of sincerity and
impressiveness, as if people believed in the duties inculcated and were striving to order their lives by them *in all
respects;* as if society was not by custom, by law, by general consent setting those precepts continually at naught; as
if states and nations, even those priding themselves most
on being called Christian, in their relations to and treatment of each other, in their dealings with the more
dependent classes within their borders, in their maintenance of capital punishment and the gigantic system of
war, which Channing declared to be the last vestige of
barbarism, with its complex and mighty enginery for
maiming and destroying the children of God and multiplying the sorrows and distresses of mankind, were not
systematically and persistently bidding them defiance, and
trampling them without compunction, remorse, or shame
into the dust. One may laud Christ to the skies, nay,
exalt him to a place in the Godhead, he may lavish
encomiums upon his precepts and example without stint,
but must not follow him too closely or apply his teachings too rigidly, in matters pertaining to the acquisition
and use of property, methods of trade, the wage system,
the relations between capital and labor, treatment of the
criminal and perishing classes, caste distinctions, and

concerns of kindred nature. Members of different religious sects may vie with each other upon each returning
Christmas time in singing anew the angelic song of
" Peace on earth and Good Will to men" and in making
vocal with anthems and hallelujahs the anniversary of
the day when its words of promise and of cheer first
echoed " o'er Judea's star-lit plains," even while the
nations to which they belong are multiplying the instruments and agencies of human slaughter, and preparing to
" let slip the dogs of war" upon the children of the
heavenly Father, with scarce a voice or murmur of protest or condemnation on their part. So utterly at variance are so-called Christian profession and practice in
this fundamental regard.

In thus animadverting on what I deem the unfaithfulness and shortcoming of the Christian Church, as it is
called — on its failure to comprehend and appreciate the
full significance and purpose of the Gospel of its acknowledged Lord, and its neglect to make the sacred principles
and precepts of that Gospel the rule of conduct in the
social and civil affairs and relations of men, I do not intend
to be understood as saying or implying that it is of no use
in the world — a cumberer of the ground, and ought to
be abolished. This conclusion is farthest from my thought.
I have no doubt that the Church, as a whole, and in its
manifold departments and activities, plays a most important part in the drama of humanity and in the providential
economy of the world — is an indispensable factor in the
problem of human progress and redemption. I have no
doubt that it is an invaluable agency for holding in check
and overcoming the evil and sorrow that exist in the
earth, for conserving and promoting the good and happiness of mankind, and a most needful instrumentality in
improving human condition and human character; in *preparing the way* for the building up of a true social order,
for the coming of the kingdom of God. I only mean to

affirm that, from my Practical Christian point of view, its
testimonies are too superficial and pretentious; that its
champions and controlling spirits are too well satisfied with
an incomplete, fractional righteousesss or too tame and
compromising in their testimonies against popular abuses
and wrongs; that its attitude is too subservient to the
civil authority and power, too complaisant and indifferent
in respect to the vindictive and unchristian features of
existing human governments and of society as it now is.
Its members are bound by social and civil ties and obligations, no less real and commanding because unwritten and
unrecognized, not to uphold or practice an ethical code
essentially truer and nobler than that which holds sway in
the Community at large, and not to undertake to devise,
advocate, or inaugurate any reform or movement which proposes to supersede the established system of human society
by one radically better and upon a moral plane distinctively
higher than that occupied by the ruling forces of the
world around, or by the politico-military patriotism of the
particular country in which they reside. My depreciation
of the Church is of this nature and goes to this extent,
but no further. Cheerfully and gratefully acknowledging
its importance and value within certain self-appointed
limits, and the good it has done and may still do thus
circumscribed and handicapped, I yet deny its claims to
being a true Church of Christ, a faithful exponent of the
religion of the New Testament, a trustworthy representative and teacher of what Christianity was designed in the
providence of God to do for the children of men, or of
what it is intrinsically capable of accomplishing in the
way of enlightening, renewing, and transforming the world.
What is needed and what will some day be realized is *a
regenerated Church*, which shall have a clearer insight
concerning the truths declared and duties enjoined in the
Gospel, which shall proclaim a loftier and more perfect
righteousness than is now taught and required by its

ministers and evangelists, which shall assert its freedom from all commercial, political, military domination and entanglements, and which shall enlist its communicants and confessors in the transcendant work of shaping all human institutions, laws, customs, practices, by the infallible standard of Practical Christianity, of readjusting the social and civil relations of men and making them conform to the order of the divine kingdom, of initiating, organizing, and practically illustrating an all-embracing, universal reform movement, based upon the great fundamental ideas of the Fatherhood of God and the Brotherhood of Man, pursuant to and in fulfillment of the prayer of Jesus, so often repeated by his avowed disciples, " Thy kingdom come, thy will be done on earth as it is in heaven."

And what I have said in regard to the shortcomings of the Church as now organized, equipped, and operated, and of its incompetency for the work which a *true Christian* Church would be able to perform for the enlightenment, moral uplifting, and harmonization of the children of men, may be affirmed of all classes of so-called Reformers and of the organizations instituted for the more effective prosecution of their respective missions. However much good they do in their chosen fields of effort, (and I would not deny but affirm that they do much) they yet are too limited and fragmentary in their objects and methods to serve the largest needs of humanity and bring the better era in. Moreover, Reformers, as a rule, are personally unfitted for a task so disinterested and sublime as that we assumed at Hopedale, besides being involved, like the members of the Church, in the maintenance and perpetuation of certain great chronic abuses and wrongs of social and civil life, their own special object of attack and extermination excepted, which render such a task essential to human welfare and happiness. To others rather then to them, and to other agen-

cies than they employ, must we look for the world's
complete redemption.

It will be seen by what appears on the foregoing pages
that it is my deliberate and solemn conviction that the
predominating cause of the failure of The Hopedale Community was a moral and spiritual, not a financial one —
a deficiency among its members of those graces and
powers of character which are requisite to the realization
of the Christian ideal of human society, such as that
enterprise was designed to represent and exemplify. In
other and more general terms, the movement was too far
ahead of and above the world, in its then existing or
present state of advancement, to be practicable.

But this, though the chief was not the only source of
its weakness and instability — was not the only agency
concerned in the suspension of its leading organic activities and in its final extinction. Other defects there were
that I am persuaded hastened and accentuated the crisis.
They were of less moment than the one named, relating,
as they did, to means and methods, to organization and
general polity, to financial resources and embarrassments,
to industrial arrangements and to forms of administration;
but they were of a serious nature, and in due time, I
have reason to believe, would of themselves have brought
disaster to all our plans, labors, and aspirations. They
need not be stated at great length, nor need it be shown
by what processes they would have wrought eventually
our ruin. It is sufficient to simply tabulate them for the
guidance of future explorers of the field on which we won
many gratifying victories, as we suffered there also a
final deplorable defeat.

Of the secondary causes of trouble and discomfiture to
us, against which I would give due warning to all concerned, the following are deemed of such importance as
to be worthy of mention in this connection, to wit: —

1. We began operations without sufficient funds for our immediate and prospective needs. We incurred a debt at the outset, which, with subsequent enlargement, proved a vexation, a burden, and a hindrance to us during our entire career. And at every stage of our experience we were annoyed and embarrassed by want of means to establish and prosecute our manifold industries advantageously, maintain our educational, religious and missionary activities liberally, build houses, open streets, supply all our public necessity, and meet easily all our obligations.

2. Our domain was in some essential respects unsuited to the purposes of such an undertaking as that in which we enlisted. Naturally infertile and difficult of cultivation, it had for the most part become exhausted by many years of neglect and imperfect tillage when we took possession of it, and so required unusual expenditure of labor and money to render it easy of management and productive to a desirable extent. For this reason our farming interests, which should have contributed largely to our prosperity, were an extra care to us and an obstacle in the pathway of ultimate success.

3. We commenced operations with too few and incommodious public and private buildings — houses, barns, stables, shops, etc., etc., — for the convenience, comfort, freedom, seclusion, retirement, essential to the common well-being and happiness. The disorder, confusion, and friction incident to the crowded condition in which we were placed at the start and for a long time afterward, wrought us irreparable injury.

4. Instead of retaining the management of our domain in the hands of the Community exclusively, as was our policy, it should have been divided into sections or lots of varying size, for the occupancy and improvement of such of our members, probationers, and dependents as might desire them, to be loaned at a moderate

charge for ground rent. This would have enabled a
goodly number of our people whose tastes and capabilities fitted them for tilling the soil, to have subsisted
themselves and their families more easily and satisfactorily than they could otherwise do; it would have developed the spirit of self-reliance and a sense of personal
responsibility, and in many ways enhanced the general
harmony and happiness.

5. Our Constitution and general polity under it were
too rigid and inflexible, making too little allowance for
individual tastes, capabilies, adaptations, judgments, choice
of action and occupation, etc.   They should have provided
for subordinate associations or communes to be instituted
by different classes of persons — Individualists, Joint-Stock
Proprietors, Communists proper, and Eclectics — the members of each privileged to occupy separate territory, establish industries of their own and manage their business
affairs in their own way, while owning a general moral
allegiance to the Community itself as the Federal Head
of all associated interests and undertakings.

6. It was a source of complication and embarrassment
as well as dissatisfaction and irritation that we allowed
seceding members to withdraw invested capital from our
treasury without proper and definitely expressed restrictions.   In seeking to be just and honorable in our dealings with such, we went to unwarrantable extremes and
jeopardized our own safety as well as our own peace.
Well understood conditions of investment from the beginning would have obviated many difficulties in that respect,
as ample means would also have done.   In our circumstances the course pursued was perilous.

7. There was always a tendency among us, stimulated
by contact with the community at large, to subordinate
our declared standard of principles and duties to expediency, money-making, worldly success, and other forms of
self-seeking, which was calculated to sap both our indi-

vidual and public virtue and to undermine the sublime structure we essayed to build. A further remove from the allurements, temptations, and downward currents of existing society would have been greatly to our advantage.

8. We allowed too large a percentage of persons among us as employes, boarders, and temporary residents, who were not only incompetent to understand and appreciate our work and so commend it to others, but were unwilling to yield cheerfully to Community requirements, thus breaking down respect for Community authority; and who by their contumacy and criticism incited in others the spirit of unrest and incipient contempt of what we deemed vital and sacred. Moreover, the conversation and conduct of such persons were often such as to corrupt the morals of our children and youth as well as of the more susceptible and easily influenced of our adult population. This condition of things necessitated a resort to restrictive legislation, to scrutinizing vigilance, and to a system of moral judicature, which, by a different policy in this particular, would have been avoided, in the interest of good feeling, harmony, and the common welfare.

Had our Community not fallen into these and kindred errors, and had its membership been composed of men and women firmly established in the principles and thoroughly imbued with the spirit of the Gospel of Christ, this History would have been very different from what it now is. Instead of being a record of mingled hope and fear, prosperity and adversity, victory and defeat, exultation and humiliation — the latter of these alternatives predominating at the last and culminating in utter disaster, it would have been one of varied experiences no doubt, joyful and sad, but all ending in a grand, triumphant success. Instead of being as a whole a warning and an admonition to future explorers and laborers in the field of social progress and reconstruction — to other

builders of a new order of society, it would have been a
guide and an inspiration to more wisely planned and
directed efforts than ours and to a sublimer consummation
than we ever sought for ‘ or conceived. As it is, it will
go out to the world and down to coming generations a
plain unvarnished tale of a disinterested, noble endeavor
to benefit mankind and bring God's kingdom in — of a
laudable but ill-fated experiment entered upon and prosecuted, not to advance any selfish or unworthy interest or
cause, but rather to show the way of a better, truer life
to individuals, communities, peoples, states, and nations,
to aid in the re-formation of the social relations of men,
the re-adjustment of industrial and commercial affairs, the
harmonizing of conflicting class interests, and the fraterni-
zation of the world. It has been written and is now
commended to all lovers of their fellowmen and especially
to all friends of Social Reform in the sincere hope — nay,
with the assurance, that somehow or other in the divine
order it may be instrumental in promoting the great
objects for which the Community was established and to
which the author in good conscience towards God and
man has devoted his life.

In bringing to a close the History of a movement with
which my name was more closely indentified than that of
any other single individual, I desire to re-affirm in
positive and unmistakable terms my continued and unwavering faith in the principles out of which that movement
sprang into being and upon which it was based, and in
the excellence and grandeur of the work which it attempted
to do in the service of God for the good of mankind.
Believing, as I have done from my early youth, in the
Religion of Jesus Christ as he taught and exemplified it,
I am confident beyond all doubt that the truths inculcated
and requirements enjoined by that religion are applicable
to human life in all its multiform and complex depart-

ments, activities, and relations, and that only by such
application in the broadest and most inclusive sense can
God's purpose in the creation of the world be accomplished or the human race become truly wise, righteous,
harmonious, and happy. Moreover, I also firmly believe
that, while the progress and ultimate redemption of mankind are greatly promoted by the broadcast diffusion of
divine truth and its gradually renewing and uplifting
effect upon the world, like leaven hid in measures of
meal, definite and radical methods of reform, similar to
that represented in the Hopedale Community, are essential
to the highest and most far reaching results and will
some day be inaugurated and carried forward to triumphant issues.

Nothing is more obvious or incontrovertible to my mind
than the need of such methods. The existing order of
human society is not simply imperfect and defective —
it is fundamentally unchristian and wrong in many of its
characteristic features, and requires organic reconstruction
and an administration of affairs along new lines, in order
to bring it into accord with the everlasting law of God
and secure to all conditions and classes of men the most
perfect equity, and the most permanent enjoyment. The
great question involved in our Hopedale experiment is
not yet settled; only postponed to a wiser and better
future. The work of Social Reform is by no means
abandoned; it is only suspended till the world is fitted
by intellectual growth and spiritual elevation to take it
up again and prosecute it to successful results, — till
some more auspicious day in the slowly but surely advancing years of the calendar of God. To doubt this would
be to set at nought the surest conclusions of human
reason, the best aspirations of the human heart, the suggestions derived from the progress of the race in past
ages, the prophetic intimations of the Hebrew Scriptures
and of the great seers of all lands and times, and the

glorious promises of the Gospel of Christ. It would be to discredit the unfathomed possibilities hid in the soul of humanity, to remand to the realm of myths and shadows the grandest ideals that have ever gladdened and inspired the great teachers and moral heroes of the world, and to deny the significance and potency of the prayer of Jesus, " Thy kingdom come, thy will be done on earth as it is in heaven."

When those possibilities are in some large degree developed; when those ideals are in good measure realized, and that prayer substantially fulfilled in a regenerate and glorified humanity and in a divine order of society, then will the meaning of The Hopedale Community and its place in the ongoings of the Providence of God be fully interpreted and understood, its distinguishing features will have become factors and characteristics of universal human life, and its ultimate purpose will have reached its consummation. Then will unrighteousness be done away, unkindness, hatred, wrath and war will be unknown, and every unhallowed usage, custom, institution be abolished; the reign of justice, love, brotherhood, peace, will be established, men will dwell together as one great family in harmony and happiness, and God even in this world will " be all in all."

APPENDIX A.

CONSTITUTION,
BY-LAWS, RULES AND REGULATIONS
OF
THE HOPEDALE COMMUNITY.

IN order to establish a state of society governed by divine moral principles, with as little as possible of mere human constraint, in which, while the members may be sufficiently free to associate or separate their secular interests, according to inclination and congeniality, no individual shall suffer the evils of oppression, poverty, ignorance or vice through the influence or neglect of others, we, whose names are hereunto subscribed, do unite in a voluntary Association to be called

THE HOPEDALE COMMUNITY.

ARTICLE I.

SECTION 1. No person shall be a member of this Community who does not cordially assent to the following

DECLARATION, *Viz.*:

I believe in the religion of JESUS CHRIST, as he taught and exemplified it, according to the Scriptures of the New Testament. I acknowledge myself a bounden subject of all its moral obligations. Especially do I hold myself bound by its holy requirements, never, under any pretext whatsoever, to kill, assault, beat, torture, enslave, rob, oppress, persecute, defraud, corrupt, slander, revile, injure, envy or hate any human being — *even my worst enemy;* never in any manner to violate the dictates of pure chastity; never to take or administer an oath; never to manufacture, buy, sell, deal out or use any intoxicating liquor *as a beverage;* never to serve in the army, navy or militia of any nation, state or chieftain; never to bring an action at law, hold office, vote, join a legal posse, petition a legislature or ask governmental interposition, *in any case involving a final authorized resort to physical violence;* never to indulge self-will, bigotry, love of pre-eminence, covetousness, deceit, profanity, idleness or an unruly tongue; never to participate in lotteries, games of chance, betting or pernicious amusements; never to resent reproof or justify myself in a known wrong; never to aid, abet or approve others in anything sinful; but, through divine assistance, always to recommend and promote, with my entire influence, the holiness and happiness of all mankind.

SEC. 2. Any person assenting, after satisfactory probationship, to the foregoing *Declaration*, and recommended in writing by seven members *as sponsors*, may be admitted into the membership of this Community by ballot-vote at any regular meeting; provided that he or she shall thereupon, in open meeting, subscribe this Constitution.

SEC. 3. Any person may resign membership at discretion by entering a minute on the Records to that effect.

SEC. 4. Any unworthy member may be discharged by vote at any regular meeting.

SEC 5. Any member having no investment of property in this Community, who shall attend none of its regular meetings, nor otherwise manifest any fraternal interest in its welfare for *two* years, shall be deemed to have relinquished membership.

SEC. 6. No meeting shall be deemed regular unless held pursuant to a public Notification from the executive authority of the Community, announcing the time, place and principal purposes of the meeting, and posted seven days previously in one of the Community's places of general concourse.

SEC. 7. Every member shall have one and but one vote on all questions; and the concurrence of two thirds of the members present and acting shall be necessary to the decision of every question, except the election of officers after repeated unsuccessful trials, the whole process of which shall be regulated by special enactment.

SEC. 8. Nine members shall constitute a quorum.

ARTICLE II.

SECTION 1. The members of this Community shall own and manage such real and movable estate in Joint-Stock proprietor-

24

ship as they may deem necessary to the maintenance of a neighborhood exclusively inhabited and controlled by persons honestly endeavoring to conform to the principles of the foregoing *Declaration*. And no person habitually setting at naught those principles shall permanently reside within the territorial limits of the Community by public consent.

SEC. 2. This Joint-Stock property shall consist of shares of the value of fifty dollars each, for which the owner shall hold certificates responsibly signed, in the form following, to wit:

For value received, A. B. or order is hereby entitled to —— shares in the Joint-Stock property of The Hopedale Community, valued at —— dollars, together with such dividends as may from time to time be declared thereon.

SEC. 3. All the real estate of this Community shall be held, managed and disposed of for the use and benefit thereof by five Trustees, always acting in conformity with the Constitution, By-Laws, Rules and Regulations, and Instructions of the Community for the time being. Three of these Trustees, but never a less number, shall be competent to receive and execute conveyances of real estate. It shall be their duty to take the utmost care that all titles to lands and tenements conveyed to or from them, as Trustees of The Hopedale Community, be so executed and recorded as to preclude all ulterior controversy either at law or in equity. And for the security of all parties concerned in their official transactions, they shall execute and cause to be recorded in the Registry of Deeds for the county of Worcester an explicit Declaration of Trust, setting forth their power and obligations; which Declaration shall be in the form following, to wit:

To all persons to whom these presents shall come: We, A. B., C. D, E. F., G. H., I. J., all of the village of Hopedale, in the town of Milford, in the county of Worcester and Commonwealth of Massachusetts, Trustees of The Hopedale Community, send Greeting: — Whereas certain lands and tenements in said Hopedale have been conveyed, and certain other lands and tenements may hereafter be conveyed, to us, as Trustees as aforesaid, or to our successors in trust, as joint tenants; Now this present Declaration of trust witnesseth: That all such lands and tenements, with their appurtenances, are to be held, managed and disposed of for the use and benefit of The Hopedale Community, so called and known, and in conformity with the

Constitution, Resolves, By-Laws and Regulations thereof, as the same are now, or may hereafter be duly established.

Provided nevertheless, that for the purpose of regulating and clearly establishing and defining the rights and powers of ourselves and our successors in trust, and of perpetuating the evidence of the same, more especially with reference to any contracts, conveyances or other instruments to be executed, or any processes to be commenced, defended or carried on by us or them, it has been mutually agreed and is hereby declared, that the following are and shall remain fundamental Articles of said trust, viz.:

ARTICLE 1. Whereas it is contemplated that the number of Trustees shall at all times be five, and that all vacancies therein shall be filled as soon as may be; Now for the purpose of ascertaining at all times in future who the Trustees are, it is declared and agreed that any three or more of the above-named Trustees, or of their successors in trust, may, as often as they shall find occasion, execute and cause to be recorded in the Registry of Deeds for the county of Worcester a Certificate setting forth who the Trustees for the time being are, and the persons so certified as Trustees shall be thenceforth deemed and taken to hold said office until a subsequent change shall be, in like manner, certified and recorded.

ART. 2. The said Trustees, or their successors (not being less than three in number), shall have the right from time to time, and at all times, as often as they shall think proper, to convey and re-convey in fee simple, or for other less estate, absolutely or conditionally, any of said lands and tenements to such persons, for such valuable or nominal considerations, on such terms of cash or credit, and in trust or wholly discharged therefrom, as they shall in each case think proper ; and their Certificate or recital, in any Deed, Lease or other instrument, that the same is executed under the authority of The Hopedale Community, shall be full and conclusive evidence thereof to all intents and purposes. And in no case shall any purchaser, mortgagee or lessee be bound to see to the application of the moneys paid by him.

ART. 3. Any Trustee now or hereafter appointed, may divest himself of the trust by executing to his co-Trustees an instrument in writing resigning his office, and releasing in due and proper form to them, as joint tenants in fee simple, all his interest in the Trust Property.

And in testimony of the foregoing we have hereunto set our
hands and seals this —— day of —— in the year ——

	A. B.	[L. S.]
Executed and delivered	C. D.	[L. S.]
in presence of	E. F.	[L. S.]
K. L.	˙G. H.	[L. S.]
M. N.	I. J.	[L. S.]

ARTICLE III.

SECTION 1. The legislative powers of this Community shall be
vested in the members thereof present and acting in regular
Community meeting. The executive powers, not necessarily
appertaining to the Trustees, shall be vested in a President
and Directory. The Directory shall consist of at least three
members besides the President. The judicial powers shall be
vested in such tribunals as the Community may from time to
time establish.

SEC. 2. It shall be the duty of the Directory to conduct the
prudential affairs, industrial operations and general interests
of the Community in such manner as to insure to every member, probationer and dependent adequate employment, educational advantages and exemption from the evils of poverty,
ignorance and vice; and also, at the same time, if possible, to
secure to the stockholders their capital unimpaired, with a clear
annual profit thereon of four per cent.

SEC. 3. Any excess of profits on the Joint-Stock operations,
over the said four per cent., shall be devoted to educational
and other purposes, for the benefit of the whole Community.

SEC. 4. The Directory, concurrently with the Trustees, shall
have power to extend and improve the Village Site, to open
and keep in order streets, commons and cemeteries, and to sell
house-lots to members who will come under obligations that
such lots, with all their buildings and betterments, shall revert
to the Community at a fair appraisal, whenever the same shall
cease to be owned within its membership, or whenever, in the
opinion of the Community, expressed through their Trustees,
the premises shall have been perverted to uses obviously repugnant to the principles of the *Declaration*.

SEC. 5. It shall be the duty of the Directory, as well as of
the Trustees, to keep accurate and permanent records of their
official transactions, and to hold their books always subject to

the examination of any member or stockholder desirous of inspecting them. And the Directory shall present to the Community an explicit report of the Joint-Stock finances at least once a year.

SEC. 6. All contracts and obligations entered into by or with this Community under any former Constitution, so far as the same may affect any right or title to property, shall be held inviolate.

ARTICLE IV.

SECTION 1. This Community shall annually elect, on the second Wednesday in January, their President and Directors, a Recorder, a Treasurer, and all other officers for the time being required.

SEC. 2. Special elections, rendered necessary by any unusual contingency, may take place as occasion shall require, but no officer thus specially elected, excepting a Trustee, shall hold over the annual election; provided nevertheless, that all Community officers shall continue to discharge their public duties until successors shall have been chosen and consented to serve in their places.

SEC. 3. Neither legislation, nor the administration of government within this Community, shall be brought into conflict with the fundamental principles set forth in the *Declaration*, or with the explicit stipulations of this Constitution.

SEC. 4. This Constitution may be altered or amended by two-thirds of the members present and acting at any regular meeting subsequent to the one first notified for the consideration of such alteration or amendment.

Now, therefore, in full ratification of this Constitution in all its Articles, Sections and Clauses, we have hereunto subscribed our respective names; mutually, jointly and severally promising faithfully to observe, respect and support the same, together with all legitimate enactments of the Community thereunder made, according to the best of our knowledge and ability, so long as we shall continue in membership; and especially covenanting. each with the Community, for himself or herself, his or her heirs, executors and administrators, never to withdraw property contrary to the stipulations of this Constitution, or of any By-Law, Rule or Regulation thereunder legitimately established. In testimony whereof, witness our respective signatures, with the dates indicated.

BY-LAWS, RULES AND REGULATIONS.

ENACTMENT I.

Respecting the Process of Electing Community Officers.

SECTION 1. All the officers of this Community shall be elected by ballot according to the process hereinafter prescribed.

SEC. 2. The presiding officer of the Community meeting at which any officer is to be elected, shall distinctly announce the office to be filled and immediately cause to be distributed among the voters an ample supply of blank paper slips suitable for use as ballots. The voters shall inscribe, each on his or her respective slip, the name of the person preferred for the office. The votes shall then be collected, assorted, counted and announced. And if any candidate shall have received two-thirds of all the votes cast, he or she shall be declared elected.

SEC. 3. If no candidate shall be found to have received two-thirds of the votes cast on the first trial, then there shall be a second trial, with the same order of proceedings. And if the second trial shall fail, then the two highest candidates shall be voted for with white and colored balls. The presiding officer shall distinctly announce for whom the white and for whom the colored balls are to be cast. Thereupon the balls shall be distributed, collected, assorted and counted. And the candidate having a majority shall be declared elected.

SEC. 4. If, on the second trial, no two, or but one of the candidates shall be found to have the highest number of votes, so as to be candidates for election by the balls, as contemplated in section 3, then the presiding officer shall proceed to determine who are the highest candidates by calling on the nominators of each nominee to rise and be counted. This process shall be continued till the two highest candidates shall have been incontestibly ascertained; and thereupon they shall be balloted for, as prescribed in section 3.

SEC. 5. If the trial to elect by the balls shall fail in consequence of a tie, it shall be repeated until successful; provided that if unsuccessful the third time, the presiding officer shall give the casting vote.

ENACTMENT II.

Respecting the Joint-Stock.

SECTION 1. All Certificates of Joint-Stock issued by the authorities of the Community, shall be carefully numbered in their proper order, and also the shares covered by such Certificates. The numbers of both shall appear on the Certificates, and all Certificates, as likewise all transfers of the same, shall be recorded in a book to be kept for the purpose.

SEC. 2. This Community shall be considered under no obligation whatsoever to redeem its scrip at par to an aggregate amount exceeding four per cent. of its entire Joint-Stock property per year, commencing with January; nor to redeem over five hundred dollars worth of said scrip for the accommodation of the same stockholder in any one year at whatsoever time commencing. Redemption money shall be so apportioned to the four quarters of the year, as that each quarter may have at least its own equitable share of resources to meet demands, and all disbursements from the Treasury shall be arranged accordingly.

SEC. 3. The notices of stockholders demanding redemption of scrip shall be made in writing and addressed to the President, Directory or Treasurer of the Community. All such notices shall take precedence by the calender month of their date, not the particular day of the month; those of the same month being placed on an equal footing with each other in respect to their proportionate dividends of the then available redemption funds.

SEC. 4. Hereafter the Treasurer of this Community shall deliver out no scrip for Joint-Stock (unless by authority from the Directory under a special agreement with some non-resident investor) without taking an Obligatory Receipt therefor expressed substantially as follows, viz.:

Received of A. B., Treasurer of The Hopedale Community, for property invested in the Joint-Stock thereof, the following specified scrip, viz.: [Here shall be inserted an accurate description.] Now be it remembered that I receive and hold this scrip, knowing, consenting and agreeing that said Community shall be considered under no obligation whatsoever to redeem its scrip at par to an aggregate amount exceeding four per cent. of its entire Joint-Stock per year, commencing with January; nor to redeem over five hundred dollars worth of said scrip for the accommodation of the same stockholder in any one year, at whatsoever time commencing; that redemption money shall be so apportioned to the four quarters of the year as that each quarter may have its own equitable share of resources to meet demands; that notices of stockholders demanding redemption of scrip shall be made in writing and addressed to the President, Directory or Treasurer of the Community at least sixty days before the expected payment of redemption money; and that all such notices shall take precedence by the calender month and not by the particular day of the month. Moreover, I do hereby bind myself, my heirs, executors, administrators and assigns, never to demand or require the redemption of the above specified scrip contrary to these conditions.

Signed at —— this —— day of —— A. D. ——.

In presence of E. F., G. H. —— C. D.

Sec. 5. All Joint-Stock scrip not redeemed by the Community within two years after the prescribed notice of demand, and which shall be due to a claimant not resident on the Community domain, shall draw interest at the rate of six per cent. per annum till redeemed. And nothing in this enactment shall be construed to hinder the redemption of Joint-Stock script to any amount, at any time, by the Community's authorities, provided it be done without inconvenience and entirely at their own option.

ENACTMENT III.

Respecting the Village Site, House Lots and Reverted Estates.

SECTION 1. It shall be the duty of the Trustees to arrange and name the Streets, Lanes, Squares and public places of our Village Site; to number all the lots and parcels of land comprised in said site, and to appraise such as shall be for sale; to prepare an accurate Plan of the whole Site and revise the same as occasion may require; to keep two or more copies of said Plan for exhibition to members and inquiring friends; and to cause the same, with all important additions or changes successively made to be entered for record in the County Registry of Deeds.

SEC. 2. Whenever any House Lot shall be sold in accordance with the Constitution, the Trustees shall execute a conveyance and title of the same to the purchaser, in the form following, to wit:

Know all men by these Presents: That we, A. B., C. D., E. F., G. H., I. J., all of the village of Hopedale, in the town of Milford, in the county of Worcester and Commonwealth of

Massachusetts, acting as Trustees of The Hopedale Community pursuant to the terms of a certain Declaration of Trust executed by Adin Ballou and others, Trustees, dated June 1, 1850, and recorded in the Registry of Deeds for the county of Worcester, in consideration of —— dollars to us paid by —— —— of said Hopedale, a member of said Community, the receipt of which sum is hereby acknowledged, do hereby grant, sell and convey to the said —— —— all our right, title, interest and estate in and to a certain parcel of land situated in said Hopedale, bounded, described and measuring as follows, viz.: [Here give full particulars] with all the buildings thereon and all the privileges and appurtenances to the premises belonging; intending hereby to convey a part of the real estate which was conveyed to said Trustees by the Deed of David A. Mundy, dated June 1, 1850, and recorded in Worcester county Registry of Deeds.

To have and to hold the granted premises to the said —— ——, his heirs and assigns, to his and their use and behoof forever; but subject nevertheless to the condition that, if at any time or times hereafter any three or more of the Trustees of The Hopedale Community (for the time then being, their identity and official character being shown in manner stated in said Declaration of Trust) shall, by their certificate in writing, under their hands and seals, to be recorded in the Registry of Deeds for said county of Worcester, set forth and declare, either that, in the opinion of the Trustees and of The Hopedale Community, the premises are then perverted to purposes notoriously inconsistent with the principles of said Community, or that, in said opinion, the premises have then ceased to be owned within the membership of said Community; and if the Trustees for the time then being shall, moreover, within three months after the recording of said certificate, pay, or tender in money, to the owner or owners of the premises for the time then being, his or her guardian, agent or attorney, for a full reconveyance of the granted premises, the reasonable value thereof, to be ascertained as hereinafter stated; and if the owner or owners for the time then being, by themselves or their respective guardians, agents or attorneys, shall upon such payment or tender, fail to release and convey the granted premises to the said Trustees for the time then being, in fee simple, free from all incumbrances to be hereafter made or suffered thereon, then, and on the foregoing condition, this Deed of conveyance shall be null and void, both at law and in equity.

And provided moreover, that such reasonable value shall, in each case, be ascertained by the written award of a majority, at least, of appraisors, to consist of the County Commissioners of the county of Worcester, or of such other persons as the parties in interest, for the time then being, shall, within one month after the recording of said certificate, mutually agree upon in writing.

In testimony whereof, and that this Deed is executed under the authority of The Hopedale Community, we, the Trustees above-named have hereunto set our hands and seals, this —— day of ——, in the year of our Lord eighteen hundred and ——.

	A. B.	[L. S.]
Executed and delivered	C. D.	[L. S.]
in presence of	E. F.	[L. S.]
K. L.	G. H.	[L. S.]
M. N.	I. J.	[L. S.]

SEC. 3.   Whenever any member of this Community, holding Real Estate in the Village Site under the title prescribed in the preceding section, shall convey the same to another member, the Instrument of conveyance shall be substantially in the form following, to wit:

Know all men by these Presents: That I, C. D., of the village of Hopedale, in the town of Milford, in the county of Worcester and Commonwealth of Massachusetts, ——, in consideration of —— dollars to me paid by —— —— of said Hopedale, ——, a member of The Hopedale Community, and for other valuable and sufficient considerations, the receipt whereof is hereby acknowledged, do hereby give, grant, bargain, sell and convey unto the said —— ——, a certain parcel of land situated in said Hopedale, and bounded, described and measuring as follows, viz.: [Here give full particulars.] with all the buildings thereon and all the privileges and appurtenances to the premises belonging; intending hereby to convey the same estate which was conveyed to me by the Deed of A. B. and others, Trustees of The Hopedale Community, dated —— —— ——, and subject to all the conditions, reservations and restrictions therein contained or referred to.

To have and to hold the above granted premises to the said —— ——, his heirs and assigns, to his and their use and behoof forever. And I, the said C. D. for myself, my heirs, executors and administrators do covenant with the said —— ——, his heirs and assigns, that I am lawfully seized in fee simple of the aforegranted premises, that they are free from all incumbrances, except as aforesaid*, that I have good right to sell and convey the same to the said —— ——, his heirs and assigns forever, subject as aforesaid, and that I will, and my heirs, executors and administrators shall warrant and defend the same to the said —— ——, his heirs and assigns forever, against the lawful claims and demands of all persons, except as above mentioned.

In witness whereof, I, the said C. D., and also my wife E., who executes this deed with me in token of her relinquishing all right to dower in the premises, have hereunto set our hands and seals this —— day of ——, in the year of our Lord ——.

Executed and delivered in presence of   C. D.   [L. S.]
     K. L.   M. N.   E. D.   [L. S.]

SEC. 4. The Trustees, when requested by the Directory, shall execute Bonds for Deeds of House Lots to members and probationers, conditioned according to contract made between the parties, always subject to existing Regulations respecting the reversion of Estates to the Community.

SEC. 5. No Real Estate owned by any member of this Community within its general Domain shall ever be encumbered by mortgage or bond, without the consent of the Directory, or of the Community on appeal from the Directory's refusal. And record shall be carefully made of all votes giving consent to such encumbrances.

SEC. 6. Whenever any Real Estate shall revert to this Community, as contemplated in Section 4, Article III of the Constitution, reference shall not be had in the appraisal thereof to expenditures of any description laid out thereon by the owner or owners, but only to its actual value, for the time being, to the Community; unless it shall be proved by written evidence that the Directory had given their consent to particular outlays, with the understanding that the Community should share the risk thereof; in which case the appraisal shall be made accordingly.

---

* If there are others they must be specified here.

SEC. 7. In order to prevent all misunderstanding and diffi-culty respecting the appraisal of Real Estate on its reversion to the Community, it is hereby made the duty of every individ-ual proprietor, before erecting any building or constructing any appurtenance on his or her House Lot, at a cost of one hundred dollars or more, to give notice thereof to the Trustees, and obtain their certificate of consent to the proposed outlay. If the Trustees shall refuse their consent, an appeal may be made to the Community. If neither the Trustees nor the Community shall give a certificate of consent, then the individ-ual proprietor may proceed to make the outlay at his or her own risk; in which case the Trustees shall demand a certificate of such proprietor's determination. And the Trustees shall take care that all such proceedings and certificates be faith-fully recorded.

ENACTMENT IV.

Respecting the Contraction of Debts, etc.

SECTION 1. The authorities of this Community shall con-tract no debt against it whatsoever, in the name thereof, except for reverted Real Estate, without the unanimous consent of the members present and acting in a regular meeting duly notified for that purpose.

SEC. 2. The Trustees shall never sell, alienate nor encumber any portion of the Community territory, excepting House Lots in accordance with the Constitution, without the positive instructions or formal consent of the members in regular meeting assembled.

SEC. 3. No funds of the Community shall ever be expended by the official authorities thereof, without having first been placed at their disposal by some vote of specific or general appropriation, passed by the members present and acting in regular Community meeting.

SEC. 4. There shall be a uniform settlement of business accounts, and a punctual payment of current demands, through-out this Community on or about the fifteenth of every month. And it shall be the imperative duty of the President and Directory to see that this system of Monthly Settlements is strictly observed in the several Branches, by all persons con-cerned.

SEC. 5. All officers of this Community shall be entitled to compensation for their official services, never exceeding the average compensation of working men at large in the several Branches as reckoned by time or by piece. And it shall be the duty of the Directory to append to their annual financial report a separate and specific statement of all charges allowed for official services, showing who have received compensation and to what amount.

ENACTMENT V.

Respecting Industry, Purveyance and Trade.

In order to distribute, define and intensify the oversight of business; to encourage useful talent and skill; to give every member of the Community, if possible, an appropriate sphere of enterprise; to increase productive industry and income; to facilitate the necessary purveyance and exchange; and to establish a well-ordered system of trade,—it is enacted as follows, viz.:

SECTION 1. Every general department or kind of Community operations, which naturally and practically admits of subdivision into two or more branches, shall be so subdivided, and each branch confided to the management of some person or persons evincing a hearty interest therein, and competent, in the judgment of the Directory, to prosecute its affairs efficiently.

SEC. 2. All industrial, managemental, commercial and official business performed for this Community, by the members, probationers and dependents thereof, shall be compensated by the piece, the quantity, the job or the per. cent., according to terms mutually agreed upon between the parties concerned for the time being; extremely impracticable cases alone excepted.

SEC. 3. Whenever two or more members of the Community shall apply to the Directory, as an association or co-partnership to take charge of any particular kind of business open to such application, and shall give satisfactory assurance of their trustworthiness, it shall be the duty of the Directory to comply with their request on such terms and for such period of time as shall not be incompatible with pre-existing engagements nor with the general welfare. In all such cases the applicants shall designate their foreman or manager, who shall officially subscribe a written statement, obligation or contract setting forth the principal particulars agreed on; which document shall be recorded by the Directory in a book to be kept for such purposes.

Sec. 4. Whenever any member, probationer or dependent of this Community, performing service in any department, branch or kind of business thereof, shall request the privilege of undertaking any piece-work, job or specific operation requiring more skill, risk or responsibility than ordinary, or affording more scope for practical discretion, it shall be the duty of the superintendent, manager, foreman or other authority having the power of disposal, to grant such request; provided it can be done consistently with pre-existing engagements, and without detriment to the general welfare.

Sec. 5. A central branch of business operatives shall be established, to be called *The Hopedale Commercial Exchange.* It shall consist of competent and responsible persons voluntarily associated for the purpose of purchasing the productions of the various branches of Community industry at fair, specific prices, selling the same for cash or goods as they may deem expedient, supplying raw materials for manufacture, also necessaries for consumption, and thus, by skillful exchanges, ensuring ample, well-compensated employment to all Community operatives. No branch or individual shall be required to deal with or through this Commercial Exchange, except as may be deemed mutually satisfactory to the parties concerned. It shall have power to constitute and organize itself in such a manner and under such regulations as two thirds of the associates may, from time to time, determine. It shall keep reliable records of its proceedings, well-arranged account books, and carefully-perserved files of all papers necessary either to the proof or explanation of its commercial transactions. Its affairs shall at all times be subject to the inspection of the Directory, who shall require well-avouched reports of its financial standing during the first weeks in January and July, semi-annually. It shall be amply paid for its commercial services and risks, by a certain percentage on all purchases and sales made for the Community and *actually realized*, as the amount thereof shall be ascertained, semi-annually, in January and July. This percentage shall be fixed, from time to time, as justice may require, by mutual agreement between its authorized officers on the one part, and the Directory on the other part. All property actually sold and delivered by the Community to the Exchange, and by the latter to the former, shall be receipted for at the date of delivery by some authorized person, and shall thenceforth be considered at the sole risk of the party holding the same. Property not actually sold by the Community to the Exchange, but delivered merely for sale on commission, shall be receipted for as such, and shall remain at the risk of the Community until sold. The Exchange shall be held under a perpetual guaranty to make seasonable payment to the Community for all property purchased thereof under this Enactment, together with a minimum per cent. profit on the cost valuation of so much of said property as it shall actually realize sales upon. Also, to return duly whatever values it shall realize on commission sales made for the Community, deducting the stipulated compensation for services. Also, on the first of January, annually to pay over all net profits, if any, which shall have been realized on the sale of Community property above the stipulated compensation and the aforesaid minimum per cent. profit. Also, to conduct all its affairs in such an upright, conscientious and honorable manner as shall not bring just reproach on the great cause of Practical Christianity espoused by this Community, but on the contrary, commend it to the respect and confidence of all well-disposed men.

SEC. 6.   No superintendent, manager, foreman, agent or commercial exchanger shall be at liberty to contract any debt whatsoever in the name of The Hopedale Community; but all notes, bills, receipts, accounts and securities necessary to the proper transaction of business with persons not belonging to the Community, shall be so expressed as to guard the Community effectually, if possible, against legal liabilities as a party under contract.

ENACTMENT VI.

Respecting Religious Meetings, Instruction and Discipline.

SECTION 1.   This Community shall hold public religious meetings regularly on the first day of the week, forenoon and afternoon; at which such devotional exercises and ministrations of the gospel shall be sustained as the Community may from time to time approve. All members, probationers, dependents and residents of the Community, not prevented by conscientious scruples, indispensable duties, sickness or other justifying necessity, shall be expected punctually and regularly to attend these meetings. Also, to abstain from all uses of the day not obviously promotive of physical health, social order, humane sympathies, moral improvement, spiritual progress and the regeneration of mankind.

SEC. 2. This Community shall hold a regular Monthly Meeting for discipline and improvement, in conformity with the principles of Practical Christianity; and, through the appropriate action of said Monthly Meeting, shall exercise the entire responsibility of directing and sustaining public religious instruction, as well as internal moral discipline. Also, the responsibility of promulgating the principles of Practical Christianity abroad, by means of the press and of the living voice, as the Community may from time to time determine.

SEC. 3. The Community shall annually elect the following officers, viz.: a Steward, a Promulgation Committee and a Council of Religion, Conciliation and Justice. The Recorder shall keep accurate and faithful records of all Monthly Meeting proceedings in a book provided exclusively for that purpose. The Steward shall have charge of every thing pertaining to the comfort and accommodation of Community meetings. The Promulgation Committee shall consist of five members. It shall be the official duty of this Committee to execute all orders and instructions given them by the Community in Monthly Meeting; to superintend the operation of all instrumentalities approved and employed for the promulgation of Community principles, whether at home or abroad; to take charge of all property devoted to such promulgation of principles; to attend to all contracts authorized by vote of said Meeting; to collect and disburse all funds raised for promulgation purposes; to keep reliable accounts and records of their transactions; and to make a detailed report of their doings at least once a year. The Council of Religion, Conciliation and Justice shall consist of not less than three nor more than seven members, who shall be subject to such instructions and restrictions as the Community, in Monthly Meeting, may, from time to time, impose. Their official duties shall be hereinafter specified.

SEC. 4. This Community shall never assume to commission, appoint or forbid any person to preach the gospel or to act as a public religious and moral teacher, but shall always leave that matter to the conscience and judgment of individuals as between themselves and God. Yet, through the action of their Monthly Meeting, the Community may invite any preacher or teacher in whom they have confidence to minister to them, or to aid them in promulgating Practical Christianity abroad. In all such cases, it shall be considered the duty of the Community to place their invited preachers or teachers on a level of temporal subsistence with the generality of their fellow-members who are otherwise employed, and to guarantee to them pecuniary succor proportionate to time expended and services rendered.

SEC. 5. The funds necessary to sustain public religious meetings and the promulgation of Practical Christianity, whether at home or abroad, shall be provided in such ways as the Community may from time to time determine.

SEC. 6. It shall be the official duty of the Council of Religion, Conciliation and Justice, to supervise all matters of religion, morality and Christian discipline; to reprove, admonish and endeavor to correct all anti-Christian customs, habits and practices springing up within the Community; to advise, mediate, conciliate and adjudicate in all cases of controversy between member and member, and between members and officers of the Community; to examine and certify their opinion of the religious and moral fitness of all applicants for probationship or membership; and, generally to exercise the proper functions of a Judicial Council, on Christian principles, concerning all matters of controversy not otherwise seasonably adjusted; provided that all decisions of said Council shall be subject to a final appeal to the Community.

SEC. 7. Hereafter no person shall be received as a probationer of this Community by the Directory, without a Certificate from said Council that he or she has been examined in respect to religious and moral qualifications, and is approved.

SEC. 8. It shall be the special duty of said Council to acquaint themselves with the views, wishes, feelings and character of all probationers; to interest themselves in their improvement and general welfare; to render their probationship as useful and satisfactory as possible; to suggest and facilitate seasonable action respecting their admission as members, discharge or continued probation; and, when proposed for membership by Sponsors (as provided in Sec. 2, Art. 1, of the Constitution), to endorse officially the sponsorial recommendation as approved or disapproved.

25

ENACTMENT VII.

Respecting Public Education and Mental Improvement.

Whereas the Constitution of this Community declares it to be a fundamental object of our Association to prevent the evils of ignorance; and whereas we cannot faithfully discharge the obligation thus assumed without making adequate provision, at the common expense, for educating the young and facilitating the mental improvement of all classes of our resident population, therefore it is enacted as follows, viz.:

SECTION 1. No child or youth connected with this Community shall be permitted to grow up without a decent education in the common branches of useful learning. Public Schools, Libraries and other requisite facilities for mental improvement shall be established and maintained for the common benefit, by means of an Education Fund annually replenished by the Community in such ways as may from time to time be determined.

SEC. 2. A Board of Education and Mental Improvement shall be annually chosen by the Community, consisting of at least three responsible members. This board shall have general charge and supervision of all Schools, Seminaries, Libraries, Cabinets, Philosophical Apparatus, etc., maintained by the Community; also of all Funds, Legacies, Donations, Lands, Buildings, Rooms, Fixtures and conveniences devoted to these purposes. It shall be their duty to take such care of all property, and to make such expenditures of all moneys entrusted to their charge, as shall render the educational and intellectual advantages of this Community eminently subservient of their intended uses. They shall take particular care that no child, youth or person neglect, or be prevented improving, these advantages. They shall keep reliable records and accounts of their transactions, and make an annual Educational Report to the Community.

ENACTMENT VIII.

Respecting a Community Post Office.

SECTION 1. For the convenience of this Community and all persons interested, a Post Office is hereby established at Hopedale for the regular transmission, reception and delivery of all mailable matter.

Sec. 2. The said Post Office shall be located in some cen_tral part of the Community village, and shall have a regular daily communication with the United States Post Office at Milford, excepting on Sundays. It shall have a competent Post Master, be kept in good order, be accessible at all reasonable hours, and be supported by postage on all mailable matter (except newspapers, periodicals and pamphlets) transmitted through it.

Sec. 3. The Directory of this Community, for the time being, are hereby empowered and required to appoint the Post Master, prescribe his particular duties, and determine his compensation; to contract with a mail-carrier and fix the hours for closing, transmitting and delivering the mail; to determine the rates of postage on all mailable matter not exempted from charge; and to make such regulations concerning said Post Office as may be found necessary to the public convenience and welfare.

Sec. 4. No person, other than the Post Master or his authorized substitute, shall meddle with the mail on its arrival, until it shall have been opened, assorted, taken account of and prepared for distribution. Nor shall any person overhaul or disturb the mailable matter deposited in the Post Office, except by permission of the Post Master, or in accordance with established regulations.

ENACTMENT IX.

Respecting a Community Lyceum.

Section 1. All the inhabitants of Hopedale over twelve years of age are hereby constituted a Community Lyceum, to be called The Hopedale Lyceum.

Sec. 2. The said inhabitants, without exception or distinction, exercising equal rights and privileges in all things pertaining to the Lyceum, are hereby authorized to organize the same by the choice of a President, Senior Vice-President, Junior Vice-President, and Secretary, who together shall constitute an Executive Council. The President shall serve for three months, and be succeeded by the Senior Vice-President; who shall be succeeded by the Junior Vice-President in regular order of promotion; and the latter by a newly elected incumbent. The Secretary, as well as the Junior Vice-President, shall be elected once in three months. These officers shall be elected by ballot, unless otherwise determined by the Lyceum at the time of election. In the absence of the President, his duties shall be discharged by the Senior Vice-President, and in *his* absence by the Junior Vice-President.

Sec. 3. It shall be the duty of the President to preside over all meetings of the Lyceum with Christian dignity, impartiality and courtesy, according to such rules as may have been adopted and the requisites of good order. He shall promptly repress all disorder, indecorum and obvious impropriety, whether of action, language or temper, and constantly endeavor to preserve a generous freedom of speech without its abuse. It shall be the duty of the Secretary to record faithfully the proceedings of the Lyceum, and to render such other service in the vocation of Scribe, as may from time to time be required. It shall be the . duty of the Executive Council to procure the delivery of at least one instructive, scientific or literary lecture every month; to provide suitable questions for public discussion, from which the Lyceum may make selections; to encourage the writing of brief essays by the members, in connection with choice readings and occasional declamation; to promote the formation of congenial classes for the prosecution of useful studies; and in general to execute its orders and administer its affairs in such a manner as to render it an efficient instrumentality for mental improvement.

Sec. 4. The Lyceum shall meet regularly once a month from the first of April to the first of October, and once a week during the rest of the year. Regular meetings may be suspended, and special ones held, whenever the Lyceum or the Executive Council may deem the same expedient. Twelve members shall constitute a quorum and a vote of two-thirds present and acting be necessary to the decision of every contested question.

Sec. 5. The Lyceum shall have ample power to determine the order of its own proceedings, and to establish such rules and regulations as may be deemed salutary — not repugnant to the Constitution or By-Laws of this Community.

Sec. 6. The Board of Education and Mental Improvement are hereby charged with the general supervision of this Lyceum; to see that it steadily pursues its declared objects; that it performs its legitimate functions; that it maintains a wholesome internal discipline; that its various exercises are so conducted

as to promote the real progress of the members in useful
knowledge; and that it fulfils the just expectations with which
it has been instituted. They are fully empowered to afford it
such accommodations and facilities as may be at their command, and for its benefit to make such expenditures of educational funds, not otherwise appropriated, as they may deem
necessary to its success. And they shall include in their Annual
Report to the Community a distinct statement of its general
operations and condition.

ENACTMENT X.

Respecting a Community Savings Bank.

SECTION 1. The Treasury of this Community is hereby constituted a Savings Bank, in which all persons residing on the
Community domain may deposit such parts of their earnings
and income as they can conveniently save for future use, subject to the conditions and regulations hereinafter prescribed.

SEC. 2. On the 16th day of each month, or on the 17th
when the 16th shall fall on Sunday, between the hours of ten
and eleven o'clock A. M., the Treasurer of this Community shall
regularly hold himself in readiness to receive for the Community's use such sums of money, not less than one dollar, and
excluding all fractions of a dollar, as may be offered for
deposit, and duly credit the same in books to be kept exclusively for this Savings Bank. And all depositors shall be
entitled to interest on their deposits, at the rate of four per
cent. per annum.

SEC. 3. Depositors may withdraw their deposits or any part
thereof, on the said 16th or 17th day of the month, between
the hours of eleven and twelve o'clock A. M., by giving notice
of one week for all sums over 5 and not exceeding 20 dollars,
of thirty days for all sums over 20 and not exceeding 100
dollars, of sixty days for all sums over 100 and not exceeding
300 dollars, of six months for all other sums not exceeding
500 dollars, and of one year for all higher sums: Provided,
nevertheless, that for the accommodation of persons desiring to
withdraw their deposits, the Treasurer may waive the conditions of notice, whenever the funds in the Treasury will admit
of it without detriment to the general welfare.

SEC. 4. Depositors shall keep a suitable book, in which the
Treasurer shall carefully note down all sums deposited or with-

drawn. And this book shall always be exhibited to the Treasurer upon occasion of the deposit or withdrawal of moneys, that the proper entries may be made.

SEC. 5. It shall be the duty of the Treasurer to present a distinct statement of the condition of the Savings Bank, in the Financial Report of the Directory annually made to the Community.

ENACTMENT XI.

Respecting a Community Fire Insurance Company.

SECTION 1. This Community is hereby constituted a Mutual Fire Insurance Company, to guarantee against all losses that may accrue by fire to any buildings or other specified property on the Community domain, not exceeding three-fourths of the fairly appraised value thereof.

SEC. 2. The Directory are hereby authorized and empowered to open Insurance Books, to appraise property needing to be insured, to determine the relative risk thereof, and to issue Certificates of Insurance on such terms and conditions as are prescribed by the best conducted Mutual Fire Insurance Companies, so far as the same may be applicable to the circumstances of this Community; provided that the insurances made in pursuance hereof shall render no public or private property liable for the payment of losses by fire, other than premium money and what may be covered by deposit notes given for that purpose.

SEC. 3. The Directory, after maturing their arrangements and methods of proceeding under this Enactment, shall publish a suitable compend of the same. And they shall regularly subjoin to their Annual Financial Report a concise statement of Insurance affairs.

SEC. 4. The following precautionary regulations against fire shall be strictly observed throughout the Community Domain. [These regulations were ten in number, but as they were what a wise and cautious prudence would suggest and can be easily imagined, it is not deemed advisable to insert them. Ed.]

ENACTMENT XII.

Respecting an Industrial Union.*

SECTION 1. In order to promote the cheerful prosecution of public improvements and a generous assistance of persons

---

* First called Industrial Army.

needing occasional aid, all the members, probationers, and dependents of this Community, capable of useful service, are hereby constituted a co-operative body to be called The Hopedale Industrial Union.

SEC. 2. This Industrial Union shall be organized in two general Departments — a *Male* and a *Female* Department. Each Department shall have power to determine and adjust its own roll of members, organize itself in such divisions, elect such officers and establish such rules as may from time to time be deemed promotive of its orderly, energetic, harmonious and successful operation. Also, to determine when, where, and to what extent its services shall be rendered. Fifteen members shall constitute a quorum for the transaction of business, and all questions shall be settled by a two-thirds majority of the members present and acting in regular Department meeting. Provided, nevertheless, that nothing shall be done by either Department repugnant to the Constitution or any Enactment of this Community, or insubordinately to the legitimate executive authority of its Directory.

SEC. 3. Whenever the Male Department of this Union shall make requisition for the use of any working vehicles, teams, implements, or alien employes of the Community, such requisition shall be promptly complied with; provided, always, that at least three days notice shall be given to the superintendent or manager in charge of such vehicles, teams, implements, or employes; and provided, also, that no serious detriment shall be done to the Community property by insisting on such requisition. And whenever the said Male Department shall find it necessary to furnish implements of labor to members unable to equip themselves, or shall have occasion to expend money for the prosecution of their legitimate undertakings, all such burdens shall be borne by the Community, subject to such limitations as the Directory may at any time deem it their duty to interpose.

SEC. 4. Each Department through its proper official organs, may, for warrantable reasons, excuse any member temporarily from actual service, or commute such service for cash equivalents in cases where the same shall be deemed especially convenient.

SEC. 5. The Directory are hereby authorized and required to carry this enactment into full and perpetual effect.

ENACTMENT XIII.

Respecting a Guaranty Against the Evils of Poverty.

Whereas this Community has solemnly pledged its general guaranty to all its members against the evils of poverty, therefore, in order to a definite and practical fulfillment of the same, in cases to which it is applicable, it is enacted as follows:

SECTION 1. An annual contribution shall be levied on all resident members, probationers and dependents of this Community owning property to the value of one hundred dollars clear of debt; which contribution shall be equal to two mills, at least, on every dollar possessed clear of debt, as nearly as the same can be ascertained. This contribution shall be assessed and collected by the directory, on or before the first day of April in each year, and the proceeds shall be credited by the Treasurer to the Relief Fund, subject to orders hereinafter prescribed.

SEC. 2. This Community, at the annual meeting every year, shall choose a Relief Committee, consisting of not less than four members, taken equally from the two sexes, whose sacred duty it shall be to make themselves acquainted with every case in which a member, probationer or dependent of this Community may need pecuniary assistance. It shall also be the duty of every member, probationer and dependent, having knowledge of any such case, to report the same without delay to some member of said Committee. And the Relief Committee, proceeding always with Christian kindness and delicacy, shall cause timely and proper assistance to be rendered to every person needing relief; either by interesting the Industrial Union in the case, or by drawing on the Relief Fund for such a sum of money as the circumstances, in their judgment, demand; provided, nevertheless, that no person or family, possessing property clear of debt to the value of one thousand dollars, shall receive aid from such Fund.

SEC. 3. So much of this Enactment as relates to the levying of the annual contribution may be suspended by vote of the Community, for one year at a time, whenever the Relief Fund shall be deemed adequate to its design without such contribution.

ENACTMENT XIV.

Respecting the Community Cemetery.

The Trustees are hereby empowered and instructed to carry into effect the following specified measures relating to the Hopedale Cemetery, viz.:

1. To appraise the Burial Lots now laid off, and which hereafter may be laid off, in said Cemetery, at some just and definite valuation, not under two dollars nor over five dollars per lot.

2. To reserve and set apart suitable portions of ground for the interment of transient residents and strangers who may have need to be buried within our Community Domain.

3. To sell Burial Lots, at their appraised valuation, with the right of perpetual occupancy for burial purposes alone, to members of the Community, and also to such other persons as may be permitted by vote of the Community to become purchasers; and to give deeds or certificate titles of the same.

4. To expend all funds arising from the sale of Burial Lots, or otherwise, in fencing and improving said Cemetery; also in erecting and maintaining a Receiving Tomb for general convenience.

5. To make and publish such Regulations relating to said Cemetery as they may deem necessary and the Community approve.

6. To appoint a Superintendent of said Cemetery, with such powers, and subject to such instructions, as they may consider judicious.

7. To cause proper Records and written evidence of all their transactions, under this Enactment, to be made and preserved for perpetual reference.

ENACTMENT XV.

Respecting Residence by Permission, etc.

SECTION 1. The protracted residence of persons on the Community Domain, who are not sympathetically interested in our objects, principles and social order, shall be steadily guarded against as of demoralizing tendency. And no person excepting acknowledged members, probationers, dependents, visiting friends, medical patients, nurses, scholars or tenants holding under unexpired contract, shall be employed, boarded or harbored on the Community Domain for a longer time than one month, *unless by special vote of the Community;* which vote shall in no case extend permission of residence beyond the period of one year without a renewal.

SEC. 2. No fire-arms, or deadly weapons of any description, shall be owned, kept, or used, either for offense, defense or sport, within the territorial limits of this Community, except by express permission of the Council of Religion, Conciliation and Justice; and then only for the purpose of killing very mischievous and dangerous animals. And it shall be the duty of every member, probationer and dependent of this Community to remonstrate, *kindly* but *firmly,* with persons from abroad, against gunning on the Community Domain, and especially against the shooting of harmless birds; and also to discountenance utterly among our children the use of all warlike, savage-like or ruffian-like toys, playthings, sports and amusements, however harmless in themselves.

ENACTMENT XVI.

Respecting Certain Official Duties.

SEC. 1. It shall be the duty of the President of this Community to see that all its Enactments are duly respected, and particularly that none of them become inoperative through the negligence of official servants on whom the responsibility of their execution immediately devolves. And he shall be expected, at the opening of every Annual Meeting, to lay before the Community a written Address or Statement, reviewing the workings of their social polity during the previous year, and suggesting such improvements as he may judge necessary.

SEC. 2. It shall be the duty of the Trustees to keep reliable Records of all their principal transactions, together with such minutes and files of written documents as shall enable them to exhibit at any time the actual condition of all the Community lands and tenements, both public and private, in respect to Layings off, Ownership, Title, Incumbrance or Claim. And the senior Trustee, for the time being, shall be considered responsible for the proper keeping of such Records and Documentary Files.

SEC. 3. It shall be the duty of the Recorder to keep, in an orderly condition, a reliable Community Registry, in which each member's name, admission, death, resignation or discharge, may be duly entered, according to date, and forever remain on record. Also to keep in like condition another Registry in which the names, reception and discharge of all probationers and dependents may distinctly appear on record. Also to keep a Catalogue, exhibiting the names of all persons permitted to reside on our Domain by special vote of the Community, and the cessation of their residence under such vote.

SEC. 4. It shall be the duty of the Directory, Council of Religion, Board of Education, and every annually elected Committee of this Community, to keep full and reliable Records of their official transactions, and to preserve carefully on File all written documents and papers which may be of evidential or historical use.

SEC. 5. It shall be the special duty of the Recorder to publish in *The Practical Christian* all new Enactments of this Community as soon as may be conveniently done after their passage. Also, with the advice of the President to publish such of the Proceedings of all regular Community meetings as shall appear proper for publication and likely to keep up a salutary interest among our friends abroad.

SEC. 6. It shall be the imperative duty of the Recorder to watch over the Community Archives with the most scrupulous vigilance; to record all transactions with promptitude; and to preserve all Books, Registers, Catalogues, Documents and Files of papers with perpetual fidelity. And no officer, member, probationer or other person, shall carry out of the Recorder's immediate custody, for examination or use elsewhere, any original Record, Minute or Paper whatsoever, without first entering the fact, with name and date, briefly, in a Minute Book to be kept in the office exclusively for that purpose.

SEC. 7. It shall be the duty of the Treasurer to keep the Directory duly informed of all moneys on hand in the Treasury, and of all moneys required to meet demands or appropriations to be paid out of the same; also, to make up the Annual Financial Report in season for the Directory's examination.

GENERAL ADOPTION AND APPROVAL.

The foregoing Revised Constitution and Enactments having been severally read, carefully considered and passed upon, are hereby collectively adopted, approved and ordered to be published. And all Enactments, sections, sentences, clauses and particular votes of this Community, on record, which are in any wise repugnant to this Revision, or superseded by it, are hereby repealed.

Done at Hopedale, this thirty-first day of August, A. D., one thousand eight hundred and fifty-three.

E. D. DRAPER, *President.*

MARY A. WALDEN, *Secretary.*

APPENDIX B.

CONSTITUTION

OF

THE PRACTICAL CHRISTIAN REPUBLIC.

A NEW Order of Human Society is hereby founded, to be called THE PRACTICAL CHRISTIAN REPUBLIC. It shall be constituted, organized and governed in accordance with the following fundamental articles, to wit:

ARTICLE I. *Objects.*

The cardinal objects of this Republic are and shall be the following, viz.:

1. To institute and consolidate a true order of human society, which shall harmonize all individual interests in the common good and be governed by Divine Principles as its Supreme Law.

2. To establish local Communities of various grades and peculiarities, all acknowledging the sovereignty of Divine Principles and so constituted as to promote the highest happiness of their respective associates.

3. To confederate all such local Communities wheresoever existing throughout the earth by an ascending series of combinations in one common Social Republic.

4. To insure to every orderly citizen of this Republic a comfortable home, suitable employment, adequate subsistence, congenial associates, a good education, proper stimulants to personal righteousness, sympathetic aid in distress, and due protection in the exercise of all natural rights.

5. To give mankind a practical illustration of civil government maintained in just subordination to Divine Principles; which shall be powerful without tyranny, benignant without

weakness, dignified without ostentation, independent without defiance, invincible without resorting to injurious force, and pre-eminently useful without being burdensome.

6. To institute and sustain every suitable instrumentality for removing the causes of human misery and promoting the conversion of the world to true righteousness.

7. To multipy, economize, distribute and apply beneficently, wisely and successfully, all the means necessary to harmonize the human race with each other, with the heavenly world and with the universal Father; that in one grand communion of angels and men the will of God may be done " on earth as it is in heaven."

Article II. *Principles.*

We proclaim the absolute sovereignty of Divine Principles over all human beings, combinations, governments, institutions, laws, customs, habits, practices, actions, opinions, intentions and affections. We recognize in the religion of Jesus Christ as he taught and exemplified it a complete annunciation and attestation of essential Divine Principles.

We accept and acknowledge the following as Divine Principles of Theological Truth, viz.:

1. The existence of one all-perfect, infinite God.
2. The mediatorial manifestation of God through Christ.
3. Divine revelations and inspirations given to mankind.
4. The immortal existence of human and angelic spirits.
5. The moral agency and religious obligation of mankind.
6. The certainty of a perfect divine retribution.
7. The necessity of man's spiritual regeneration.
8. The final universal triumph of good over evil.

We accept and acknowledge the following as Divine Principles of Personal Righteousness; viz.:

1. Reverence for the Divine and spiritual.
2. Self-denial for righteousness' sake.
3. Justice to all beings.
4. Truth in all manifestations of mind.
5. Love in all spiritual relations.
6. Purity in all things.
7. Patience in all right aims and pursuits.
8. Unceasing progress toward perfection.

We accept and acknowledge the following as Divine Principles of Social Order; viz.:

1. The supreme Fatherhood of God.
2. The universal Brotherhood of man.
3. The declared perfect love of God to man.
4. The required perfect love of man to God.
5. The required perfect love of man to man.
6. The required just reproof and disfellowship of evil-doers.
7. The required non-resistance of evil doers with evil.
8. The designed unity of the righteous.

We hold ourselves imperatively bound by the sovereignty of these acknowledged Divine Principles, never, under any pretext whatsoever, to kill, injure, envy or hate any human being, even our worst enemy.

Never to sanction chattel slavery or any obvious oppression of man by man.

Never to countenance war or capital punishment, or the infliction of injurious penalties, or the resistance of evil with evil in any form.

Never to violate the dictates of chastity by adultery, polygamy, concubinage, fornication, self-pollution, lasciviousness, amative abuse, impure language, or cherished lust.

Never to manufacture, buy, sell, deal out or use any intoxicating liquor, *as a beverage.*

Never to take or administer an oath.

Never to participate in a sword-sustained human government, either as voters, office holders or subordinate assistants, *in any case prescriptively involving the infliction of death or any absolute injury whatsoever by man on man;* nor to invoke governmental interposition in any such case, even for the accomplishment of good objects.

Never to indulge self-will, bigotry, love of pre-eminence, covetousness, deceit, profanity, idleness or an unruly tongue.

Never to participate in lotteries, gambling, betting or pernicious amusements.

Never to resent reproof or justify ourselves in a known wrong.

Never to aid, abet or approve others in anything sinful; but, through divine assistance, always to recommend and promote with our entire influence the holiness and happiness of all mankind.

ARTICLE III. *Rights.*

No member of this Republic, nor Association of its members,. can have a right to violate any one of its acknowledged Divine Principles; but all the members, however peculiarized by sex, age, color, native country, rank, calling, wealth or station, have indefeasible rights as human beings to do, to be and to enjoy whatsoever they are personally capable of that is not in violation of those Principles. Within these just limits no person shall be restricted or interfered with by this Republic, nor by any constituent Association thereof, in the exercise of the following declared rights; viz.:

1. The right to worship God, with or without external ceremonies and devotional observances, according to the dictates of his or her own conscience.

2. The right to exercise reason, investigate questions, form opinions and declare convictions, by speech, by pen and by the press, on all subjects within the range of human thought.

3. The right to hold any official station to which he or she may be elected, to pursue any avocation or follow any course in life, according to genius, attraction and taste.

4. The right to be stewards, under God, of his or her own talents, property, skill and personal endowments.

5. The right to form and enjoy particular friendships with congenial minds.

6. The right to contract marriage and sustain the sacred relationships of family life.

7. The right to unite with, and also to withdraw from, any Community or Association, on reciprocal terms, at discretion.

8. In fine, the right to seek happiness in all rightful ways and by all innocent means.

ARTICLE IV. *Membership.*

SECTION 1. Membership in this Republic shall exist in seven Circles; viz.: the Adoptive, the Unitive, the Preceptive, the Communitive, the Expansive, the Charitive, and the Parentive. The Adoptive Circle shall include all members living in isolation, or not yet admitted into the membership of an integral Community. The Unitive Circle shall include all members of Rural and Joint-Stock Communities. The Preceptive Circle shall include all members specially and perseveringly devoted to Teaching; whether it be teaching religion, morality or any branch of useful knowledge, and whether their teaching be done with the living voice, or with the pen, or through the press, or in educative institutions. All such teachers, after having proved themselves competent, devoted and acceptable in the Communities to which they belong, shall be considered in this Circle. The Communitive Circle shall include all members of integral Common-Stock Communities or Families, whose internal economy excludes individual profits on capital, wages for labor and separate interests. The Expansive Circle shall include all members who are especially devoted to the extension of this Republic, by founding and strengthening new integral Communities; who have associated in companies for that express purpose and are employing the principal portion of their time, talents or property in that work. The Charitive Circle shall include all members who are especially devoted to the reformation, elevation, improvement and welfare of the world's suffering classes, by furnishing them homes, employment, instruction and all the requisite helps to a better condition; who are associated in companies for that express purpose and are employing the principal portion of their time, talents or property in such works. The Parentive Circle shall include all members who, on account of their mature age, faithful services, great experience, sound judgment or unquestionable reliability, are competent to advise, arbitrate and recommend measures in cases of great importance. They shall be declared worthy of a place in the Parentive Circle by their respective integral Communities, in a regular meeting notified for that purpose, by a unanimous vote.

SEC. 2. The members of no Circle shall ever assume to exercise any other than purely moral or advisory power, nor claim any exclusive prerogatives, privileges, honors or distinctions whatsoever over members of other Circles; but shall be entitled to respect and influence in consideration of intrinsic worth alone. Nor shall there be any permanent general organization of these Circles *as such*. But the members of either may unite in co-operative associations, companies and partnerships, for the more efficient prosecution of their peculiar objects; and may also hold public meetings, conferences and conventions, at pleasure, for the promotion of these objects.

SEC. 3. Any person may be admitted a member of this Republic by any constituent Community or other authorized

26

body thereof in regular meeting assembled. And any twelve or more persons adopting this Constitution from conviction may render themselves members of the Republic by uniting to form a constituent and confederate Community thereof.

SEC. 4. Any person may resign or withdraw membership at discretion, or may recede from either of the other Circles to the Adoptive Circle, by giving written notice to the body or principal persons concerned. Any person uniting with a society of any description radically opposed in principle, practice or spirit to this Republic, shall be deemed to have relinquished membership; likewise any person who shall have ceased to manifest any interest in its affairs for the space of three years.

SEC. 5. Any constituent Community or other organized body of this Republic competent to admit members shall have power to dismiss or discharge them for justifiable reasons. And no person shall be retained a member after persistently violating or setting at naught any one of the sovereign Divine Principles declared in Art. II of this Constitution.

ARTICLE V. *Organization.*

SECTION 1. The constituent and confederate bodies of this Social Republic shall be the following; viz.: Parochial Communities, Integral Communities, Communal Municipalities, Communal States and Communal Nations.

SEC. 2. Parochial Communities shall consist each of twelve or more members belonging chiefly to the Adoptive Circle, residing promiscuously in a general neighborhood, associated for religious and moral improvement and to secure such other social advantages as may be found practicable.

SEC. 3. Integral Communities shall consist each of twelve or more members inhabiting an integral territorial Domain, so held in possession and guaranteed that no part thereof can be owned in fee by any person not a member of this Republic.

There shall be three different kinds of Integral Communities; viz.: Rural, Joint-Stock and Common-Stock Communities. Rural Communities shall hold and manage the major portion of their respective Domains in separate Homesteads, adapted to the wants of families and to small associations under a system of individual proprietorship. Joint-Stock Communities shall hold and manage the major part of their respective Domains in Joint-Stock proprietorship, with various unitary economies, under a system of associative co-operation; laying off the minor portion into Village House Lots, to be sold to individual members under necessary restrictions. Common-Stock Communities shall hold and manage their respective Domains and property in Common-Stock, without paying individual members profits on capital or stipulated wages for labor. Common-Stock Families may also be formed within Rural and Joint-Stock Communities when deemed desirable and practicable; in which case such Families shall not be considered Integral Communities, but as constituent portions of the Communities on whose Domain they respectively reside.

Sec. 4. Communal Municipalities shall consist each of two or more Communities, whether Parochial or Integral, combined, as in a town or city, for municipal purposes necessary to their common welfare, and impracticable or extremely difficult of accomplishment without such a union.

Sec. 5. Communal States shall consist each of two or more Communal Municipalities combined for general purposes necessary to their common welfare, and impracticable or extremely difficult of accomplishment without such a union.

Sec. 6. Communal Nations shall consist each of two or more Communal States combined for national purposes necessary to their comnon welfare, and impracticable or extremely difficult of accomplishment without such a union.

Sec. 7. When there shall be two or more Communal Nations, they shall be represented equitably, according to population, in a Supreme Unitary Council by Senators elected for the term of —— years.

Sec. 8. The several constituent bodies of this Republic herein before named shall be organized under written Constitutions, Compacts or Fundamental Laws not inconsistent with this General Constitution, and shall exercise the governmental prerogatives and responsibilities defined in the next ensuing Article.

Article VI. *Government.*

Section 1. Self-government in the Individual, the Family and the primary congenial Association, under the immediate sovereignty of Divine Principles, being the basis of moral and social order in this Republic, shall be constantly cherished as indispensable to its prosperity. Therefore all governmental powers vested in the confederate bodies of this Republic shall be such as are obviously beneficent and such as cannot be conveniently exercised by the primary Communities or their component Circles. And such confederate bodies shall never assume to exercise governmental powers not clearly delegated to them by their constituents.

SEC. 2. Each Parochial and each Integral Community shall exert its utmost ability to insure all its members and dependents a full realization of the guaranties specified in Object 4, Article 1, of this Constitution; viz.: a comfortable home, suitable employment, adequate subsistence, congenial associates, a good education, proper stimulants to personal righteousness, sympathetic aid in distress and due protection in the exercise of all natural rights. And whereinsoever it shall find itself unable to realize the said guaranties, it may unite with other Communities to insure them, by such means as shall be mutually agreed on for that purpose. Each Community shall have the right to frame, adopt and alter its own Constitution and laws; to elect its own officers, teachers and representatives; and to manage its own domestic affairs of every description, without interference from any other constituent body or authority of this Republic; excepting always the prerogatives which it shall have specifically delegated or referred to others.

SEC. 3. Each Communal Municipality shall be formed by a Convention of delegates chosen for that purpose by the Communities proposing to unite in such Municipality. The delegates shall be chosen equitably on the basis of population. These delegates shall frame a Constitution or Fundamental Compact, clearly defining the governmental powers to be exercised by the Municipal authorities, which, having been submitted to the voting members of the Communities concerned and adopted, the Municipality shall be considered established and go into organized operation accordingly. But either of the Communities composing such Municipality shall have the right to secede therefrom, after giving one year's notice, paying all assessments due the corporation at the time of such notice, and relinquishing its share of public property therein. Or the union of two or more Communities constituting a Municipality may be dissolved at any time by mutual agreement of the federative parties.

SEC. 4. Each Communal State shall be formed by a Convention of delegates from the Municipalities proposing to unite in

the same, by a process substantially similar to the one prescribed in the preceding Section, but without the right of
secession therein reserved. And each Communal Nation shall
be formed by the States proposing to unite therein in general
accordance with the same process.

SEC. 5. The duties and powers of the Supreme Unitary
Council shall be defined in a Fundamental Compact, to be
framed by delegates from all the Communal Nations then
existing and adopted by at least two-thirds of the citizen members of the Republic present and acting in their respective
primary Communities, at meetings duly notified for that purpose. And all questions throughout this Republic, excepting
the election of officers, shall be determined by a two-thirds
vote.

SEC. 6. No official servant of any grade in this Republic
shall ever assume to distinguish him or herself by external
display of dress, equipage or other artificial appliances above
the common members; nor shall receive compensation for
official services beyond the average paid to the first class of
operatives at large, with a reasonable allowance for incidental
expenses; but every official servant shall be considered bound
to exemplify the humility, modesty and benevolence inculcated
in the Christian precept. " Whosoever will be chief among
you, let him be the servant of all." Nor shall it be allowable
for any of the constitutional bodies of this Republic to burden
the people with governmental expenses for mere worldly show
or for any other than purposes of unquestionable public utility.

ARTICLE VII. *Religion.*

SECTION 1. Acknowledging the Christian religion as one of
fundamental Divine Principles, to be practically carried out in
all human conduct, this Republic insists only on the essentials
of faith and practice affirmed in Article II of this Constitution.
Therefore, no uniform Religious or Ecclesiastical system of
externals shall be established; nor shall any rituals, forms,
ceremonies or observances whatsoever be either instituted or
interdicted; but each Community shall determine for itself,
with due regard for the conscientious scruples of its own members, all matters of this nature.

SEC. 2. Believing that the Holy Christ-Spirit will raise up
competent Religious and Moral Teachers, and commend them,

by substantial demonstration of their fitness, to the confidence of those to whom they minister, this Republic shall not assume to commission, authorize or forbid any person to preach or to teach Religion; nor shall any constituent body thereof assume to do so. But each Community may invite any person deemed worthy of confidence to be their religious teacher, on terms reciprocally satisfactory to the parties concerned.

SEC. 3. It shall be the privilege and duty of members of this Republic to hold general meetings, at least once in three months, for religious improvement and the promulgation of their acknowledged divine principles. In order to this, Quarterly Conferences shall be established in every general region of country inhabited by any considerable number of members. Any twenty-five or more members wheresoever resident shall be competent to establish a Quarterly Conference whenever they may deem the same necessary to their convenience. In so doing they shall adopt a written Constitution subsidiary to this general Constitution and no wise incompatible therewith, under which they may make such regulations as they may deem promotive of the objects they have in view. All such Conferences shall have power to admit members into the Adoptive Circle of this Republic, and also, for sufficient reasons, to discharge them. And each Quarterly Conference shall keep reliable records of its proceedings, with an authentic copy of this general Constitution prefixed.

ARTICLE VIII. *Marriage.*

SECTION 1. Marriage, being one of the most important and sacred of human relationships, ought to be guarded against caprice and abuse by the highest wisdom that is available. Therefore within the membership of this Republic and the dependencies thereof, Marriage is specially commended to the care of the Preceptive and Parentive Circles. These are hereby designated as the confidential counsellors of all members and dependents who may desire their mediation in cases of matrimonial negotiation, contract or controversy; and shall be held pre-eminently responsible for the prudent and faithful discharge of their duties. But no person decidedly averse to their interposition shall be considered under obligation to solicit or accept it. And it shall be considered the perpetual duty of the Circles named to enlighten the public mind relative to the requisites of true matrimony, and to elevate the marriage institution within this Republic to the highest possible plane of purity and happiness.

SEC. 2. Marriage shall always be solemnized in the presence of two or more witnesses, by the distinct acknowledgment of the parties before some member of the Preceptive or Parentive Circle selected to preside on the occasion. And it shall be the imperative duty of the member so presiding to see that every such marriage be recorded within ten days thereafter in the Registry of the Community to which one or both of the parties shall, at the time, belong.

SEC. 3. Divorce from the bonds of matrimony shall never be allowable within the membership of this Republic except for adultery conclusively proved against the accused party. But separations for other sufficient reasons may be sanctioned, with the distinct understanding that neither party shall be at liberty to marry again during the natural life-time of the other.

ARTICLE IX. *Education.*

SECTION 1. The proper education of the rising generation being indispensable to the prosperity and glory of this Republic, it shall be amply provided for as a cardinal want; and no child shall be allowed to grow up anywhere under the control of its membership without good educational opportunities.

SEC. 2. Education shall be as comprehensive and thorough as circumstances in each case will allow. It shall aim in all cases to develop harmoniously the physical, intellectual, moral and social faculties of the young: — to give them, if possible, a high-toned moral character based on scrupulous conscientiousness and radical Christian principles; a sound mind, well stored with useful knowledge and capable of inquiring, reasoning and judging for itself; a heathful, vigorous body, suitably fed, exercised, clothed, lodged and recreated; good domestic habits, including personal cleanliness, order, propriety, agreeableness and generous social qualities; industrial executiveness and skill in one or more of the avocations necessary to a comfortable subsistence; and, withal, practical economy in pecuniary matters. In fine, to qualifiy them for solid usefulness and happiness in all the rightful pursuits and relations of life.

SEC. 3. The Preceptive Circle of members shall be expected to distinguish themselves by a zealous, wise and noble devotion to this great interest of education. And every individual, family, private association and constituent body of this Republic, in their respective spheres, shall co-operate, by every reasonable effort, to render its educational institutions from the nursery to the university pre-eminently excellent.

ARTICLE X. *Property.*

SECTION 1. All property, being primarily the Creator's and provided by Him for the use of mankind during their life on earth, ought to be acquired, used and disposed of in strict accordance with the dictates of justice and charity. Therefore, the members of this Republic shall consider themselves stewards in trust, under God, of all property coming into their possession, and as such imperatively bound not to consume it in the gratification of their own inordinate lusts, nor to hoard it up as a mere treasure, nor to employ it to the injury of any human being, nor withhold it from the relief of distressed fellow creatures; but always to use it, as not abusing it, for strictly just, benevolent and commendable purposes.

SEC. 2. It shall not be deemed compatible with justice for the people of this Republic, in their pecuniary commerce with each other, to demand, in any case, as a compensation for their mere personal service, labor or attendance, a higher price per cent., per piece, per day, week, month or year than the average paid to the first class of operatives in the Community, or general vicinity where the service is rendered. Nor shall it be deemed compatible with justice for the members, in such commerce, to demand, as a price for anything sold or exchanged, more than the fair cost value thereof, as nearly as the same can be estimated, reckoning prime cost, labor or attention, incidental expenses, contingent waste, depreciation and average risks of sale; nor to demand for the mere use of capital, except as partners in the risks of its management, any clear interest or profit whatsoever exceeding four per cent. per annum.

SEC. 3. It shall not be deemed compatible with the welfare, prosperity and honor of this Republic for the people thereof to owe debts outside of the same exceeding three-fourths of their available property rated at moderate valuation by disinterested persons; nor to give or receive long credits, except on real estate security; nor to manufacture, fabricate or sell sham and unreliable productions; nor to make business engagements, or hold out expectations, which are of doubtful fulfillment.

SEC. 4.   Whenever the population and resources of this Republic shall warrant the formation of the first Communal Nation, and the government thereof shall have been organized, a uniform system of Mutual Banking shall be established, based mainly on real estate securities, which shall afford loans at the mere cost of operations.   Also, a uniform system of Mutual Insurance, which shall reduce all kinds of insurance to the lowest terms.   Also, a uniform system of reciprocal Commercial Exchange, which shall preclude all needless intervention between producers and consumers, all extra risks of property, all extortionate speculation, all inequitable profits on exchanges, and all demoralizing expedients of trade.   Also, Regulations providing for the just encouragement of useful industry and the practical equalization of all social advantages, so far as the same can be done without infringing on individual rights. And all the members shall be considered under sacred moral obligations to co-operate adhesively and persistently in every righteous measure employed for the accomplishment of these objects.

ARTICLE XI.   *Policy.*

It shall be the fundamental, uniform and established Policy of this Republic:

1.   To govern, succor and protect its own people to the utmost of its ability, in all matters and cases whatsoever not involving anti-Christian conflict with the sword-sustained governments of the world under which its members live.

2.   To avoid all unnecessary conflicts whatsoever with these governments, by conforming to all their laws and requirements which are not repugnant to the Sovereignty of Divine Principles.

3.   To abstain from all participation in the working of their political machinery and to be connected as little as possible with their systems of governmental operation.

4.   To protest, remonstrate and testify conscientiously against their sins on moral grounds alone; but never to plot schemes of revolutionary agitation, intrigue or violence against them, nor be implicated in contenancing the least resistance to their authority by injurious force.

5. If compelled in any case by Divine Principles to disobey their requirements, or passively to withstand their unrighteous exactions and thus incur their penal vengeance, to act openly and suffer with true moral heroism.

6. Never to ask their protection, even in favor of injured innocence or threatened rights, when it can be interposed only by means which are condemned by Divine Principles.

7. To live in peace, so far as can innocently be done, with all mankind outside of this Republic, whether individuals, associations, corporations, sects, classes, parties, states or nations; also to accredit and encourage whatever is truly good in all; yet to fellowship iniquity in none, be enslaved by none, be amalgamated with none, be morally responsible for none; but ever be distinctly, unequivocally and uncompromisingly *The Practical Christian Republic* until the complete regeneration of the world.

Article XII. *Amendments.*

Whenever one-fourth of all the members of this Republic shall subscribe and publish a written proposition to alter, amend or revise this Constitution, such proposition of whatsoever nature shall be submitted to each Community for consideration. Returns shall then be made of all the votes cast in every Community to the highest organized body of the Republic for the time being. And the concurrence of two-thirds of all the votes shall determine the question or questions at issue. If the proposition shall have been a specific alteration or amendment of the Constitution, it shall thenceforth be established as such. If a Convention shall have been proposed to revise the Constitution, a Convention shall be summoned and held accordingly. But no alteration, amendment or revision of this Constitution shall take effect until sanctioned by two-thirds of all the members present and acting thereon in their respective Communities, at regular meetings duly notified for that purpose.

INDEX.

THE AMERICAN UTOPIAN ADVENTURE

sources for the study of communitarian socialism in the
United States 1680–1880

Series One

Edward D. Andrews THE COMMUNITY INDUSTRIES OF THE SHAKERS (1932)

Adin Ballou HISTORY OF THE HOPEDALE COMMUNITY from its inception to its virtual submergence in the Hopedale Parish. Edited by W. S. Heywood (1897)

Paul Brown TWELVE MONTHS IN NEW HARMONY presenting a faithful account of the principal occurrences that have taken place there during that period; interspersed with remarks (1827)

John S. Duss THE HARMONISTS. A personal history (1943)

Frederick W. Evans AUTOBIOGRAPHY OF A SHAKER and revelation of the Apocalypse. With an appendix. Enlarged edition (1888)

Parke Godwin A POPULAR VIEW OF THE DOCTRINES OF CHARLES FOURIER (1844) DEMOCRACY, CONSTRUCTIVE AND PACIFIC (1844)

Walter C. Klein JOHANN CONRAD BEISSEL, MYSTIC AND MARTINET, 1690–1768 (1942)

William J. McNiff HEAVEN ON EARTH: A PLANNED MORMON SOCIETY (1940) With "Communism among the Mormons," by Hamilton Gardner

Michael A. Mikkelsen THE BISHOP HILL COLONY. A religious, communistic settlement in Henry County, Illinois (1892) With "Eric Janson and the Bishop Hill Colony," by Silvert Erdahl

Oneida Community BIBLE COMMUNISM. A compilation from the annual reports and other publications of the Oneida Association and its branches, presenting, in connection with their history, a summary view of their religious and social theories (1853)

Marianne (Dwight) Orvis LETTERS FROM BROOK FARM 1841–1847. Edited by Amy L. Reed (1928)

Robert A. Parker A YANKEE SAINT. John Humphrey Noyes and the Oneida Community (1935)

A. J. G. Perkins & Thersa Wolfson FRANCES WRIGHT: FREE ENQUIRER. The study of a temperament (1939)

Jules Prudhommeaux ICARIE ET SON FONDATEUR, ÉTIENNE CABET. Contribution à l'étude du socialisme expérimental (1907)

Albert Shaw ICARIA. A chapter in the history of communism (1884)